BITTER FEAST

BITTER FEAST

*Amerindians and Europeans in
Northeastern North America, 1600-64*

DENYS DELÂGE
*translated from the French
by Jane Brierley*

UBC PRESS / VANCOUVER

Originally published as *Le Pays renversé*
© Les éditions du Boréal 1985

ISBN 0-7748-0434-3 (hardcover)
ISBN 0-7748-0451-3 (paperback)

Canadian Cataloguing in Publication Data

Delâge, Denys.
Bitter feast

Translation of: Le pays renversé.
Includes bibliographical references and index.
ISBN 0-7748-0434-3 (bound). – ISBN 0-7748-0451-3 (pbk.)

1. North America – History – Colonial period, ca. 1600-1775. 2. Indians of North America
– History – Colonial period, ca. 1600-1775. 3. Europe – Commerce – North America –
History. 4. North America – Commerce – Europe – History. 5. Indians of North America
– Commerce – History – 17th century. I. Title.

E38.D4513 1993   970.02   C93-091414-7

This book has been published with the help of a grant from the Social Sciences Feder-
ation of Canada, using funds provided by the Social Sciences and Humanities Research
Council of Canada. Publication was also made possible by ongoing support from the
Canada Council, the Province of British Columbia Cultural Services Branch, and the
Department of Communications of the Government of Canada.

The translator wishes to thank the Canada Council for its generous help in awarding a
grant-in-aid for preparing this translation, and to express gratitude to the author for his
unfailing cooperation in the preparation of the English edition of this work.

UBC Press
University of British Columbia
6344 Memorial Rd
Vancouver, BC V6T 1Z2
(604) 822-3259
Fax: (604) 822-6083

To the memory of my parents
To the memory of Charles

Contents

Preface and Acknowledgments / ix

Maps / xii

1 Europe in Transition at the Heart of an Economic World-System / 3

2 North America before European Settlement / 36

3 The Question of Unequal Exchange / 78

4 Huronia and Iroquoia / 163

5 Conquer America and Conquer the Atlantic / 238

6 The Rebirth of European Societies in North America / 301

Conclusion / 333

Notes / 343

Bibliography / 371

Index / 389

ILLUSTRATIONS

Page 3: detail of 'Cantino' map of the world (1502). In Henry Harisse, *Les Corte-Real et leurs voyages au Nouveau-Monde* (Paris: E. Leroux 1883). Courtesy National Archives of Canada

Page 36: detail of drawing by Samuel de Champlain depicting Huron deer hunt. In Samuel de Champlain, *Les voyages de la Nouvelle France occidentale, dicte Canada ...* (Paris: Pierre Le-Mur 1632). Courtesy National Archives of Canada, C113066

Page 78: detail of wampum etching, engraved by I.B. Scotin. In Claude Charles Le Roy Bacqueville de la Potherie, *Histoire de l'Amérique septentrionale ...* (Paris: J.-L. Nion & F. Didot 1772). Courtesy National Archives of Canada, C10891

Page 163: detail of etching on the cover of *Le grand voyage du pays des Hurons ...* , by Gabriel Sagard (Paris: Chez Denys Moreau 1632). Courtesy National Archives of Canada, C113480

Page 238: detail of etching depicting the English capture of Quebec. In Louis Hennepin, *Nouveau voyage d'un pais plus grand que l'Europe avec les réflections des entreprises du Sieur de la Salle ...* (Utrecht: A. Schouten 1698). Courtesy National Library of Canada, C115063

Page 301: detail of a drawing of a habitation constructed to house Samuel de Champlain and others at Quebec. In Samuel de Champlain, *Les voyages du sieur de Champlain Xaintongeois, capitaine ordinaire pour le roy, en la marine ...* (Paris: Chez Jean Berjon 1613). Courtesy National Library of Canada, NL 8759

Preface
and
Acknowledgments

> Some say to us, 'Do you think you are going to succeed in overturning the Country?' Thus do they style the change from their Pagan and Barbarous life to one that is civilized and Christian. *Jesuit Relations* (1936), 10:27

To write the history of northeastern North America, we must begin by looking beyond the political framework and artificial boundaries that various European powers imposed on the continent. We must consider this huge territory as it was, well before the first European contacts – an economic unit, an area in which people and goods circulated, bordered by the Atlantic seaboard, the Saint Lawrence River basin, and Hudson Bay – a world in which the division of labour, although rudimentary, was a characteristic trait. We must then analyze the process by which this area was brought into the Atlantic economy.

Contact and exchange presuppose the existence of two parties, and we must therefore look at the relationships that developed between Amerindians and Europeans. All too often, only a brief introductory chapter is devoted to this aspect of Amerindian history in North America, after which writers turn to the question of how European societies took shape on this continent. This obscures the fact that Amerindians played a determining role in the historical period. The history of the conquest of North America cannot be fully told unless it includes the history of the conquered peoples. Similarly, commentators have frequently focused too much attention on the influence of France and England in North America, forgetting the presence of Sweden and Holland – a particularly serious omission where Holland is concerned, since this country exercised a determining influence in the fullest sense.

We are therefore embarking on a study of the history of these various powers, but with a difference. It is not so much the political acts of their leaders that interest us as the transition of these social groups to capitalism. We will look at their position in the economic world-system centred on the Atlantic and evaluate their standing in the wider European world-system, bearing in mind that Europe, in order to generate profit, had organized a global economy linking continents and oceans in a single entity.[2] World-system theory is based on the premise that all world-systems have a characteristic, hierarchical organization consisting of a core or centre, a semi-periphery, and a periphery. Consequently, each of the social groups under consideration has a place in this perspective.

At the beginning of the seventeenth century, Holland occupied the central, hegemonical position. (Incidentally, for the purposes of this book, Holland means the Low Countries or United Provinces of the period, unless the actual province of Holland is specifically mentioned.) Amsterdam was at the heart of both the Atlantic and European world-systems. England hovered on the semi-periphery, although near the central zone, and a little farther off were Sweden, France (the cities of the western coast, at any rate), the countries of the Iberian Peninsula, and Italy. North America lay in a distant periphery, as did Africa and India.

The globe has experienced a phenomenal expansion in economic life since the sixteenth century. The underlying mechanism behind this movement toward the integration-subordination of the world into one vast economic system is, without any doubt, the process of accumulation of capital on a global scale.

Despite the fact that northeastern North America formed an entity, it was impractical within the scope of this book to carry out a detailed study of each of the first peoples or even each of the major families of peoples. A choice had to be made, and we will therefore be looking mainly at Iroquoian rather than Algonkian societies. Similarly, the Inuit do not fall within the scope of this study.

The wealth of available documentation and analyses of the

Iroquoians – and more particularly the Hurons – made this a logical choice. Among the studies in this area, Bruce G. Trigger's masterwork, *The Children of Aataentsic*, has exercised a marked influence on my work – one that goes far beyond the few direct references given in the course of this book.

Because it was mainly the fur trade that established relations between Europeans and Amerindians during the period under discussion, and because Albany and Montreal polarized this trade, I have focused more attention on interracial relations in New Netherland and New France, only alluding to those in New England by way of reference. From another perspective, however, we will be closely following the development of the English colonies' position in the Atlantic economic system.

I have chosen to insert long citations in the text. Although this is not customary in works of this kind, I felt it would give the reader more direct contact with rich and little-known sources (in particular the *Jesuit Relations*), and also allow the various historical actors a chance to speak for themselves.

I would like to thank all those who helped me bring this work to completion, as well as those whose advice I asked and who provided both assistance and encouragement. I especially want to thank Gilles Bourque, Michel Leblanc, Emmanuel Le Roy Ladurie, Pierre Mignault, Marie Laure Pilette, Gertrude Robitaille, and Sylvie Vincent for their invaluable contribution, as well as Paulette Poulin and Jocelyne Larochelle, who typed the original French manuscript. Finally, my thanks go to Micheline Dejordy for her indispensable support and close collaboration, and to my two sons, Paul and Éric.

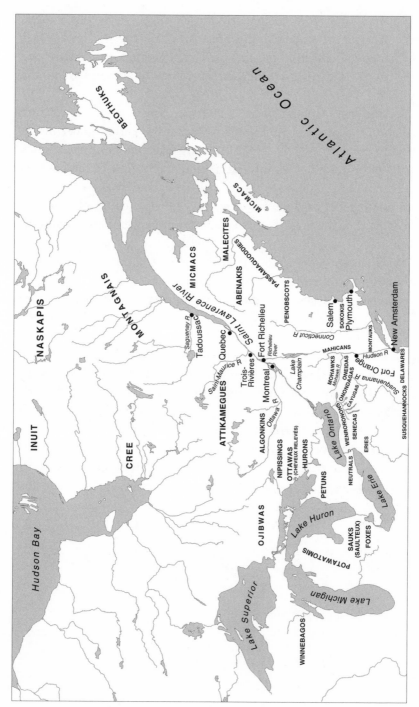

MAP 1: TRIBES OF NORTHEASTERN NORTH AMERICA

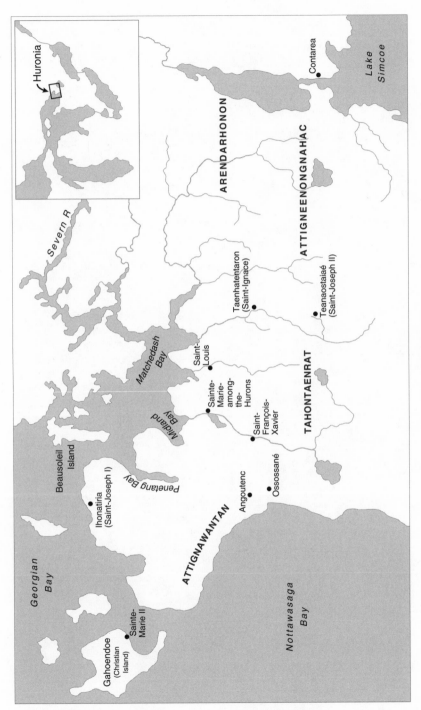

MAP 2: HURONIA

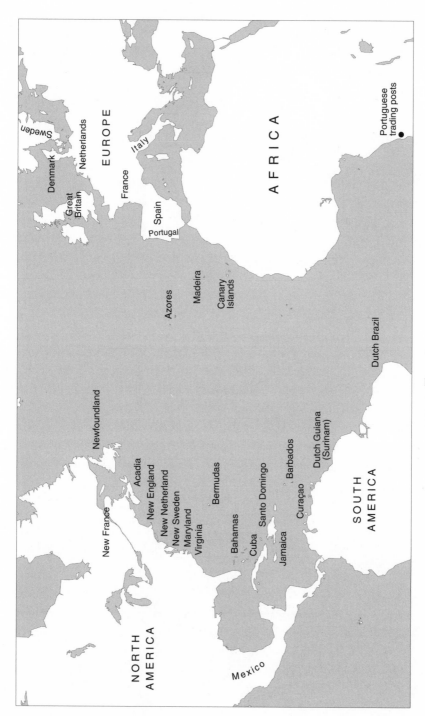

MAP 3: The Atlantic

BITTER FEAST

EUROPE IN TRANSITION AT THE HEART OF AN ECONOMIC WORLD-SYSTEM

1

The colonies of seventeenth-century North America were born as a result of the workings of merchant capital and the rivalry among imperial powers for a share of the world market. For this reason, any study must examine how these colonies were articulated and integrated with Europe and the global economy of the day, and in particular, with the underlying process of accumulation of capital. The colonies represent elements in a greater whole that, like pieces of a jigsaw puzzle, can only acquire coherence and meaning when assembled. However, again like a jigsaw puzzle, the picture exists before the pieces: it is the whole that determines the elements, not the other way around. This means that North American colonial history cannot be explained in concrete terms without taking into account the European economic conjuncture, demographic cycles, phases of growth and decline, and also the bumpy and irregular transition from the feudal to the capitalist mode of production.

To posit the hypothesis that causality in history goes beyond the frontiers of each colony, and even the continent itself, presupposes not only linking the study of colonial history to a wider perspective, but also setting our inquiry within a specific time frame. Major economic cycles occur in century-long spans and need to be viewed with a wide-angle lens, so to speak. Moreover, colonial history can only be really understood in the light of an economic world-system. A world-system is a huge socio-economic entity that covers and integrates regions, countries, continents, and empires, and one that functions according to the exigencies of an economic conjuncture common to all parties. It is a system where the ebb and flow of prices, wages, and populations affect all these parties, despite discrepancies among them. On another level, it is also a system characterized by the international division of labour with a core that monopolizes finance, commerce and manufacturing, and a more rural, primitive periphery that supplies raw materials. In the fifteenth century, the system centred on Europe. It spread to South America and Africa in the sixteenth century, and to North America in the seventeenth, finally encompassing the Mediterranean, the Baltic, and the Atlantic. A common mechanism for establishing prices had already developed, therefore, against the backdrop of the major transition from feudalism to capitalism – advanced in some areas, at a standstill in others. Capitalism involved the development of production forces, expansion of markets, accumulation of capital, and dispossession of small producers who were transformed into 'free' wage-earning workers.

THE CONJUNCTURE

Economically speaking, the whole sixteenth century is characterized by expansion, the phase A of a long cycle, despite intermittent slowdowns (1525-30, 1540-60) and even catastrophes (1585-1600).

The cycle opened around the years 1460-80, before the conquest of the Americas. What is immediately striking is the revolution in prices. At first they rose gradually, then, around 1525, the movement accelerated. Wages did not follow suit, however, and price inflation was soon accompanied by inflated profits. Over the century, real wages shrank by over half.[1]

The conquest of Africa and the Americas, their insertion into the European market, and the plundering that accompanied these conquests contributed enormously to this expansive thrust of economic life, as well as to soaring prices. The theft of great quantities of gold, the systematic exploitation of silver mines using new extraction techniques (the mercury amalgam process), and the use of slave Amerindian labour inundated the European market with precious metals. Low production costs contributed to this abundance of metals, which in turn contributed to the rise in prices. However, in those European societies that were still 85 to 90 per cent rural, transformations linked to major commerce did not yet constitute the standard variable. We must turn to agricultural production to understand the great economic fluctuations.

During this whole period, the European population was growing. It went from sixty or sixty-five million persons at the end of the fifteenth century to about 100 million at the end of the sixteenth century. The opposite was the case on the periphery, however. At the time of conquest, the Americas had a greater population than Europe (at least seventy million inhabitants at the end of the fifteenth century), but a century later it had fallen to between twelve and fifteen million. In Europe, demographic recovery involved a gradual occupation of marginal land and a consequent drop in agricultural yield. A farmer on marginal land puts in longer than average working hours while reaping a smaller crop. Under demographic pressure, agriculture spreads to poorer land, and farm prices tend to rise in both absolute and relative terms compared to non-farm prices. It was this process, active throughout the sixteenth century, that proved to be the main cause of inflation.

The tragic drop in American native populations and the exhaustion of the best lodes put a curb on the low-cost production of gold and especially of silver. Profits were subsequently reduced by the unification of markets and competition. It has been noted that following the second half of the sixteenth century, both economic and demographic growth slowed down. The seventeenth century, while not a period of decline, can nevertheless be qualified as phase B of a long cycle – a period of hesitant growth and stabilization. This was by no means uniform, either in time or space. The first two decades were difficult everywhere, followed by an upswing between 1625 and 1650, and a subsequent marking time from 1650 to 1700.[2] The Spanish and Italian economies were out of control from the beginning of the century, the French economy proved more stable, and the Dutch and English economies performed best.[3] Not only was there an economic chill: the climate itself added to the general difficulties. The seventeenth century, particularly the last half, experienced a global cooling – the little ice age.[4]

Another factor was the decline in the overall population of the world market during this century. Africa maintained its demographic level, but in the Western Hemisphere disaster struck. In central Mexico alone, the population fell from twenty-five million in 1519 to about one million a century later.[5] Nowhere else was the drop so drastic. In Germany especially, but also in southern Europe, populations dropped severely, possibly by as much as 25 per cent. France and Switzerland barely maintained their numbers. Only the countries in the northwest – Holland, England, and the Scandinavian group – registered some demographic growth, although this was very slow after 1650.

Margins of profit dwindled and competition grew. The change in conjuncture – that is, in short-term circumstances – affected the various powers in different ways. Some emerged as winners, others as losers, as the countries of Europe experienced upheavals in the balance of power, the division of labour, and in their positions on the international chessboard. We can already see that the powers taking part in the race for colonies in the early seventeenth century differed from those of the sixteenth century.

THE RISE OF NORTHWESTERN EUROPE AND THE DECLINE OF SOUTHERN EUROPE

Geography and Inflation

In the emerging world market, the conditions of the lengthy economic cycles were experienced by all. We can nevertheless detect numerous differentiation factors that helped shift the centre of gravity, contributing to the advance or the retreat of this or that country, and to its movement from the centre to the periphery or vice versa. Among these factors, two were crucial: the first, which was the result of the phenomenal geographic expansion of the European world-system, was the displacement of the major axes of economic activity from the Mediterranean to the Atlantic; the second was the inflation current throughout the sixteenth century.

Venice had been the centre of the European world-system during the fifteenth century, but the great discoveries of the following century dislodged the major axes of modern life. Seville, Lisbon, and Antwerp began to compete for the central position. The Flemish city was successful for a short period, until Amsterdam moved into the spotlight between 1590 and 1600.[6] The centre of gravity had therefore moved from southern to northwestern Europe.

The sharp rise in prices did not affect all regions of the world market with equal force – quite the contrary. The hardest hit were the two powers that had monopolized the New World's precious metals – Spain and Portugal – and consequently their principal suppliers of manufactured products, the Italian and Flemish cities. The closer the economic ties that any city or country had with Portugal and Spain, the harder they were hit by inflation. In this way, the very active role of sixteenth-century French merchants who were involved in trading American products contributed largely to inflation, and in the short term made their own products less competitive in various markets. French participation in Spain's rapid development was therefore to create the actual conditions for its own downfall. By the beginning of the seventeenth century, French products were no longer as competitive as English or Dutch products. The same was true for several Italian and Flemish products.

The Development of Forces of Production
The great powers were those with the most advanced – that is, the most efficient – production organization. The forces of production grew most rapidly in northwestern Europe.

The Dutch moved to the fore in communication techniques when they developed the *fluyt*, a vessel conceived for commercial purposes. A crew of only ten could man a 200-ton *fluyt*, whereas an old-style English ship of the same tonnage needed about thirty hands on board.[7] Shipbuilding methods progressed rapidly, particularly in Holland. The labour time needed for production was reduced by the use of cranes, by windmills that provided the power to run saws, and also by the division and standardization of labour. Any country that could take the lead as maritime builder and transporter held one of the keys of power. Holland took this lead in the seventeenth century, followed with some delay by England. These two countries were also the most innovative in the field of energy. The Dutch applied wind-driven energy to all kinds of sectors, from pumping the sea out of their fields to running flourmills, sawmills, and various grinding machines. The English, from 1540 on, rapidly increased their charcoal production. This was accompanied by a whole series of inventions unknown in continental Europe, such as ovens heated with coal or coke.[8] Mining, metallurgy, brewing, and construction demanded an ever greater input of constant capital, which was beyond the ability of artisans to accumulate. As a result, a capital-labour relation gradually developed.

The production of non-agricultural commodities formed the basis of the sixteenth-century urban economy. Labour was organized within the framework of the guilds, which kept strict watch over artisans' working conditions as well as the whole labour process: wages, size of workshops, quality control, and prices. This production system reached the height of its development in Italian and Flemish cities, which completely dominated the world market in the sixteenth century. The skills of their artisans and their control of the market enabled these countries to take over the main production sectors: textiles (including cloth, silks, garments, and tapestries), leather goods, glassware, printing, and metalworking. The Flemish and Italians had cornered the market for high quality and luxury products, leaving to other countries the commodities of lesser quality. Since the artisanal production methods were similar, it was more profitable to produce luxury merchandise than to compete for the ordinary commodity market.

England and Holland were therefore limited to producing lesser quality textiles, as was France to some degree. These countries marketed lighter, less durable, and less expensive products, engaging in mass rather than luxury production. The labour involved was more stereotyped, and the entrepreneurs reacted to the least profit fluctuation in mediocre goods by breaking down work into individual operations, extending the work day, and above all by pushing down the wage level. In England, instead of buying textiles from urban artisans, the merchants used rural workers in poor and overpopulated agricultural regions – a system variously referred to as 'putting out' or 'cottage industry.' These workers, who had not enough land for subsistence, spun, carded, and wove textiles in their homes for itinerant merchants. In the seventeenth-century economic context, when the market for luxury goods was virtually saturated, textile production on the putting-out basis was to completely outmode the guild system of production. The number of artisans involved in Venetian textile production dropped from 22,430 in the first decade of the seventeenth century to 2,640 in the final decade.[9]

Let us look at the most basic sector, agriculture, which determines the fate of all others. During the sixteenth and seventeenth centuries, two countries were to revolutionize agriculture. Holland was by far the leader in this area, followed once again by England. Little or nothing changed in all other countries. One seed of wheat sown yielded four or five grains. Throughout Europe, the system of allowing fields to lie fallow every three years prevailed, which meant that a third of the arable land was unproductive each year. The Flemish and Dutch were the first to break with traditional agricultural methods. Without letting the land lie fallow or exhausting the soil, they succeeded in producing greater yields by diversifying – mainly by alternating cereal and vegetable crops. The latter (hulled vegetables such as peas or broad beans, and fodder plants such as clover and alfalfa) are considered to be 'improving' crops because they fix atmospheric nitrogen and enrich the soil.[10] Furthermore, growing leguminous and root crops (mainly turnips) provided fodder for cattle, which made it possible to increase herds. More animals meant more manure and better soil fertilization. This modern form of agriculture enabled a small country like Holland, with a million and a half inhabitants, to become the great power of the early seventeenth century.

Such agricultural developments also served as the basis of England's power. It was this change in rural production techniques that was needed to set things in motion, to provide the thrust for the growth of cities, trade, manufacturing, and, in a word, the division of labour. By 1600, the Dutch peasantry probably made up less than half of Holland's population.[11] In England, around 1650, the peasantry made up about 50 per cent of the population. Apart from these two exceptions, the general proportion was over 80 per cent.

Production Modes and Transitions

In a Europe divided into powers competing to share (plunder) the wealth of the world market, the ultimate key to success lay in developing capitalist relationships in agriculture and industry. The secret of power and the basis for establishing a hegemony were to be found in countries where the capitalist mode of production ousted the feudal mode, and where the capitalist class was even able to control government. Throughout the period dealt with in this book, and in fact since the fourteenth-century crisis in feudalism, Europe as a whole had been engaged in a process of changing production relations. The speed and form of such changes differed according to region, but the basic context was identical. However, what interests us in this study are precisely the differences among countries; stagnation in some and forward movement in others is often a factor in the retrogression of the former and the progress of the latter. These differences, although they may be minimal to begin with, are pivotal in the process of transition. Insofar as they objectively play a key role in the positions occupied by different coun-

tries and regions in the centre, semi-periphery, or periphery, these differences have what is called a multiplier effect: a small initial advantage
which is transformed into an immense superiority, and vice versa.[12]
During the first half of the seventeenth century, it was in northwestern
Europe (mainly in Holland and England, but also in France) that capitalist relationships developed.

REFEUDALIZATION OF SOUTHERN AND EASTERN EUROPE

Spain

Strange as it may seem, the phenomenal wealth accumulated by Spain in
the sixteenth century, after it had plundered the Americas, actually
pushed the country backward. It caused an excessive rise in government
spending, while at the production level it merely stimulated the manufacture of luxury commodities, thus causing an enormous waste of time
and labour and entrenching old-fashioned working methods. Other
types of manufacturing, especially for medium quality textiles, disappeared. Since wealth is a source of inflation, money fled abroad to places
where its purchasing power was greater, and this in turn stimulated production in foreign countries.

Even though sheep-raising grew significantly in rural areas during
the sixteenth century, it did not have the same effect as in England. In
Spain, raising animals required the seasonal movement of livestock to
winter and summer feeding grounds, and this was such an important
factor that the monarch had accorded the exclusive right (*Mesta*) for
sheep-raising to the nobility, who successfully opposed land enclosure as
well as the regrouping of parcels of land and their transformation into
private property. The nobles' right of passage for their herds was thus
preserved, but at the same time agriculture was condemned to stagnation.[13] The Valencia region was the exception. Here the Moors had developed a state-of-the-art form of agriculture, using irrigation to produce
rice, sugar, and mulberries. However, with the expulsion of the Moors
between 1609 and 1610, this form of agriculture vanished. In Catalonia,
only the peasants were able to develop a more modern type of agriculture, since they exercised real property rights and were not crushed by
the burden of seigneurial rights. This region was also the only one to
experience relative prosperity in the seventeenth century.[14]

The textile industry of Castile, the country's main industrial sector, collapsed in 1590. The decline was absolute. 'Maritime activity between Spain and its American colonies, which amounted to 55 ships and 22,000 metric tons per year between 1600 and 1604, fell to 27 ships and 9,000 tons per year between 1640 and 1650, and to 8 ships and 2,500 tons per year between 1701 and 1710.'[15] A contemporary French source mentions the statistics recorded for total freight arriving at Cádiz at the end of the seventeenth century: 25 per cent French, 22 per cent Genovese, 20 per cent Dutch, 10 per cent English, 10 per cent Flemish, 8 per cent German, and only 5 per cent Spanish.[16]

Italy

The Italian cities were extremely prosperous from the Middle Ages to the sixteenth century. However, although their merchants had invested considerable capital in production, this sector never really assumed a truly capitalistic mode characterized by a capital-labour relationship. The guilds maintained their control over production, which was almost exclusively devoted to luxury commodities. In rural areas the feudal system remained dominant, and social relationships continued as before, much as they did in the cities. Close ties existed between capital and the major feudal powers, who formed an important clientele for luxury goods. At the time of the artisans' revolt, the bourgeoisie in Italian cities (like its counterpart in the cities of Flanders) allied itself as always with the feudal powers, thus undermining its own future as a class.[17] Moreover, Italian capital looked for shelter in finance and real estate investment, which helped to re-establish feudalism in rural areas. In addition to being organized on an overly constricting family basis, Italian merchant bankers lacked a strong consumer industry[18] and the support of a government powerful enough to help them realize their ambitions. As a result, their capital went largely to financing development in neighbouring countries.

Eastern Europe

For eastern Europe, the sixteenth century marked the beginning of a second period of serfdom. Even free settlers east of the Elbe were transformed into serfs. This region was condemned to retrogression because of the bourgeoisie's weakness and the peasants' inability to maintain their rights, even when labour was scarce and the demand for grain was high in western Europe, for which the east became the main supplier. The seigneurs monopolized trade and blocked peasant access to markets. At the same time, the peasants bore the brunt of taxation, and taxes grew at a dizzying rate. The results were disastrous for the entire economy.

THREE MODELS OF TRANSITION TOWARD CAPITALISM

Three great powers – Holland, England, and France – confronted one another in the seventeenth century. Holland had a mere million and a half inhabitants, England five million, and France twenty million. Despite such great disparities in population, it was Holland that dominated the world market at the beginning of the century. Its fleet ruled the seas and its products were competitive everywhere. A century later, England was on the point of overtaking Holland, while France, with its greater population, still lagged behind. The secret of the two smaller countries' success lay in the development of capitalism, which freed forces of production in agriculture and manufacturing. This gave them material superiority, with resulting commercial and military superiority. Furthermore, the development of capitalism breathed new life into the economy and society as a whole, providing a veritable kick-start that had an undeniable effect on colonial policy.

The Originality of the Dutch Model

The Dutch model of transition is interesting on several counts. In the first place, it demonstrates a transition to genuine capitalism, although this is disputed by some writers.[19] Holland was not only a republic of merchants. Production took forms that were definitely capitalist. There is a tendency to see only two models of transition: the English model for rural history and the French model for political history. Holland was original in more ways than one, however, and although it did not win out internationally in the long term, it nevertheless provides a model that cannot be ignored when discussing the question of transition.

In the Middle Ages, the feudal mode of production never gained the hold on the Dutch rural areas that it had elsewhere in Europe, whether in France, Germany, or even Flanders. Actually, Holland had been little more than a swamp-ridden zone on the outposts of the Roman and Carolingian empires. The soil was not good for growing cereals, so Holland became a land of livestock farmers. Because of their mobility, these farmers were able to resist the imposition of feudal relationships better than the sedentary peasants. Throughout the Middle Ages, the Dutch pushed back the sea to build their country. Peasant settlers in all the new polders shared the land as free men. Each peasant had his own parcel of land. Egalitarian traditions, especially those of the Friesians in the north, continued to exercise a strong influence. For example, elected representatives supervised the watch kept over the dikes. In general, land was sold to the settler in return for a cens – a form of ground rent – that was usually very low. The parcels were in a single block, and consisted of long, narrow strips.

Despite some formal constraints that were feudal in appearance, Dutch peasants were in fact free and most owned their own land.[20] In addition, Charles v's policy in the sixteenth century was to weaken the nobles of the Low Countries, in whom he saw a rival power. He took away their rights to dispense justice and to collect taxes and transferred them to the central power. Even aristocratic property became taxable. Small proprietors, on the other hand, found themselves freed from heavy social constraints and thus able to improve their work methods without fear of the seigneurs skimming off all the profits of their labour. They achieved better yields, specialized their farming, and participated intensively in marketing their surplus products and buying what they had previously made inefficiently for themselves in a self-sufficient economy.

This increase in agricultural yield, as well as the beginning of a division of labour within the rural world, was the basis of the Dutch economic development. On this basis, cities could grow and an internal market could emerge and expand, supported by the peasants' buying power. From then on, parcels of land remained intact instead of being broken up into smaller portions as the population grew. The surplus population worked in other sectors such as fishing, the navy, peat-gathering, and drainage. The peasantry became a class among other rural and general classes – a class that could, through its labour, accumulate enough capital to improve land drainage and buy more livestock.

During the sixteenth and seventeenth centuries, the size of herds on farms tended to grow, thereby producing more manure. A whole body of legislation existed to encourage better livestock breeding. Cows produced much more milk, which stimulated the production of butter and cheese. Several farms also specialized in industrial farming, growing such things as sea-kale and rapeseed, from which oil for soap, lighting, and cooking was extracted while the residues were fed to cattle. Among other products were flax for linen, hops and barley for beer, and plants for dyeing.

Horticulture, although limited to the gardens of the wealthy elsewhere in Europe, took great strides forward in Holland. Large scale production of fruit and vegetables developed in all rural areas. The Dutch were the only Europeans who ate fruit and vegetables. Farmers throughout Holland abandoned the fallow system that required a third of the land to remain unproductive. With draft animals, they could practice deep tilling. The land was systematically enriched with animal and vegetable fertilizers and urban waste. They grew leguminous plants, which fixed nitrogen in the soil. Windmills provided motor energy and canals accelerated transport. Produce was easily sold. Cereal production, which was already marginal, diminished in favour of more intensive farming. Wheat, barley, and rye, of which the Dutch ate less than other Europeans, were more frequently imported from the Baltic.

Contrary to what was the case elsewhere, the Dutch peasantry was prosperous and even had a literacy rate of over 50 per cent. After the Reformation, possessions seized from the Roman Catholic church (about 20 per cent of which was land), were used for public service projects such as education, health, and welfare. Schools popped up like mushrooms, and by the end of the sixteenth century there was a school in every village.[21] Purchasing power extended to the peasant masses, instead of being concentrated in the hands of a few noble families who bought luxury products, as it was in eastern Europe. Inventories after death confirm this, showing that the Dutch peasant bought all kinds of textiles, various copper, pewter, and iron objects, and construction materials.[22] This provided a sound material base for the manufacturing sector.

Dutch farming was specialized and commercial, but in the strict sense it was not capitalist. Although profit was a criterion in farming, and considerable capital was invested, a wage-earning class hardly developed at all, except in rare instances. In the same way, no great estates developed. Unlike England, the Dutch peasantry was not dispossessed, and rural dwellers did not need to take on piece work at home in order to survive. However, although agriculture itself was not capitalist, it was the basis for the development of capitalism in other sectors of production and for the circulation of goods and capital. It encouraged the growth of cities and, in general, the division of labour everywhere, even in rural areas. In certain regions such as Friesland, farming families made up only 38 per cent of the population. What did rural people do if they didn't farm? They were artisans, merchants, or wage-earners – unlike their English counterparts, who formed a kind of rural subproletariat that lived in poverty, barely surviving from one putting-out order to the next. The Dutch wage-earners congregated in the peat-growing areas (peat being a fuel), and where labourers for drainage were needed. In the Groningen and Friesland regions, capitalist enterprises constructed canals, built villages to lodge the thousands of temporary workers, and exported enormous quantities of peat to various cities in the province of Holland.[23] The majority of young rural dwellers migrated to cities to work in production, commerce, or service. Many others became herring fishermen, sailors, or workers in ship-building yards.

The sea fed the country. Fish, particularly herring, was a basic food for the whole population. Throughout this sector, capitalist relationships quickly became established. The fishing fleet included several hundred ships in the North Sea (over 200 whalers sailed to the Arctic annually).[24] Several thousand sailors worked either on these boats or in commercial shipping. During the sixteenth century, fishing boats belonged to their captains, who hired a crew of about twelve men. By the beginning of the seventeenth century, however, things had changed. Fishing businesses with several ships would hire both captain and crew. This development resulted from the need to centre fishing in two major ports (because of the war against Spain), combined with growing marketing difficulties and the rapid rise of equipment costs.[25]

Although heavily involved in the fishery business, the Dutch were above all traders. At the end of the sixteenth century and the beginning of the seventeenth, Holland's commercial supremacy was unrivalled. It controlled the world market's major circulation axes. The merchants speculated in time and space, buying cheaply and selling at a profit. Everything passed through Holland, mainly through Amsterdam, which became an immense warehouse. There were never less than 800,000 to 1,000,000 bushels of cereal in stock, ready to be sold when prices rose.[26] In 1670, the Dutch fleet's tonnage stood at around 568,000, a volume far superior to the combined volumes of the Spanish, Portuguese, French, English, Scottish, and German fleets.[27] The Dutch fleet employed 120,000 sailors,[28] and it controlled the entire Baltic trade, importing wood, hemp, peas, vegetable oils, and cereals. By the second half of the six-teenth century, the price of cereals on the international market was being set in Amsterdam. Dutch mercantile enterprises bought, transported, transformed, refined, and resold commodities. Louis xiv bought the Italian marble for Versailles in Amsterdam. The Dutch East India Com-pany, founded in 1602 with an initial capital of 65 million florins or ten times the initial capital of its English rival, controlled half of the Euro-pean trade with Asia once it had ousted the Portuguese from most of their trading posts. The Dutch West India Company, founded in 1621 with a similar capital, occupied Brazil and controlled most of the Atlantic trade in African slaves. These great companies generated capitalist relation-ships. At the end of the seventeenth century, the Dutch East India Company was hiring 12,000 men for its warehouses, shipbuilding yards, arsenals, and ships. Most of these were wage-earners. During its two centuries of existence, this company was to transport a million men on its ships bound for Asia. Only a third of the crews survived the five-year round trip.[29]

Merchant capital entered production, and a whole manufacturing section developed (*Verkeersindustrien*),[30] linked to major commerce. In this country with no forests, the greatest shipbuilding yards of the period sprang up. These in turn exercised a powerful stimulus on other activi-ties – the manufacture of sails and cables, nails, and precision instru-ments. Also involved were all those enterprises with a high percentage of constant capital, which transformed imported raw materials into fin-ished products for export – distilleries, foundries, sugar and salt refiner-ies, tobacco and soap factories, cloth-bleaching houses, printing plants, and glass factories. The cost of these installations eliminated the artisan-entrepreneur from the start. Wage-earners were the general form of labour, and the guilds were completely excluded. Briefly put, the process of division of labour was under way in Holland.

Alongside this first sector, and dominated by it, grew what Dutch historians call *fabrieken*, an older manufacturing sector which was less directly linked to the phenomenal rise of major commerce. The *fab-rieken*, with a high percentage of variable capital, hired specialized labour working mainly in textiles but also in leatherwork, pottery, and, to a lesser degree, in brickmaking. The capital-labour polarization in this older sector was not complete. The guilds were still active but were unable to block the development of wage-labour. Nevertheless, they still managed to maintain trade skills as the basis for division of labour, and to prevent the transfer of activity from town to country. In the early seventeenth century, the textile industry of Leiden dominated all the others, even the English, with its 'new draperies,' a lighter, lower quality fabric made of long staple wool.[31] However, England became especially competitive, thanks to the compulsory purchase of Irish wool at low prices, and to the development of the cottage industry due to the poverty of the English peasantry. England finally overtook Holland, which had to fall back on producing mainly luxury fabrics. The 'new draperies' – the sector of the future that would bring about a new, capitalist division of labour – moved to England.

Holland, centre of world trade and, for a long time, the leader in manufacturing, also played a major financial role through its enormous accumulation of capital. Its stable currency was for many years the universal money, that is, the general equivalent in international trade. The first real bank in Holland was founded in 1609, as was the first exchange – signs of maturity in the financial sector. In peacetime, the mass of available capital brought the interest rate down to 3 per cent, whereas in wartime it kept the rate between 4 and 6.5 per cent, which favoured investors. By way of comparison, the kings of France and England at this time payed an interest rate of 15 and 10 per cent, respectively.[32]

The bourgeoisie, which had acquired control of the national liberation movement in 1580, created and controlled a flexible, centralized government. The bourgeoisie had also done away with feudal constraints and had infused all social life with its own criteria of success. The country was highly urbanized. Amsterdam's population grew from 30,000 inhabitants around 1580 to 100,000 in 1620. Leiden and Haarlem each had 40,000 inhabitants; Rotterdam 20,000. The internal market was solid, and division of labour between town and country well developed. Unlike the rest of Europe, where the economic crisis of the seventeenth century served as an excuse to hound out dissidents, religious tolerance prevailed in Holland. As a result, Jews and Huguenots arrived by the thousands to work and invest there. People from Scandinavia, Germany, and Scotland also came to look for work. Emigration was low as there was no lack of work, salaries were the highest in Europe, and some social measures were already in place to reduce poverty, including free handouts of bread and clothing, and shelters for poor people. In the early seventeenth century, the Dutch republic was therefore a capitalist social organization – the only one in existence at that time. Later, Holland would be overtaken by its rival, England, where the development of capitalism followed a different course. This was the emergence, in rural areas, of a less sophisticated model that tended to focus more on changes in the production process.

The English Way

The English development toward capitalism is distinguishable from the Dutch mainly because of the agrarian question. Although the country followed the Dutch and Flemish model, thus acquiring the indispensable infrastructure for getting started, it moved away from the Dutch model as far as social relationships in agriculture were concerned. Instead of developing a peasant land-owning class that was active in the market, true capitalist relationships were established within agriculture itself, according to what is now the classic model: landowners and capitalist farmers on one side and wage-earning rural workers on the other. The yield from the English capitalist farm compared well with that of the Dutch peasant-proprietor's farm. The basic difference lay in the fact that the English model favoured the development of cottage industry by dispossessing the rural proletariat.

Unlike Holland, England had a well-established feudal mode of production. Here, as elsewhere on the European continent, this mode of production experienced a crisis in the fourteenth century that brought about a major readjustment of class relationships. Since the system had used up all the available arable land, and because productivity tends to diminish when marginal land is opened up, the dominant classes were unable to guarantee the maintenance of their revenue.[33] These classes therefore tended to increase surplus labour and exactions of all kinds, bringing about a rise in peasant unrest. The peasants succeeded in freeing themselves from serfdom – that is, they obtained the removal of corvées and arbitrary taxes, and acquired the right to move about freely. The amount of the feudal rate known in England as the cense became fixed. Nevertheless, despite many revolts during the first half of the sixteenth century,[34] this class never succeeded in acquiring a genuine right to ownership of its lands.

The tendency for feudal rents to drop reached a critical point. The feudal landholders were unable to bring about a return to serfdom and thus an increase of peasant exploitation. They began evicting the peasants in the sixteenth century, when market conditions were more favourable for agricultural production, particularly sheep-raising for the textile industry. Enclosure – the movement that dispossessed rural populations by appropriating common land as well as by transforming land in feudal domains into enclosed private property – was not confined to England. The same phenomenon occurred throughout continental Europe, with the exception of Holland. It was more noticeable in England, however, where the movement was of unparalleled magnitude.

While the gentry, in particular the large landholders, took over common lands, the yeoman class, consisting of freeholders under the rank of gentleman, also participated by annexing waste land and by regrouping adjoining parcels of land. The poorest peasants were forced out, unable to live by farming any longer. They thus became wage-earning farm labourers for wealthy landowners or for rural domestic industry, urban wage-earners, or, as was the case for 80,000 peasants between 1620 and 1642, they emigrated to New England and the West Indies. Regrouping and specialization of the land resulted in greater yields, while the new wage-earners increased the consumer market. Gradually, people from rural areas swelled the ever-growing urban population. By the beginning of the seventeenth century, 10 per cent of the English population was already concentrated in London, compared to 2 per cent of the French population in Paris.[35] The monarchy opposed this phenomenon at first for military and fiscal reasons.[36] Legislation against it was ineffective, however, and in 1608 the major landholders were already powerful enough to get initial legislation passed in favour of enclosure.[37] Cromwell's revolution of 1640-50 finally abolished all vestiges of feudalism in rural areas, benefitting the large landholders and thus sealing rural capital-labour relationships. This decade represented far more than a civil war for English society; it was a break with the old order, a profound and irreversible transformation of the whole society. The capitalist mode of production had succeeded to such a degree that England, which had been a second-ranking power at the beginning of the century, became the great power of the two following centuries.

The English bourgeois revolution is a crucial event in explaining this country's rise to power, and more particularly, the resulting success of its colonial policy. By looking at England before and after the revolution, we will see how important it was for capitalism to be already well developed in the sectors of agricultural and non-agricultural production, thus providing the bourgeoisie with enough power to end feudal relationships and take over the government. It would use this government to further its own ends, despite certain concessions to the aristocracy.

Between 1500 and 1640, the English countryside changed slowly. At the time of the Reformation, the large landholders took over a very sizeable portion of the lands confiscated from the Roman Catholic church. They then continued to enlarge and regroup their properties by enclosure. Men were evicted for sheep, in fact. Behind this extension of sheep-pastures at the expense of peasant land, another reality was beginning to take shape. The large landholders, in the manner and according to the interests of their class, were changing English rural society to accommodate the demands of wool production, a sector dominated internationally by the Dutch. The transformation of English society thus took place in a context of dependency. In the longer term, the changes eventually brought about the conditions that took England from the semi-periphery to the centre of the Atlantic market and, ultimately, of the world market.

Between 1610 and 1640, England's external trade increased tenfold.[38] In the first half of the sixteenth century, agricultural change brought a sharp rise in English cloth exports mainly destined for finishing in Antwerp. When the international economic circumstances changed and the market shrank at the beginning of the seventeenth century, production in England was maintained, despite numerous difficulties, by being oriented toward coarser cloth produced in rural areas by dispossessed peasants. Only the English social structure could accommodate this new division of labour, in which merchant capital entirely dominated domestic labour. In this way, commercial capital penetrated the production sector and was oriented toward mass production rather than the production of luxury goods. The process of rural evictions led to the formation of a national market and encouraged the development of consumer industries within the country.

In effect, the dispossessed peasants, poorer than their self-sufficient ancestors, were forced to buy food and clothing. Moreover, in England the development of commerce gave rise to the creation of industries such as sugar refining, the production of saltpetre, copper, and so on. It might be said that this 'backward' country was merely catching up with the rest of Europe. Nevertheless, it was precisely in these new sectors that capitalist relationships developed – something that was not always the case across the Channel. Where England did make innovations, however, was in the energy field. By the sixteenth century, coal had begun to replace wood as a fuel.

The new industries required such large investments that artisan-entrepreneurs were excluded at the outset. It was therefore on a clearly capitalist basis that this leading sector developed. The monarchy tried various means of limiting the concentration of land as well as extending and imposing the town guild system for organizing labour.[39] In general, however, these government measures, and others designed to stop the use of new machinery, could never be effectively and strictly applied – unlike in France, where the monarchy, having provided itself with a servile bureaucracy, exercised far more real power than in England.[40]

As a rising power and Holland's rival, England already had several advantages: a superior energy source (coal rather than peat), a larger internal market because of its population (five million compared to one and a half million), and capitalist production relations that were becoming established even in rural areas. At the beginning of the seventeenth century, England seemed as much a colony as a rival of Holland. Cromwell's bourgeois revolution was to demolish the two major obstacles blocking the rise of English capitalism: the vestiges of feudalism and Dutch supremacy.

The English revolution, like the French revolution a century later, assumed the dimensions of a gigantic social conflict in which the various social forces of the country confronted one another in every direction. These forces were the aristocracy, which opposed the loss of its privileges and the excessive centralization of power in the hands of the monarchy; the levellers, made up of peasants opposed to enclosure and artisans opposed to the disappearance of the guilds; the merchants of the great monopolies, often linked to the old order; and finally the rising bourgeois classes, wealthy as a result of their investments in farming, manufacturing, and commerce. Following the severe tensions of the English civil war, it was the bourgeoisie that emerged victorious by insuring the political and social conditions of its own success.[41]

The feudal regime was done away with in 1646, a move that benefitted large landholders. Feudal land became private property, but ownership was not guaranteed to copyholders (holders of parcels of manorial land), who could, therefore, be evicted by former feudal authorities who now owned the land. This marked the end of institutional obstacles to enclosure. Feudal privileges were eliminated, as were commercial monopolies, both of which had been barriers to the free circulation of men and merchandise in what became the greatest internal market in Europe. Feudal courts of justice were also done away with, as well as sumptuary laws (laws regulating expenditure, mainly with regard to conspicuous consumption according to rank). Although the craft guilds were not legally abolished, obstacles to the penetration of capital in business disappeared and the artisans gradually became members of the proletariat.

The revolution also did away with absolute monarchy and transferred power to a parliament controlled by the bourgeoisie. The old tax system, which was mainly a burden on agricultural production, disappeared. Parliament created two taxes: a property tax and an indirect tax on consumption. Since it had acquired control of these taxes, it was able to use this power to benefit industry. The sale of public administrative posts (barratry) was abolished. The revolution also affected all forms of religious life. The Church of England lost part of its lands and courts, its monolithic control of education, and its power of censorship. The many religious sects emerged from hiding and were able to hold public meetings and discussions. True, the Church of England remained the official church, but competition among doctrines became an established fact. This breach in official dogmas and the mechanisms of censorship encouraged the rapid expansion of intellectual and scientific life.

Cromwell's revolution guaranteed the rising bourgeoisie control of government by lifting the internal institutional obstacles to the development of capitalism. The battle was not yet won, however. English capitalism and the class that brought it about – the bourgeoisie – could not develop unless they broke free from their semi-colonial dependence on Holland. It was therefore no accident that the English revolution was accompanied by an offensive against Holland that took concrete form in the Navigation Acts of 1650-51, and later of 1660. The aim of the Acts was to weaken the Dutch monopoly on shipping by insisting that all goods entering and leaving English ports be carried by English ships or by those belonging to either the country in which the goods originated or to which they were going. The Acts also prohibited foreign ships from having access to colonies, thus greatly assisting Britain's development as a naval power. To this was added a series of protectionist measures designed to encourage local textile production at the expense of the Dutch textile industry. The commercial confrontation developed into a military standoff. It took three wars – 1652-54, 1665-67, and 1672-74 – for England to gain a decisive victory over its rival. The Dutch international trade monopoly was broken, and London, like Amsterdam, became a warehouse for international commerce. Although Holland retained control of the Baltic trade, it was nevertheless gradually ousted from the Atlantic.

The double victory of the English bourgeoisie over the old regime and its Dutch rival accelerated the development of capitalism. In 1651, the Venetian ambassador to London was already noting that 'trade and traders are making great strides, for the government and commerce are in the same hands.'[42] Capital controlled agriculture and imposed its laws: polarization of capital (land, livestock, and equipment) against labour (wage-earners), the search for maximum profit by increasing productivity (relative surplus value), along with a wage squeeze and the extension of the working day (absolute surplus value). Toward the end of the seventeenth century, the large landowners controlled about three quarters of the agricultural land.[43] The percentage of the labour force devoted to farming diminished, while total production increased and prices dropped. The country became an exporter of cereals and meats. Toward the end of the 1660s, 30 per cent of the population lived in towns, which was less than in Holland, but twice the French figure. Finally, while manufacturing on the continent tended to decline with the various crises, particularly after 1650, it made rapid progress in England.[44] Large businesses were founded, operating outside the guilds and employing many wage-earners in glassworks, mines, foundries, breweries, shipbuilding yards, and so on. A proletariat was developing, its members poorer than their artisan ancestors. The latter took fourteen to fifteen weeks to earn enough to pay for a year's bread, whereas in 1730 their descendants took fifty-two weeks.[45] Workers, as well as farm and manufacturing products, could circulate freely in a huge internal market that had no domestic barriers. Holland, the only great capitalist power at the beginning of the seventeenth century, finally lost its lead to England, the second country to experience a bourgeois revolution. England in turn had to face a third power, France. However, despite the fact that France was four times greater in area and population, it was never able to compensate for its outmoded socio-economic regime.

The French Way

France was the most populous country in Europe, with twenty million inhabitants in 1600. No other country, not even Russia, had even half this number. England had five million at most. As Fernand Braudel has described it, 'France was as full as an egg.'[46] Its strength lay in the density of its population, its strategic geographic position, and its centralized government. Its great weakness was agriculture. Yields were low and methods out of date. Techniques that were already known to Flemish and Dutch farmers could not take hold the way they had in England because the French farmers had no available capital to improve yields. Furthermore, it was difficult to feed cities if the countryside was barely subsisting, nor was it possible to foster the growth of a wage-earning class if farm prices shot up with every crisis in agricultural production. If agriculture could not advance, neither could anything else. But why was French farming so continually bogged down? The answer to this question is best seen by looking at the specific history of the French transition from feudalism to capitalism.

In the Middle Ages, France built the classic feudal structure. The system, like that in England and elsewhere, was severely shaken by the crisis of the fourteenth century. The result was very different in France, however, because limited peasant production on a family basis had almost supplanted seigneurial production, and this had enabled the French peasantry to withstand the crisis of expropriation by feudal landholders better than their English counterparts.[47] Unable either to evict the peasantry or return them to serfdom, a form of labour that was too inefficient due to peasant resistance, the aristocracy had no choice but to compensate for the drop in revenue that, as a rule, accompanied all phases of decline. It therefore increased pressure on peasant families in order to force them into surplus production. This additional feudal oppression provoked more peasant resistance and led to numerous revolts. These were a serious threat to the feudal system, as they put into question the very existence of the seigneury. The revolts in turn stimulated a movement designed to benefit the monarch by centralizing power and putting down resistance. The disappearance of serfdom did not, therefore, mean the end of the feudal mode of production, but merely the end of a phase. Once the crisis was over, this mode of production was restructured along different lines, the main one being the increase in the monarch's power to shore up a crumbling feudal authority.[48]

In the seventeenth century, French agriculture continued to be plagued by recession and numerous production crises. Cereal crop yields hovered between a ratio of 4 grains harvested to 1 seed sowed, and at best 6 to 1, or in bad years a scant 2 to 1. On the other hand, in Flanders, Holland, and somewhat later in England, yields regularly reached a ratio of 15 to 1.[49] If we take 5 to 1 as an average, which is probably higher than the actual yield, and if we remember that farmers had to put aside the seed for the following year, this gives an average yield for consumption of 4 to 1.[50] Before the sheaves had even been harvested, however, the Church took a tithe of approximately 1 in 10. Further payments took their toll: the champart (a fixed share of the produce) where applicable, the cens (a form of ground rent), and other seigneurial dues, usually payable in money. In the case of métayage (a form of tenure in which the landowner supplied seed and equipment, and the farmer paid a portion of his produce), the landowners kept half the harvest. There was also tallage, a tax levied by the Crown on feudal dependants. In addition, there was often rent to pay, because few labourers owned enough land.[51] The collection of fiscal dues for king, clergy, and seigneur was usually entrusted to a financier called a 'farmer general,' who bought the right to gather taxes. This guaranteed the dominant classes regular revenues while giving free rein to the farmer general to use the harshest methods. The tax collectors meanwhile accumulated their own capital out of the difference between what they collected and what they had to hand over. Finally, there was the whole range of seigneurial rights: *lods et ventes* (taxes on the sale of land), *droits de justice* (the right to dispense justice), *droits de pigeonnier* (rights regarding dovecotes), and all sorts of regulations forbidding free access to forests and water courses.

With such a heavy feudal burden, it is not surprising that France underwent eleven general famines in the seventeenth century and sixteen in the eighteenth century, not taking into account the hundreds of regional famines.[52] Nor is it surprising that 85 per cent of families owned less than five hectares of land, this being the threshold above which a peasant family could live without fear of starving or going into debt, even in years when prices were high.[53] Further, in contrast to the Dutch peasant family, which made a comfortable living and had purchasing power as well, the French peasant family lived in squalid, unpartitioned huts with no hope of putting money by to improve its land, to drain it, or to purchase animals and equipment. Not only were there few animals, but those that did exist were skinny beasts. Cows, for example, gave half as much milk as those in Holland. As a result, manure was scarce, and the existing supply was badly preserved and badly used; nor was anything known about using such substitutes as vegetable fertilizers or urban waste.

Farming methods had stagnated. But how could they evolve when the land was broken up into tiny parcels, and subject to feudal regulations such as the *vaine pâture* (rules concerning the use of common land)? In any case, the farmer had little incentive to change his methods when the results of any increase in productivity were appropriated by the parasite classes, to be used for war, spent on luxuries, or accumulated as capital. Why buy a horse for ploughing merely to have it requisitioned by passing soldiers in the next war? Why invest in land burdened with all sorts of taxes, land for which the limits and rights of ownership were not even established, or land that might be subject to *main morte*, that is, which had to be returned to the Church upon the death of the holder? The feudal lords had tried to take over common land and absorb the peasant parcels, but enclosure had never reached a critical threshold. In general, there were few large landholders and few totally landless families. However, the peasantry did not possess the majority of arable land. Church and aristocracy were the great landowners, but instead of farming their land as a unit, they broke it up into parcels to be contracted out to peasants under the métayage system.

The poorest peasants had to take on piece work at home to survive, generally work related to the textile industry, thus creating a kind of semi-proletariat. In the strict sense, however, the mass of peasants were not radically cut off from their means of production. There was little development of a wage-earning class. Consequently, France did not develop a labour market or a genuine internal consumer market, as was the case in Holland with its specialized, prosperous peasantry, or in England with its dispossessed peasantry transformed into a wage-earning class. In France, the proportion of agricultural produce marketed remained small, on the whole, and self-sufficiency continued to be the principal objective.

Viticulture – growing grapes for wine – was the exception. This labour-intensive sector required low capital input, although as a general rule, despite a high degree of commercialization, the old social relationships persisted. This was the case in the La Rochelle region, in particular, where vineyards and salt marshes were rented out in métayage. The mode of production continued on traditional lines and the relationship between the proprietor and his métayers was more that of a feudal lord and his serfs than of a capitalist entrepreneur and his labourers.[54]

Although the bourgeoisie invested large amounts of capital in rural areas throughout the century, these were generally investments that fed off the old structures and had little effect on the growth of a wage-earning class, the concentration of ownership, or the development of production forces. All in all, the division of labour between rural dwellers who worked on the land and those who did not, or between rural and city dwellers, progressed slowly, even though the population of Paris doubled between 1600 and 1650, growing from 200,000 to 400,000.

Like agriculture, industry showed little progress and was unable to free itself from its traditional carapace. Capitalism had difficulty penetrating industry, and there was no sudden growth. We should not be deceived by the existence of numerous and renowned royal factories – nearly 300 of them – that enjoyed preferential status.[55] These were marginal in relation to overall production. Furthermore, they were usually models of their kind only in relation to luxury products that were generally destined for conspicuous consumption. Most of these factories ran on a deficit budget and developed nothing new in the way of production techniques and methods or labour organization, since they were based on the guild system of medieval industry. To paraphrase one of Braudel's comments, although opulence may effectively captivate a society, it is a poor means of supporting or promoting an economy.[56] France had no gold or silver mines, nor any coal mines. Wood was almost its only source of energy. Metallurgy played a minor role, and there was almost no quality steel production.[57] Papermaking, chemistry, and glassmaking continued to be marginal.[58] The navy was not much help as it lagged technically and did not have the stimulating effect seen in Holland and England. The building sector, occupied a fairly important place. However, in the non-farming sector it was the textile industry that had the highest production level and provided by far the greatest employment,[59] even though it only accounted for about 5 per cent of the gross national product and employed only 5 per cent of the population. Linen, hemp, wool, silk, canvas, fine and coarse cloth were produced by artisans in the towns and by peasants in the countryside. In other words, artisanal labour, not manufacturing, dominated urban areas. In rural areas, the impoverished peasant who produced textiles at home remained too poor to have any significant buying power. As he was not entirely destitute, he managed to stay self-sufficient and could avoid using the market to feed, clothe, and lodge himself.

A shaky internal market hardly encouraged improved means of communication. Conversely, poor roads discouraged an internal market. Until about 1660, roads were bad, bridges rare, and tolls innumerable. Most of the trade was limited to local roads and paths for a population of peasants bound to their lands, trying to live off what they possessed, and rarely going beyond two or three leagues for their needs. Family, the weekly market, the notary, and the local tribunal – either that of the seigneur or the king – formed their small world.[60] Before Colbert, the network of major roads was largely inadequate and used only for post-horse traffic and the transport of luxury goods. Beyond a distance of 'five or six leagues' (twenty to twenty-four kilometres), no provisions or merchandise, however light, could offset transport costs.[61] Waterways were a popular alternative although geography did not favour all regions, and canals were not built until the late 1660s. To all intents and purposes, then, no true internal market existed, economic life was fragmented and dispersed, and communications were poor.

France's state of international commerce was not much better. France traded mainly with the Middle East and Spain. Although a good third of its trade was with northern Europe, this was entirely controlled by the Dutch. France's port cities were beyond the main sea routes. Unlike Holland and England, both determined seafaring nations, France remained divided between land and water, and there was not the necessary concentration of capital to organize Atlantic traffic.[62] Trade with the

Americas was meagre, consisting of the Newfoundland fisheries, Canadian furs, and the slave trade, particularly with the West Indies (this last providing the basis for the greatest fortunes). Only Saint-Malo and Le Havre were able to outfit some fifty ships of 100 tons or more.[63] France had a total of only 350 in 1664.[64] This was probably about ten times less than the Dutch figure. In Holland, a similar number of ships would have three times the tonnage.[65] French currency was unstable and subject to frequent devaluations; it could only handle a small fraction of trade, and barter was therefore the main form of exchange. Furthermore, throughout the seventeenth century the monarchy did not yet have the monopoly for minting coinage, and 'little princes' who were more or less independent continued to mint their own money.[66] Even though the Italians, followed by the Dutch and the English, set the example, the French bourgeoisie was unable to acquire the two indispensable tools for ✓ the rise of capitalism – banking and an exchange. France cared mainly for commerce and very little for industry. Numerous foreigners were involved, most of them Protestants. The bourgeoisie, which represented a fraction of the population dominated by the upper classes, was drained from the top. In fact, whoever succeeded in commerce or industry ceased to be bourgeois and bought land, seigneuries, government posts, or noble titles. Once acquired, these symbols masked 'lowly' origins and the bourgeois shed his spirit of enterprise.[67] Richelieu is reported to have expressed the paradoxical opinion that if honours, and especially offices, were to be had without money, commerce would be abandoned.[68]

Behind the bourgeoisie, which acted as the vehicle of capital, capital itself became dominated and diverted from its proper aims in order to serve as a tool for social promotion in the old order. I say capital rather than capitalism here because the latter did not emerge until capital entered the production sector. This was rarely the case in seventeenth-century France. Merchant capital did indeed develop, but had little or no effect on production relations. There is no basic contradiction between the feudal system and merchant capital, as historian Maurice Dobb has pointed out,[69] because even though the latter tends to dissolve feudal relationships, it feeds on the old social order by living on concessions, monopolies, speculation in regional disparities, and subcontracts for gathering royal or seigneurial taxes. This means that the accumulation of merchant capital does not necessarily lead to capitalism. As long as capital makes few inroads into production, there is little development of the mechanisms by which peasants and owner-artisans are dispossessed and converted into wage-earning workers. Nevertheless, two groups did come closer to being actual wage-earners. These were the artisans, who were increasingly dependent on merchants, and, in particular, those peasants who lived on parcels of land too small for subsistence and who eked out a living with piece work done at home. It was only after the 1660s, however, that this process began to have a real effect.

In Holland, the rising bourgeoisie was the first to defeat a monarchy – in this case, the Spanish monarchy. In England, Cromwell's civil war ended in the execution of Charles I, whose successor lost any real power. Things were very different in France, where the monarchy had twice emerged victorious from severe social conflicts. The first of these occurred during the Wars of Religion in the second half of the sixteenth century. Here as elsewhere, religious motives acted as catalysts for deeper antagonisms – rivalry between nobles for control of the monarchy, social demands by artisans, economic and political demands by city merchants, and peasant struggles against the feudal system and taxes. The royal victory was a harsh blow to opposition forces, which included provincial parlements and independent towns and cities. Although the Huguenot stronghold of La Rochelle managed to obtain guarantees of considerable autonomy, Richelieu besieged it and forced it to capitulate in 1629. The policy imposed by him illustrates well the process of centralization within the yoke of feudalism. This comprised the imposition of royal taxes, the control of salt-works for the benefit of the monarchy, the interdiction of municipal councils, the restoration of municipal corporations, the sale of charters and public posts, and the appointment of nobles to key positions.[70] All in all, the monarchy succeeded in conquering and taming a merchant bourgeois stronghold and neutralizing its members. By thus affirming its authority throughout the country, the Crown was subsequently able to increase taxes by a coefficient of four between 1630 and 1640,[71] and even managed to severely restrict religious dissidence, that is, Protestantism.

The second confrontation took place during the civil war known as La Fronde, which for a time brought together the forces of opposition – provincial parlements, city artisans and merchants, and starving peasants. The outcome of this struggle destroyed the last obstacles to an absolute monarchy ruling by divine right. A central administration replaced the local parlements and (a fact worth noting) the army increased from 40,000 soldiers at the beginning of Louis xiv's rule to 300,000 by the end.[72]

Internally, France faced intense and frequent peasant[73] and urban struggles, a divided nobility, and pressure from minority segments of the bourgeoisie to do away with guilds and feudal relationships (in favour of enclosure and private ownership). Externally, it faced the meteoric rise of rival powers (Holland and England) and a socio-economic system that was qualitatively superior. None of these conditions, however, could prevent France's absolute monarchy from upholding the aristocracy's pre-eminent position by assuming and centralizing political power in its interests. Nor did they prevent the monarchy from stimulating economic development, although this was done within a framework of feudal relationships and in a contradictory manner. On one hand, economic development tended to obliterate the old structures, while on the other, the continued existence of these old structures inhibited economic development.[74]

THREE MODELS OF COLONIZATION

At first glance, it seems surprising that Holland, which controlled the seas during the entire first half of the seventeenth century, was unable to establish an Atlantic colonial empire. In fact, it was precisely this country's advanced commercial and industrial state, its prosperity and hegemony, which induced it to stick to commerce and transport on an international scale rather than engage in colonial enterprises. In particular, Dutch merchants could find wood, potash, cereals, metals, and furs at the best prices in the Baltic. It was precisely because Holland controlled Europe, commercially speaking, that seventeenth-century English merchants became interested in wood from Virginia for shipbuilding. Their choice was that of a second-ranking power.

This phenomenon is best illustrated in the fisheries. Shifts in the balance of power among European rivals in this sector were to have an absolutely determining effect on the colonial history of North America. The Dutch fleet took the lion's share – complete control of the North Sea. Moreover, they even controlled the inshore fishing along the British Isles and, in the sixteenth century, were the main suppliers to the British market. In 1600, 500 of such fishing boats plied British coasts.[75] West coast English fishermen were ousted from their own territorial waters and markets. The herring catch alone brought Holland at least two million pounds sterling, almost the equivalent of British textile exports.[76] Rather than crossing the Atlantic, the British might have found closer and therefore more profitable fishing grounds in the abundant waters around Iceland, the Jan Mayen islands, and Spitsbergen on the edge of the Arctic Ocean. However, between 1610 and 1630, the Dutch managed to push all rivals out of this area as well.[77]

Among such rivals was the Muscovy Company of London, also forced out of the most lucrative commercial fishing sector of the time, Arctic whaling. About 250 whalers sailed to the Arctic each year, the crews for these perilous expeditions largely made up of foreigners (Friesians and Germans). Processing stations were set up in Spitsbergen. The Geschiendenis der Novidische Company secured the fishing monopoly for the Arctic Circle, that is, from Novaya Zemlya, north of Russia, to Baffin Bay. Dutch sailors in the Davis Strait took possession of the Labrador coast in the name of the states-general of Holland and forced out all rival powers. The latter included France, which was interested in the area but was refused a permit to rent Dutch boats for this enterprise.

Under the circumstances, English, Basque, French, Portuguese, and Spanish fishermen had no choice but to go farther afield – to Newfoundland, in fact. There, the French and Portuguese had the upper hand during the first half of the sixteenth century. They started with two assets. Coming from salt-producing countries, they had access to cheap salt for preserving the cod catch on board. Moreover, these Roman Catholic countries were large consumers of fish. English fishermen not only had to pay more for salt, but their market had been taken over by the Dutch, and their boats were inferior. As a result, they dried their cod on shore, building drying racks for this purpose. This method required less salt but more men – about ten more per crew. The semi-permanent camps established for drying fish became the nuclei of future settlement. At the end of the sixteenth century, only the English had camps in Newfoundland. They exported their dried cod to Spain, bringing back wine and salt.[78]

The use of drying racks tended to concentrate the English fishing fleet, which originated in a few west coast ports. The method of salting the fresh cod on board, on the other hand, tended to disperse the French fishing fleet all over the fishing banks and the Gulf of Saint Lawrence.

French boats were therefore more open to attack by English ships, which managed to exploit the weaknesses in the French defence and monopolize the best fishing grounds. This drove the French ships farther into the Gulf.[79] It was therefore in spite of themselves that the French explored the Gulf and discovered a rich resource that they had not originally sought – furs. To begin with, they traded sporadically on the Nova Scotian shore, and then, around 1580, moved into the Gulf as far as Tadoussac, combining fishing and fur trading. It was only at the beginning of the seventeenth century that fur trading became a separate commercial activity. In 1605 the French established a permanent trading post in Acadia – Port-Royal on the Bay of Fundy. The site was not well chosen. Port-Royal was on a peninsula with limited access by river to a fur-producing hinterland. Moreover, it was vulnerable to pirate attacks by the English. In 1608, the French decided to move to Quebec, a site that commanded a view of the river and acted as a port of entry to northeastern North America, as well as being a refuge from rival navies.

Initially, the Dutch reacted to the French appropriation of a new source of supply by purchasing shares in French trading companies. The Dutch merchant Lambert Van Tweenhuyzen controlled 20 per cent of the shares in the de Monts Company, which in 1603 held the monopoly for Acadia.[80] Later, however, the Dutch intervened directly. In 1609, the English navigator Henry Hudson explored, on behalf of the Dutch, the river to which he gave his name. After this, the Dutch established themselves in the Hudson River area and attempted to siphon off the furs from the interior of the continent to the detriment of the French at Quebec. In any event, the furs that went from Quebec and Tadoussac to La Rochelle, Rouen, or Bordeaux ended up in Amsterdam before being shipped to Russia. The 'Muscovy' artisans knew better than anyone how to remove the short hairs of the beaver pelt in order to make felt for hats, while keeping the pelts and the guard hairs for other purposes.[81] The Dutch merchants would deliver one form of merchandise and leave with two others that they sold throughout Europe. In a word, all merchandise circulated through Dutch channels.

The Dutch did very little actual fishing on the Newfoundland banks, but they were present nevertheless. They left the work of production – that is, fishing and processing – to others and specialized in transport. Between 1589 and about 1670, they bought the product directly from the fishing boats and transported it faster and better than anyone else, reselling the fish throughout Europe.[82] However, they never established themselves in Newfoundland. There as elsewhere, rather than found colonies, they left the expense of such endeavours to other powers, since their competitive prices enabled them to penetrate every market. We must also realize that the Dutch had very little reason to emigrate from a religiously tolerant country with the highest standard of living in Europe and a prosperous peasant class engaged in intensive farming. When they did emigrate, they spread out in small settlements connected to their trade in various ports and cities of Germany, Poland, Scandinavia, France, and England. In any case, their main thrust was in the direction of the lucrative Asian trade.

It was a very different story on the other side of the North Sea. It was the jerky development, the crises, and the general difficulties of early seventeenth-century English society that, almost fortuitously, enabled Great Britain to establish the basis of a colonial empire. To begin with, peasants were evicted by enclosure, which was sanctioned by law as of 1608. This was followed by the general economic quagmire of 1620-30, during which Dutch production drove English production to the wall, so to speak. The English civil war and the bourgeois revolution sealed the fate of peasant struggles for free ownership of land. It was a violent process since the peasants were not evicted on an individual basis, but as a group. However, the relative toleration given to religious sects, which were agents of social as well as religious confrontation, made a certain amount of regrouping possible. The only option, however, was to leave: but for where? For Holland? That is what the Puritans did. For the great commercial centres of Europe? The Dutch had monopolized all of them. For Spain? But that was a Roman Catholic country, and in any case the French had long been the suppliers of cheap labour there. That left the Atlantic coast of North America or the West Indies, to both of which people from the British Isles emigrated in search of land and food.

From the colonial perspective, France started out as a loser and finished as a loser. This was not for lack of potential emigrants – far from it. In the sixteenth, seventeenth, and eighteenth centuries, large numbers of people emigrated from overpopulated France – thirty-four inhabitants per square kilometre in the sixteenth century, twice the rate of Spain. It was less than the Low Countries (forty per square kilometre) and Italy (forty-four per square kilometre), but these two were urbanized,[83] indus-trialized countries. Where could emigrants go? Spain was the main desti-nation. As cheap labour, French artisans, workers, and peasants took the place of the Spanish who left for the Americas. Braudel has defined this French emigration as 'abundant, permanent, and socially mixed, a clear sign of French overpopulation. Jean Herauld, sire de Gouberville, says in his *Mémoires* that there were 200,000 French in Spain in 1669, an enor-mous but not inconceivable figure.'[84]

In the sixteenth century, the Huguenot Wars exterminated or hounded out numerous dissidents. After the relative religious peace of the seventeenth century, the revocation of the Edict of Nantes in 1689 provoked fresh waves of wholesale emigration. However, by forbidding all religious dissidence, the French monarchy diverted emigration to Protestant countries. The founding settlers of French North American colonies amounted to about 10,000 Roman Catholics. It is very likely that almost as many Huguenot settlers came to the Dutch and English colonies of North America. In any case, with an economy that had little interest in the Atlantic, and a navy that was anything but vigorous, French colonists had not much incentive to go far afield. Furthermore, without competi-tive merchandise, how was it possible for the French to establish trade and make profitable inroads into the international market?

North America before
European Settlement

2

'My father well recalls the time when the white man came to look for minerals here in the interior,' wrote An Antane Kapesh in the spring 1975 number of *Recherches amérindiennes au Québec*, in an article entitled 'Ces terres dont nous avions nommé chaque ruisseau' ('These lands where we have named each stream'). 'The surveyor began measuring the Indian lands, but the Indian had long ago measured his own territory with his legs. There was not a piece of it that he had not seen and on which he had not set foot.

'When the Indian left the Moisie River, going as far as Fort Chimo on his own legs and finding his Indian food each day, he walked over this territory from one sea to another. And throughout the length and breadth of his territory he had given a name in his own language to each river and each stream. When he set off in a canoe for the George River from the mouth of the Moisie, he knew the Indian name for every single portage on his route.

'But these days no one knows the Indian way of naming the Indian land. Today, when you look at a map, all the rivers, all the lakes – the whole Indian country – have French names.'

NORTH AMERICA

An Antane Kapesh, a forty-nine-year-old Montagnais woman living in Schefferville, speaks to us of the dispossession of her people over the past forty years. It is a dispossession that is part of a process begun in the sixteenth century, and one that continues today – witness the current claims of Amerindian and Inuit communities. Need we remind ourselves that the Europeans did not discover the Americas? They conquered these continents that had been inhabited for over 40,000 years. The occupation of northeastern North America followed the retreat of the last ice age 10,000 years ago. North America is therefore an 'old continent.' What European navigators discovered was how to reach it.

We cannot conceive of North American history as the creation of new white societies in a new continent. The history of North America is first that of the Amerindians. Before studying the mechanism whereby this continent was integrated and subordinated to the world market and the process of accumulation of capital, we must take a moment to get to know this land, to learn who inhabited it, and what societies developed there.

Plant and Wildlife

The continent was covered with forest comprising vast stands of cedar, oak, pine, ash, and maple. According to Pierre Boucher, there were 'all the widths and heights of pine needed to make masts for ships, with strong elms, large and tall, and oaks that were tall, thick, and straight.'[1] The Jesuits remarked of the Richelieu that 'its banks are clothed with beautiful pines, through which it is easy to walk.'[2] The shores of the Saint Lawrence above Montreal 'are usually shaded with great oaks and other full-grown forest-trees.'[3] All observers remarked on the magnificence of the forest.[4]

The continent teemed with wildlife.[5] Such abundance was unheard of among Europeans, and the first white men were all overwhelmed by the wealth of game on the land and in the water. In North America, the number of bison alone has been estimated in the tens of millions.[6] Bison roamed not only the western plains, but the whole Great Lakes region. There were fairly large numbers even in New Netherland, especially in the southwest.[7] By the beginning of the twentieth century, all that remained of these immense herds was a mere dozen or so animals. Similarly, the white-tailed deer *Odocoïleus virginianus* existed in countless numbers in New Netherland,[8] although there were none in the Saint Lawrence valley below Montreal.[9] It was actually one of the rare species whose territory increased rather than shrank with colonization. The wapiti (*Cervus canadensis*), which once inhabited the temperate forests from the Atlantic to the Pacific, now only survives in the Rocky

Mountains.[10] Pierre Boucher, who called it the *vache sauvage* or wild cow, tells us that it could be found above Trois-Rivières and in increasing numbers as one moved upriver.[11] Travellers journeying from Montreal to Lake Ontario regularly spotted herds of wapiti swimming from island to island.[12] He also mentions encountering moose farther north, 'the most common and widespread of all animals in this land.'[13] Beyond this range, there were large numbers of caribou. South of Montreal, it was usual to see wild turkey, a fowl that is practically extinct on this continent today.[14] Van der Donck notes that these were the most widespread type of bird, and that they were found in flocks of twenty or thirty, large and plump, weighing between twenty and thirty pounds each.[15] Then there was the now extinct passenger pigeon *Ectopistes migratorius*, the *tourte* of New France. Their numbers were so prodigious that Van der Donck wrote, 'The pigeons ... are astonishingly plenty. Those are most numerous in the spring and fall of the year, when they are seen in such numbers in flocks, that they resemble the clouds in the heavens, and obstruct the rays of the sun.'[16]

De Vries has this to say: 'Pigeons, at the time of year when they migrate, are so numerous, that the light can hardly be discerned where they fly.'[17]

Figures of speech? Not at all. Here is Pierre Boucher: 'There is another kind of bird called a *tourte* or a *tourterelle*, if you will, almost as big as pigeons, with greyish plumage. The males have a red throat and taste excellent. Their quantities are prodigious, and one can kill forty or forty-five with a single gun shot. This doesn't always happen, but it is common to kill eight, ten, or twelve in this way. They usually arrive in May, and leave in September, and are found throughout this country. The Iroquois catch them in nets, sometimes taking three and four hundred at a time.'[18] For the reader who still thinks the descriptions in these few citations are exaggerated, the journal of the celebrated naturalist, John James Audubon, states that in 1813 on the Ohio River, a southbound flight of migrating passenger pigeons stretched out of sight from east to west, filling the air with a strong smell and obscuring the daylight for three consecutive days.[19] Pierre Boucher, who was the seigneur of Boucherville near Montreal, described the common birds of the region, among them the native swan, of which only a handful now survive: 'But I will only name those that are near by, such as swans, bustards, wild geese, cranes, ducks, teals, more than ten kinds of diving birds, [among them] loons, bitterns, herons, woodcocks, snipe, sandpipers, plovers, [and] dunlins.'[20]

On several occasions the Jesuits marvelled at the multitudes of bustards, ducks, swans, and wild geese.[21] Quail and partridge were everywhere. Sagard tells us that 300 horned larks (*alouettes*) were killed on the island of that name with one shot of a musket.[22] According to De Vries, in 1633 there were hundreds of thousands of wild geese all along the Atlantic seaboard, from New Netherland to Virginia.[23]

Throughout the continent, the limpid lakes and rivers, great and small, teemed with wildlife.[24] In 1644, the Dutch pastor Megapolensis noted that the waters of the Hudson River were as clear as crystal and that all sorts of fish could be caught in abundance: pike, sturgeon, burbot, carp, eel, and perch, among others.[25] The salmon swam upriver as far as Oneida country, to what is now called Orishany Creek.[26] Van der Donck states that 'all the waters of the New Netherlands are rich with fishes.'[27] 'There is much salmon and trout from the entrance to the Gulf up to Quebec,'[28] said Boucher, and beyond this the salmon went upriver as far as Niagara Falls. There were also large numbers of white beluga whales between Tadoussac and Montreal, and 'one saw admirable quantities' downriver from Quebec. At Trois-Rivières, the Jesuits mentioned a 'Savage' who caught twelve or fifteen sturgeon as tall as a man.[29] Father Le Jeune wrote in 1636:

> As to the fish, he is here, as it were, in his empire. There are a great many Lakes, Ponds, and Rivers, filled with them. The great river is full of Sturgeon, Salmon, Shad, Pike, Flounders, goldfish, whitefish, Carp of different kinds, Eels, etc. Not that they can be caught everywhere in the same abundance, but there are places where the quantity of fish seems marvelous. While I am writing this, here comes a boy bringing twenty-five or thirty Flounders, caught in one night. There are some Lakes where one could live on fish, winter and summer. This last winter our French caught Pike there three or four feet long, Sturgeons of four or five feet, and other fish in abundance. It was a Savage who made me acquainted with this trade. It is now being enjoyed by our French at the three Rivers, where the fishing, to tell the truth, exceeds all ideas that we may have of it; but it is not that way everywhere.[30]

Pierre Boucher wrote of the Quebec region, 'Fish are plentiful everywhere in this region, and of many kinds, such as sturgeon, salmon, brill, bass, shad, and several others. But I must also mention the eel fishing in autumn, so abundant that those who have not seen it for themselves could not believe it. One man caught over fifty thousand. They are big and plump, and very tasty, far better than those in France. We salt them all year long and they keep perfectly, being an excellent food for working men.'[31] Anthropologist Harold E. Driver estimates that, in terms of food supplied, the yield per fresh water acre exceeded that of hunting and gathering.[32] Large whales were frequently sighted in the Gulf as well as along the New Netherland coast, although they are now only found in the Arctic Ocean.[33] The shores of New Netherland also yielded a plentiful supply of lobsters, oysters, clams, mussels, cockles, and other seafood.

After this brief description of the flora and fauna of North America, let us travel for a few moments in Father Lalement's canoe on a 1663 journey up the Saint Lawrence between Lac Saint-Pierre and Montreal.

Continuing our route, we had not sailed quite an hour when we entered a Lake fed by six large Rivers which empty into it, besides the river Saint Lawrence which flows through its middle. These Rivers form, at their mouths, Islands and peninsulas so pleasing to the view and so adapted to human habitation, that nature seems to have gathered together a portion of the beauties of the habitable globe expressly to display them here. The banks, partly prairies and partly groves, appear from a distance like so many pleasure-gardens, having nothing of Savagery about them but the tawny [i.e., wild] animals, such as Elk, Deer, and Wild Cows, which are seen in herds and in large numbers.

We crossed this Lake in a calm broken only by the leaping and the noise of sturgeon and other fish unknown in Europe, which sprang up by the hundred about our Vessel. In this Lake we encountered a Moose swimming across – an animal exceeding in height the tallest mules of Auvergne, and possessed of incomparable strength and unequaled agility, both on land and in the water, where it swims like a fish. We straightway despatched a little bark canoe in pursuit, manned by two Frenchmen and by two Algonquin Savages who were accompanying us. These men, being still more dexterous in the water than the animal, made it turn and double many times in that great Lake, where its actions were like those of a Stag chased by Hunters in the open country. It was a pleasure to see how, by dint of bursts of speed and convulsive movements, he tried to gain the land, and how the Hunters at the same time, tossing on the water in their Canoe, blocked its way and guided him despite himself toward the Bark, where men were waiting to despatch it – which they finally did.

No sooner was he killed than opportunity was offered to kill three more in the same manner, and with fresh incidents, such as render this one of the pleasantest modes of hunting in the world.

Meanwhile, those who busied themselves with fishing did their part not less acceptably, so that we soon had the means of regaling our company with fish and flesh.

We had no sooner reached the end of this Lake than those famous Richelieu Islands were disclosed to us. When the settlers of these regions need venison and game, they have only, during a certain season, to repair hither, where the only money required to buy them is lead and powder. These Islands are fully a hundred and fifty in number, some being four leagues in circumference, and others two or three leagues. Some are like prairies, with no trees but plum-trees, whose fruit is red and of fairly good flavor. Others are covered with trees and Wild vines; these climb the former, which bear fruit that is always tolerably palatable. Other Wild fruits are found here, such as strawberries, raspberries, cherries, blueberries of exquisite flavor, blackberries, currants, both red and white, and many other small fruits that are unknown in Europe, among them being some species of little apples or haws, and of pears ['poires,' i.e., berries] which ripen only with the frost. But nothing seems to me so curious as certain Aromatic roots and some Simples of great virtue, which are found here.

These Islands are separated from one another by canals of great diversity of form. Some extend in a straight line, as in pleasure-resorts, and are two leagues in length and a quarter of a league in width; others are narrower, and only admit of being traversed in the shade of trees, which almost meet from either side in the form of an arbor. These latter canals become insensibly lost, and vanish in a pleasing manner from one's view, until they rejoin the River whence they started. But they are all wonderfully stocked with fish of every species, which find their living there.

The River, after thus pursuing its tortuous path through such pleasant regions, resumes its course and keeps thenceforth to but one channel, which the observer would rather take for a great canal made by the hand of man than for the bed of a River, so straight is it, and with banks so symmetrical, clothed on either side with very beautiful trees rare in Europe – as far as an Island four leagues long. It is rather a cluster of Islets than a single one, so remarkable for channels and streams that those who have attempted to count them reckon more than three hundred. They merge into one another, and form labyrinths of such surprising beauty and so rich in fish, Otters, Beavers, and Muskrats, as almost to surpass belief. The Iroquois cause this abundance by preventing our Algonquins from hunting in these beautiful regions.

On the shore of this fair Island we found a herd of Wild Cows, which are a kind of Deer, but much more savory than ours – and so easy to kill that they have only to be driven by being frightened into the River, into which they immediately plunge and begin to swim; and then the hunters in their Canoes are at liberty to catch them by the ears and kill them with the knife, or to lead them alive upon the bank. Occasionally two or three hundred of them are seen together.

This prey was offered us too fortunately for us not to profit by it. Meanwhile we were constantly advancing toward Montreal, and despite the rapidity of the current, which flows with great strength in that vicinity, we ascended as far as the River des Prairies, which flows from the North and empties into the Saint Lawrence river.

This spot even exceeds all the others in beauty; for the Islands met with at the junction of these two streams are so many large and beautiful prairies, – some oblong and others round, – or so many gardens designed for pleasure, both because of the various fruits found there, and because of the shape of the gardens themselves and the artifice wherewith nature has prepared them with all the charms possible for Painters to depict in their landscapes. Birds and wild animals are there without number, and the fishing is excellent. This used to be a general resort for every Nation before the Iroquois had tainted all these regions; and hence it will some day be a place most suitable for the site of a large and wealthy city.[34]

An Inhabited Continent

The Amerindians arrived in North America in successive waves during the ice ages, when the level of the oceans had dropped. They travelled by a strip of land that would normally be submerged beneath the Bering Strait. Referred to as Beringia, this strip linked Siberia and Alaska. A first wave of people might have come at least 40,000 years ago. Then, 35,000 years ago, the climate began to warm up again, the oceans rose, and Beringia was submerged for 10,000 years. Subsequently, a new cooling enabled other groups of humans to cross the sea. Finally, 10,000 years ago, the passage was cut off, and only maritime migrations were possible. This was the route taken by the last of the early migrants 5,500 years ago – the Inuit. The first inhabitants gradually occupied the two Americas, moving southward through a long corridor beside the Rockies. Initially, these people of Mongol origin settled in the southern portion of North America before moving northward as the climate became warmer and the Champlain Sea retreated. They occupied the Saint Lawrence lowlands about 8,000 years ago. The Inuit moved east from Alaska along the Arctic coast, and occupied Quebec's far north 4,000 years ago.[35]

How many of these first peoples inhabited the Americas when Columbus arrived? Between 70 to 100 million, more than the total population of Europe – a relatively 'empty' old continent with only 60 or 65 million inhabitants. A century later, the population of the Americas had been reduced catastrophically to a mere 12 to 15 million and by the end of the seventeenth century to between 11 and 13 million. This descending curve only began to move upward in the eighteenth century, when the white populations began increasing by leaps and bounds.[36] South America took over three centuries to recover its pre-Columbian population level. It is possible that population loss in North America was equally great. Although it varied greatly in intensity, since horticultural peoples were much more vulnerable than hunter-gatherers, it seems that the demographic shrinkage in the two continents was comparable – that is, in the range of 90 to 95 per cent.

How large was the population of North America at the beginning of the sixteenth century? For a long time, estimates were in the neighbourhood of less than a million, even a great deal less, perhaps as little as a quarter of a million. As historical and especially archeological research progressed, this estimate climbed constantly. Twenty years ago, it still hovered around the million mark. Today, most specialists in the field agree on a minimum figure of three million (although some have suggested figures of between ten and twelve million) with the following spread: two and a half million on the present territory of the U.S., and one million on the present territories of Canada, Alaska, and Greenland.[37] The population of Canada would not reach similar numbers until the second quarter of the nineteenth century. In other words, Canada also took about three centuries to recover its prehistoric population. The Amerindian population of Canada continued to decline until the beginning of the twentieth century, when it reached its nadir of about a quarter of a million. It has since begun moving on an upward curve.

The Amerindian population of New England has been estimated at between 72,000 and 90,000.[38] On Long Island alone, the population stood at about 6,000,[39] and on Martha's Vineyard, at about 3,000,[40] that is, a density of 43 inhabitants per square kilometre. The explorer Verrazano reported seeing fires all along the coast of tiny Block Island, and in 1662 there were still 1,200 Amerindians living there.[41] Jacques Cartier visited Hochelaga, on the site of the future Montreal, and found an Iroquoian village fortified by a triple stockade in the middle of fields of sweet corn. The village consisted of some fifty longhouses and had about 1,500 inhabitants, while the village of Stadacona near Quebec had nearly 600 inhabitants.[42] The Huron population has been estimated at a minimum of 20,000.[43] The Iroquois confederacy included as many people as the Huron confederacy. According to the Jesuits, the Neutrals may have numbered 12,000 people in forty villages, while the less numerous Petuns lived in nine villages.[44] In total, the Iroquoian peoples numbered over 100,000.

The Jesuits were always careful to ask their Amerindian hosts about the identity of various peoples, where they lived, and how they were spread over the territory as a whole. The Hurons told them that they (the Hurons) were surrounded by other peoples.[45] The Jesuits soon realized that Huronia was only the entrance to the territory. 'Toward the south, we see other Peoples beyond number.'[46] After 1650, that is to say, after the destruction of Huronia, the missionaries set off westward to spread the Gospel. As they travelled along the old trade routes through the Great Lakes, they constantly remarked on peoples who until then had been 'unknown.' Father Gabriel Druillettes tried to make a superficial estimate of the peoples that could be reached beyond Sault Sainte Marie. He listed fourteen nations, some of them sedentary, others gatherers 'of a kind of rye' (wild rice) who lived in villages of three to five thousand souls. These nations might have had between 8,000 and 20,000 people living in sixty villages. To this we must add all the far larger nations, all of them sedentary, to be found to the south and southwest.[47] Such estimates are necessarily imprecise, and might as easily be doubled as halved. One thing is certain, however: the Amerindian was everywhere in North America. In whatever direction the missionaries moved, even on reaching the 'northern sea,'[48] they always spoke of the multitude of peoples.[49]

At the beginning of the sixteenth century, therefore, several hundred tribes occupied North America. They spoke 190 different languages belonging to forty-three different families, these being attached to nine phyla. If we add thirty-one unclassified languages, we get a total of 221 mutually unintelligible languages. With the exception of Inuktitut of the Aleutian Islands, which is related to the language of Siberia, and (although this is less certain) with the exception of Arthabaskan, which is thought to originate from the Sino-Tibetan phylum, no relationship between Amerindian and Asiatic languages has been successfully proved.[50] Three large language families occupied northeastern North America: Inuit, Algonkian, and Iroquoian.[51]

The Inuit occupied the entire coast of the Arctic Ocean, including the Arctic coast of the Quebec-Labrador peninsula. These people were nomad hunters whose migrations followed the marine animals that they hunted.

The Algonkian family occupied the Atlantic coast from North Carolina to Labrador and westward to the Rockies, covering the entire territory of present-day Canada. This family included countless tribes with related dialects. These can be divided, for the sake of convenience, into two sub-groups: sedentary tribes on the east coast of the present-day United States – Delawares, Pequots, Montauks, and so on – who lived mainly by farming and fishing; and migrant hunting tribes which included Passamaquoddies, Malecites, Abenakis, and Micmacs in Maine and the Canadian Maritimes, and the Beothuks of Newfoundland, probably of the same family, who were exterminated. There were also the Montagnais along the north shore of the Gulf and up the Saint Lawrence as far as the Saint Maurice River, and the Attikamegues of the upper Saint Maurice. The Algonkin tribe (not to be confused with the

Algonkian family) inhabited the Ottawa River basin up to the Abitibi region, and the Crees occupied the James Bay area beyond this. The Ottawas occupied a huge territory that included Manitoulin Island, the northern and eastern shores of Georgian Bay, and the peninsula between Lake Huron and Lake Michigan. The Nipissings were concentrated around the lake that bears their name. North of Lake Superior one met Ojibwas, Blackfeet, Gros-Ventres, and the bison-hunting Plains Cree.

The Iroquoian family covered a territory of over 100,000 square kilometres around Lake Erie, Lake Ontario, and part of Lake Huron. It was divided into six confederacies: Hurons, Petuns, Neutrals, Eries, Susquehannocks, and Iroquois. These were semi-sedentary horticultural peoples. In the sixteenth century, the Iroquoians also occupied the Saint Lawrence valley from the mouth of Lake Ontario to the Île d'Orléans. There were over a hundred villages in all.[52]

None of these peoples had ever been completely self-sufficient. As far back as we are able to go, archaeologists find proof of exchanges between the populations of the continent. For example, in Saint Lawrence valley burial grounds several thousand years old, objects have been found that come from the four corners of North America – pendants made from conch shells from the Gulf of Mexico or the Atlantic coast, copper tools from lodes west of Lake Superior, quartzite arrowheads from the tip of northern Labrador, jasper from Pennsylvania, and so on.[53]

Subsistence Modes
How could three million inhabitants of the palaeolithic age, lacking metals and efficient tools and techniques, manage to get their food, clothing, lodging, and means of transport from nature? Horticultural peoples rarely suffered from famine, and their population grew slowly but steadily. Around the year AD 1000, the Iroquoians lived in small villages with a few houses about seven to nine metres long. They subsisted mainly by hunting and a little farming. In the fourteenth century, sweet corn and the newly introduced haricot bean provided a guaranteed source of protein, generating a new kind of life and the appearance of villages of 2,000 people.[54] We also know that the peoples of the Algonkian family were not always scattered. They were more numerous along the coast where the climate favoured horticulture and they could specialize in fishing. Even the Algonkian populations of Canada, who were mainly hunters, were

generally well fed. All in all, the absence of famine and the slow but regular increase in population is explained by the development of horticulture with an extraordinarily high yield, coupled with a flora and fauna that were unimaginably abundant. A National Geographic Society study estimates that sixteen square kilometres of Illinois forest could provide an annual supply of hundreds of kilos of acorns and nuts, 100 deer, 10,000 squirrels, 200 turkeys, and even 5 bears.[55]

On the horticultural level, it should be remembered that the rate of yield in France for cereals was 1 for 1 in poor years and 6 for 1 in better years. The record rate for Holland reached 15 for 1. In North America, the rate of yield for sweet corn easily reached 200 for 1 (27 bushels per acre, or 2,425 litres per hectare).[56] In South America, this miracle plant, which required little attention, had already enabled its growers to accomplish great things. The free time gained by the Mayas from the easy cultivation of sweet corn enabled them to devote time to architecture and to building cities far more populous than the cities of Europe. In addition to sweet corn, North American Amerindians cultivated haricot beans, squash, pumpkins, and sunflowers, all with high yields, but not the potato or the tomato, which were South American plants.[57] They gathered small fruits such as blackberries, strawberries, raspberries, and blueberries.[58] They harvested maple and birch syrup and wild rice in the west. They also gathered the bark of birch, oak, and whitewood, and combined them with acorns, which they soaked in hot water to eliminate the toxic tannic acid,[59] to make a flour.

The Amerindians knew of the properties of over 1,000 species of wild edible plants.[60] Their ingenuity in this area is undeniable. The many uses they made of the bulrush (*Typha latifolia*)[61] offer a good example. Its rhizomes, dried and pulverized, were used as sweet flour to make bread and pancakes. The fresh rhizomes were also crushed and boiled to make a syrupy gluten that was then either mixed with flour made from sweet corn or else used to thicken broths and sauces. (Flour production has been estimated at 5,500 pounds per acre.)[62] The lower part of the bulrush stalk can be eaten boiled, like leeks, if the tough outer layers are removed. The young, green spikes taste like sweet corn if well boiled.[63] The ripe fruit provides a kind of cotton, and when mixed with lard, makes an ointment for burns. The Amerindians used this cotton to make disposable diapers for their babies, placing it inside a pair of leather

pants and replacing it as needed. The leaves of the bulrush were also useful for weaving wicker baskets.

HURONIA

We have drawn a broad picture of North America before its conquest,
briefly describing the land and its inhabitants. This picture would be
incomplete without a brief analysis of how Amerindian societies worked.
As it would be impossible to study each of them here, we have chosen to
explore in detail only one – the Huron society.

This choice is based on the fact that the Jesuit writings dealt mainly
with this society, and because the studies of Élisabeth Tooker, Conrad
Heidenreich, and above all Bruce G. Trigger[64] now enable us to make a
distinctive analysis of the workings of Huron society and the changes it
underwent with the impact of the fur trade.

A Word about Sources

Letters, travel accounts, and missionary reports such as the *Jesuit
Relations* together form the major documentary sources on Amerindian
societies during the period under consideration, and they are therefore
of inestimable value. These are the first written observations about these
societies, which had an oral tradition. Such 'relations' were generally
addressed to a devout French public, and the narrators were also actors
in these accounts. As missionaries, their aim was to convert the peoples
whom they were observing to Christianity. The individual narrator
therefore assumed the stance of a judgmental spectator vis-à-vis these
societies, which he posited as pagan. From such a perspective, the narrator obviously cannot give a 'neutral' ethnographic account of the habits
and customs of the American peoples. Such an account would compare
Hurons and French on an equal basis, as two sovereign 'nations' with
respective traditions, manners and customs, rituals, prayers, and so on –
in other words, two ethnic groups viewed from a perspective of cultural
relativism. The missionaries' position could not have been more dissimilar.
Their proselytizing zeal prohibited them from taking a relative approach
in matters of religious belief. As a result, the narrative voice was constantly invaded by the Christian and French message: the Huron supernatural became the forces of evil, the devil, Satan; the Amerindian
became 'our Savage,' and 'our barbarian.' Instead of inviting the reader to

a meeting of Huron and Frenchman, the narrator presented a scenario in which pagan met Christian, the savage met civilized man. Take, for example, such chapter titles as 'On the treachery of the Hiroquois,'[65] or references to 'songs and other ridiculous [Huron] ceremonies,' or the 'reign of Satan in these countries, and divers superstitions.' This omnipresent mode of discourse effectively depreciates its subject and introduces a value judgment that makes any fair comparison between the beliefs and practices of Amerindians and Europeans impossible. On the other hand, insofar as no critique of colonialism existed in those days, this approach is obvious and explicit, and it is fairly easy to decode the narration in order to make an ethnohistorical analysis.[66]

History and Geography

The Hurons, whose real name was 8endat or Wendat,[67] were concentrated within a relatively confined territory – fifty-five kilometres east-west and thirty kilometres north-south – between Lake Simcoe and the shores of Georgian Bay. 'The Huron country is not large, its greatest extent can be traversed in three or four days,'[68] according to the *Jesuit Relations*. There must have been about 20,000 Hurons, although this figure may have been as high as 25,000 to 30,000.[69] They lived in some twenty villages of varying sizes, with the largest having about 1,500 to 2,000 inhabitants. We should recall that, by comparison, a European village of the same period rarely had more than 500 inhabitants. These villages were usually surrounded by a stockade made of stakes, enclosing 10 to 15 houses built in a tunnel shape, each between 7 and 8 metres high, 8 and 10 metres wide, and an average of 25 metres long, although this varied between 10 and 65 metres, according to the size of the clan that inhabited it. Each of these longhouses contained a row of fireplaces around which the various menages lived.[70]

The Hurons belonged to four or perhaps five different tribes joined by a confederacy dating back to 1440, when the Attignawantan and Attigneenongnahac tribes sealed their first alliance. The Arendarhonon tribe joined in 1590, followed by the Tahontaenrats in 1610. We do not know whether a fifth group, the Ataronchronons, was an actual tribe, nor whether it was in or out of the confederacy.[71] Huronia lay at the northern limits of the corn-growing region (sweet corn at that time needed 120 days to ripen, and the number of days without frost in this area ranged between 135 and 142)[72] in a very rich agricultural belt. It occupied a frontier zone between horticultural peoples and hunters, an area from which communication lines spread over the entire North American northeast.[73]

Nature and the Division of Labour

The division of labour, apart from some activities suitable for children and old people, was drawn exclusively and very strictly along gender lines. Except under extraordinary circumstances, the men were never seen to share in women's work, nor women to share in men's work.[74] Tasks requiring much travelling fell to men, whereas more sedentary activities were reserved for women. On a more fundamental level, activities that were symbolically clustered around life were the domain of women, while those connected with death fell to men. Women planted, cultivated the fields, cooked, sewed, kept house, gathered nuts and other food, and educated the children, while the men felled trees, fished, hunted, traded, built canoes, houses, and fortifications, and waged war.[75]

Using hoes of wood and stone, the women loosened the earth, heaped it up in mounds, planted the seed for corn, squash, broad beans of various kinds, and sunflowers,[76] then kept them free of weeds, and harvested them. Each woman worked her allotment in a kind of community garden where mutual aid was the byword. Children could make themselves useful by weeding and chasing away the birds. Women also milled a good part of the corn that, with its derivatives, constituted 65 per cent of the Huron diet. One person required about 215 kilograms per year.[77] The women produced much more than this, however, because large quantities were needed for trade.[78] Cornmeal was stored in big containers inside the longhouses. Women also made rope,[79] wove baskets, made pottery for preserving and cooking food, and gathered firewood.

Although men's agricultural labour was secondary, it was nevertheless indispensable. They were responsible for clearing land. The procedure was as follows: if the tree was a small one, they would use stone axes, hitting repeatedly with short little blows; if the tree was larger, they tore or burned off the bark from the trunk, then cut the main branches in order to kill the tree and let light through. Since fields gradually became exhausted, despite the use of fish as fertilizer, and the sources of wood became increasingly distant, the Hurons would move their village

after a dozen years. The work of clearing a section of forest and rebuild-
ing houses and a stockade had to begin again.[80]

Men took no other part in farming, except for growing tobacco,
which was their exclusive domain. However, they spent a lot of time,
particularly in winter, making stone tools (scrapers, drills, arrowheads of
Niagara flint, clubs, and axes) which had to be polished, tapered, and
sharpened. Animal bones were also used to make needles and spoons. In
turn, these stone tools were used to work on wood and leather for the
production of arrows, toboggans, bowls, puzzles, wooden armour, moccasins, and snowshoes, as well as canoes, some of these being 'eight and
nine strides [metres] long or a [metre] and a half wide in the middle,'[81]
easily able to accommodate six men. They were usually made according
to the Algonkian method, using birch bark sewn with leather thongs and
laid over a framework of light cedar. A mixture of pine gum and animal
fat was used to make the joints waterproof. Canoes could also be made
out of a single large elm, from which the bark was delicately removed in
a single piece. This was then fitted, smooth side out, over a framework of
appropriate dimensions and only the ends had to be sealed.[82] Two men
could make such a canoe in two days. Canoes enabled the Amerindian to
navigate lakes and rivers and consequently to fish, hunt, trade, and
undertake all sorts of journeys. Fishing went on all year long, and ice
fishing was as popular as the summer variety.[83] The Hurons used spears,
seines, hooks and lines, and nets, even in the winter. Fish and meat were
preserved only by being dried or smoked, since salting techniques were
unknown to the Hurons.[84]

Hunting, the exclusive domain of the men, was a collective activity.
When they beat the forest for game, the men would drive the animals
into a cul-de-sac where nets had been stretched in readiness, and then
kill them.[85] For the Hurons, however, hunting was a marginal activity
compared to fishing. They raised no animals except dogs, which were
fattened for eating or trained for hunting.[86] Occasionally they would
tame wild creatures such as a duck or a bustard[87] to be used as decoys, or
even a bear, as mentioned by Champlain in 1616 and the Dutchman
Bogaert in 1634, the latter describing a small cabin in a Mohawk village
where a bear had been in the process of being fattened for three years.[88]

The land was the collective property of the community. Private ownership was generally limited to a few tools, weapons, and personal cloth-

ing. There was no obligation to work and no hierarchy involved with work. No one watched the women in the fields or the men building stockades. Everyone shared in all the tasks that were the responsibility of his or her sex, and such tasks were generally decided upon collectively, either informally or in council. There were no coercive measures to force anyone to work, and yet everyone worked.

Although work was often hard for both sexes, it was never onerous, especially since the workers moved on to other things once the needs in question were satisfied. This left plenty of time for talking, puttering around, smoking, dancing, carving, singing, playing with the children, and feasting. Also, both men and women devoted a great deal of time to decorating their houses, leather clothing, and domestic objects with a variety of motifs, using various pigments as well as animal and vegetable fibres and *wampum* beads. They also decorated parts or all of their bodies with geometric, animal, or anthropomorphic designs using bright pigments mixed with animal fat.[89] They covered their bodies with animal fat for protection against the sun, the cold, and insects.[90] Their feasts were prodigious: 20 deer and 4 bears cooked in 30 kettles, or 50 large fish and 120 smaller varieties in 25 kettles.[91] The American Stone Age was indeed an age of plenty![92] The advent of the fur trade, however, was to increase work time and reduce free time and leisure activities.

THE RULE OF GIVING

The product of work belonged to the producer. Nevertheless, in order to forestall inequalities, the Hurons had established a code of giving that involved generosity, hospitality, and ceremonial exchange so as to share the goods produced without the need of a market. In fact, no Huron village ever had a marketplace, not even a temporary one. Goods, whether local or foreign in origin, circulated exclusively within the sharing and redistribution networks. Although these networks favoured the individual clan, they also extended to the whole community. In other words, within the Huron community, there were no commercial transactions, properly speaking. Goods acquired were spontaneously shared within lineages (or segments of clans). This generalized practice of giving insured equality and accounted for the disdain with which the accumulation of goods was viewed; it governed the rules of courtesy at all times as well as the Huron penchant for games of chance, contributions to feasts, rituals, and carnivals, and the obligation to satisfy any desire expressed by a member of the community.[93] As a result, there were neither sellers nor buyers among the Hurons, neither commanders nor commanded, neither rich nor poor. 'You note, in the first place, a great love and union, which they are careful to cultivate by means of their marriages, of their presents, of their feasts, and of their frequent visits. On returning from their fishing, their hunting, and their trading, they exchange many gifts; if they have thus obtained something unusually good, even if they have bought it, or if it has been given to them, they make a feast to the whole village with it. Their hospitality towards all sorts of strangers is remarkable.'[94]

Giving was the key to the Huron social universe – the obligation to give, the obligation to receive, and the obligation to give in return. As in other primitive societies observed by Marcel Mauss, receiving a gift in Huronia meant giving a gift in return.[95] Giving was far more than a social rule; giving and, consequently, exchanging constituted a basic rule of Huron social relations. Giving also had great symbolic and religious significance. The spirit of giving was invested in the person of the donor and the thing given, and it required that the receiver make a gift in return. In other words, the receiver owed the giver a gift. The number of transactions did not matter; the spirit embodied in the gift must, in one form or another, return to its original home. The gift must come full circle. Once the receiver had acquitted himself of his debt to the giver, he thereby acquired a hold over the donor; hence the mandatory circulation of wealth.[96] Any failure in this system of reciprocity gave the injured party a magical power over the offender.

Commerce

What the Hurons were unable to produce at home they acquired by trading with neighbouring or distant tribes. A network of footpaths or packed-earth trails connected Huron villages for a distance of over 300 kilometres.[97] Beyond the borders of Huronia, the trail continued for another 300 kilometres as far as the Neutrals in the direction of Niagara. By crossing the Niagara River, it was possible to connect with the Iroquois trail network. This ran from the site of present-day Buffalo to Albany via the Genessee valley, Lake Cayuga and Lake Seneca, the Onondaga valley, and the present-day sites of Rome and Schenectady. It took only three

days for a team of runners to cover this span.[98] Southward below Lake
Erie lay the trail network of the Susquehannocks that covered Pennsylvania. They were the Hurons' commercial allies. It was these trails that
the European colonists used when settling the central part of
Pennsylvania.[99] The Amerindians kept maps of the water routes, and we
know that, starting from the huge inland sea formed by the Great Lakes,
it was possible to travel by water over the whole continent – from the
Arctic to the Gulf of Mexico, from the Atlantic to the Rockies. One could
leave Huronia by canoe, for example, and reach the Ottawa River via
French River and Lake Nipissing.[100] From the Ottawa River, one could
travel to the lower Saint Lawrence, James Bay, or follow a network of
rivers and lakes to reach Lac Saint-Jean and down the Saguenay to
Tadoussac, without using the Saint Lawrence. In the prehistoric period,
the actual merchandise always moved around more than the men themselves, and trading goods circulated mainly through a chain of middlemen. The Hurons got their wampum largely from the Susquehannocks,
who in turn got it from producers on the Atlantic seaboard (wampum
also came via the Mississippi from the Gulf of Mexico). Catlinite (pipe
clay) from South Dakota probably reached the Hurons through the
Sioux-Ottawa chain. Copper, extracted from surface veins west of Lake
Superior, came through the Ottawas and the Nipissings.

The Hurons sold their own products (sweet corn, nets, and rope) to
neighbouring peoples but also acted as middlemen themselves. Flint,
tobacco, and black squirrel pelts were purchased from the Neutrals,
Eries, and Petuns, and some were resold to the Algonkian peoples of the
north. Going in the reverse direction, the Hurons traded furs, dried
fruit, reed mats, and medicines from the north. The Ottawas traded
around Lake Superior and Lake Michigan, while the Nipissings traded
northward with the Cree.[101] The first European products from ships at
Tadoussac in the sixteenth century reached the Hurons through the
Montagnais-Cree-Nipissing chain of exchange. The Hurons apparently
did not travel regularly as far as the Ottawa River before the beginning of
the fur trade. The French saw the Hurons for the first time in 1609.
During their journeys, the Hurons found what food they needed by
hunting and fishing. In addition, they left caches of food all along their
route and carried with them toasted cornmeal known as *sagamité*, a kind
of ready-to-eat concentrated food.[102]

At the end of the prehistoric period, tribes began to specialize in their economic activities, and the Hurons became strongly active in the exchange network. The fur trade, which was grafted onto the existing exchange networks, increased the amount of travelling and the number of transactions, as well as conferring on the middleman a far greater strategic role than had previously existed.

This specialization in commerce had, in many respects, an influence on the internal workings of Huron society. Although equality had always been the rule with respect to the products of farming, gathering, hunting, and fishing, rights of ownership over trade routes were to benefit the owners of such routes. Huron custom accorded the discoverer of a new trade route rights over it for himself and his lineage. Only the discoverer had the right to use the route, and anyone else must obtain his permission to do so. This permission was given in return for valuable gifts. Le Jeune noted that

> several families have their own private trades, and he is considered Master of one line of trade who was the first to discover it. The children share the rights of their parents in this respect, as do those who bear the same name; no one goes into it without permission, which is given only in consideration of presents; he associates with him as many or as few as he wishes. If he has a good supply of merchandise, it is to his advantage to divide it with few companions, for thus he secures all that he desires, in the Country; it is in this that most of their riches consist. But if any one should be bold enough to engage in a trade without permission from him who is Master, he may do a good business in secret and concealment; but, if he is surprised by the way, he will not be better treated than a thief, – he will only carry back his body to his house, or else he must be well accompanied. If he returns with his baggage safe, there will be some complaint about it, but no further prosecution.[103]

This right gave rise to inequality in the acquisition of trade goods – an inequality that ran counter to a whole series of measures designed to assure redistribution for consumption. In the long term, however, the development of commerce implied more frequent use of redistribution systems (commerce) than of sharing (production). Although redistribution guaranteed sharing after the fact, it had latent tendencies that contributed to social inequality. In effect, it conferred symbolic prestige on individuals and lineages possessing greater wealth, a prestige of which other members of the society, who lacked access to the same wealth, were deprived. Furthermore, it became possible for holders of wealth to choose not to redistribute it.

prestige

Hurons acquired social prestige in two ways, first by their capacity for redistribution and second by their ability to show courage in war. This last point was a very important component in the internal equilibrium of Amerindian societies, and I will be dealing with it in a separate section. Apart from the question of prestige, however, other signs of symbolic inequality appeared in relationships among trading tribes. For example, Hurons married Algonkian women as a means of sealing commercial alliances, but the reverse was not the case. Commercial exchanges were also marked by numerous feasts. When invited by the Hurons, the Algonkians ate the food offered by their hosts, but when the Algonkians were the hosts, the Hurons brought their own food. Lastly, the Huron language was the language of trade. Some Algonkian tribes, such as the Nipissings who wintered over in Huronia, were bilingual, whereas the Hurons never were.[104] In other words, although the principle of equality always prevailed on the material level in Huron society and, it would seem, among trading partners, latent forces leading to relationships of subordination were nevertheless already present. Later, the fur trade would play on this contradiction and activate the latent forces that would destroy this ancestral tradition of equality.

As with exchange within Huron society, external exchange (commerce) linked people and collectivities, both of which attributed meanings to this kind of commerce that went far beyond the material nature of observable relationships.[105] Trade with the outside represented material and symbolic exchange for the Hurons, and was both an economic and a political activity. The Hurons only had commercial relations with tribes with which they were at peace and, as a result, could not trade with enemies or strangers. Commerce was conceived of as an exclusive relationship with a partner-collectivity. It was the representatives of a collectivity who met, not individuals. Alliances between trading partners were indispensable prerequisites for commerce and were always restated in a ritual way (gifts, speeches, and dances) before the actual commercial exchange took place. 'It is the custom of these people to speak through presents, and through feasts.'[106]

Commerce was also practised in dangerous zones beyond Huron

control, where war and peace were unpredictable factors. Under these conditions, trade had to take on forms that would allay any uncertainty and threat of hostility. How could one make sure one's trading partner was well intentioned? Basically, the answer lay in exhibiting reciprocal generosity. The rates of exchange were stable, fixed by custom, and part of the trading arrangement. There was never any question of haggling or niggardliness.[107] This would have revealed suspect intentions. Trading therefore took place in an atmosphere of generosity. *A* made a show of prodigality, thereby placing *B* in his debt. *B* returned the gift a hundred-fold, thus putting *A* in the position of debtor. *A* in turn was again obliged to show great generosity to *B*, and so on. To give more was to prove one's friendship and one's willingness to maintain good relations, to say nothing of establishing a reserve of credit for the future. If a trading partner left a gathering owing a debt, he would acquit himself at the next. In the long term, the balance would be restored; in the short term, the concern for showing excessive generosity acted as a precaution against hard-nosed dealing, which was a source of friction.[108]

These rules of mutual generosity could nevertheless be accompanied by a relationship of unequal exchange. In effect, the criteria of generosity operated mainly with respect to the evaluation of the labour and time required for production (value of labour power) on the side of the givers, and with respect to the estimated usefulness (use value) on the part of the receivers. One could therefore pass for being generous by playing on the lack of information of one's partner. To give a large quantity of goods to a neighbouring allied tribe could seem as generous as giving less to an allied tribe that was far from the centres of production and poorly informed as to the real value of the goods. It is difficult to say whether the Hurons tried to enrich themselves at the expense of their allies in their traditional commercial activities. It is probable that they did so at the expense of distant tribes. They were, in any case, well placed to know the real value of the merchandise exchanged and to develop a means of controlling the exchange networks – and in fact they did this with the development of the fur trade.

Huron Society
Like most Iroquoian societies, Huron society was matrilinear and matrilocal, that is, its kinship system was based on maternal ascendance

and the fact that the new spouse went to live in his wife's house. In matrilinear kinship systems, the basic unit is not the nuclear family but the clan. In this system, biological paternity is dissociated from cultural paternity. In fact, a man exercises the affectionate and educational functions of a father toward his sisters' children, while his own children are brought up by their mother and her brothers or close male kin (maternal uncles). The feeling of belonging to the clan takes priority over belonging to the nuclear family. In the periods preceding the development of agriculture in North America, the nuclear family (as was the case among the northern Algonkians) was the basic economic unit. Hunting and gathering had led to a scattered occupation of the territory. Horticulture, on the other hand, favoured concentrations of people and the construction of large dwellings related to clans, thereby providing greater security.[109]

The clan brought together all the descendants of a common ancestor, a common grandmother. A village included people from several lineages. Since marriage was exogamic, that is, it took place between people of different clans, it was impossible for all the members of one clan to inhabit the same village. Within the village, the unit of affiliation was therefore lineage. This could be the basis for grouping some one hundred people and occasionally far more, as opposed to the nuclear family which included only a few people. Siblings and cousins belonged to the same big 'family,' although a distinction was made between the two levels of kinship. When people moved to another village, they were normally taken in by their kin, that is to say by the members of another lineage within their clan.

What were the particular effects of this system of filiation in a society where private property and social classes were nonexistent? Belonging to a lineage imposed rules of reciprocity (sharing and exchange) between a large number of people. This was particularly evident in the case of inheritance. The few goods amassed by the deceased were distributed among a large number of heirs on the maternal side.[110] One of the functions of this kinship system was therefore to make the sharing of wealth obligatory and to forestall any process that might lead to the concentration of wealth in the hands of a few.

This system also had major implications for sexual life, marriage, divorce, and the education of children. The clan took precedence over the nuclear family, the maternal uncles assumed the cultural functions of paternity, and there were no social classes to incite men of the dominant classes to transmit their goods to an eldest son in order to keep the legacy whole. As a result, women had control of their own bodies. This meant that the clan valued motherhood, whoever might be the biological father. The important thing was to have children. It is worth noting that the birth of girls was slightly more valued than that of boys, and, in the case of compensation for murder, a sharing of thirty presents was required for a man and forty for a woman.[111]

In Huronia, premarital sexual relations were considered normal from puberty onward, and the girls were as active as the boys in such liaisons. At this stage, sexual relationships were not exclusive.[112] When a young girl became pregnant, she chose from among her lovers the one she wanted to marry. Although the parents played an important role in the choice of a spouse, they could not impose their will. When the young people were agreed, the boy's parents made a gift to the parents of the girl.[113] If they accepted it, the couple slept together for several nights in a sort of trial marriage,[114] after which the girl was free to accept or refuse her husband. Only when she actually accepted did her parents organize a marriage feast for the two families. Once married, and above all after the birth of a child, Huron couples became monogamous.[115] If there were no children, divorce was very easy. The right to divorce also applied to couples with children, but such cases occurred more rarely because relatives and friends would try to save the marriage. Sometimes a wife repudiated her husband, generally because of his inability to provide. As far as the children were concerned, the departure of their biological father merely meant the disappearance of a provider. Since the cultural function of paternity was assumed by the maternal uncles, divorce did not have the same emotional impact that it would in nuclear families in patrilinear filiation systems.

Like the Iroquoians and most of the Algonkians, the Hurons had a deep respect for children. Never under any circumstances would they strike a child or inflict any form of corporal punishment.[116] They were extremely patient with the young. The Europeans were scandalized to see the undisciplined way in which the Hurons brought up their children, and the Hurons were equally horrified to learn that the Europeans slapped, hit, and whipped their offspring.[117]

The education of boys and girls in Huronia followed the male and

female models particular to this civilization. Boys were to become warriors, hunters, and fishermen, and were therefore trained to bear arms
and conditioned to bravery, stoicism, endurance, and resourcefulness. In
order to harden themselves, some deliberately burned themselves or wore
scanty clothing in winter.[118] Boys, like men, must never cry. 'Tears are so
rare in these countries, with respect to what concerns men, that I do not
remember, in almost nine years that I have lived among the Savages, to
have seen one of them weep, – except in sentiments of piety.'[119] A boy
must also learn to talk without expressing strong emotions and to avoid
gesticulating while speaking, which was considered effeminate.[120] Boys
did not take part in domestic activities, because this 'was not man's
duty.'[121] 'If a mother asked her son to go to the shore or to the woods, or
to do some other similar household chore, he would reply that it was a
girl's work and do nothing.'[122] Conversely, girls did not take on either the
role or the 'character traits' particular to boys. In both cases, this prohibition was aimed at preventing people from stepping outside sexual roles.

Young girls, always in the company of their mothers, learned to work
hard, cultivate the land, prepare food, and care for children. Women were
in charge of the young children. Later on, the maternal uncles took charge
of the boys' education, often taking their nephews to live with them.[123]

Although men and women paid equal attention to their bodies,
wearing jewels and dressing their hair,[124] in everyday life they lived in relative separation, whether at work or at play. The men sought the company of other men, and the women gathered among themselves.[125]

The Huron and Iroquoian political system in general offers an interesting example of 'democracy.' Founded on the kinship system, political
power effectively represented the whole population. In the villages, each
lineage elected a peace chief or *sachem*, also referred to as 'captain' in the
Jesuit Relations. Each lineage could also elect, if need be, a war chief. The
civil and military powers were completely separate. The sachems or captains were elected and could be removed from power. They generally
came from the same line within a lineage and were chosen for their
courage, their ability to speak well and remain cool under stress, and
their generosity. Those who were too anxious for personal prestige were
kept from power.[126] These elected officials had no coercive powers and
acted more as spokesmen and coordinators.

They reach this degree of honor, partly through succession, partly through election; their children do not usually succeed them, but properly their nephews and grandsons. And the latter do not even come to the succession of these petty Royalties, like the Dauphins of France, or children to the inheritance of their fathers; but only in so far as they have suitable qualifications, and accept the position, and are accepted by the whole Country. Some are found who refuse these honors, – sometimes because they have not aptitude in speaking, or sufficient discretion or patience, sometimes because they like a quiet life; for these positions are servitudes more than anything else ... These Captains do not govern their subjects by means of command and absolute power; they have no force at hand to compel them to their duty. Their government is only civil; they represent only what is to be done for the good of the village, or of the whole country. That settled, he who will takes action. There are, however, some who know well how to secure obedience, especially when they have the affection of their subjects.[127]

A village council was made up of all the village sachems, the tribal council was made up of all the village councils, and similarly the confederacy council was made up of all the tribal councils. These councils approved the election of new sachems and regulated all community life – respect for customs and laws, the coordination of activities, relocation of villages, commercial affairs, feasts, dances, and games. Decisions had to be unanimous, reflecting a consensus that could only be acquired through eloquence and the capacity to persuade. The Jesuits felt the Hurons had no policy at all and that their 'captains' had about as much power as a town crier.[128]

Although each tribe considered one of its sachems as the first or principal sachem, there was no real 'great chief.'[129] The principal sachem did not have the right to interfere in the affairs of clans to which he did not belong, nor the power to command other sachems. Any sachem could call a meeting, and, in fact, meetings were held on an almost daily basis, attended by all who wished to do so.

This is the picture of the council of the Hurons, only they are seated a little lower still, that is to say, flat upon the ground, all pellmell without any order, unless it be that the people of one tribe or village are placed near those of another. While in France they are discussing precedence, and amusing themselves in offering a chair to one whom they would consider impertinent if he accepted it, here they will have held and concluded three councils among the Savages, who, upon the whole, do not cease to be very grave and serious in their rather long speeches. There were about sixty men in their assembly, without counting the young men who were scattered here and there.[130]

The councils, too, held almost every day in the Villages, and on almost all matters, improve their capacity for talking; and, although it is the old men who have control there, and upon whose judgment depend the decisions made, yet every one who wishes may be present, and has the right to express his opinion.[131]

Van der Donck wrote that the Dutch who lived and traded with the Indians were amazed to see how such societies could run themselves without any judicial institutions. In Holland, he pointed out, the crime rate was greater than among the Indians, despite a zealous police force.[132] Chiefs possessed symbolic privileges, for the most part. They did not consume more than their fellow tribesmen and had the same dwellings and clothes. If anything, they had less time for subsistence activities such as hunting and fishing, because they had to travel regularly to councils. 'A Captain must always make it a point to be, as it were, in the field; if a Council is held five or six leagues away for the affairs of the Country, Winter or Summer, whatever the weather, he must go. If there is an Assembly in the Village, it is in the Captain's Cabin; if there is anything to be made public, he must do it; and then the small authority he usually has over his subjects is not a powerful attraction to make him accept this position.'[133]

As they moved around, sachems were fed and lodged according to the rules of hospitality. As sachems, and frequently as proprietors of trade routes, they received a larger share of gifts, and their prestige was therefore increased by redistribution.[134]

Like sachems, the war chiefs were grouped in village, tribal, and confederacy councils. They dealt with military matters, and military power was exercised in the same way as civil power – on the basis of consensus, without coercion or material privileges. Military chiefs traditionally possessed only marginal political powers compared to the civil powers of the sachems, although the increase in wars that accompanied the fur trade was to change this.

There being no 'state' and no power of coercion over individuals, social order and peace were regulated by the rule of giving. It established social relationships and guaranteed the flow of goods and services, while acting as a barrier to the existence of privileged groups. Trade was the basis of peaceful relationships; beyond that lay war.[135]

Before the first contacts with Europeans, economic motives seem to have been fairly unimportant in the conduct of wars, although such motives did exist. After all, there were trade networks and routes to be protected. Furthermore, trade zones had become larger over the centuries, bringing changes in tribal relationships. The Huron tribes had gone from being enemies to being members of a confederacy. Similarly, Hurons, Petuns, Neutrals, and Algonkians had become allies. Gradually, as nearby enemies had become allies, war relationships had been transferred to more distant tribes. The object of war was not to subjugate the enemy totally or to take possession of his territory. War was confined to a vicious circle of vendettas in which each side took its turn at exacting revenge for the death of its own. Traditionally, at the request of grieving families, war chiefs would organize expeditions, always on a voluntary basis, in order to ambush the enemy, bring back a scalp, and take prisoners. Enemy bands frequently confronted one another and fired off arrows until one of the two decamped.[136] The confrontation ended with the taking of a few scalps and/or a few prisoners. Villages were not sacked, populations were not exterminated. War was a means of demonstrating bravery, ingenuity, endurance, and skill.[137] This 'heroism' in war was so important that war was an indispensable condition for providing a social role model. This was the most vulnerable aspect of Amerindian societies: internal peace and harmony rested on external violence. Prestige was largely due to one's merit within the social group, but such merit was for the most part acquired through war, vendettas, and, in a word, violence.

Nevertheless, there may have been deeper motives for war than an emerging economy or the desire to have a male role model. What primitive or modern society has not known war or the threat of war or owed its existence to war? Is war not a means of structuring antagonism? Is the 'other,' the foreigner, the enemy, not indispensable to the definition and creation of a collective 'we'? Is it not a question of affirming oneself by opposing another? Is war not a social cement? Does war not maintain and invigorate the social fabric? This hypothesis seems borne out by the rituals of torture, for torture is the outcome – the macabre, celebratory feast – of war.

Why didn't the Amerindians simply kill their prisoners, since they didn't use them as slaves? Why take the enemy captive and leave themselves with the choice of either adopting them, thereby replacing lost compatriots, or torturing them to death? And why torture them according to a slow but increasing scale of calculated suffering when there was no question of forcing the victim to confess? Why do it in a flamboyant way, in the centre of the village, where the whole community – men, women, and children – took an active part in the ordeal? Why make the 'other,' the outsider, the focus of an entire ceremony leading up to the ultimate cannibalistic rite?[138] And finally, why must the victim taunt his butchers throughout his torment, or sing and dance to emphasize his identity and his difference? Torture might be conceived of as a ritual designed to ward off the threat of the alien, the unknown, and to bind a whole people together with the fear of suffering the same fate. It might also be a ritual designed to take away the enemy's strength through cannibalism. This was symbolic when the prisoner was adopted in place of a lost member of the tribe, thus passing from alien status to become part of the communal 'we.' There was also straightforward cannibalism where the Hurons devoured the victim's body in order to appropriate his strength and courage. It might also be suggested that the uncertainty in which the Hurons left their prisoner as to his fate – adoption or torture and death – manifested the omnipotence of the sovereign 'we,' which had the power to give life or inflict suffering and death on the alien, and to literally reduce him to pieces. We may further ask whether it suggests, as a corollary, the well-being to be gained by belonging to the collective 'we.' Consider the choice of site for torture. Except for the actual putting to death, which took place outside the village, the ordeal was held in the middle of the village, in the heart of the communal territory. Does it not show to what degree the 'other' represents only pain and death when he attacks the 'we'? What about the victim who sings in his suffering, who is not only displayed, but who becomes by his very endurance the hero of a ritual turned against himself? Does he not show in his otherness the irreducible nature of both parties? Of victim versus executioners? A tormented but brave victim against his aggressive, fearful executioners? Do not both ward off fear?

The comparison between torture in the New World and in Europe at the same period is enlightening, for in the 'old' continent, torture was carried out even more systematically, according to methods which, in their 'refinement', gradation, public display, and sadism equalled and even surpassed Amerindian customs. To be convinced of this, one has only to read Michel Foucault's *Surveiller et punir*, which contains the description of an execution carried out in 1757 on the scaffold in the main square. The criminal was 'tortured with red-hot pincers tearing the flesh off his nipples, arms, thighs, and calves. His right hand, holding the knife with which he had committed the said parricide, was burned in sulphur fire; molten lead, boiling oil, burning resin, and hot wax combined with sulphur were thrown on the pincer wounds, after which his body was drawn and quartered by four horses, his limbs and trunk burned to ashes in the fire, and his ashes thrown to the wind.'[139] Another example is the execution of the assassin of William of Orange (1584). After undergoing constant torture for eighteen days, he was condemned to 'the sum of all possible suffering' in the main square.[140]

Torture was practised in both Europe and America. The basic difference was noted by a Huron named Savignon while travelling in France. He remarked that 'the French whipped, hanged, and put to death men from among themselves, without differentiating between the innocent and the guilty.'[141] *Among* – that is the key word which shows the difference. War was not waged against the outside only, but *among* Frenchmen. The enemy was also on the inside. For the Hurons, all members of the tribe were part of the collective 'we.' This was not the case for the French, for whom suffering on the scaffold, by incarnating the omnipotence of the king, served to inculcate fear and resignation in the dominated classes. Beyond the apparent similarity between torture on both sides of the Atlantic, the choice of victims as well as the whole symbolic aspect of the rituals had completely different functions.

In Europe, torture was presented as an instructive ritual (torture to extort confession) and a ritual of punishment for all 'criminals.' Criminals liable to the death penalty included servants guilty of petty larceny, thieves, blasphemers, and vagabonds. There were 160 capital crimes in English law in 1760 and 223 in 1819. In Europe, almost all punishment, including the death penalty, involved severe physical suffering: wearing an iron collar, being whipped, having a hand cut off, or being branded.[142] In Huronia, by contrast, except for cases of witchcraft, the criminal was never punished; rather, reparation for the crime was required. The Jesuits mention specifically that murders were extremely rare. Although it was the crime rather than the criminal that was punished, which might seem 'unjust' to readers of the *Jesuit Relations*, it was the most effective method possible to prevent the recurrence of such 'disorders.'[143]

In Europe, brutal punishment was aimed at an enemy within the walls. It was a ritual that manifested power in a conspicuous way, thereby revealing the existence of an internal war. The sovereign incarnated a superior power that transcended his subjects, one that they were compelled to recognize. Punishment for crimes, in particular, was not the business of the people at large. Only the state could legitimately carry it out. The European ritual accurately reflected reality: on one side stood the people, reduced to the status of spectators, and on the other stood military power. The parades, various halts, including stops for religious ceremonies at church doors, and public readings of sentences were all more symbolic of the sacrilegious affront to the sovereign's power than of the seriousness of the criminal act itself. While Amerindian cannibal rituals showed the desire to take over the strength and courage of the alien so as to combat him better, the European ritual revealed the existence of a dissymmetry, an irrevocable imbalance of power.[144] For example, in addition to the acts of aggression on the body of the condemned man, the cadaver was then mutilated and reduced to pieces, and each piece was displayed like butcher's meat.[145] In this ritual, the alien is less than nothing, and the politics of power is fear.

The cannibal ritual, on the contrary, symbolized the solidarity of all the members of a community against the stranger, to whom strength, intelligence, and courage were attributed. These qualities must therefore be taken from him. In the Amerindian tribe, the 'we' referred to all the members of the community. In Europe, the 'we' did not group all the individual members of one people, but those who, within this people, recognized the legitimacy of a sovereign whose sword they feared. It was a 'we' of people on their knees, set in a context of domination.

The Hurons
Living in a society where coercive power did not exist, the Hurons, like the Iroquoians or the Algonkians in general, were proud,[146] strongly individualistic, tolerant, and free. This applied to both men and women.

'They are never in a hurry,'[147] noted the Jesuits – that is, they were not in the habit of rushing to keep up. They were capable of unusual feats of endurance, fearing neither hunger, cold, nor heat.[148] They could work very hard but detested heavy, servile work more than anything.[149] They ate when hungry but could control hunger so well that they could go two, three, or even four days with little or no food.[150] They had infinite patience. 'What shall I say of their strange patience in their poverty, famine, and sickness?' wrote Le Jeune. The astonishingly peaceful atmosphere of everyday life struck most observers. 'It is wonderful how well they agree among themselves, and how ... the larger [i.e., greater] ones do not command the others in an imperious or dictatorial manner,' said Le Jeune. 'If so many families were together in our France, there would be nothing but disputes, quarrels, and revilings.'[151] Contemporary ethnological literature has provided us with similar testimony in numerous cases.[152] The Hurons' reserve, generosity, and patience were counterbalanced by the hate, sadism, and unbridled fury expressed during the rituals of torture enacted upon the bodies of their enemies.

The Hurons, like Amerindians in general, were very reserved in public and careful not to display affection, aggressivity, or love. Men and women generally dressed modestly, although they had none of the shame of nudity common among the missionaries.[153]

Amerindians were generally in remarkable physical condition. The Jesuit F. du Peron considered them to be a robust people, all much taller than the French,[154] a comment confirmed by recent studies of Iroquoian burial grounds on the lower Saint Lawrence. These revealed tall men and women, averaging 1.72 metres in height.[155] The Huron diet usually supplied a daily ration of about 3,000 calories per person and was well-balanced, as indicated by the absence of tooth decay and associated disease.[156] Father Le Jeune described them as 'all well made men of splendid figures, tall, powerful, good-natured, and able-bodied.'[157]

The study of human bones contained in various North American ossuaries tells us that life-expectancy must have been between twenty and twenty-five years. These figures are apparently comparable to those in Europe for the sixteenth century. Nevertheless, they are unreliable, because these averages are not based exclusively on the average age of skeletons. They also include an estimate (necessarily approximate) of infant mortality, and it is known that the deaths of children under a year

are always under-represented in ossuaries. This estimated infant mortality is the source of such a low average age of death, and the corresponding life-expectancy at birth is, in these circumstances, a poor indicator of
the average age of death among adults. We know that it was not unusual
to live to over fifty years.[158] The comparison between Europe and North
America on the basis of quantitative data is too unreliable in this regard
to draw any firm conclusions, but we do have numerous sources which
note that physical condition and health were better in the New World.

Huron women had fewer children than women of the white race,
mainly because there was no animal substitute for maternal milk. They
nursed their children for anywhere up to two or three years and probably
abstained from sexual relations during this time.[159] Women bore an average of three or four children, instead of six, as in Europe. In addition,
women gave birth in a crouching or kneeling position, as did all
Amerindian women. Births were generally easy, and the mothers
resumed their normal activities as soon as the baby was born. Was this
an indication of the harsh conditions imposed on women – not being
given any rest – or rather of an excellent physical condition?[160] Women
ate adequately and performed regular work that exercised all their muscles, that was diversified, and not excessively fatiguing. Psychological factors were also involved: maternity was not considered an illness, nor was
sexuality considered a sin.

A somewhat mythical conception of the status of women in primitive societies in general, and in Iroquoian society in particular, has
resulted from the writings of various authors. These include Engels, who
wrote on the Iroquois 'gens' (referring specifically to matrilinear kinship
groups) in *The Origin of the Family, Private Property, and the State*.[161] The
oppression of women has been a characteristic of several classless primitive societies. Maurice Godelier's analysis of relationships between men
and women among the Baruyas of New Guinea[162] is an excellent example. If men and women have been far from equal in primitive societies as
a whole, it is nevertheless true that, among the Algonkians and
Iroquoians, the relative role of women was clearly superior to that of
women in European societies, as observed then or even now. The Jesuits
remarked of the Montagnais women, 'The women have great power
here. A man may promise you something, and if he does not keep his
promise, he thinks he is sufficiently excused when he tells you that his

wife did not wish to do it. I told him then that he was the master, and that in France women do not rule their husbands.'[163]

In Huron society, the women did not have such an important position as among the Iroquois, where women often accompanied their husbands on journeys.[164] Nevertheless, in a society where mythical history went back to an original woman, Aataentsic, the reputed creator of the earth and men,[165] women organized everything concerning their work independently, without any unwarranted male interference.[166] Although they were excluded from some festivities, such as certain feasts,[167] they played an important role in the election of sachems, although the latter were obligatorily men. They may well have had the power to both elect and dismiss sachems.[168] They also had relative sexual freedom. They could, like men, refuse to conform to general opinion, refuse to accept certain of the sachems' decisions, and adhere to their own views. They could, again like men, although this was less frequent, become shamans or even members of curing societies.[169] One of these societies, Atirenda, composed of eight members including six women, was renowned for the treatment of fractures.

As far as the relative importance of the activities of one sex or the other was concerned, relations between men and women were to change. A case in point is the development of the fur trade. At the end of the prehistoric period, the economic activities of each sex were fairly equal in importance.[170] But with the development of the fur trade, an exclusively male activity, the relative weight of the economic role of men increased, giving them more power in this sector. It also took men away from their village more often and for longer periods, leaving the women greater opportunity for taking care of community matters. However, the fur trade was not possible unless women increased their production of sweet corn and its derivatives. These surpluses enabled the Hurons to provide cereals for friendly tribes in exchange for furs, and these in turn were used in trading with the whites. As far as women were concerned, their increased role as providers, their predominance in the organization of village life, and the maternal filiation system gave them power of their own. This was certainly equal to that of the men, although the women paid for this power with a greater amount of labour. The social importance of Huron women was therefore linked to their position at a given moment in the social division of labour. Should this position change, their fate would be very different.

Characteristics of Huron Civilization

Huron medicine combined magic (religious rituals, charms, and invoca-
tions) and empirical knowledge (a remarkable knowledge of the medicinal properties of wild plants as well as precise anatomical knowledge).
Examples of empirical knowledge included the use of teas: some made
from cedar bark (*Thuya occidentalis*), rich in vitamin C to fight scurvy;
and one made from purple foxglove (*Digitalis purpurea*), which was used
as a cardiac stimulant. Similarly, their birthing methods were very effective.[171] In addition, the Huron practice of bathing in rivers, and the use
of 'hot rooms and sweat boxes,'[172] which were forms of sauna that
insured a minimum of cleanliness, contributed to good health. Basically,
medicine conformed to the Hurons' traditions and beliefs. Depending
on the circumstances, it employed three different approaches: empirical
(involving the use of medicinal plants), physiological, and psychological
or magical (which involved either consideration of the sick person's
desires or the performance of magic rituals). The Jesuits supplied some
convincing testimony in this respect:

> The Hurons recognize three kinds of diseases. Some are natural, and
> they cure these with natural remedies. Others, they believe, are caused
> by the soul of the sick person, which desires something; these they cure
> by obtaining for the soul what it desires. Finally, the others are diseases
> caused by a spell that some sorcerer has cast upon the sick person;
> these diseases are cured by withdrawing from the patient's body the
> spell that causes his sickness.[173]

Unlike the Europeans, the Amerindians danced and made a great
deal of noise and music around the sick person.[174] Apart from removing
spells or fending off witchcraft, these rituals communicated the sympathy and support of the community. As mentioned earlier, shamans, both
men and women,[175] often formed curing societies, the members being
skilled in both magic rituals (songs and dances) and technical knowledge
in treating the sick. They diagnosed illnesses, cast out spells, prescribed
teas, set broken bones and treated dislocated limbs, removed projectiles,
and organized collective rituals like the *Andacwander*. In this ritual,
unmarried young people came to make love around the sick person in
order to provide comfort. Gabriel Sagard recorded that

in the country of our Hurons, there are also gatherings where all the girls of a village gather about a sick person, either at his wish, as a result of a dream, or at Loki's behest, for his health and cure. The girls thus assembled are all asked which of the young men of the village they wish to sleep with the next night; they each name one, and these are immediately informed by the masters of ceremony. They all come in the evening to sleep with the girls who have chosen them in the presence of the sick person, from one end to the other of the longhouse, and spend the whole night thus while two captains, one at each end of the dwelling, sing and bang their tortoise shell rattles from the evening until the next morning, when the ceremony ends. Pray God that such a damnable and lamentable ceremony be abolished.[176]

Generally, great importance was accorded to listening to dreams and gratifying desires in the curing process.

The religious world permeated all Huron social life, as much in the acts of daily life as in celebrations, feasts, carnivals, dances, curing rituals, and the telling of myths. 'And such observances are called among them "Onderha," that is to say "the ground," as one might say, the prop and maintenance of their whole State. "These," the old men and the Captains say to us, "are what we call affairs of importance."'[177] Missionaries and travellers at first greatly underestimated the importance of religion in Amerindian societies, because they found no official creed,[178] no place of worship, no institutionalized church, and no clergy. Nevertheless, the Amerindians conferred a spiritual reality on everything around them. 'They address themselves to the Earth, to Rivers, to Lakes, to dangerous Rocks, but above all, to the Sky; and believe that all these things are animate.'[179] Of these spirits or *oki*, that of the sky was the most powerful, because it ruled the seasons, the winds, and the tides. Because these spirits could be good or bad, mere vows were not enough. Offerings were made to them, usually a small amount of tobacco thrown into the fire. This was done on countless occasions – before going to sleep, when asking for a cure, and so on. During a long journey, while travelling to Quebec, for example, tobacco was put in the crevices of a large boulder in a river to obtain protection from capsizing and against enemies.[180] Exceptionally, one could burn a body as a sacrifice, but there was never any human sacrifice, properly speaking. Hunting and fishing involved the killing of animals and the risk of losing the friendship of the animal spirits. The Hurons therefore killed only what they needed, never wasted anything, and disposed of certain bones in ritual fashion, making a point of never throwing them to the dogs.[181]

Although the Hurons had shamans, these cannot be considered the equivalent of a clergy, because they had no monopoly of access to sacred things or any institutional legitimation. Furthermore, there was no strict division of labour between the sacred and the profane. The shaman's role was to ensure long-distance communication with the spirits beyond the visible world. Since humans communicated with the supernatural through dreams, the shaman was basically a decoder of dreams.[182] Let us hear what Jean de Brébeuf had to say on this subject:

> They have a faith in dreams which surpasses all belief ... They look upon their dreams as ordinances and irrevocable decrees, the execution of which it is not permitted without crime to delay ... The dream is the oracle that all these poor Peoples consult and listen to, the Prophet which predicts to them future events, the Cassandra which warns them of misfortunes that threaten them, the usual Physician in their sicknesses, the Esculapius and Galen of the whole Country, – the most absolute master they have. If a Captain speaks one way and a dream another, the Captain might shout his head off in vain, – the dream is first obeyed. It is their Mercury in their journeys, their domestic Economy in their families. The dream often presides in their councils; traffic, fishing, and hunting are undertaken usually under its sanction, and almost as if only to satisfy it. They hold nothing so precious that they would not readily deprive themselves of it for the sake of a dream. If they have been successful in hunting, if they bring back their Canoes laden with fish, all this is at the discretion of a dream. A dream will take away from them sometimes their whole year's provisions. It prescribes their feasts, their dances, their songs, their games, – in a word, the dream does everything and is in truth the principal God of the Hurons. Moreover, let no one think I make herein an amplification or exaggeration at pleasure; the experience of five years, during which I have been studying the manners and usages of our Savages, compels me to speak in this way.[183]

Religion played an objective ecological role by manifesting in mythical form, through discourse and practice, a reciprocal relationship between man and nature. It situated man as part of nature rather than transcending it, as in the Judeo-Christian tradition. The afterlife was a harmonious world where relatives and friends would be found again. Farming, fishing, and hunting would be easy. There was no last judgment, no hell.[184] The Jesuits remarked that Hurons 'make no mention either of punishment or reward, in the place to which souls go after death,' all being equal in the afterlife as they were in their own society.[185]

In addition to specifying the relation of man to nature, religious ceremonies (the Feast of the Dead, the interpretation of dreams, rituals for casting out spells, and acts of witchcraft) were aimed at both developing a sense of belonging to Huron society and imposing redistribution practices in order to guarantee the equal sharing of goods. Briefly, witchcraft, dreams, and feasting were powerful means of redistribution.

It was the custom when someone died to give gifts to the dead person's family. Every ten or fifteen years, when the village moved to a new site, a Feast of the Dead was organized. This was the occasion for digging up bodies and placing them in an immense common grave, thereby symbolizing the integrity of Huronia in the afterlife.[186] Each lineage brought gifts to the memory of the dead, gifts that were then redistributed, 'for they spare nothing, not even the more avaricious.'[187] 'Now all these presents do not follow the dead man into the grave ... A large share goes to the relatives, to dry their tears; the other share goes to those who have directed the funeral ceremonies, as a reward for their trouble.'[188] Through fear of sorcery (and because jealousy was believed to be the main motive for the use of witchcraft), those who were luckier than others in hunting or commerce hastened to share their gains.

> They say that these sorcerers are ruining them: for if anyone has succeeded in any enterprise, if he has been fortunate in trading or hunting, these wicked ones immediately put a spell on him, or on someone of his house, so that he will consume all in doctors and medicines. Thus, to remedy these kinds of maladies, there is an infinite number of doctors which they call *arendiwane*. These people are, in my opinion, true sorcerers with access to the devil. Some only judge of the evil, in various ways, through pyromancy, hydromancy, necromancy, feasts,

dances, and songs; others try to cure the evil by blowing, or with beverages, and other ridiculous mimicking, which has no virtue or natural effectiveness. But none of them will do anything without large gifts, and without generous rewards.[189]

The Hurons believed that dreams expressed the desires and messages of the soul.[190] It was therefore necessary to satisfy dreams, otherwise one might fall ill or die.[191] Sometimes the desire expressed by the dream went beyond the Huron social code. If it was a question of killing or humiliating someone, for example, the Hurons usually satisfied the desire with some symbolic object such as a charm. When the expressed desire exceeded material possibilities, the village council proposed a reasonable solution. Nevertheless, generally speaking, the desires of the dreamer were respected, particularly if he was sick.

> In addition to the desires that we generally have that are free, – or, at least, voluntary in us, – which arise from a previous knowledge of some goodness that we imagine to exist in the thing desired, the Hurons believe that our souls have other desires, which are, as it were, inborn and concealed. These, they say, come from the depths of the soul not through any knowledge, but by means of a certain blind transporting of the soul to certain objects; these transports might in the language of Philosophy be called *Desideria innata*, to distinguish them from the former, which are called *Desideria Elicita*. Now they believe that our soul makes these natural desires known by means of dreams, which are its language. Accordingly, when these desires are accomplished, it is satisfied; but, on the contrary, if it be not granted what it desires, it becomes angry, and not only does not give its body the good and the happiness that it wished to procure for it, but often it also revolts against the body, causing various diseases, and even death.[192]

In this passage, Father Ragueneau is speaking of the main superstitions of the Hurons. We learn, through the nebulous vocabulary of the period, that above and beyond the importance attached to desires and dreams, the Hurons knew of the existence of what we call the conscious and the unconscious. The missionary went on to say:

In the same manner, the Hurons believe that there are certain persons more enlightened than the common, whose sight penetrates, as it were, into the depths of the soul. These see the natural and hidden desires that it has, though the soul has declared nothing by dreams, or though he who may have had the dreams has completely forgotten them. It is thus that their Medicine-men, – or rather, their Jugglers, – whom they call *Saokata*, acquire credit, and make the most of their art by saying that a child in the cradle, who has neither discernment or knowledge, will have an *Ondinnonk* – that is to say, a natural and hidden desire for such a thing; and that a sick person will have similar desires for various things of which he has never had any knowledge, or anything approaching it. For, as we shall explain further on, the Hurons believe that one of the most efficacious remedies for rapidly restoring health is to grant the soul of the sick person these natural desires.[193]

How can one describe this society where the body received so much attention, and where desire and celebration were so important? 'They are born, live, and die in a liberty without restraint; they do not know what is meant by bridle or bit. With them, to conquer one's passions is considered a great joke, while to give free rein to the senses is a lofty Philosophy.'[194] It was a society in which the logic of attending to desire even extended to the rituals surrounding death. On the occasion of these rituals, the dying person could give a 'farewell feast' and insist, while alive, that he be clothed in the garments he would wear for the last, great journey.[195]

Freud has taught us that all social life (civilization) is incompatible with the uninhibited satisfaction of instinctive needs, and that all social life rests on the repressive organization of instincts.[196] Despite the emphasis on desire and celebration, social life in Huronia was no exception to this rule. The demands of work, war, kinship, political organization, and so on, imposed on everyone a whole series of constraints on the pleasure principle. However, as Herbert Marcuse has pointed out in *Eros and Civilization*, one must distinguish between repression and *surplus repression* – 'the restrictions necessitated by social domination.' It must also be distinguished from what he refers to as '(basic) repression,' that is, 'the modification of instincts necessary for the perpetuation of the human race in civilization.'[197]

Although basic repression and surplus repression are always inextri-

cably entwined, it can be said that, in the main, both forms were characteristic of European society. In Huronia, however, although everyone
worked, such work did not require excessive time, there was no hierarchical division of labour, the social product was collectively distributed
according to individual needs, and production was keyed to such needs.
Surplus repression was therefore relatively nonexistent.

To paraphrase Marcuse, any form of the reality principle already
requires an extremely wide and intensely repressive control of instincts.
In Huronia, because of the specific historical institutions and the
absence of relationships of domination, additional controls did not
develop, except for those indispensable to all human association.[198] The
aim of additional controls would have been to designate and impose distinction, the alienation effect, and exclusion. Since these did not exist,
interpersonal relationships were marked by a spontaneity, immediacy,
and a closeness evident on many levels. Doors were always open, and
people came and went at all hours.[199] Physical contact was frequent and
normal – people touched each other,[200] ate and drank from the same kettle, and threw the leftovers back into it,[201] for there was no disdain for
oneself or for others. Marcuse has noted that the senses of smell and
taste are more 'proximity senses,' more 'bodily,' closer to sexual pleasure
than other senses, and that they tend to fade in relation to the senses of
sight and hearing[202] when surplus repression is reinforced.

Among the Amerindians, we do not observe this specialization of, or
reduction in, the senses. 'The French do not trust their own eyes so much
as those of the Savages,'[203] noted the Jesuits, and the same was true of the
sense of hearing. The ritual 'eat-all' or 'leave-nothing' feasts involved the
whole body. The missionaries reported that on these occasions, the
Amerindians 'give full liberty to their stomachs and bellies to utter whatever sounds they please, in order to relieve themselves.'[204] They were
aware of their bodies in everything they did. The whole body of a man or
woman was erotic.[205] The Amerindians painted it, oiled it, wore jewels
around their necks, in their ears, around their elbows, on their legs and
ankles, and so on.[206] The whole body was violently involved in the movements of dances (frequently held with masks for the sick, and during
carnivals).[207] 'A good dancer in France does not move his arms much,
and holds his body erect, moving his feet so nimbly that, you would say,
he spurns the ground and wishes to stay in the air. The Savages, on the

contrary, bend over in their dances, thrusting out their arms and moving them violently as if they were kneading bread, while they strike the ground with their feet so vigorously that one would say they are determined to make it tremble, or to bury themselves in it up to the neck.'[208]

As is always the case, the reality principle imposed restraints on sexuality (by nature polymorphous-perverse) through numerous bans against such things as incest (within the clan) or sexual relations during the nursing period; nevertheless, sexuality was neither sublimated nor channelled into monogamous institutions. We should remember that sexual relations were considered normal from puberty onward, rape was nonexistent,[209] divorce was easy, and sexuality was not exclusively aimed at reproduction, as was made clear by such ceremonies as the Andacwander.

The immense amount of attention paid to desires and dreams ('Dreams are indeed the God of these poor Infidels')[210] is indicative of a society in which one *could* desire things, because sharing and mutual help featured prominently. Thus, if anyone fell sick, the others sought to satisfy his desires.[211] If a warrior dreamed he had been taken prisoner, the next day his fellows would reenact the nightmare in order to ward off its ill effects.[212] This betokens a society in which Eros is not totally in chains, where each man or woman is attentive to the pleasure principle within himself or herself, where people recognize and accept their instincts and impulses, where the manifestations of pleasure are not the 'flowers of evil,' and where 'nature' is not something to be conquered but to be heard.

'In France, if any one fall into a fit of anger, or harbor some evil purpose, or meditate some harm, he is reviled, threatened, and punished; there [among the Amerindians] they give him presents, to soothe his ill-humor, cure his mental ailment, and put good thoughts into his head again.'[213] For the Hurons, this sickness of spirit and mind originated in a failure to reciprocate generosity and in the absence of counter-offerings. Anger was a sign that the spirit wanted to return to its place of origin. In this way, exchanges of gifts, which assumed a whole symbolic and collective dimension, were an ever-present factor of social life.[214]

By attacking native medicine, shamans, religion, and beliefs, the Jesuits would not only throw a whole society into disarray but would shake the entire structure of the Huron and Amerindian personality.

The Question of
Unequal Exchange

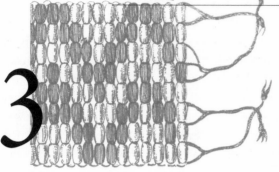

3

In order to understand the history of North America more fully, we first had to look at Europe before the colonial period and then get a basic picture of the 'new' continent prior to European settlement. In this third chapter we consider the equally essential aspect of relationships between colonizers and colonized, particularly from an economic perspective. More precisely, we are looking at these relationships in relation to the whole question of exchange, which was an underlying factor of the seventeenth-century fur trade. As this analysis progresses, we will get a clearer view of the implications of exchange for Amerindian societies as a whole.

At this period of merchant capitalism, it was not so much the fur trade as the phenomenon of unequal exchange that established the basic structure for the entire subsequent history of northeastern North America. Moreover, unequal exchange disrupted the reproduction mechanisms of Amerindian societies, upsetting relationships not only among themselves but also between man and nature.

Throughout the century, the development of the fur trade rapidly integrated the Amerindians into a market economy. From then on, they were prisoners of an implacable process that led to impoverishment and dependency, while their labour allowed the merchants to build fortunes and set in motion a military machine that would be turned against them. How did this exchange lead to wealth for some and poverty for others? A clear answer to this question should emerge from a detailed analysis of the mechanics of unequal exchange in this context.

Let us begin by establishing the theoretical framework for analyzing unequal exchange. Then, following a brief history of the first contacts between Amerindians and Europeans, we will look at the issue in detail.

EXCHANGE PRODUCTS

Exchange is not by definition unequal. For example, commerce can be directed toward exchange of use value, but only among producers (c-m-c, that is, commodity-money-commodity).[1] In this type of exchange, there is neither accumulation of capital nor enrichment of one party at the expense or to the detriment of the other. In the prehistoric period, commerce among tribes generally took this form. This was clearly not the case in the fur trade, which involved Amerindian producers, merchants, and European producers. The merchant was not a producer of wealth; consequently he did not share the same interests as his two producing partners.

Insofar as exchange between primitive societies and merchant capital involves products unknown to one of the parties, that is, products for which they have no terms of comparison for production costs, the subjective-value theory applies.[2] In other words, the merchants knew the value of furs in Europe, but the Amerindians did not. Moreover, the merchants' woollen blankets, knives, axes, and guns were priceless acquisitions for the Amerindian. Why wouldn't he be willing to exchange large piles of beaver skins for a gun? From the standpoint of use value, it seemed normal that the Amerindian would consider a gun worth more than a bow. Because the products offered in exchange were unknown to the primitive producers, they could be subjectively satisfied with an exchange that was objectively unequal.

Apart from an exchange of use values (furs for metal objects, textiles, arms, and so on), the fur trade presupposed a process of accumulation of capital characterized by an unequal exchange in labour time. This great commercial enterprise brought together two areas in which productivity was unequal: a stone-age continent and a manufacturing-age continent. Furthermore, merchandise circulating on the world market acquired an exchange value related to the average labour time in the production zones of that market. For example, given the development of agriculture in Europe and the shrinking of great forests to beyond the Ural Mountains, the production of furs demanded more labour time than in

North America, where vast stretches of virgin forest were filled with fur-bearing animals. In the case of manufactured products, however, the reverse was true. Generally, labour time was lower in Europe, and, consequently, average productivity was higher there than in North America. We can compare Amerindians with Africans in this respect, even though the respective periods of colonization were different. Even today, Africans export raw material that represents a greater number of working hours than it takes to manufacture the products obtained in exchange. Briefly put, when the productivity of the respective parties is unequal,[3] so is the exchange.

What is the point of circulating merchandise if not to make a profit for the middleman? The merchant possessed capital in the form of money; he invested it in the purchase of trade goods, for which he acquired furs to be sold at a profit in Europe. The motivation for the operation was therefore the transformation of M into $M + \Delta M$, ΔM being surplus value (given $M - C - M'$, the general formula for capital in circulation).[4] Ultimately, it didn't matter what the use value was of the circulating merchandise; the essential thing was to augment capital.

Merchant capital was therefore intent on the terms of exchange. It had to buy cheaply and sell at the best price. As a result, merchants always took advantage of the coexistence of plenty and scarcity. They sold when and where scarcity pushed up prices. Fur was rare in Europe and abundant across the Atlantic. The value of furs would therefore be greater in Europe than in North America. The merchant naturally tried to take advantage of this difference. However, in this context, fur was like gold, in that the more one imported, the more its value declined. Also, the more the merchant controlled the terms of exchange, the higher the profits; but as they became higher, more investors were attracted and competition would increase, causing profits to drop. To combat this general tendency for prices to drop, and thus preserve a good profit margin, a commercial monopoly was the best solution. In the economic crisis of the seventeenth century, the monopoly made it possible to limit competition among Europeans and to augment it among Amerindians, as well as to keep the latter relatively uninformed about the value of the merchandise involved and the techniques of production. The monopoly was also a means of concentrating repressive force by maintaining a garrison and building forts.

With the initiation of the fur trade, Amerindian societies can no longer be understood in isolation. The distance at which they traded became the major factor in the changes affecting them. To apply the theory of unequal exchange properly in this context, we need to list the major implications of exchange for Amerindian societies.

(1) The fur trade placed two economies in direct contact: a market economy, based on the accumulation of capital, and a primitive economy, in which commerce was based on contractual trading arrangements. In principle, however, exchange can only take place between mutually compatible forms of commerce.

(2) As the fur trade developed and created links among the communities that it integrated into the world market, the primitive producer gained more and more information about the real value of the merchandise, and was less and less willing to let himself be duped.

(3) The development of trade soon altered the division of labour toward greater specialization, in turn bringing about imperialistic and hierarchical relations among tribes and even within tribes.

(4) The more that trade developed, the greater the penetration of trade goods, thereby increasing the Amerindians' dependency on European products.

(5) From being autonomous, Amerindian societies became first the economic periphery, then the political and cultural periphery of the centre – Europe.[5] Exchange between two such poles ended, as always, with a transfer of assets from the periphery to the centre.[6]

(6) Merchant capital established relationships among regions with unequally developed production forces. However, links created by trade inevitably resulted in a technological transfer, and the peoples of the periphery attempted to appropriate the developed production techniques of the centre.

(7) The permanent transfer of wealth to the centre forced the peoples of the periphery into ever-increasing production in order to obtain the products of the centre. What followed was a spiralling exploitation of resources and a shift in the balance between man and nature, all of which led to the exhaustion of wealth in the periphery.

(8) The resulting scarcity of resources heightened competition and increased war among the peoples of the periphery.

(9) Furthermore, the collective impoverishment of the peoples of the

periphery in relation to the enrichment of the central powers posed a
threat, insofar as it might provoke a total overthrow of the system of
domination. The army was therefore an important component of such
domination. It was also true that European leaders in North America
feared for many years that, following some reversal, the Amerindian
peoples would drive the newcomers back into the Atlantic.

FIRST CONTACTS

Apart from very early encounters between Vikings and Amerindians,
commercial exchange between Amerindians and Europeans started in
the sixteenth century, when fishing boats began working in the Gulf of
Saint Lawrence. These exchanges continually increased. When Jacques
Cartier dropped anchor in Chaleur Bay, some fifty Micmac canoes
approached, laden with furs to trade. The Micmacs' behaviour clearly
indicated that they were accustomed to trading. As the European fur
market expanded, so did the importance of fur trading over fishing, to
the point where fishermen began to specialize in the fur trade instead.
Several ships sailed to Tadoussac, the northeastern tip of a prehistoric
copper route running from Lake Superior (where the surface copper
veins were exploited), through Georgian Bay, Lake Nipissing, the Ottawa
valley, and, after threading through numerous lakes and rivers, to Lac
Saint-Jean and the Saguenay River. In the opposite direction, European
products were carried along this trade artery to reach Huronia (on Lake
Huron) and Lake Superior. European products reached Huronia around
1580,[7] before Hurons and Europeans had ever met. European merchandise also followed the wampum route to Iroquoia, either by the Saint
Lawrence River, the Richelieu valley, Lake Champlain and the Hudson
River, or by the Saint Lawrence, Sault Saint Louis, Lake Ontario, and
overland to three of the Finger Lakes – Oneida, Cayuga, and Seneca.[8]
The first European products reached the Senecas (the most westerly
Iroquois tribe) between 1550 and 1575. This tribe had discarded its stone
axes and flint knives for metal tools by 1590.[9]

European trade made use of pre-existing exchange networks, which
covered the entire river system of northeastern North America. It is
therefore not surprising that Saint Lawrence Iroquoian pottery has been
found along the Ottawa River and its tributaries as far inland as the
Abitibi region, the upper Saint Maurice region, and around Lac Saint-

Jean, Fort Rupert on James Bay, and Kuujjuarapik on Hudson Bay.[10] The
Jesuits wanted to find a passage to China, which they hoped would lie
across the saltwater 'northern sea' – Hudson Bay – and learned from the
Amerindians that it could be reached by several waterways leading from
the Saint Lawrence basin. The first two routes took two weeks. They
began at the Saguenay River and Lac Saint-Jean, where a fair was held
annually at a place called Nekouba.[11] Here, Amerindians came from the
Great Lakes, the Ottawa River, the Saint Lawrence, and Hudson Bay. A
second connecting route started at the Saint Maurice River. A third, also
a two-week route, linked Lake Nipissing, the Ottawa River, and the
Temiscaming River to the northern sea. A fourth began at the western
end of Georgian Bay and a fifth, which took only a week, started from
Lake Superior.[12] It was possible to criss-cross the continent by canoe.
One simply had to keep paddling and know the required portages join-
ing the various water networks. In 1656, twenty-five 'Nipissirinien'
canoes 'laden with men, women, children, and furs,'[13] arrived at Trois-
Rivières via the Saint Maurice River. They had travelled by the Lake
Huron-Trois-Rivières link, avoiding the Saint Lawrence. The journey
had reportedly taken one month, during which time the travellers had
lived by hunting moose and beaver and by fishing. They told the French
how to follow this route.

Although Amerindians and Europeans each had trading interests –
the former in order to acquire more efficient tools, the latter to make a
profit – there was nothing equal about the relationship between these
trading partners. To begin with, the Europeans were better armed. Also,
they alone knew the terms of exchange and the value in Europe of furs
and trade goods. Moreover, they had no compunction about kidnapping
Amerindians and carrying them off to Europe, either as gifts for kings
and nobles or to be sold into slavery, as Esteban Gomez did in 1525 following an expedition to the Bay of Fundy. Corte Real in 1502 and
Thomas Aubert in 1509 each brought back seven captives from their
explorations of the Gulf of Saint Lawrence.[14] At this period, merchants
gave the Amerindian almost nothing in return for the fortunes in fur.
They made fabulous profits, and this attracted a growing number of
traders. Gradually, however, the Amerindians realized that they were
receiving far too little in return for their goods.

When, in 1534, Jacques Cartier erected a cross at Honguedo (Gaspé) with the arms of the king of France, in whose name he took possession of the territory, the Iroquoian chief Donnacona objected. Cartier reported in his journal that Donnacona made a 'great speech' to the French. 'He indicated the land all around us, as though he wished to say that it all belonged to him, and that we must not erect our cross without his permission.'[15] By way of response, Cartier showed him an axe, pretending to want to trade it for the chief's old bearskin. Donnacona approached to conclude the exchange but was taken prisoner along with his entourage. Cartier explained in mime that the cross was simply a navigating mark for ships and that the French would be back to trade. He nevertheless kept two of Donnacona's sons as prisoners and took them back to France. When these sons returned in 1535, they lost no time in telling their compatriots that they were being cheated with trade goods of little worth.[16] Cartier then went up the river known as Hochelaga (also called Ga-na-wa-ga in the Oneida dialect), which would later be known by its French name, the Saint-Laurent or Saint Lawrence River.[17] He followed the river, passing the canoes of the Iroquoian populations of Quebec who went each summer to fish off the Gaspé Peninsula.

At the beginning of the next century, Champlain would travel seated in the middle of a canoe manned by Amerindians, who took him westward, past rapids and over portages, to the lake of the Attignawantans,[18] that is, Lake Huron, which he called the 'freshwater sea,' and also southward to O-ne-ä-dä-lote,[19] the lake to which he pretentiously gave his own name. The missionaries followed his example when going up the Saguenay from Tadoussac to Lake Piwakwami, which they renamed Lac Saint-Jean.[20] Without the Amerindians, neither Champlain nor the Jesuits would have been able to draw maps of northeastern North America.

Overall, the Saint Lawrence Iroquoians remained sufficiently strong to successfully oppose European attempts to settle on their territory. Their hostility forced Cartier to abandon his settlement at Cap Rouge. Roberval's attempt in 1642 met with a similar fate.[21] Moreover, the fact that the territory had neither gold nor diamonds put an end to these rather half-hearted efforts at French colonization until the final years of the century. The French then turned to the coast of Brazil and what is now the southeast United States, but without success, finally returning to the Gulf of Saint Lawrence.

The Epidemics

Trading between ships and canoes included not only merchandise but also microbes. Regular commercial exchanges helped spread microbes around the globe. Here, too, the exchange was unequal, but this time it was the Amerindians who had nothing to give but everything to receive. They succumbed to illnesses against which they had almost no resistance. Without the necessary antibodies, they died like flies.

What were these new diseases for which the Amerindians had no immunity? Smallpox, typhus, cholera, typhoid and yellow fever, influenza, gonorrhoea, syphilis in its European form, and all the children's diseases that were often fatal to Amerindians: measles, roseola, German measles, chickenpox, scarlet fever, diphtheria, and whooping cough.[22] Of course, death by disease was nothing new in North America. Paleontological studies of pre-Columbian skeletons have revealed cases of hepatitis, encephalitis, poliomyelitis, non-pulmonary tuberculosis, rheumatism, arthritis, the American form of syphilis, intestinal parasites, gastrointestinal ailments, and respiratory infections, among others. Nevertheless, none of these appear to have had devastating effects on Amerindian populations, which also suffered very little from malnutrition or tooth decay.[23]

What accounted for the absence of many diseases found elsewhere in the world? Since very little livestock was raised in the New World compared to other continents, the general level of health must have been very high. However, it seems that the determining factor was the way in which palaeolithic man entered North America. The migrating peoples spent several centuries in the Arctic tundra. The rigorous climate apparently protected them from Eurasian diseases, 'filtering out' a great many of the germs originally carried by the migrants. It is also possible that several infectious agents did not become widespread in the Ancient World until after the major migrations had crossed Beringia.[24]

In 1535 a large-scale epidemic struck the Stadaconans.[25] When Champlain returned in 1608, not a single soul was left of the people who lived in the villages on the shores of the Saint Lawrence. These were people who had cultivated sweet corn, haricot beans, tobacco, squash, and sunflowers, who had fished for mackerel and cod in the Gaspé, and caught marine mammals in the Gulf. It is possible that the climate cooled, affecting crops in this region, which was at the northern limit of the area in which sweet corn could be grown. The epidemics may have greatly

diminished the inhabitants of Stadacona. Later, they may have fallen victim to the Iroquois, who may have exterminated them to gain access to
their trade.[26] Epidemics and intertribal wars turned the Saint Lawrence
into a sort of no man's land by removing these sedentary Amerindians,
and created a vacuum that enabled the French to establish themselves
there permanently. The Mayflower Puritans took advantage of a similar
vacuum when they arrived in Plymouth in 1620. Between 1617 and 1619,
an epidemic had struck the native populations of the coast. It varied in
intensity from region to region, but had drastically reduced the population of the Patuxet (Plymouth) area. The Narragansetts profited from
the weakened state of the Pokanokets, being thus able to attack and drive
them away. However, the latter allied themselves to the European newcomers in the hope of getting help against their traditional enemies.[27]

    In the same way that European epidemics had attacked the Inca
empire and halved its population long before the arrival of Pizarro,[28] epidemics had wreaked havoc on the shores of the Saint Lawrence before
the French could establish themselves there. The same phenomenon
occurred in Acadia, where the Jesuits reported in 1611 that the Micmacs
'are astonished and often complain that, since the French mingle with
and carry on trade with them, they are dying fast, and the population is
thinning out. For they assert that, before this association and inter-
course, all their countries were very populous, and they tell how one by
one the different coasts, according as they have begun to traffic with us,
have been more reduced by disease.'[29]

    In the seventeenth century, the continued presence of Europeans on
the shores of North America, where they traded, settled, and evange-
lized, led to an increase in epidemics. Algonkins and Micmacs were
struck by an epidemic in 1611 and several died. During the winter of 1623-
24, a fever ran through the Ottawa valley.[30] However, there was no actual
pandemic in northeastern North America before 1634. That year, smallpox took a severe toll of several tribes. The Dutch surgeon, Harmen
Meyndertsz van den Bogaert, visited an Iroquois village and observed
that 'a good many Savages here ... died of smallpox.'[31] In 1635, the epidemic affected the Montagnais, the Algonkins, and the Hurons. Father
Brébeuf noted that it was so universal 'among the Savages of our
acquaintance that I do not know if one has escaped its attacks.'[32] In 1636-
37, a second pandemic hit the Amerindian population. It was more

severe and more often fatal than the 1634 epidemic. This time it was influenza that took its toll. In mid-August of 1636 it was raging in the Saint Lawrence valley. A month later it had reached Huronia. The Amerindians then connected the spread of disease with the circulation of trade goods.[33] The malady even reached populations that had no direct contact with Europeans. In 1637, a new epidemic appeared, probably a childhood disease. Again, the Amerindians were hard hit, whereas the Europeans (even the French[34] living in Huronia) emerged relatively unscathed and rarely died. In 1639, a new pandemic of smallpox occurred.[35] The *Jesuit Relations* of 1639 stated that the Algonkins 'are dying in such numbers, in the countries farther up, that the dogs eat the corpses that cannot be buried.'[36] A year later, the Jesuits wrote, 'Of a thousand persons baptized since the last Relation, there are not twenty baptized ones out of danger of death ... more than 260 children under seven years.'[37] Of all the epidemics, this was the greatest killer. In 1641, smallpox reappeared for the third time. In 1645, 'maladies succeeded one another' in Huronia, 'then famines had their turn.'[38] In 1646-47, an epidemic struck the Iroquois and, almost at the same time, worms attacked the fields of sweet corn.[39] The Iroquois saw in all this the results of witchcraft practised by Father Isaac Jogues, whom they put to death along with his companion, Jean La Lande.[40]

A period of calm lasting a few years followed this wave of epidemics. In the winter of 1656-57, the missionaries noted a 'great mortality' among the Iroquois.[41] The following year, while they were counting the 'spoils wrested from the powers of Hell,' they wrote, 'We bear in our hands more than five hundred children, and many adults, most of whom died after Baptism.'[42] From 1660 to 1663, another epidemic stretched from the Atlantic coast to Lake Superior,[43] then in 1675 it broke out again.[44] In 1661, a Jesuit missionary described the symptoms as follows:

> We were detained three weeks at Tadoussac by a kind of contagious disease, hitherto unknown, which swept away the greater number of those whom it attacked. Their death, however, was due only to the violence of the convulsions, by which they were shaken in the strangest manner, yielding up their lives as if desperate, – or, at least, with contortions of the limbs which rendered a patient stronger than three or even four men together; and that, too, when his soul was hovering on his very lips.[45]

The pattern of epidemics was simple. The first epidemic weakened the population of a region, which was then unable to continue its various productive activities properly, and the poorly nourished survivors became easy prey for subsequent epidemics.[46]

Together, these various waves of epidemics killed at least half the Amerindian population, but some tribes, such as the Montagnais, were harder hit than others. The Huron population was reduced by half between 1634 and 1640 alone, as were the Iroquois and the Neutrals. In his *Jesuit Relations* of 1643-44, Father Vimont noted that 'where eight years ago, one could see eighty or a hundred cabins, barely five or six can now be seen.'[47] It is estimated that on the New England coast, for every Amerindian who died in war, three died of disease.[48] Adriaen Van der Donck commented on the Amerindians of New Netherland:

> The Indians also affirm, that before the arrival of the Christians, and before the small pox broke out amongst them, they were ten times as numerous as they now are, and that their population had been melted down by this disease, whereof nine-tenths of them have died ... We deem it worth our attention to treat concerning the nature of the original native inhabitants of the land; that after the Christians have multiplied and the natives have disappeared and melted away, a memorial of them may be preserved.[49]

The epidemics varied in their effects on different age groups. People between fifteen and forty suffered most. As a result, they had an equally severe effect on nursing infants.[50] But epidemics did more than halve the Amerindian population; they put the very future of their societies seriously at risk. At the same time that disease attacked the most productive age group, it also killed a large number of adults before they had time to transmit their knowledge to the young.[51] Traditional medicine was powerless in the face of these new diseases, people being unaware of their exact course or how they should be treated. In general, the epidemics spread a variety of microbacteria and struck at short intervals. There would be a brief respite, and then they would break out again. The use of steam baths followed by immersion in cold water – a technique frequently used in traditional medicine – often resulted in the sick person drowning because he or she had become too weak.[52]

It was long believed, as can be gathered from the *Jesuit Relations*, that there was an epidemiological disparity between Hurons and Iroquois. The trading at Trois-Rivières, but more especially the prolonged presence of the missionaries among the Hurons, apparently exposed the latter to contagion to such a degree that they were conquered by disease before being vanquished by the Iroquois.[53] However, it now seems that the Huron defeat was caused less by a difference in the intensity of the epidemics and more by the different conditions in which the two Amerindian communities endured the disease. The Huron community began to disintegrate as a result of the disruptive effect of the missionaries – a foreign element living in its midst. Their presence caused deep divisions in Huron society as well as a loss of self-confidence following the process of acculturation – all at the very moment when the Huron confederacy was confronting the gravest dangers. Before following this train of discussion, however, we must identify the origin of the epidemics more specifically.

For the Amerindians, only one question arose: why do we die when the Europeans survive? The Montagnais were convinced that the French, and especially the missionaries, only wanted 'the ruin of the country and the death of all the inhabitants.'[54] Most of the Hurons thought the same way. In 1636-37, many of them suspected the Jesuits of witchcraft. The Ottawas thought the same.[55] Who were these celibate shamans who often closed their doors to visitors?[56] What did they do behind their closed doors? They hid themselves in the woods, it was said, with pictures of children, which they pierced with a needle in order to throw a spell over them and make them die.[57] The missionaries wrote; could it be the writing that made the Amerindians die? 'No [said a Huron], it is not these drinks that take away our lives, but your writings; for since you have described our country, our rivers, our lands, and our woods, we are all dying, which did not happen until you came here.'[58]

And why did the missionaries harass the dying, threatening them with torments of hell worse than the most horrifying tortures, instead of comforting them?[59] The 'French snow' (sugar) that they gave sick people – was it poison? Several were persuaded that it was.[60] Finally, since the French taught that 'the first woman who ever lived brought death into the world,' did that mean that the women of their country were similarly malevolent?[61] The Hurons found themselves attacked by disease as never

before and facing death, while the newcomers, the intruders, survived.
They sought an explanation – any explanation. However, all the rumours
and theories led to the same general conclusion: there was a link between
these new diseases and the presence of the missionaries as well as the
general presence of the French and the Europeans. In 1637, the Jesuits
were forced to appear before the Huron grand council, where they were
accused of being 'the authors of this so universal contagion.'[62] The council considered either expelling the Jesuits or condemning them to
death.[63] Finally, however, it made no decision, preferring to wait until
the canoes from Trois-Rivières returned. By a curious coincidence, the
Jesuits' dwelling caught fire.[64]

During the epidemic of 1639, the Jesuits again fell under suspicion of
witchcraft because of their relentless insistence on baptizing sick children, by force if necessary and against the parents' wishes. These newly
christened children died. Could it be the result of baptism? Many
Hurons said that there were more deaths in the village with the most
Jesuits, where they had managed to baptize the largest number of people.
Were such suspicions justified? Probably. According to the following
quotation, the Jesuits appear to have carried the disease:

> They observed, with some sort of reason, that, since our arrival in these
> lands, those who had been the nearest to us, had happened to be the
> most ruined by the diseases, and that the whole villages of those who
> had received us now appeared utterly exterminated; and certainly, they
> said, the same would be the fate of all the others if the curse of this mis-
> fortune were not stopped by the massacre of those who were the cause
> of it ... Wherein truly it must be acknowledged that these poor people
> are in some sense excusable. For it has happened very often, and has
> been remarked more than a hundred times, that where we were most
> welcome, where we baptized most people, there it was in fact where
> they died the most; and, on the contrary, in the cabins to which we were
> denied entrance, although they were sometimes sick to extremity, at the
> end of a few days one saw every person prosperously cured. We shall
> see in heaven the secret, but ever adorable, judgments of God therein.[65]

The tension rose to a fever pitch and the Jesuits' lives 'depend[ed]
upon a single thread.'[66] Two of them, Brébeuf and Chaumonot, escaped

an assassination attempt and fled eastward to a more isolated village. The smallpox spread with their arrival, affecting converts more than others. As soon as they realized this, the new converts recanted, and 'the Faith [was] in disgrace.'[67] In 1647, Father Jérôme Lalemant, superior of the Jesuit missions in New France, transcribed Father Jogues's account of his captivity among the Iroquois. In passing, he mentioned that the

> Algonkins and the Hurons – and next the Hiroquois, at the solicitation of their captives – have had, and some have still, a hatred and an extreme horror of our doctrine. They say that it causes them to die, and that it contains spells and charms which effect the destruction of their corn, and engender the contagious and general diseases wherewith the Hiroquois now begin to be afflicted. It is on this account that we have expected to be murdered, in all the places where we have been; and even now we are not without hope of one day possessing this happiness ... Moreover, it is true that, speaking humanly, these Barbarians have apparent reasons for thus reproaching us, – inasmuch as the scourges which humble the proud precede us or accompany us wherever we go, as they have preceded and accompanied those who have gone before us in the publication of the Gospel; but, in token of the soundness of the adorable truths which it contains, the result is that finally these peoples will not fail to yield themselves to Jesus Christ; although he comes to them only with scourges in his hands.[68]

In the light of such comment, we can now better understand the repeated refusal of the French to sell weapons to the Hurons, with the exception of converts. The Jesuits lived in Huronia under threat of expulsion and even death. When epidemics struck, anger against them mounted. It is interesting to note that in Iroquoia there was neither pastor nor Dutchman.

Although it is a fair supposition that the 1634 epidemic was caused by the presence of ships from France, the cause of disease in subsequent years is more difficult to pinpoint. Nevertheless, there seems to be a link between the increase of epidemics and the rapid growth of a European population on the eastern seaboard, particularly in New England.[69] It is not unlikely that some diseases were carried by animals who ultimately transmitted them to humans. This, in any case, was the theory put for-

ward by Calvin Martin in *Keepers of the Game*.[70] He also suggested that
animal epidemics that were fatal to humans may have affected North
American wildlife by the sixteenth century, but such a hypothesis must
remain pure conjecture until paleopathology has given us proof. In the
period we are looking at, there is only one possible indication of such a
phenomenon. It involves three members of the Petite Nation, an
Algonkian tribe that took refuge in Montreal, terrified after seeing sick
caribou. 'They added that there had arisen a certain disease among the
Caribous, which made them vomit blood through the throat, remaining
quite still when they were pursued. They have seen as many as five, six,
or seven fall stiff in death in a moment: that has so terrified them that
they have resolved to leave their country in order to come and live near
the French.'[71] This was probably a case of pasteurellosis, according to
Calvin Martin.[72] The other reported case dates from much later, in the
autumn and winter of 1781-82, in the northern plains and Great Lakes
area. There, a smallpox epidemic cut down more than half the
Amerindian population, and, at the same time, an animal epidemic
struck the bison, caribou, moose, swans, ducks, and seagulls. The animals died in as great numbers as the humans. Could humans have transmitted the disease to animals? Wolves who ate human remains
contracted alopecia (mange). Could animals have transmitted disease to
humans? If, as is probable, the animals were infected with tularaemia
and/or sylvatic plague, these two diseases could have been transmitted to
humans.[73] On the other hand, there may have been a human epidemic
running parallel to a separate, unconnected animal epidemic. Between
1796 and 1803, some disease (probably tularaemia) was rampant among
the beaver while smallpox was killing humans. Was there a connection?
All this is pure speculation, but it is not unreasonable to suppose that the
arrival of global microbes in North America also affected wildlife.[74] For
example, tiny animal life and rats introduced by European ships may
well have transmitted infected ticks to North American animals.[75]

There is no doubt that the missionaries carried disease. What is
equally certain is that interethnic relationships (commerce, exchange,
war, diplomacy, and marriage), which had developed considerably, were
also largely responsible for the microbian unification of northeastern
North America. The Iroquois, even with no missionaries among them
(the first Jesuit mission in Iroquoia dated from 1656), fell sick and died in

large numbers in the pandemics of the winter of 1634-35 and after,[76] during the same period as the Hurons. In 1636-37, their neighbours, the Susquehannocks, fell victim to an epidemic, and the Senecas were struck by smallpox in 1640-41.[77] As we know how frequent contact was among the various tribes of the Iroquois confederacy, disease must certainly have run through all the villages. The 1646-47 epidemic affected all Iroquoia, but not Huronia.[78] The Iroquois, like all Amerindian peoples of the northeast, must have lost about half of their population between 1634 and 1640 and more between 1640 and 1650. Although the Iroquois and the Dutch did not have as close ties as the Hurons and the French, the Iroquois travelled regularly to Fort Orange to exchange furs, and there they came into contact with European inhabitants. In 1644, the Dutch pastor, the Reverend Johannes Megapolensis, Jr., said of Mohawk women that they were 'exceedingly addicted to whoring; they will lie with a man for the value of one, two, or three *schillings*, and our Dutchmen run after them very much.'[79] Although the author is clearly confusing the sexual freedom of the Iroquois men and women with prostitution (although the introduction of money into sexual relations may indicate a transition to prostitution), the point here is the development of physical contact between the Dutch and the Iroquois. Father Ragueneau, in speaking of an Iroquois raid at Trois-Rivières in 1650, wrote that 'their commander, the most prominent among these enemies of the faith, was a Hollander, – or, rather, an execrable issue of sin, the monstrous offspring of a Dutch Heretic Father and a Pagan woman.'[80] Speaking of the Amerindian women in New Netherland in general, Van der Donck notes that 'several of our Netherlanders were connected with them before our women came over, and remain firm in their attachments.'[81]

PARTNERS IN EXCHANGE

Trade and Merchant Capital in New France
The French were the first to find themselves in a position to trade for furs in the Saint Lawrence. In terms of the weather, however, the choice of the shores of the Saint Lawrence for a European colony in North America had many drawbacks compared to other sites along the Atlantic coast. In general, the land around Quebec was free of frost for only about 130 days per year, and for only about 100 days downriver, northeast of Baie-Saint-Paul. The river froze over for four months of the year.

This factor complicated trade with the West Indies. Furthermore, navigation on the Saint Lawrence was difficult. However, the French did not take these factors into account, as they merely intended to trade, not to colonize or farm the land. In 1608, a fort at Quebec offered distinct advantages for trade. Quebec had a commanding view of the river, and ships venturing into the narrows would come within range of French cannon. The Saint Lawrence and its tributaries covered an immense watershed, draining half the continent and providing access, especially northward, to the best furs. Also, because the French had arrived first and were well situated, they had established commercial alliances with the Algonkians and the Hurons, tribes that since pre-Columbian times had exchanged merchandise over a territory stretching from the Great Lakes to Hudson Bay. The French were the first Europeans to graft their activities onto this exchange network. At Quebec itself, trade took place with the Montagnais, using a sort of pidgin language that was half Montagnais, half French.[82]

We may ask why, when intensive trading already took place at Tadoussac, the French wanted to establish themselves at Quebec and run the risk of the dangerous navigation involved in sailing upriver. It was precisely because trading was so intensive that the French sought another site. At Tadoussac, trading had been going on for almost a century, attracting numerous French and Basque ships as well as Dutch vessels. Competition had brought prices and profits down all over the Gulf, from the Acadian coast to Tadoussac.

In the seventeenth century, profits dropped drastically in North America, just as in Europe. The solution was to penetrate the interior in order to make contact with other Amerindians who were less familiar with trade, and to exclude European rivals by effectively establishing a monopoly. When Champlain came to Quebec in 1608, he did so in the name of the monopoly of Sieur de Monts and proceeded to build the first fort to block passage upriver, thereby excluding commercial rivals. The Basque merchants from Tadoussac tried to foil this plan by attempting to kill Champlain and gain entry to the fort, using the locksmith Jean Duval as a would-be assassin.[83]

The French merchants who had been excluded – traders from La Rochelle, Saint-Malo, Saint-Jean-de-Luz, and Dieppe – applied pressure at home, and the monopoly was revoked in 1609. Free trade was restored between 1610 and 1612, and competition increased, as would be expected. The Montagnais, who were already seasoned traders, took advantage of the situation. At Tadoussac in 1611, these Amerindians, who had become 'clever and crafty,' refused to trade until 'several ships had come together, in order to have better terms.'[84] This attitude, which ran counter to the rules of contractual commerce, can only be accounted for by the fact that a century of trade had been practised in a context of dog-eat-dog competition among fishing boats – transactions in which no one side could get the upper hand. The Montagnais had been forced to alter their traditional mode of exchange, as they had been unable to form a long-term alliance with a stable European partner, and probably because, in addition, they had been unable to obtain gifts that corresponded to their own generous presents.

The merchants then moved upriver to Montreal, where the Europeans' rapacious habits angered the Algonkins and Hurons, who were still unaccustomed to direct dealings with the newcomers. The large number of traders resulted in a surplus production of furs in France, followed by a drop in prices.[85] However, the Amerindians were also competitive. For some years European products had been arriving via the Gulf, from where they were distributed through the ancient trade networks. The Montagnais and Micmacs were the initial middlemen, and at the turn of the century they were joined by the Algonkins and Hurons. The Iroquois (mainly the Mohawks), who were far from trading sites or boxed into their territory, managed to get trade goods by raiding and pillaging the Algonkin and Huron canoes. The latter tribes asked Champlain for military aid in driving off their rivals. Champlain and his men made two armed incursions against the Mohawks, one in 1609 and the other in 1610, reaching Mohawk territory via the Richelieu River.[86] The surprise effect of French muskets made victory easy.

In the meantime, rival merchants from Rouen and Saint-Malo agreed to launch a new monopoly called the Société des Marchands. This new monopoly made the price of European products rise, much to the displeasure of the Montagnais, who now sought every opportunity to trade with smugglers downriver from Tadoussac. The Hurons and Algonkins, unfamiliar with the rules of international trade, were not yet aware of the connection between a monopoly and prices. For them, exchanges were carried out in an almost ritual fashion, in a context of celebration with speeches and dancing. There was no question of driving a bargain. The French profited from this ignorance. Around 1610, the Mohawks stopped raiding the Saint Lawrence valley. Champlain's victories notwithstanding, this was mainly because European goods could now penetrate the interior via the Hudson River, where the Dutch had begun to trade.[87] However, the Oneidas and the Onondagas, Iroquois tribes that were still without easy access to European goods, continued to raid the Algonkins and the Hurons, who had to gather a thousand warriors to repel the attackers. These raids forced the Algonkins to ally themselves with the Hurons, who assumed leadership of the alliance. The Algonkins had a smaller, more dispersed population and were dependent on Huron corn for their survival; they were therefore obliged to give up their role as middlemen to the Hurons.[88] In 1615, during a journey to Huron country, Champlain undertook a third military offensive against the Iroquois, and this sealed the alliance between the French and the Hurons – the most powerful Amerindian confederacy.[89] From this moment on, soldiers armed with muskets lived among the Hurons to guarantee effective military defence against the Iroquois. A few missionaries and company agents joined them. In all, there were some thirty Europeans living with the Hurons.[90]

In this way, the French assumed a position of strength in the fur trade. They had an excellent geographical position with access to the best source of furs in terms of quality and quantity, they had conducted a successful military campaign against the rivals of their Amerindian allies, they were associated with the most powerful Amerindian confederacy in the northeast, and finally, they held a monopoly with no immediate challengers in their trade with relatively naive Amerindian commercial partners.

Champlain, more than anyone, understood that simply being a trader was not enough when engaging in the fur trade. Amerindian mores must be taken into account. This was the secret of his success – not just the force of his personality, but his ability to organize the fur trade in ways that were compatible to the two economies. It was not a question of prices. For example, at the request of the Hurons, who met the French for the first time in 1609, an alliance was formed, then a common military expedition undertaken. There was an exchange of people who became both hostages and interpreters. An exclusive relationship was established between the two trading partners. In this respect, the French monopoly of the fur trade, although objectively disadvantageous to the Hurons in terms of the world market, was exactly what the latter sought. If trading also meant making peace, practising diplomacy, and creating friendships, then it was impossible to conclude treaties with a large number of competing sellers. The Hurons had no desire to trade with Champlain's competitors who went up the Saint Lawrence as far as Lac Saint-Louis just above Montreal.[91] The Hurons refused to trade with merchants on whom they could not count for military support, and they formed an alliance with Champlain because he agreed to accompany them on military expeditions against the Iroquois.[92] In more general terms, European powers gained a substantial foothold in North America because Amerindian societies insisted that the Europeans participate in their wars as a condition of trade.

When the French and Hurons met, whether at Sault Saint Louis, the mouth of the Richelieu, Trois-Rivières, or Quebec, their encounters were always accompanied by festivities that lasted several days. The merry-making included shooting contests (with muskets), the exchange of presents, feasts, speeches, the actual trading, farewell presents, and so on.[93] Quite apart from the ritual of exchange,[94] Champlain had comprehended a more fundamental aspect of Amerindian society – the spirit of giving. To get a picture of this, we must look at two passages, one describing the beginning of a trading session in 1611, and another describing the end of one in 1633.

The 1611 trading session opened thus: 'After they had spun and danced enough, the others [Hurons], who were in their canoes also began to dance by several movements of their bodies. When the song was over, they came on land with a few furs and gave gifts similar to those offered by the others. We reciprocated with presents of equal value. The next day, they traded what little furs they had, & again gave me a special present of thirty beavers, for which I recompensed them.'[95]

The closing of the 1633 session was described thus: 'Sieur de Champlain made his presents, which corresponded in value to those that the Hurons had made him. To accept presents from the Savages is to bind oneself to return an equivalent.'[96]

What is striking about these two citations is the insistence on exchanges of equal value, on reciprocity. Merchants were usually looking for surplus value and often boasted of having bartered shoddy goods for the furs received. In both the operations described above, Champlain made no profit – a circumstance that seems amazing at first glance. In the first round of giving, Champlain gave generous gifts, which obliged the Hurons to be more generous in the second round. However, the real trading took place in this second round – that is, the bartering of furs for French merchandise. With the exchange finished, Champlain showed renewed generosity on the last day by offering gifts that encouraged the Hurons to come back the next year. Thus, 'without breaking with the custom of the country,'[97] Champlain turned the Huron rules of exchange to his advantage.

Rivalry between French port cities, however, was not about to disappear. The excluded merchants of Saint-Malo, Saint-Jean-de-Luz, and La Rochelle applied all kinds of pressure either to get rid of, or get around, the monopoly. In 1621, Guillaume and Emery de Caën were able, thanks to strong friends at court, to oust the Société des Marchands and secure the monopoly for their own company, known as the Compagnie de Caën or de Montmorency. The ousted company used its own influence, and the two companies merged in 1622.[98] 'The Savages were visited by many people, to such an extent that an Old Man told me he had seen as many as twenty ships in the port of Tadoussac. But now since this business has been granted to the association, which to-day has a monopoly over all others, we see here not more than two ships which belong to it, and that only once a year, about the beginning of the month of June.'[99]

At the suggestion of the Dutchman de Bruck,[100] Richelieu, taking his inspiration from the Dutch model, intervened directly in 1627 to create a company called the Compagnie de la Nouvelle-France or the Compagnie des Cent Associés. Richelieu personally directed the new company, which was mainly made up of nobles connected to the machine of state, such as treasurers and receivers, as well as some twenty Catholic merchants, most of whom were from Paris and Rouen, none from La Rochelle. The large number of nobles and various functionaries who were permitted to engage in business as shareholders without losing rank insured that Richelieu's goals for the company would meet little opposition. Merchants like those from La Rochelle would have had difficulty supporting the cardinal's objectives, being hardheaded businessmen rather than statesmen given to grand political schemes. In fact, as far as internal politics were concerned, Richelieu was intent on eliminating an old political enemy, the Huguenots. For the past ten years, a religious and civil war had been laying waste to southern and southwestern France, including the Languedoc and Cévennes regions and La Rochelle. With regard to foreign policy, Richelieu planned to send 4,000 settlers to North America to establish the basis of an empire. In 1627, the Compagnie des Cent Associés spent 164,000 *livres* sending a first contingent of 400 settlers to New France. Foreigners, non-Catholics, and criminals were excluded.[101]

The problem now arose of how to get these settlers across the Atlantic. The French navy was, in fact, the weakest among the powers vying for imperial power in North America. The expedition left France at a time when the king's troops and the navy were busy blockading La Rochelle. The besieged city succeeded in getting England to come to its aid, and the two countries found themselves at war. Jarvis Kirke, a London shipowner, heard of the colonization project and organized an expedition to intercept the French fleet. He caught up with it in the Gulf of Saint Lawrence, after destroying Miscou on the Acadian coast and a trading post at Cap Tourmente on the Saint Lawrence. Throughout the summer, English ships raided French fishing ships in the Gulf and set up a blockade to prevent food getting through to Quebec. The 400 immigrants went back to France. Kirke slipped back to London and helped found an Anglo-Scottish company to trade in the Saint Lawrence, to which the king of England gave the monopoly for trading and the authority to destroy French establishments in the region.[102]

In 1629, Kirke took Quebec, imprisoned the garrison, then seized the French ships bringing provisions to the settlement. By this time, there were only about twenty Frenchmen left in the colony. Kirke's capture of Quebec is a good indication of how the British navy was growing in strength. In fact, the English dislodged the French from Port-Royal in 1613, but the French returned in 1615. The English came back in turn, capturing Acadia in 1628-29. However, since the English had taken Quebec and Acadia after the signing of a peace treaty between France and England, these were returned to France (but not to the Amerindians) in 1632. La Rochelle, the Protestant stronghold of France, succumbed to the long siege and famine and surrendered to the king's Catholic army.[103]

In that same year, the Compagnie des Cents Associés gave up its ambitious projects because it was on the brink of bankruptcy. It subcontracted the monopoly in exchange for a third of the revenue. It is not clear whether the few people who had settled in New France had the right to act as middlemen between the company and the Amerindians from 1632 to 1645. A clause in the company by-laws of 1627 stated that established settlers could trade freely with the Amerindians, on condition that they took all the beaver pelts to the company store, which undertook to buy them for two livres each.[104] During that period, a pelt was worth ten livres when it arrived in France. This clause probably remained a dead letter until 1636, when the 'habitants' were allowed to trade with the Amerindians (always on condition that they bring the furs to the company store). La Chesnaye notes in his memoir of 1677 that before 1645, the fur trade was forbidden 'very severely to the inhabitants, except for the fruits of the country, in order to encourage such crops as peas, corn, and wheat for bread.'[105]

In 1645, the most important people in the colony formed the Compagnie des Habitants, taking advantage of the difficulties experienced by the Compagnie des Cent Associés, whose shareholders had come to realize that they would never recuperate the money already invested.[106] The new company obtained the trading subcontract until 1663. In return, it was obliged to bring out twenty couples a year to settle in New France as well as see to the 'government' of the territory and pay 1,000 livres annually to the Compagnie des Cent Associés, which retained all seigneurial rights. As had been the case since the colony's founding, the new arrivals could not escape seigneurial relationships, inasmuch as they would settle on a parcel of land. The intention was to transplant the social relationships of France and thereby reduce the conflict between settlement and the fur trade. Settlers who were obliged to stick to their land (since they had to produce crops in order to keep it) would not devote too much time to trading.

For the first time, control of the trading monopoly was now centred in the colony instead of the home country. In principle, all habitants (that is, colonists) who were heads of families in the colony could join the new Canadian company. There were to be three divisions however: the first included 'the nobles and those in authority,' the second included 'businessmen and master tradesmen,' and the third, 'the commonality' of the remaining habitants.[107] What actually happened is a perfect example of the conditions in which transplanted European societies were reborn in the New World. Far from being open to all habitants, free trade was immediately stopped by the company directors, who published a ban in September 1645. 'All persons, of whatever quality and condition, be they habitants, soldiers, workers, sailors, or others,' were forbidden 'to trade any beaver or other pelts,' under pain of confiscation and a fine.[108] However, a secret clause allowed the Jesuits to take part in trading. Money came into the colony, but mere settlers had no more access to it than to trading, since the Communauté des Habitants defined by the company included only 'four or six families,' and these, 'after being poor, found they were handling considerable amounts [of capital], and therefore enlarged their houses and indulged in much spending, which was greater for their vessels and cargoes, and the wealth from beaver had to pay for it all.'[109]

The 'small habitants' united around the colonist Maheu and the interpreter Marsolet in order to mutiny against the privileged few, but Governor Montmagny intervened, and the guilty were punished.[110] Order was restored – that is, the fur trade continued to be controlled by a few families to the detriment of the majority. The company directors did have to make one concession, however: colonists were allowed to trade, on condition they only used products of the colony as trade goods – in other words, agricultural products – and that the pelts be resold at a fixed price to the company store.[111] The situation now reverted to what it had been before 1645.

The fur trade operated under these conditions until 1663. Nevertheless, with the exception of the first two years when the beaver catch had been plentiful, the yield in subsequent years was fairly poor. The members of the Compagnie des Habitants had financed themselves with high interest loans of between 25 and 30 per cent negotiated in La Rochelle. The merchants of this city, who had been excluded from the fur trade since 1628, again became involved, this time permanently, alongside the Rouen merchants. The loans came due just as the Hurons, the fur-supplying allies of the French, were decimated in the 1648-49 epidemic, and while the French market was being rocked by the civil war known as La Fronde. The Compagnie des Habitants returned to Tadoussac and to the inflexible monopolistic formula. In 1660 – just before the beaver pelt market jumped from five to twenty livres – the company had to hand over the sale of merchandise in France to the Rouen merchants.[112] In 1661, the company cancelled its agreement and reverted to the old system.[113] All in all, the Amerindians had to deal with a monopoly from 1608 to 1663, despite successive companies.

Each year the Hurons would come down from their country to meet the French. On the day of arrival, they settled in and built longhouses. On the second day, they held council and made gifts to the French to reaffirm their friendship. Speeches and presents were always symbolically linked. A gift was one's word, and one's word was a gift.[114] To refuse a gift was to refuse the word that accompanied it.[115] The French accommodated themselves to this and to other customs of the country,[116] and learned the language of gifts and metaphors.[117] They in turn gave presents that spoke of friendship and hospitality and offered a great feast to their trading partners: 'sagamité, composed of peas, of bread-crumbs or powdered sea biscuit, and of prunes; all this was boiled together in a great kettle which is used for making beer, with water and no salt.'[118] During the third and fourth days, the Hurons exchanged their pelts and tobacco for blankets, axes, kettles, cloaks, iron arrowheads, little glass cannons, shirts, and similar articles.[119] A council was again held on the fifth day, to the accompaniment of dancing and singing. The French gave a farewell feast and displayed their gifts in the middle of the meeting place.[120] The governor usually took the opportunity of insisting that the Hurons convert to Christianity, giving more presents to new converts,[121] and finally wished them a good journey. 'Monsieur le chevalier had these people [the Hurons] told that he presented them a barrel of hatchets and of iron arrow-heads. Part of this was to waft their canoes gently homewards, part to draw them to us next year.'[122]

At last, the Hurons left, or as the *Jesuit Relations* described it, 'The next morning they disappear like a flock of birds.'[123] There was little of the European marketplace in all this. Trading was carried out largely according to the forms of primitive commerce: an alliance that joined the partners in a pact of generosity,[124] carried out in a highly symbolic ceremony; the absence of competitive bargaining on either side; trading sessions lasting several days, and so on. Despite appearances, however, trading was dominated by the market economy. The French offered lavish hospitality, and the Hurons were obliged to do the same. At precisely the moment when the Hurons were the debtors according to their system of giving, they entered the company trading post for the exchange of goods. The French had been generous in diplomacy; now the Hurons must be generous in 'business.' Champlain's strategy continued to prevail – no profit in the public arena, all the profit during trading in the company store. The company was obliged to maintain fairly fixed prices, nevertheless, because the Hurons would have interpreted any fluctuation in relation to the market as trickery and treason.

The French had decoded the Amerindian system of exchange. They had understood that gifts circulated and were sure to bring a return, but that by definition time was needed to produce any reciprocal benefit.[125] Since the idea of a term (in the sense of a payment at a later date) was current in primitive commerce, the French were able to link this with extending credit, which they did following the destruction of Huronia. Merchants made increasingly large advances of merchandise to resident Amerindians.[126] What was a financial transaction for one party was a transaction of honour for the other.

Trade and Merchant Capital in New Netherland

The Dutch, who controlled the fur trade in Europe, did not leave the French to enjoy sole exploitation of the new American source of furs for long. In 1609, some merchants chartered a boat piloted by an English captain named Henry Hudson, intending both to discover a passage to the Orient via North America and to trade in the territories lying between Virginia and the Gulf of Saint Lawrence. Hudson went up the river that bears his name as far as the tide or as far as the neighbourhood of present-day Albany. He bartered various goods for a large number of furs. His success attracted many other ships, which traded on the coast and went up the Hudson, Connecticut, and Delaware rivers in order to escape competition. Up to and including the year 1613, trade was open to all. Four companies sent several ships into the area and shared the commerce. These were companies equally interested in the fisheries. Among them, the Van Tweenhuyzen Company had interests in the Rouen fur trade and had already sent ships to trade in New France.[127]

In 1613, the lack of profits forced Holland to resort to a monopoly. Two companies were interested, and they divided the territory between them in 1614, each holding half the monopoly. In other words, rivalry continued, and at the end of 1614 the New Netherland Company was formed by the four principal companies that had been previously involved in the New Netherland trade. This merging of several rival companies was not new. The Verenigde Oostindische Company, that is, the United East India Company, was created in this way in 1602, as was the Noordse Company or the Northern Company in 1614. These mergers followed the reduction of profit margins typical of major commerce in the early seventeenth century.

The New Netherland Company built Fort Nassau on the site of present-day Albany, just as the French had built a fort at Quebec. Here, too, strategic reasons governed the choice of location. Any unwanted boats reaching Fort Nassau could be repulsed by cannon fire. Although the Hudson River froze over at Albany, it remained open from there to the sea. The Hudson and its tributary, the Mohawk, together made up the largest water network on the east coast and the main water route to the Great Lakes. The Dutch were therefore in a position to reach the Hurons, who were the major fur suppliers, but the route was, on the whole, more difficult than the link between Montreal and Georgian Bay. In any case, the Hurons had already sealed their alliance with the French.

The Dutch first traded with the Mahicans on the territory around their fort. The Mohawks initially raided the Mahicans but were later able to trade directly with the Dutch. Like the French, the Dutch tried to gain prestige by providing military aid to their allies. An attempt to help the Mohawks against the Susquehannocks proved a failure, however. From then on, the Dutch were loath to get involved in Amerindian tribal wars. To make up for initial disadvantages, the Dutch tried to attach their trade to the pre-Columbian wampum trail, which ran from Long Island (the principal producer of wampum), to the Richelieu via the Hudson, then up the Saint Lawrence to the entire Canadian shield inhabited by the Algonkian peoples. An alliance between Mahicans and Algonkians would have made it possible to drain off northern furs to Fort Nassau. The Mohawks foiled the Dutch plans, fearing that an alliance between their northern enemies and the Dutch would squeeze them out. In 1624, after concluding a tactical pact with the French and the Algonkians, the Mohawks succeeded in a major strike against the Mahicans,[128] even though the latter had the military support of some of the Dutch.[129] In 1628, the Mohawks completely subjugated their adversaries, forcing them to emigrate eastward into the Connecticut River valley,[130] and established themselves as the sole middlemen in trade with Fort Nassau.

In the meantime, merchants who had been excluded from the monopoly, but were attracted by the profits, applied pressure. Their tactics were much the same as those that broke the de Monts monopoly in 1609 in New France. They finally succeeded in getting the New Netherland fur trade reopened to all comers in 1617. The New Netherland Company was unable to keep its highly profitable monopoly. Nevertheless, it continued to trade, sharing the territory so as to forestall the drop in prices caused by the presence of several traders in one place.[131]

After years of vacillation and diminishing profits, the Dutch states-general promoted a concerted, global policy aimed at creating a single great company out of the numerous companies possessing ships, crews, and trading posts on the shores of Africa, Brazil, and New Netherland. This was to be the Dutch West India Company, modelled on the United East India Company. In doing this, the states-general wanted to make the new company the spearhead of Dutch commercial interests by abolishing competition among the Dutch and concentrating their forces in order to combat rival powers – mainly Spain and Portugal, but also England and France. New Netherland was therefore integrated into a much greater entity. The company established itself there in 1623, and held sway until 1664. It imposed a new monopoly over trade, and built a new trading fort – Fort Orange – to replace Fort Nassau and a further fort at Manhattan called New Amsterdam. The intervention of Dutch political power in the affairs of companies was designed to reduce internal rivalry and create a genuine, concerted commercial strategy. This marked an important phase in the history of North American commerce, for it would now be empires rather than companies that confronted each other on this continent.

Between 1623 and 1629, the Dutch West India Company had sole trading rights, and only company agents could actually trade. Nevertheless, profits were attractive and everyone wanted a piece of the action, to use a modern expression. The struggle to gain a preferential share of the fur trade erupted first within the company itself. Two opposing factions supported divergent personal aims and interests. The first felt that there was only one way of making profits in the fur trade: maintain a rigid monopoly and keep settlement by Europeans to a minimum, because settlers were inevitably attracted to the fur trade and always ended up

taking part legally or illegally, thereby altering the exchange relationships.[132] Like the directors of the Amsterdam company, this faction
wanted maximum short-term profit.

The second faction supported a long-term strategy. From this standpoint, settlement was indispensable in order to consolidate the colony's
interests in the face of the virtual threat posed by the English colonies,
particularly Virginia, where the population was growing by leaps and
bounds. This faction therefore suggested that settlement enterprises be
set up, with seigneuries directed by company shareholders who would
have the right to trade. This meant that apart from the normal dividends
proceeding from the company's overall activities, some shareholders,
who would become seigneurs or *patroons*, would have direct access to
the exchange relationship in the fur trade. This was a blatant conflict of
interest, but the need to populate the territory with Europeans continued to be important, otherwise everything might be lost to the English.
This second faction, led by Killiaen Van Rensselaer, finally succeeded in
imposing its views. It had the support of the states-general, for which a
global strategic policy carried more weight.

An initial breach had been opened. The principal shareholders
obtained a *Vryheden ende Exemptien* or Charter of Freedoms and Exemptions giving them the right to take part in the fur trade if they became
patroons. Several patroonships were created, all near places where trading occurred. Immense territories were conceded in return for an under-
taking by the patroon to transport and settle fifty adult colonists in four
years.[133] The patroons also had to respect company policy, which insisted
that such territory first be purchased from the Amerindians. Most of
these attempts at setting up patroonships failed. Van Rensselaer was the
exception. The main reasons for failure were the continued opposition of
many of the company's directors, Amerindian raids, and highly unpredictable profits. Van Rensselaer's success lay in the fact that his patroonship surrounded Fort Orange, which was the largest trading centre. At
the outset, he managed to get around the monopoly. Although in principle he had no access to the fort's trade, which was reserved for company
agents, he was able to trade directly with Amerindians who crossed his
land to reach the fort.[134] Also, he supplied goods to his tenants, who
bartered them with the Amerindians for furs that they were obliged to
resell to Van Rensselaer.

It may seem surprising that, when Holland itself no longer had a seigneurial system, settlers could be integrated into patroonships in New Netherland. The explanation lay in the way the seigneurial system operated in the fur trade. All free colonists were excluded from trading, because the settlers in patroonships had a dependent relationship with the patroon. Moreover, the patroon could use his settlers as a semi-captive labour force in the fur trade. Contracts signed with feudal tenants contained clauses specifying how they could participate in the fur trade.[135] Van Rensselaer obtained a large number of furs in this way and broke the monopoly of the company at Fort Orange.[136] However, as time went on, the tenants in turn wanted to get a share of the trade. David P. De Vries described the situation at Fort Orange during his journey of 1639, remarking that the company 'had nothing but an empty fort,' while the patroons (Godyn, Van Rensselaer, de Laet, and Boemart) had built themselves fine farms at the company's expense. They engaged in so much fur trading on their farms all around the fort that 'every boer was a merchant'.[137]

At the end of the 1630s, the colony had become a financial failure for the company. Moreover, the thrust of English settlement (more than 20,000 colonists in New England, and an equal number in Virginia), was not only a general long-term threat, but also a threat to the fur trade. Traders from Plymouth went up the Connecticut River and tried to compete with the Dutch. In 1637, the New Sweden Company got a foothold on the Delaware River, and Swedish merchants went up this river to trade. Despite this company's Swedish allegiance, however, a large part of its capital came from Holland. It was supplied by Dutch merchants who were interested in the fur trade but excluded from the West India Company, and by Dutch manufacturers who were shareholders in Swedish-Dutch copper-finishing businesses. A copper price war between the Dutch West India Company and the Swedish-Dutch copper manufacturing interests had resulted in a surplus production of copper goods. The Amerindian market offered an opening for such goods.[138] Although the Dutch West India Company looked on this venture with disapproval, it tolerated it, for fear the English might get into the business of selling copper to the Indians instead. The old dilemma of monopoly versus settlement reared its head once again. Van Rensselaer described the company's impasse, noting that if it wished to keep the fur trade to itself, thereby limiting it to a few (the most profitable solution), it would have no means of protecting the territory. On the other hand, a large number of inhabitants would lead to profit losses. In any case, no one would be bothered coming there to settle if the fur trade was not open to everyone.[139]

In 1639, under pressure from the states-general, the Dutch West India Company gave up its monopolistic leanings and opted for a policy of settlement, realizing that this was the only way of keeping the New Netherland territory under its control. The directors thought they could make the colony profitable in the long term by developing cereal crops.[140] A new Charter of Freedoms and Exemptions opened trade to everyone, with the company reserving the right to charge a 10 per cent customs tax on fur exports. The company kept Fort Orange for a few years as the only trading post, allowing private traders to compete with its agents. In 1643, Van Rensselaer's nephew and manager, Arent Van Curler, stated that even when fur trading had been particularly good, neither he himself nor the company had been able to get pelts because private traders had garnered them all. In 1644, the company closed its store and simply maintained the fort, which from then on was used exclusively by private traders.[141]

With trading thrown open to all, a scramble for furs began. Many settlers abandoned their farms. People who had no domicile in New Netherland came into the colony for the sole purpose of trading. Everyone was out to make a fortune, and as a result the price of trade goods rose on the colonial market followed by a rise in the price of furs sold by the Amerindians. The following excerpt, with its shocked tone, is an excellent indication of how the terms of exchange had altered to the relative benefit to Amerindians:

> We have already stated that the cause of the population of New Netherland was the liberty to trade with the Indians. We shall now prove that it also is the cause of its ruin, producing two contrary effects, and that not without reason as shall appear from the following.
>
> This liberty then which in every respect should have been most gratefully received, of which use should have been made as of a precious gift, was very soon perverted to a great abuse. For every one thought that now the time had come to make his fortune, withdrew himself from his comrade, as if holding him suspect and the enemy of

his gains, and sought communication with the Indians from whom it appeared his profit was to be derived. That created first a division of power of dangerous consequence, in opposition to Their High Mightinesses' motto – produced altogether too much familiarity with the Indians which in a short time brought forth contempt, usually the father of hate.[142]

At Rensselaerwyck, the patroon's delegates tried to ruin traders who were not feudal tenants by paying higher prices for pelts. This had a boomerang effect. In 1642, the patroons and the company proclaimed by ordinance that there would be a fixed maximum price for furs. They were unable to impose this price, however, and in 1643 Van Rensselaer resorted to force. He built a fortified trading post on Barren Island below Fort Orange in order to stop ships coming upriver to trade – with the exception of his own and the company ships. He made no bones about the conflict of interest between traders and Amerindians, stating that prices must be so advantageously fixed that the patroon, the traders, and even the colony's settlers would get a share of the profits. The only losers, he concluded, would be the Amerindians, whom he described as currently profiting from the situation at the patroon's expense, due to the excessive prices obtained.[143]

Because of competition, traders began going further afield in order to meet the Amerindians away from the usual trading places. Thus was born what the Dutch called the *bosloper*. The methods of these men often bordered on robbery, kidnapping, and assault. In 1645 the company imposed a code of ethics for trading and again set a maximum price for furs. According to A.W. Trelease, this price was two and a half times higher than the price set in 1642.[144] Numerous ordinances outlawed the bosloper until, in 1660, his existence was legally recognized.[145] Van Rensselaer's efforts to limit access to the Fort Orange region met with very little success. In 1652, Director-General Stuyvesant put an end to all of Van Rensselaer's quasi-monopolist practices. He renamed Fort Orange 'Beverwyck,' which means 'beaver town,' and gave the local merchants full autonomy.

As we can see, this period in New Netherland was a highly competitive one, not only inside the colony, but outside, vis-à-vis its English and Swedish neighbours.[146] As a result, the exchange relation was more favourable to the Amerindian in New Netherland than in New France, where complete freedom to trade had never really existed. There was perhaps one exception to this overall picture. In 1653-54, during the first Anglo-Dutch war, the drop in imported trade goods had caused prices to jump at Fort Orange.[147] Father Jogues commented in 1643 on trade at Fort Orange after a stay in New Netherland, during which the Dutch had saved him from death by torture by paying a ransom. 'Trade is free to every one, which enables the savages to obtain all things very cheaply: each of the Dutch outbidding his companion, and being satisfied, provided he can gain some little profit.'[148]

The Iroquois trading system resembled that of the Hurons, with trade and peace going hand in hand. A whole ceremonial panoply surrounded the speeches and exchange of gifts – singing, dancing, feasting, even theatre and mime. Father Lalemant produced this remarkable description of a peace (which in the event did not last long) concluded among the Iroquois, French, Hurons, Attikamegues, and Montagnais:

> On the fifth day of July, the Iroquois prisoner who had been set at liberty and sent back to his own country ... made his appearance at three Rivers accompanied by two men of note among those people, who had been delegated to negotiate peace with Onontio (thus they name Monsieur the Governor), and all the French, and all the Savages who are our allies.
>
> A young man named Guillaume Cousture who had been taken prisoner with Father Isaac Jogues, and who had since then remained in the Iroquois country, accompanied them. As soon as he was recognized all threw their arms around his neck ... When the most important of the three, named Kiotseaeton, saw the French and the Savages hastening to the bank of the river, he stood up in the bow of the Shallop that had brought him from Richelieu to three Rivers. He was almost completely covered with Porcelain beads. Motioning with his hand for silence, he called out: 'My Brothers, I have left my country to come and see you. At last I have reached your land ... I come to make known to you the thoughts of all my country.' When he had said this, the Shallop fired a shot from a swivel gun, and the Fort replied by a discharge from the cannon, as a sign of rejoicing.
>
> When those Ambassadors had landed, they were conducted into

the room of the sieur de Chanflour, who gave them a very cordial reception. They were offered some slight refreshments, and, after they had eaten and smoked, Kiotsaeton [*sic*], who was always the spokesman, said to all the French who surrounded him, 'I find much pleasure in your houses' ... The Alguonquins [*sic*] and Montagnais invited them to their feasts, and they gradually accustomed themselves to converse together ...

Finally, Monsieur the Governor came from Quebec to three Rivers; and, after having seen the Ambassadors, he gave audience to them on the twelfth of July. This took place in the courtyard of the Fort, over which large sails had been spread to keep off the heat of the Sun. Their places were thus arranged: on one side was Monsieur the Governor, accompanied by his people and by Reverend Father Vimont, Superior of the Mission. The Iroquois sat at his feet, on a great piece of hemlock bark. They had stated before the assembly that they wished to be on his side, as a mark of the affection that they bore to the French.

Opposite them were the Algonquins, the Montagnais, and the Attikamegues; the two other sides were closed in by some French and some Hurons. In the center was a large space, somewhat longer than wide, in which the Iroquois caused two poles to be planted, and a cord to be stretched from one to the other on which to hang and tie the words that they were to bring us – that is to say, the presents they wished to make us, which consisted of seventeen collars of porcelain beads, a portion of which were on their bodies. The remainder were enclosed in a small pouch placed quite near them. When all had assembled and had taken their places, Kiotsaeton who was high in stature, rose and looked at the Sun, then cast his eyes over the whole Company; he took a collar of porcelain beads in his hand and commenced to harangue in a loud voice. 'Onontio, lend me ear. I am the mouth for the whole of my country; thou listenest to all the Iroquois, in hearing my words. There is no evil in my heart; I have only good songs in my mouth. We have a multitude of war songs in our country; we have cast them all on the ground; we have no longer anything but songs of rejoicing.' Thereupon he began to sing; his countrymen responded; he walked about that great space as if on the stage of a theatre; he made a thousand gestures; he looked up to Heaven; he gazed at the Sun; he rubbed his arms as if he wished to draw from them the strength that moved them in war. After he had sung awhile, he said that the present that he held in his hand thanked Monsieur the Governor for having saved the life of Tokhrahenehiaron, when he drew him last Autumn out of the fire and away from the teeth of the Alguonquins; but he complained gracefully that he had been sent back all alone to his own country ... When he had said this, he fastened his collar in the appointed spot.

Drawing out another, he tied it to the arm of Guillaume Cousture, saying aloud: 'It is this Collar that brings you back this prisoner. I would not have said to him, while he was still in our country: "Go, my Nephew; take a Canoe and return to Quebec." My mind would not have been at rest; I would always have thought over and over again to myself, "Is he not lost?" In truth, I would have had no sense, had I acted in that way. He whom you have sent back had all the difficulties in the world, on his journey.' He began to express them, but in so pathetic a manner that there is no merry-andrew in France so ingenious as that Barbarian. He took a stick, and placed it on his head like a bundle; then he carried it from one end of the square to the other, representing what that prisoner had done in the rapids and in the current of the water – on arriving at which he had transported his baggage, piece by piece. He went backward and forward, showing the journeys, the windings, and the turnings of the prisoner. He ran against a stone; he receded more than he advanced in his canoe, because alone he could not maintain it against the current. He lost courage, and then regained his strength. In a word, I have never seen anything better done than this acting. 'Again' (said he), 'if you had helped him to pass the rapids and the bad roads, and then if, while stopping and smoking, you had looked after him from afar, you would have greatly consoled us. But I know not where your thoughts were, to send a man back quite alone amid so many dangers. I did not do that. "Come, my nephew," I said to him whom you see before your eyes; "follow me, I wish to bring thee to thy own country, at the risk of my life."'[149]

The Iroquois ambassador presented fifteen other gifts and speeches, interspersed with songs and dances. The next day, the governor gave a feast, then, on 14 July, 'responded to the Iroquois gifts with fourteen gifts which all had a special meaning, and which were the vehicles of their word.' The Iroquois accepted these gifts, and the peace was concluded.

Tradition forbad competition, and Amerindian ethics dictated observance of the reciprocal rules of generosity. This being the case, how did the Iroquois manage to accommodate themselves to the competitive trading that generally prevailed at Fort Orange? It is said that as soon as the Dutch arrived in North America, they allied themselves with the tribes along the Hudson River. A rope tying a Dutch ship to a tree was meant to symbolize the alliance. The Dutch and the Mohawks concluded a similar covenant, represented in this instance by an iron chain to emphasize the solidity of the relationship.[150] The Iroquois came on foot to Fort Orange, not one by one, but in a group. Only the last director-general, Pieter Stuyvesant (1647-64), adopted the habit of going to meet them annually. Before this, the diplomatic aspects of the trading ceremonies had been directed by Van Rensselaer's manager and nephew, Van Curler. The Iroquois had therefore developed ties with these two men. Like the French, the Dutch did not come to terms until they had renewed the alliance with gifts and speeches. For many years, Van Rensselaer's patroonship assumed the cost of these presents, until Director-General Stuyvesant took it upon himself. As mentioned earlier, the first Anglo-Dutch war resulted in a scarcity of Dutch trade goods at Fort Orange, and the price of these goods rose at the same time as the price of beaver dropped at the fort. The Iroquois considered themselves betrayed, and slaughtered some cattle – the meaning of which was that the end of trade meant the beginning of war. In vain did the Dutch try to explain the laws of a market economy to their partner. The Fort Orange authorities then had to strong-arm the principal citizens of the town into contributing trade goods for gifts to the Iroquois and thus maintaining the alliance.[151] Evidently, trading at Fort Orange had borrowed much from primitive commerce – the concept of a pact between sovereign nations, the exchange of presents, and fixed prices.

Still, although the Iroquois took advantage of the low price of trade goods in the competitive context of Fort Orange, they do seem to have had difficulty adapting to the anonymous and conflictual nature of competition in this area. A 1659 document reports a Dutch-Iroquois meeting in detail, and is noteworthy for its denunciation of the trading relationship that had taken hold at Fort Orange, and for its insistence that, in the name of friendship, the Dutch should accept a delay in reciprocity:

1. They [the Iroquois] say, they had made the journey, to treat with us [the Dutch] in friendship and give a string of wampum ...

3. They say, we have been agreed here, that we had made an alliance; the *Dutch* say, we are brothers and joined together with chains, but that lasts only as long as we have beavers, after that no attention is paid to us, but it shall always be, as if we needed each other. They give two beavers.

4. The alliance is made in the country, who can break it? Let us at all times keep together what has been made one. They give two beavers ...

7. The *Dutch* must leave off their wickedness and not beat them as much, as they have done. They give one beaver.

8. We desire, that the smiths should repair our things, even when our people have no money ... They give a beaver and a string of wampum.[152]

The Dutch replied by assuring the Iroquois of their undying friendship, while making it clear that 'we cannot compel our smiths and gunmakers to repair the muskets of our brothers without receiving pay for it, as they must earn a living for their wives and children, who would otherwise perish from hunger; or they would remove from our country ... and then we and our brothers would be very much embarrassed.'[153] The long and short of it was, how were the Dutch to explain the rules of a monetary economy to partners for whom the rules of exchange involved sharing and redistribution rather than obtaining coins?

At Fort Orange, the Iroquois encountered a large number of traders, and transactions were carried out in the traders' private homes. Individual Iroquois chiefs and merchants probably developed personal bonds. It is also possible that the Amerindian expected that exchanges in private homes would be accompanied by some form of ceremony, as seems to be indicated in the following passage: 'Not satisfied with merely taking them into their houses in the customary manner, they attracted them by extraordinary attention, such as admitting them to table, laying napkins before them, presenting wine to them and more of that kind of thing, which they did not receive like Esop's man, but as their due and dessert, insomuch that they were not content, but began to hate, when such civilities were not shown to them.'[154]

This practice of trading in private houses nevertheless placed the

Amerindians in a situation of dependence in relation to their hosts. In addition, some Dutch traders, prompted by greed and the spirit of competition, enticed Amerindians into their homes then locked them in, forcing them to trade and possibly even molesting them. The Iroquois insisted that the Dutch authorities guarantee their safety during trading at Fort Orange, as well as their freedom to leave one house for another, and 'that they may barter their beavers at pleasure and ... that they may go where they please ... when they want ... to go to another place to trade.'[155]

Although the Dutch conducted trading in a manner that included some of the traditional Amerindian forms, the Iroquois, for their part, gradually adopted some of the rules of commerce current in a market economy. The above instance illustrates, in particular, how the Iroquois demanded freedom to choose among houses and trade goods. Commerce at Fort Orange therefore adopted the following pattern. The fair opened with a diplomatic meeting of the two nations who were partners in the exchange. After the ritual repetition of the covenant, the Iroquois communicated their messages and demands, each being accompanied by a present. The Dutch representatives replied with gifts to each of the Iroquois proposals. Now that they were familiar with the rule of giving in Amerindian societies, they gave feasts and lavish gifts, thereby putting the onus on the Amerindians to respond generously in the next phase, when furs were bartered in private houses. The Iroquois, too, gradually came to understand the rules of European commerce, and took advantage of the exchange of presents and speeches not only to renew ties of friendship but to talk about prices and quantify the generosity of their trading partner – a practice clearly not according to tradition. For example, during a meeting at Fort Orange in 1660, the Senecas protested that the Dutch had not answered their demand of preceding years, which called for one beaver to be worth a blanket and a piece of cloth, or '50 hands full of wampum,' or '30 hands full of powder ... They ask, that henceforth it shall be fixed, that they shall receive 30 hands full of black wampum for one beaver ... [or] 60 hands full of white wampum.'[156] Here we have Iroquois speeches aimed less at displaying their own generosity than at demanding more from their Dutch partner. In other words, the Iroquois had understood in practical terms that commercial exchange was more important than contractual exchange at Fort Orange. The Iroquois were using traditional forms of communication to defend their interests in a new economic universe: they demanded better prices and freedom of choice in trading partners, and also voiced their opposition to the practices of the boslopers, who came to meet them in order to trade before they reached Fort Orange. If such practices became general, they would deprive the Iroquois of the collective bargaining power that the ceremonial form of exchange gave them.

Two Strategies

Both France and Holland intended to accumulate capital in North America, as well as extract the continent's wealth and maintain a balance of power that was disadvantageous to the Amerindians. The complex relationships involved can nevertheless be seen, in simplified terms, as an attack by capital, intent on the accumulation of wealth, on primitive, vulnerable societies. The strategies for accumulating capital varied according to time and place. On this point, the French and the Dutch had opposing strategies, and the effects of each on Amerindian societies were correspondingly different.

Beginning in 1630, the tensions and contradictions inherent in unequal exchange were to reveal themselves in a much more violent, even disastrous way. The fundamental differences between France and Holland, in terms of their transition to capitalist production methods, were to surface in the New World. At this difficult economic juncture, it seemed as though each power reacted according to the specific articulation – that is, the connecting structure – of its production methods. Holland, like England, seemed to react by developing capitalist relationships and lowering prices, whereas France turned toward the past by reinforcing its feudal structure. It is almost no exaggeration to say that France carried on trade with catechism in hand, while Holland used low prices, weapons, and alcohol.

Holland was a capitalist country offering its merchandise at competitive prices on the world market. Bourgeois attitudes prevailed in the marketplace. It was a question of business, of profit. As early as 1625, the Dutch West India Company instructed the colony's governor to recognize the Amerindians' right of ownership to their territories. This was why the Dutch purchased land from the Amerindians before establishing themselves in the colony, thereby acquiring legal ownership. Manhattan was bought in 1626 for sixty florins, the equivalent of some ten beaver skins.[157] Things were done strictly according to the book. Of course, the agreement did not have the same significance for both parties. As the Manhattans had no conception of private property, they must have seen it as an alliance by which they gave a trading partner permission to settle on their territory. The agreement gave the company clear title that could be used as the basis for its right of ownership to the land, should any Amerindian or rival European power contest it. We should note in passing that this practice was the basis of recognition of native rights in North America, such rights being admitted insofar as they had to be ceded. Finally, in contrast to the French, the Dutch had no evangelical mission. The Dutch West India Company only brought one pastor to Fort Orange. This was Jonas Michaelius, who found the Amerindians so repugnant after a first encounter that he quickly gave up any idea of converting them. Indeed, there was no question of selecting immigrants on the basis of religion or good morals so as to give Amerindians an edifying example. When the West India Company was founded, the prime need was for at least minimal settlement in order to provide military defence and sufficient farm produce for the trading posts. Dutch, French, Walloons, Germans, Scandinavians, and English came to settle in the colony.[158] Although the European population of New Netherland numbered only 300 in 1629, its cosmopolitan and secular nature was already evident. Basically, the Dutch were conducting an economic offensive from Fort Orange. All Dutch policies in North America were part of a capitalist economic development strategy – a strategy consisting of pricing policy and the use of both monopolistic and competitive trading methods.

In New France, things were different. One of the prime factors here was the geopolitical nature of the colony. The French were less exposed to rivalries among European powers than the Dutch with their neighbouring English and Swedish rivals. The French were the only European power in the Saint Lawrence valley. However, by the beginning of the 1640s, the beaver had disappeared from Huronia and Iroquoia. From then on, there was direct competition between the Dutch and the French through their allied tribes. Geographic isolation was no longer a factor. The better armed Iroquois raided and pillaged the French allies, threatening the very existence of French outposts at the mouth of the Richelieu (Fort Richelieu) and at Montreal, where they lay in ambush, watching the movements of 'the hurons on the River and the French of Montreal on land.' Writing in 1643, Father Vimont noted that 'formerly, the Hurons had the upper hand; at present, these [the Mohawks] prevail, both in number and in strength.' Since obtaining muskets from the Dutch, they 'make incursions upon our Algonquins and Montagnais, and watch the Hurons at all places along the River, – slaughtering them, burning them, and carrying off their Peltry, which they go and sell to the Dutch, in order to have powder and Arquebuses, and then to ravage everything and become masters everywhere.'[159]

Neither the Dutch allies nor the Dutch themselves were ever threatened to this extent by the French and their allies. Nevertheless, even in such circumstances the French rarely gave their allies weapons. This apparently suicidal policy only makes sense if one identifies the two major social forces implicated in the colonization of New France: the Roman Catholic church, and the merchants.

Although French merchants came to do business, they were in missionary country, ideologically speaking. Therefore, rather than purchasing pagan land, they made themselves at home in Amerindian territories in order to convert the natives to Roman Catholicism and French culture. In 1627, the French authorities magnanimously granted converted Amerindians the status of 'French naturals' in an article of the charter of the Compagnie de la Nouvelle-France.[160] In 1615, four Recollets arrived to convert the Amerindians. Almost immediately, they denounced the Société des Marchands (which was supporting them) for lack of interest in bringing out French Catholic immigrants. To provide an example of French civilization to the Amerindians, plenty of settlers were needed.

In 1625, the Recollets brought out the Jesuits. Gradually, the Catholic party gained ground. Taking advantage of the Huguenots' military setbacks in France, they even managed to squeeze out the Huguenot-controlled Compagnie de Caëns and to impose a proselytizing colonial policy. The Jesuit Philibert Noyrot, the Duc de Ventadour's confessor, stayed briefly in Quebec then returned to France in 1626, his aim being to eliminate the Compagnie de Caën and turn the colony into a bastion of Catholicism. In 1632, when Champlain returned to the Habitation, his entourage was organized on a quasi-religious basis, with religious services, saying the rosary, and so on. He renewed the alliance with the Hurons, but this time he made the presence of Jesuits in Huronia a condition sine qua non of trade.[161] The Jesuits rid the colony of Protestants and relegated the Recollets, their rival religious order, to Acadia, thereby obtaining exclusive control of religious matters. They then attempted to establish a theocracy on the shores of the Saint Lawrence, and a missionary country in Huronia, far from all perverse influences.

A unique symbiosis developed between the interests of merchants and missionaries, which was evident in all French colonization strategies. The French empire compensated for its economic lag by making use of the religious framework. The merchant, who was dependent on an outmoded production structure, needed the missionary and vice versa, since alliances with Amerindian tribes took place in the context of the fur trade, and it was through these alliances that Jesuits were able to settle among these tribes. Moreover, only the accumulation of capital through the fur trade could maintain trading posts, pay for soldiers, and bring over a few settlers – all 'services' without which the missions could not survive. In 1635, Father Le Jeune wrote, 'The more imposing the power of our French people is made in these Countries, the more easily they can make their belief received by these Barbarians, who are influenced even more through the senses, than through reason.'[162]

The missionaries were to utilize trade for religious purposes by getting the merchants to implement pricing policies and the selective sale of weapons to encourage conversions. As of 1632, and more obviously after 1640, there were two sale prices for trade goods: a blatantly pagan price (the higher), and a Christian price (the lower).[163] In concrete terms, the governor initially gave more presents to converts than others, but after 1642 gave gifts to converts only, excluding the 'pagans.' Thus, for the same amount of furs, the convert brought back more trade goods to Huronia than the 'traditionalist.'

> In accordance with this custom, which is followed among these Peoples, Monsieur the Governor considered that the presents that had been made in the past to the Hurons who came down to Trade, were given solely on account of the alliance that we sought with them; and he judged, last Summer, that the presents which he would give them would have a better effect if they were given as a token that the Truths which we preach to them are most certain. Indeed, never have gifts been of such advantage to the Faith; for, – in addition to the fact that,

when the Canoes returned, the whole Country, on learning what had
happened down there, conceived the idea that the matters that we
come to announce to them are received throughout the World as well-
established Truths (which some frequently doubted, because, they
said, the first Frenchmen whom they had known had said nothing to
them about God), – we have derived from them this further benefit,
that never have we had larger Audiences in all the Villages and Cabins
where we have gone to teach these Peoples.[164]

The selective arms sale policy, in a context where Iroquois pressure
was becoming increasingly threatening, was the second phase of the missionaries' strategy. 'The use of arquebuses, refused to the Infidels by
Monsieur the Governor, and granted to the Christian Neophytes, is a
powerful attraction to win them: it seems that our Lord intends to use
this means in order to render Christianity acceptable in these regions.'[165]

Although selective arms sales represented an offensive tactic aimed
at getting converts, there was a defensive side to it. How could the French
arm the Amerindians when tensions were mounting as the 'work' of the
missionaries progressed? The Jesuits were living among them, and the
danger was far too great. To ensure their physical safety, therefore, the
missionaries only sold arms to men who had come under their ideological control, and even the sale of arms to converts was sporadic. In 1644,
Governor Montmagny issued an ordinance forbidding 'selling, giving,
bartering, or exchanging with savages, either Christian or not, harque-
buses, pistols, and other firearms, powder, or lead.'[166]

When the French returned in 1632, some sort of equilibrium still
existed between Hurons and Iroquois, but as time went on rivalry
became more intense. Deprived of weapons, tied to an exchange relationship that was particularly unfavourable, and prey to violent internal
tensions after the missionaries had become active, Huronia gradually
weakened. In 1649, it was to be completely annihilated by its rival.

The Place of Tribes in Trade

Even in pre-Columbian times, there was a division of labour among
tribes. However, this was regulated only by geography, climate, and the disposition of natural resources. Fishing activities were carried on by tribes
that lived near water; produce was grown by the horticulturalists in the

south; and hunting activities were the specialty of northern tribes. As the fur trade expanded, the division of labour became more complex. In other words, the more goods Amerindian societies produced for the market, the more they specialized and the more they reduced their independence.

The Micmacs, for example, who formerly devoted most of their time to fishing, and only hunted in the winter, began to spend more time hunting. In order to obtain more trade goods, they had to replace fish as their food base with biscuits, dried peas, and flour, thereby increasing their dependence on the French. The New England coastal Amerindians had very little direct contact with European fishing boats at this period, as the fur trade was carried on in the Gulf, and not along the Atlantic seaboard.[167] These Amerindians therefore used the Micmacs as middlemen to obtain European products in exchange for agricultural produce and deer skins, while the Micmacs became increasingly specialized trappers.[168] The Montagnais, who fished, hunted, and gathered their food, devoted more and more time to hunting for the fur trade. They compensated for the loss of products from fishing and gathering by purchasing flour, bread, and tea.[169] Like the Montagnais, the Algonkins gradually increased their fur production, leaving themselves less time for fishing, hunting, and gathering for subsistence purposes. Consequently they became increasingly dependent on Huron agricultural products. The Hurons, in order to attract furs into their trading network, had to produce large corn surpluses[170] on a regular basis.[171] For example, the Hurons bartered corn for furs with the Nipissings, who in turn consumed part of it and bartered the rest with the James Bay Cree. The Hurons' corn became so vital that the Nipissings, who traded directly with the French, preferred, after 1620, to trade via the Hurons in order to get corn.[172] The Nation des Bois (an Ojibwa branch), controlled the entire exchange network west of Lake Superior and Lake Michigan, and only traded directly with the French after 1653.[173] Three or four hundred Hurons took part in intertribal commerce; 250 to 300 others transported furs as far as Trois-Rivières. This represented a proportion of one in six adult males.[174] As it was necessary to produce more corn, more land had to be cleared; but as the soil became exhausted after about a dozen years, they had to move, clear, and build and fortify a new village. The relocation of a village of 1,000 inhabitants represented about 1,500 man-days, without counting the time needed to clear fields, which was much longer.[175]

Furthermore, the specialization of tribes and the resulting interdependence made exchange relationships unequal among the tribes themselves. Trade goods increased in value the farther they got from the source, since they became more scarce. For example, the Ottawas bought goods from the French and resold them to distant tribes, to whom a small quantity of goods was worth far more than to eastern tribes.[176] The Hurons did the same. As another example, the converted Montagnais bought French produce at the Christian price and sold it at the pagan price.[177] Clearly, economic incentives were spurring everyone on to become a middleman of some kind. The unequal exchange relationships, first localized at the source (where whites and Amerindians traded), gradually filtered through the chain of exchange, each tribe wanting to compensate for its loss in one exchange by a gain in another with a more distant tribe.

The specialization of tribes and the resulting interdependence went hand in hand with hierarchization. Gradually, relationships of dominance were established. The tribes who established themselves as middlemen vis-à-vis the Europeans used the military advantage conferred by the acquisition of European products to turn against tribes who had no access to these products. Thus, the Micmacs, who were among the first to acquire iron axes and knives, won their wars against their neighbours, the Echemins, who were obliged to flee in great numbers to the north shore of the Saint Lawrence.[178] The history of the Winnebagos, a sedentary, Sioux-speaking group several thousand strong, is a good example of the vicious circle in which tribes found themselves around 1630. Oral tradition tells us that the Winnebagos had always considered the Ottawas as rather weak and barbarous nomads. But the Ottawas were the first to obtain iron weapons, which they used against the Winnebagos to crush them; epidemics did the rest. Only a few hundred survivors were left.[179]

It was the Iroquois who 'succeeded' best in this respect. They had originally been tributaries of the Mahicans, who had held the monopoly over the right of access to trade at Fort Orange since 1614. The Mahicans forced the Iroquois to pay high tribute for the right of passage. In 1624, however, the Iroquois vanquished the Mahicans and drove them out of their territories west of the Hudson. Now that the Mahicans were subject to the Mohawks, they extended the chain of dependence in 1643 by in turn imposing a tribute on Amerindian communities still armed with bows and arrows – the Wiechquaeskecks and Tappans who lived near the mouth of the Hudson.[180] The Mohawks also made the Shawnee, Delaware, and Sokoki tribes tributary,[181] and decimated the Canarsees of Long Island who refused to pay tribute.[182] Father Jogues remarked, while a prisoner of the Iroquois, that at 'about that time, – some Hiroquois Captains [were] going to visit some small nations which are, as it were, tributary to them, in order to get some presents.'[183]

In New France, the Huron confederacy had gained control of the fur trade, supplying the French with two-thirds of their furs. Its central position in pre-Columbian commerce had prepared it for this role. In order to safeguard their hegemony, the Hurons maintained spies among both allies and enemies.[184] Other tribes maintained a relatively privileged position in the system of intertribal relationships by exercising control over waterways. For example, the Kichesipirinis, an Algonkian tribe, controlled the Hudson Bay, Tadoussac, and Georgian Bay routes from their strategic position on Morrison Island on the Ottawa River. They exacted tribute for the right of passage, and the Hurons had to let them have corn very cheaply in exchange for furs.[185]

Unequal exchange had a ripple effect. To begin with, although Amerindian tribes generally lost in the exchange, those who acted as middlemen were relatively better off. Secondly, although war in its traditional form was an ever present characteristic of Amerindian societies, the first tribes to trade with the Europeans were also the first to become equipped with metal weapons, which gave them indisputable superiority over their neighbours. These various conditions provoked something of a stampede toward increasingly unequal exchanges. In the final analysis, it was not so much the fur trade as this unequal exchange that provided the structure for the whole history of the transformation-disintegration of Amerindian societies.

It was a Huron of the Arendarhonon tribe who first went down the Ottawa to meet the French.[186] According to Huron tradition, sole rights to this trade belonged to his lineage, and its members could demand gifts from anyone who wished to take part in it. However, given the importance of the trade, such control would have completely disrupted the balance of power and the sharing traditions of Huron society. It was therefore decided that a chief of the tribe would control the route, and that all members of the tribe would have access to it. This important decision, made at the confederacy level, meant that the principal Huron chiefs of different tribes would take over the management of trade. These old chiefs, while not directly participating in trading, would control it.[187] The fur trade, by assuming an increasingly significant role, helped expand not only the chiefs' power and prestige, but also their wealth. Those embarking on trading expeditions had to give them gifts. The novel aspect of this phenomenon was the importance of privileges. The chiefs now had the right to the best share at banquets and curing rituals, which, incidentally, were not necessarily performed for just anybody.[188] Huron society reacted to these new forces and/or influences by reinforcing the standards of distribution and sharing, in order to counteract any possible desire on the part of the chiefs to appropriate wealth. This is doubtless what explains the growing importance accorded the Feast of the Dead in the post-Columbian period. It is true that the Huron social system was able to keep its working rules on an egalitarian basis by emphasizing the importance of social institutions for redistribution. Nevertheless, during redistribution rituals, an Amerindian acquired prestige if he shared possessions with his have-not brother, a form of symbolic recognition not attainable by the recipient. This did not lead to the emergence of social classes, however, because once the cycle of sharing was complete, material equality was assured. During the accumulation phase, however, the possession of wealth created inequality.[189] As a result, a double shift occurred. There was a tendency for the distribution relationships (unequal acquisition, equal consumption) to take precedence over the sharing relationships (equal acquisition, equal consumption). Because the process of redistribution brought inequality, there followed a growing tendency toward social inequality, at first symbolic, then material.

In 1623, there were about ten Frenchmen living among the Hurons, and later between twenty and thirty. These included soldiers for defence against Iroquois attacks, missionaries sent by monopoly-holding companies, and paid interpreters (referred to as 'truchements' in the *Jesuit Relations*). The missionaries could only make themselves understood through these interpreters. Although the French (Champlain and the Recollets) intended to get the 'Savages' to adopt French culture and Christianity, the Hurons saw things in a more pragmatic way. The presence of soldiers gave them military supremacy over the Iroquois, and, in general, they were pleased to have a few Frenchmen around, because they hoped to learn how to make the goods that they had to buy from the Europeans.[190] These Frenchmen adapted well to life among the Hurons, and, with the exception of the missionaries, often married Amerindian women and took on the manners of the country – 'because the French, who are better instructed and have been raised in the School of the Faith, become Savages themselves if they live for even a short while with the Savages, and almost lose Christian form.'[191]

The Hurons thought it perfectly normal that the French should integrate into their society, and deemed it their hospitable duty to marry the missionaries, as remarked by Sagard. He, however, considered such manners very forward – indeed, all the more so, he said, because 'in these pursuits, the women and girls were, without question, worse and more importunate than even the men, who came to ask us on the women's behalf.'[192] It is not surprising to learn that the Hurons preferred the laymen to the clerics. The laymen were armed and adapted to their society far better.[193] Apart from the few Frenchmen living in Huronia, contacts were limited to the journey undertaken annually by 200 to 250 Hurons to Trois-Rivières. During this entire period, changes in Huron society were less due to the presence of strangers in their midst[194] than to the Amerindians' collective involvement in unequal exchange relationships. Missionary influence was still marginal. It was against the companies, and in particular against Protestant interests in such companies, that the missionaries let fly their first bolts, for, as Sagard stated, 'our first design ... is to make them [the Amerindians] sedentary, & to mingle with them good and virtuous Catholic families, to show them by practice and example the things they have learned from the priests and brothers, & that they would have difficulty imagining themselves without experiencing this example of good laymen in this menagerie.'[195]

It must be remembered that the missionaries had strong backers in France. The Recollet missionary LeCaron had been the almoner of the Duc d'Orléans.[196] When, in 1625, the Jesuits arrived in New France, they were empowered to send interpreters back to France if they deemed their lives to be immoral. The Compagnie de Caën lost two experienced interpreters, Brulé and Marsolet, in this way.[197] It was only after 1634 that the missionaries' influence would be felt by the Hurons, but by 1625 the religious apparatus was already becoming increasingly significant in

Franco-Huron relations.

The Hurons recognized French technical superiority, but nevertheless considered them inferior on the physical and intellectual plane.[198]
Iron, textiles, glass, weapons, writing, cats – all these things impressed
the Hurons. Nevertheless, they were horrified by the cupidity and greedy
ruthlessness of the French traders, even among themselves.[199] In 1610,
Champlain brought a Huron named Savignon back to France. He lived
there for nearly a year. Although he had been very well received in
France, Savignon had no desire to return there, so appalled was he by the
frequent death penalties and corporal punishment, and the way adults
beat, maltreated, and jeered at children. He was also shocked by the fact
that there were people who had to beg in order to eat.[200] The Huron
chiefs considered themselves the equals of the kings of France. The
Huron language was the language of commerce, and the French used it
to trade. Although Huron society was undergoing rapid change, it had
not yet broken down, any more than the Huron personality. The fact
that the Hurons did not yet drink alcohol was a good indication of this.

EXCHANGE

Measuring Terms of Exchange

The Dutch were a little late getting into the fur race, but this initial draw-
back was political rather than geographic. Their French rivals had
already made allies of the Hurons, who controlled the largest trading
network in North America. Since the Dutch were second to arrive on the
scene, they were obliged to make allies of marginal tribes. They had
failed in their first attempts at military intervention in Amerindian quarrels. The Mohawks then moved in as their principal trading partner. The
Dutch would have preferred an alliance with the Mahicans and
Algonkins at the expense of the French and the Hurons. The Dutch still
had a hypothetical advantage – their ability to offer goods at attractive
prices. However, although we know that Dutch products were highly
competitive on the international market, before 1629 there is no reason
to suppose that the Dutch would have given more goods than the French
for a similar quantity of furs.

It is not easy to quantify the terms of exchange between Amerindians
and merchants from the various European colonies. Nothing has been
found that would provide a detailed account of exchanges between

Amerindians and the traders of New France,[201] New Netherland, and New York. For the period prior to 1629, there is not even a description of the manners and customs of the tribes allied to the Dutch. Such a description might have provided some idea about how far trade goods had penetrated the continent. Before 1629, the fur trade was not yet in full swing, nor had it led to the depletion of resources. In fact, the two European trading posts of Quebec and Fort Orange traded furs from juxtaposing zones that were not competitive to any extent. All in all, the fur market in North America was not yet completely unified.

However, after 1629 there are some data that enable us to support the hypothesis that Dutch goods from Fort Orange were more competitive than French goods from Trois-Rivières. Here, we must look at the development of the exchange relationship between the Dutch and Iroquois on one side and the French and Hurons on the other. For this analysis, it is necessary to evaluate the penetration of trade goods among the Hurons and Iroquois, as well as the Amerindians' volume of fur production, and the prices of trade goods.

The Dutch were still relatively unfamiliar with Iroquois mores, despite having traded with them for several years. The French had a distinct advantage in this respect. Thanks to the missionaries and the interpreters whom they had left with Huron and Algonkian tribes, they had acquired an excellent knowledge of Amerindian languages and mores. Father Vimont described a diplomatic meeting of 1645, which included the governor and the representatives of three tribes: 'Observe, in passing, that it was necessary to speak in four different languages – in French, in Huron, in Algonquin, and in Hiroquois; we have here Interpreters of all those languages.'[202]

According to the pastor Michaelius,[203] in 1628 no Dutchman spoke an Amerindian language fluently, and sixteen years later, in 1644, the pastor Megapolensis confirmed this fact.[204] The most experienced knew a few words that were useful for trading, but were usually content with gestures.[205] The same was true of Bogaert, the surgeon at Fort Orange, who not only did not speak a word of Iroquois, but was also blamed by the Oneida council for having come into their country without bringing gifts. Worse yet, he was treated as a good-for-nothing, unlike the six Frenchmen who came to trade several months earlier, bearing fine gifts. Bogaert was in a position to testify to this: his hosts possessed good axes for cutting, as well as shirts, coats, and razors of French manufacture. Inside the longhouses of a Mohawk village he noticed 'doors of hewn boards, furnished with iron hinges.' He also observed in 1634 the presence in several houses of fittings and objects such as 'iron chains, harrow irons, hoops, [and] nails.' On 10 January 1635, Jeronimus, one of Bogaert's companions, 'burned the greater part of his pantaloons, that dropped in the fire during the night, and the chief's mother gave him cloth to repair it.'[206] This was probably more than could be found in Huronia at the same period. In any case, the *Jesuit Relations* make no mention of doors or harrows.

In 1628, the pastor Jonas Michaelius noted that trade was disrupted by a war between the Mohawks and Mahicans, and that one needed beads and knives to trade. There was no question of firearms.[207] Six years later, Bogaert visited the Mohawks and the Oneidas, both Iroquois tribes. His observations give us a good idea of the penetration of European goods. At that time, firearms were still a curiosity. On several occasions the Iroquois asked Bogaert to give them a demonstration.[208] The Hurons were similarly lacking in firearms during the same period. They may have extended hospitality to a few French soldiers, but the weapons remained in European hands.

In April 1639, De Vries mentioned in his journal that the Amerindians of Fort Orange were in the process of replacing their traditional arms with Dutch guns.[209] In 1644, when the pastor Megapolensis visited the Iroquois, he noted that whereas their weapons formerly consisted of bows and arrows, and stone axes and mallets, they now bought guns, swords, and iron axes and mallets from the Dutch.[210]

He also noted that the Mohawks were in the habit of buying two ells of duffle cloth, which they wore like a blanket, without any sewing.[211] Nowhere in analogous documents concerning Huronia is there any allusion to such a penetration of trade goods, especially with respect to weapons.

A sign of the developing exchanges was the fact that the Mohawks called the Dutch *assirioni* (makers of cloth), or *charistooni* (ironsmiths).[212] The Hurons and Montagnais respectively dubbed the French *Agnonha* (people of iron) and *Mistogoche* (wooden canoes or boats).[213] The Senecas had no direct commercial dealings with the Dutch in 1660,[214] and yet, from the 1630s on, they had access to a considerable volume of European products. As Trigger has remarked, 'Allowing for the difficulties of dating archaeological sites to within a few decades, glass beads, brass kettles, and iron goods appear to have been at least as abundant among the Seneca as they were among the Huron by this period.'[215] However, the Hurons were the middlemen dealing directly with the French, whereas the Senecas got their goods from the Mohawks and the Oneidas, who were the principal middlemen for the Dutch. The Neutrals occupied a similar position to that of the Senecas but were heavily involved in the French exchange network and dependent on the Huron middlemen. In 1641, cloth had apparently not yet replaced leather for clothing.[216] All these details lead to the unavoidable conclusion that Dutch goods had penetrated farther into Iroquoia than French goods into Huronia.

Can this greater penetration of Dutch goods be explained by a greater production volume of furs in Iroquoia? It would seem so, judging by a remark made by Bogaert. In 1635, when the beaver reserves were exhausted in Huronia,[217] he reported seeing 120 beaver pelts in the house of a Mohawk chief, which the latter had caught with his dogs, and he also mentioned having eaten beaver meat throughout his stay.[218] Even so, everything indicates that, on the contrary, the production of furs was greater in Huronia. In 1626, the volume of exchange was clearly higher on the French side. They were getting between 12,000 and 15,000 pelts against less than 10,000 on the Dutch side. Between 1624 and 1635, exports of furs from New Netherland went from 4,700 to 16,304, but these were not all from the Iroquois. Van Rensselaer judged that between 1625 and 1640, about 5,000 to 6,000 pelts were traded annually at Fort Orange. In 1635, half the furs exported, that is, about 8,000 pelts, came from Fort Orange where the Iroquois went to trade.[219] During this same period, the Hurons supplied the French with two-thirds of their furs, or 8,000 to 10,000 pelts per year. Briefly, the Iroquois traded a smaller volume of furs than the Hurons, but obtained more European goods for them.

What accounts for this? There are two possible explanations. Either their fur production costs were lower than those of the Hurons, or the prices of Dutch goods were lower. Trigger[220] only considers the first of these two hypotheses. Huronia occupied a much smaller territory than Iroquoia, and therefore the Iroquois had larger hunting grounds with more beavers. Whereas the Hurons were faced with exhausted beaver stocks as of 1630, the Iroquois stocks were not depleted until 1640. The Iroquois were still able to obtain furs close by, and therefore cheaply, while the Hurons had been forced to look to other tribes for their supply. In other words, the Hurons had become middlemen rather than producers, and had to go ever farther away to find furs. This meant that they were giving part of the French goods acquired in Montreal to the tribes that supplied them with furs, with the result that, while Dutch goods were concentrated in Iroquoia, French goods spread through the entire network of tribes supplying the Hurons. This is a plausible explanation, but it does not account for the fact that the Senecas, who were not privileged partners of the Dutch, had as many European goods as the Hurons, even though the latter were the middlemen dealing directly with the French. Indeed, the Senecas had many more European goods than the Neutrals, although the latter's position in the Huron-French trade network was analogous to that of the Senecas in the Mohawk-Dutch network. Also, the Hurons could reduce production costs due to distance by taking advantage of the ignorance of far-away tribes to impose terms of exchange that were highly favourable to themselves. We know that the fur trade encouraged the development of hierarchical relationships among tribes. Those who had acquired a middleman role duplicated the phenomenon of unequal exchange to their own advantage and the detriment of the distant tribes.

The second hypothesis appears to involve a more determining factor: that is, compared to the Hurons, the Iroquois obtained more trade goods for an equal or lesser quantity of furs. This brings us to the differences between prices of French goods at Montreal, and Dutch goods at Fort Orange. The available data are too few and far between to draw definite conclusions, but the competitiveness of Dutch goods in relation to French is confirmed by various indicators and by testimony.

There is no doubt that a knowledge of the prices of French and Dutch trade goods could provide a far more satisfactory explanation in this respect (that is, of the depletion of beaver in Huronia). In the absence of accurate data for a comparative history of prices, we must rely on the prices of the only goods for which it is possible to establish a comparison.

In the indictment that the Oneida council addressed to Bogaert, the chiefs accused the Dutch, among other things, of being scoundrels because they did not give enough goods in exchange for beaver, whereas the French gave six handfuls and more of wampum for a single pelt. A few days later, the chiefs proposed a commercial agreement based on four handfuls of wampum and four yards of cloth. However, they complained that the Dutch were often short of trading goods (cloth, wampum, axes, and kettles), forcing them to carry their furs home again.[221] One might be immediately tempted to conclude that the French trading goods were far more competitive. On the other hand, it is possible that this was merely a shrewd move on the part of the Oneidas to play off the two European rivals against one another, something the Montagnais had done for many years in the Gulf of Saint Lawrence.

Illegal trading in smuggled goods throws additional light on this question. Oddly enough, smuggling seems to have been a one-way affair. Furs from the French trading network took the English or Dutch route – especially the latter. The reverse process never occurred. The amount of contraband goods seems to have been fairly large, as indicated by a document in the Rotterdam archives dated 1 March 1646. This mentions a shipment from New England to Holland of 1,200 beaver skins of Canadian origin.[222] This must have posed a problem for Jesuit confessors, because in 1647 the fathers put their heads together and decided that smugglers could 'dissimulate in good conscience' if the company store was not 'reasonable.'[223] In 1648, the Hurons addressed Governor Montmagny with 'a prayer that the price of the goods be reduced.'[224] Five years later, the Communauté des Habitants had to reduce their toll on incoming beaver from 50 per cent to 25 per cent for fear the Amerindians might divert their furs to the Dutch.[225]

Indirect confirmation of Dutch commercial superiority can be found in the following passage from a letter written by Father Le Mercier, dated June 1656. The priest attempted to explain why the Onondagas wanted the French to settle in their village:

> They are not content with coming to us, but for a long time they invite us to go to them, and offer us the finest land that they have, and that is to be found in this New world. Neither the necessities of trade nor the hopes of our protection induce them to do all that; for they have hitherto had and still enjoy both those things with the Dutch, much more advantageously than they can ever hope to do with the French. But it is

the act of God; he has, doubtless, lent an ear to the blood of the
Martyrs, which is the seed of Christians, and which now causes them to
spring up in this land that was watered by it.[226]

Finally, although it refers to the year 1670, which is beyond the
period that we are studying, let us look at the testimony of Governor
Courcelles. He reported that the Ottawas, having inquired of the
Iroquois the prices of goods offered by the Dutch of Fort Orange,
learned that they were much lower than the prices of French goods. For
one beaver pelt, the Dutch gave four times as much as the French.[227]

If nothing else, this tells us that the prices of Dutch trade goods must
have been lower than the prices for French trade goods. It should come
as no surprise when one realizes that Dutch merchandise was more competitive on the world market generally. Furthermore, the Saint Lawrence
valley was controlled by a monopoly, whereas free trade had long been a
feature of commerce in the Hudson valley.

Dependence on European Products

Between the time that trade began and the year 1660, trade goods varied
very little in type. Europeans generally sold much the same wares. These
included metal objects such as axes, iron arrowheads, awls, swords, ice
picks, knives, and kettles; textile products such as hooded cloaks, blankets, night caps, hats, shirts, and sheets; and food produce such as
prunes, raisins, corn, peas, crackers, sea biscuits, and tobacco.[228] To this
list must be added polychrome beads imitating wampum, firearms, and
alcohol. For this wide range of European products only a single
Amerindian product was traded: fur.

The Montagnais were among the first tribes to trade with the
Europeans. They quickly stopped making pottery and cooking their food
in bark containers. Metal replaced everything. They began buying
chaloupes – the French rowboat that could accommodate a sail – and
this type of craft gradually replaced canoes on the Saint Lawrence
River.[229] They wore cloth garments, and they, too, equipped themselves
with contraband firearms bought from traders. These were all products
that they did not know how to make themselves. Among the Hurons, the
desire to take part in trading encouraged them to concentrate in the
Georgian Bay area. After 1620, the number of European imports for

which there was a strong demand among the Hurons grew rapidly.[230] As with the Montagnais, stone implements gave way to metal tools. Iron cooking pots gradually replaced pottery, although this was still made.[231] European products were generally of poor quality and had to be replaced often, which is to say the unequal exchange had to be repeated.

Moreover, the two societies did not have equal opportunity when it came to borrowing one another's technologies. Europeans not only learned geographical, botanical, and zoological data from the Amerindians, but adopted the use of moccasins, snowshoes, canoes, and toboggans. Moreover, the whites acquired new products and were in a position to appropriate production techniques at the same time. For example, the whites not only learned how to paddle and portage, but also how to make canoes.[232] Amerindians, on the other hand, acquired metal utensils without being able to adopt the techniques of metal production. The Hurons were able to reuse old iron or copper to make scrapers, arrowheads, and so on,[233] by using the old stone-working techniques, but they still couldn't produce iron, melt it, or work it like a blacksmith. In other words, once the exchange had taken place, the Amerindian became dependent on his trading partner, because he could not reproduce what he had adopted. As a result, he had to keep on going back to the European trader, and each time he did so the exchange was unequal. Under these conditions, trade led to dependency. The greater the volume of trade, the greater the dependency.

In the beginning, all governments and companies had formally prohibited the sale of firearms to the Amerindian, for fear that the more numerous native peoples could force them back into the sea.[234] In order to enforce a relationship of unequal exchange, military superiority was necessary. Nevertheless, although European traders had a common interest in maintaining military superiority, the laws of competition drove rivals, and particularly those who were excluded from trading, to sell firearms, either to get furs more easily, or to equip Amerindian allies to destroy the allies of other, rival Europeans. Until 1629, trading was carried out on a monopolistic basis, and rivalry among Europeans had not yet spiralled as a result of depleted beaver stocks. Consequently, arms sales were limited. A few ships in the Gulf traded contraband weapons with the Montagnais. A small number of smuggled weapons were traded in New Netherland between 1629 and 1639, but, all in all, only a few weapons passed into Amerindian hands. It was after 1639, with the advent of free trade in New Netherland, that the sale of firearms began to grow. At the same time as competition increased among Fort Orange traders, the competitive thrust of the English in the Connecticut valley, and the Swedes in the Susquehanna valley, began to be felt. Rivalry among Europeans caused them to throw caution to the wind, and firearms passed into the hands of the Iroquois – mainly the Mohawks. Coincidentally, the Iroquois acquired these weapons at the very moment when they had exhausted beaver stocks on their own territory. They now had a pressing need to subject the tribes who brought them furs from more distant places.

> This Liberty caused still greater mischief: for the inhabitants of Renselaerswyck [*sic*], who were as many traders as persons, perceiving that the Mohawks were craving for guns, which some of them had already received from the English, paying for each as many as Twenty Beavers and for a pound of powder as many as Ten to Twelve guilders, came down in greater numbers than usual where guns were plenty, purchasing them at a fair price, realizing in this way considerable profit; they afterwards obtained some from their Patroon for self defence, in time of need, as we suppose. This extraordinary gain was not long kept secret, the traders coming from Holland soon got scent of it, and from time to time brought over great quantities, so that the Mohawks in a short time were seen with fire locks; powder and lead in proportion. Four hundred armed men knew how to make use of their advantage, especially against their enemies, dwelling along the River of Canada [the Saint Lawrence], against whom they have now achieved many profitable forays where before they had but little advantage; this caused them also to be respected by the surrounding Indians even as far as the Sea coast, who must generally pay them tribute, whereas, on the contrary, they were formerly obliged to contribute to these.[235]

Despite a series of ordinances aimed at prohibiting arms sales in New Netherland, guns continued to be sold at Fort Orange, on eastern Long Island, on the Connecticut River, and in Narragansett Bay.[236]

In 1641, 350 Iroquois came to prowl on 'the great River' near Montreal. Among them, thirty-six had muskets, powder, and lead, others had bows, arrows, and swords.[237] In February 1643, between eighty and ninety Mohawk warriors, with guns on their shoulders,[238] came down to the New Amsterdam region to exact tribute from the Wickquasgecks and the Tapaens. In the summer of the same year, 700 Iroquois were on the prowl near Montreal, 300 with muskets, which they were 'skilled in handling.'[239] In 1648, without actually outlawing the sale of firearms to Amerindians, Director-General Stuyvesant imposed some restrictive measures on trading at Fort Orange.[240] These had little effect, however, because the Mohawks were ready to pay up to 120 florins for arms that were worth 6.[241] Even the governor was suspected of illegal trading.[242] When the company directors in Holland were informed of what was going on, they merely advised traders not to sell firearms to the Amerindians except for hunting purposes.[243] The Amerindians, who were bound to the Dutch by the fur trade, continued to obtain arms. As a result, Fort Orange became the Iroquois arsenal, and firearms, powder, and lead became the principal trading goods.[244] In 1649 these Iroquois on the borders of Huronia numbered about a thousand men who were better armed, 'mostly with the fire arms, which they obtain from the Dutch, their allies.'[245] In 1652, a convert wrote to Father Le Jeune, who was then living in France. 'Speak to the great Captain of France, and tell him that the Dutch of these coasts are causing our destruction, by furnishing firearms in abundance, and at a low price, to the Hiroquois, our enemies.'[246]

Although English, Swedes, and Dutch were involved in this arms race – the Swedes even sold artillery pieces to their Susquehannock allies – it was the Dutch who took the lead.[247] They sold more guns than anyone else, offering the best quality at the lowest prices. Their hegemony became even more marked after 1644, when competition among Fort Orange traders intensified. As a result, the prices paid for Mohawk furs rose rapidly. They dropped during the first Anglo-Dutch war in 1653-54, but rose immediately afterward. They dropped again in 1659, but that year Director-General Stuyvesant compensated the Amerindians for this loss with presents worth 100,000 florins.[248] In 1647, Father Lalemant, reporting the aftermath of an Iroquois raid on the Saint Lawrence, mentioned that 'there were found in their reduit some arquebuses much heavier and far longer than ours.'[249] There is nothing surprising in this, since the arms industry in Sweden was the most sophisticated in Europe. Dutch capital controlled the industry. Swedish firearms were more durable and of better quality than those produced elsewhere.[250]

The French, however, refused to sell arms. In 1641, Governor Montmagny gave a musket to a Huron who had come to Quebec to trade and had agreed to being baptized. This good convert was greatly surprised, reported Father Vimont, because 'these arms are wholly new to them.'[251] In 1643, Father Jogues described an Algonkin counterattack following an attack by Iroquois armed with several muskets. His description also gives us an insight into French policy regarding firearms. 'If these Young Algonquins had powder to continue and pursue further, they would have killed most of the band; but we have always been afraid to arm the Savages too much. Would to God that the Hollanders had done the same, and had not compelled us to give arms even to our Christians, – for hitherto, these have been traded only to the latter.'[252]

The striking thing is the French determination to give Amerindians a limited quantity of arms, and these only to converts, despite the disparity in military strength and the threat which it posed to the Huron and French trading network. In 1642, 'a band of Hyroquois, armed by the Dutch with good arquebuses, which they can use as well as our Europeans,'[253] routed twelve Huron canoes on their way back to Huronia. The Jesuits noted that these ambushes happened every year, and that 'this evil is almost without remedy; for, besides the fact that, when they are going to trade their furs, they are not equipped for war, the Iroquois now use firearms, which they buy from the Flemings, who dwell on their Shores. A single discharge of fifty or sixty arquebuses would be sufficient to cause terror to a thousand Hurons who might be going down in company, and make them the prey of a hostile Army lying in wait for them as they pass.'[254] Iroquois harassment was 'the greatest thorn we have,' wrote the missionaries in 1644. 'We are now, as it were, invested and besieged on all sides.' Even so, there was still no question of arming Huron allies.[255]

Alcohol has long been considered largely responsible for the disintegration of Amerindian societies. Contemporary descriptions all paint a terrifying picture of the Amerindian and alcohol: his uncontrolled and insatiable thirst, his demented and violent behaviour, leading to calamities such as assault, murder, and suicide.[256]

From the very first contacts, alcohol had been part of the exchange between Europeans and Amerindians. The fishermen in the Gulf sold it in the sixteenth century. Henry Hudson traded it for furs on his first voyage. In 1634, Van Rensselaer hoped to get brandy to be bartered for furs all along the coast.[257] Soon alcoholism was the cause of numerous skirmishes between Amerindians and whites.[258] Before long, both French and Dutch were issuing a whole series of ordinances prohibiting the sale of alcohol to the Amerindians. The regular renewal of such prohibitions showed how ineffectual they were in New Netherland, with the possible exception of Fort Orange. Here the ban had some effect, although alcohol still continued to be sold.[259] In New France, prohibitions of the sale of alcohol went back to Champlain, but it was impossible to stop such trade with the Amerindians in the Gulf, where 'there is always some one who trades with them, or who will sell them a bottle now and then in secret.'[260] Circumstances were different among the Hurons, especially after 1630, when monopolistic trading and the presence of the Jesuits provided fairly strict supervision. Since the Hurons came down in a group to Trois-Rivières once a year, it was all the easier to monitor them. Although 'there is always found some base soul who, to gain a little Beaver fur, introduces by Moonlight some bottles into their cabins,'[261] in general, the consumption of alcohol by these Amerindians remained marginal. The brandy question gave rise to lengthy wrangling in the French colony between mercantile and religious interests. After 1660, Monseigneur Laval, the bishop of Quebec, instigated a fierce battle against the sale of brandy to the Amerindians.[262] The traders, undeterred by the threat of excommunication, kept on selling alcohol. Looking at the question on a higher plane, however, the remarkable thing is the ambivalent position of the Roman Catholic church. On one hand, the church was associated with power and domination, and on the other it was opposed to this domination being excessive.[263]

Contrary to what many may have believed in the past, the sale of brandy was never the basis of the fur trade, neither in the seventeenth century nor afterward. Generally speaking, alcohol was not bartered for furs, but offered as a gift before the actual trading took place. Historian Louise Dechêne has established the fact that brandy only accounted for 4 to 5 per cent of the total value of trading stocks at the end of the seventeenth century.[264] She points out that brandy was a complementary trade for anyone who wanted to build a solid clientele, encourage the Amerindians to hunt on his behalf, and guarantee regular returns.[265] Alcohol consumption tended to rise, primarily, as competition became more intense among greedy traders driven to use every possible means, and, secondarily, as Amerindian societies suffered increasing disruption. It is therefore not surprising to note that 'drunkenness' first spread among the Gulf tribes.[266]

All documents remark on the difference between the way alcohol affected Europeans and Amerindians. Was it, in fact, the effect or the manner in which alcohol was drunk – or was it rather the cultural differences with respect to drunken behaviour? Was it the degree of intoxication? Or the greater capacity for uninhibited expression of impulses? Perhaps all these factors played a part. The native peoples of northeastern North America produced no alcohol before the arrival of Europeans. It may be that centuries of alcohol consumption produces a certain degree of resistance to its effects, although this is by no means proven. Was diet a factor? Europeans were salt eaters, whereas the Amerindians were not, a fact that Marie de l'Incarnation thought significant.[267] True, the Great Lakes peoples had a diet entirely lacking in salt, but this was not the case with coastal tribes that ate seafood. Possibly, as has been suggested by recent medical research, there is a link between a propensity to drink alcohol and a lack of certain minerals, such as magnesium, in the diet.

In the beginning, Amerindian people used alcohol according to the logic of their own civilization.[268] Amerindians attached great importance to dreams, which dealt with a supernatural universe. At first they probably associated dreams and drunkenness. Inasmuch as messages in dreams had to be respected, a supernatural value had to be attached to the acts and words of drunken people. As for the way in which alcohol was consumed, the Amerindians probably transferred the *habitus* acquired in 'eat-all' or 'leave-nothing' feasts, described by the Jesuits as follows:

> As to their 'leave-nothing' feasts, they are very blamable; and yet this is one of their great devotions, because they make these feasts in order to have a successful chase. They must be very careful that the dogs taste nothing of this, or all will be lost, and their hunting will be worthless. And notice that, the more they eat, the more efficacious is this feast. Hence it happens that they will give, to one man, what I would not undertake to eat with three good diners. They would rather burst, so to speak, than to leave anything.[269]

The Amerindian only drank when he had enough alcohol to get completely drunk. If several Amerindians had a keg to share among themselves, they would choose a few of their number to drink and get drunk to the limit of their capacity. The others would look on.[270] Insofar as the drunken person was in communication with the supernatural, he was allowed to do as he pleased, to be unbridled, aggressive, and destructive. However, it didn't take many years for the Amerindian to comprehend the true effects of alcohol and its disastrous results: deaths, accidents, indebtedness, ruin, and dispossession.[271] In 1633, when an Amerindian was held prisoner in Quebec for having killed a Frenchman while drunk, the following argument was put forward by his fellows: 'It was brandy, and not that Savage, who had committed this murder, meaning to say that he was drunk when he struck the blow. "Put thy wine and thy brandy in prison," they say. "It is thy drinks that do all the evil, and not we."'[272]

The same scenario recurred in 1642 among the Hackensacks, an Atlantic coastal tribe. They were accused of killing two Dutchmen. They offered reparation, but Governor Kieft wanted an execution. The Amerindians replied that alcohol was responsible, and that its sale should be outlawed.[273] In 1659, the Mohawks explained that they didn't like to see their people drink in this fashion, and that the sale of alcohol had reduced their effectiveness in fighting the French. After deciding to carry home brandy one last time – a gift offered could not be refused – they demanded that the sale of brandy to their people be stopped and the brandy kegs plugged. They made it clear that they intended to denounce any Dutchmen who sold alcohol in future.[274] The Mohawks sought a negotiated solution with their Dutch trading partner. If the Dutch were allies, they reasoned, then they must stop giving gifts that killed them.

As the years went by, the social function of alcohol changed. In the beginning, it had been a way of attaining a religious experience. Later, it was a symptom of disintegration in Amerindian societies. Alcohol was also used in war. In 1652, for example, the Mohawks surprised and massacred an Abenaki village while 'all its inhabitants were intoxicated with liquor, sold to them by the Dutch.'[275] At Onondaga there was brandy from New Netherland 'in such quantities as to make [it] a veritable Pothouse,' according to the Jesuits.[276] Was there a link between mounting alcohol consumption and the presence of a great many captives in the Onondaga villages? In 1663, drunkenness had spread over the entire northeast. 'This evil is general in these regions, extending as it does from Gaspé (whence a good Ecclesiastic writes in fitting terms that Christianity is utterly ruined among the Savages, because of drunkenness) as far as the Iroquois.'[277]

As Amerindians grew increasingly dependent on Europeans and native societies continued to disintegrate, alcohol seemed to serve as a palliative, a means of escaping idleness. As might be expected, by 1646 alcohol had already become part of a way of life on the reserves.[278]

Initially, the fur trade had been grafted onto an existing economy and a traditional form of commerce. Later, the new form of commerce predominated, then totally disrupted the old economy. We can see the process at work on various levels – for example, wampum, the all-purpose money-equivalent produced by the coastal Amerindians, originally with stone and bone tools.[279] Using conch shells, they manufactured wampum 'with great difficulty and much hard work.'[280] They produced white beads in larger quantities, and blue beads in relatively small quantities – there being only one blue spot in a conch, blue wampum was worth more. The beads were strung on threads made from the bark of slippery elm (*Ulmus rubra*).[281] Wampum was used as adornment, either as jewellery (bracelets, necklaces, pendants, and so on), or ornamentation for men's and women's clothing, such as robes made of animal skins, and moccasins. It was the basis of all decorative art,[282] and was also used in religious and diplomatic ceremonies to show sincerity and attachment, as well as being an aid to memory.[283] It was used as money, and therefore circulated throughout the prehistoric trade network in northeastern North America.

Wampum does not seem to have been used as money by the settlers of New France, except for the fur trade. Instead, it was the beaver pelt that became the general equivalent, the 'coin of greatest value,' as it is described in the *Jesuit Relations*.[284] In Huronia, where wampum was the general equivalent, the missionaries introduced counterfeit money, so to speak: manufactured porcelain beads, an ersatz wampum used to buy corn and smoked fish.[285]

The Dutch had the advantage, since the wampum-producing centres for the whole of northeastern North America were located within their territory, mainly on Long Island. Although the beaver was used as the standard of exchange in New Amsterdam, wampum remained the main medium of exchange.[286] In 1653, Van der Donck mentioned that 'this is the only article of moneyed medium among the natives, with which any traffic can be driven; and it is also common with us in purchasing necessaries and carrying on our trade; many thousand strings are exchanged every year for peltries near the seashores where the wampum is only made, and where the peltries are brought for sale. Among the Netherlanders gold and silver begin to increase and are current, but still the amount differs much from that of the Netherlands.'[287]

The Dutch were quick to import beads from Venice or produce imitation wampum from porcelain or multicoloured glass made in their own factories. Large amounts were produced in far less time than it took for native producers to make shell beads. The imitations swamped the market. The Amerindians lost control of their own currency, and to cope with this they successively devaluated it. As always happens in such cases, bad money drove away good, and the imitation tended to replace the shell beads. There was even a type of imitation wampum of variable quality, made of half-finished, unperforated beads that were handled loose-packed rather than in strings or belts. In 1650, the New Netherland authorities prohibited trading in this bulk wampum, and also set an exchange rate for strung wampum: 6 white beads = 3 black = 1 stuiver for regular wampum; 8 white = 4 black = 1 stuiver for strung but roughly finished wampum. This last type of bead was imposed as legal tender, although it was refused on the market.[288] In this context of devaluation and imposed currency, it was beaver that served as the standard, even though wampum was still used as money. When beaver fell in value from 8 to 4.5 florins in 1663, wampum was devalued by half. The wage-earning employees of the Dutch West India Company, who were paid in wampum, lobbied unsuccessfully to be paid in beaver.[289]

As the Amerindians' economy became subordinated to the world market and then integrated into it, the Amerindians found themselves losing control of their own currency. The introduction of a false or imitation currency (multicoloured glass beads) forced out the true currency (wampum made of shell beads), in addition to which the places where the latter were produced fell under Dutch control. Beaver pelts became the exchange standard because of the fur trade, and the value of beaver pelts was fixed on the European market. Finally, as an internal colonial market emerged, the currency of European powers began to circulate.

The number of gold and silver coins gradually grew, and by 1653 they were even common, according to Van der Donck.[290]

THE EFFECTS OF EXCHANGE

The Fur Wars

War among Amerindians increased as a result of the subordination of Amerindian societies to European economic power. It was actually a new type of war combined with the traditional, old-style form of guerilla warfare on territorial frontiers. As we know, the beaver disappeared from Huronia around 1630 and from Iroquoia a few years later. The two major middlemen in the fur trade had no choice but to expand their sources of supply if they were to continue having access to European products.

The figures speak for themselves. After 1630, Hurons and Iroquois almost doubled their fur production, despite epidemics that cut their respective populations in half. Suddenly, the relative importance of the fur trade in these two societies increased fourfold. In New France, production rose from 15,000 pelts before 1630 to about 30,000 pelts between 1630 and 1640. Production in New Netherland climbed with equal rapidity. Before 1630, it had hovered around 7,000 pelts per year. In the decade following, it rose to about 15,000, then to 35,000 in 1656 after the defeat of Huronia, and to over 46,000 after the defeat of the Eries. There is no doubt that results of this kind, in such a critical period, could only be gained by an unprecedented jump in the number of intertribal wars in both the major trading networks.

The process of integration-subordination of Amerindian societies in relation to the world market soon added fuel to rivalry between imperialist powers. To all intents and purposes, Amerindian tribes were mere tools in this confrontation, given the fact that each power's primary aim was to appropriate its rival's allied tribes.

As of 1633, Champlain planned to conquer Iroquois territory and expel Dutch and English settlers from the regions bordering on New France. The Jesuits looked upon these plans for ousting rivals with a favourable eye, and in 1641 submitted to Richelieu their own plan for driving out the Dutch from New Netherland.[291] In 1643, the Jesuits expressed the fear that 'the design of the Dutch is to have the French harassed by the Iroquois, to such an extent that they may constrain them to give up and abandon everything, – even the conversion of the

Savages.'[292] In 1653, the Dutch governor envisaged the expulsion of English settlers from territories contested by New Netherland.[293] English and Dutch accused each other of using Amerindian allies for hostile purposes. Each of the European powers tried to get hold of the others' assets, be they ships or territories. In 1653, for example, the English captured a valuable prize, an event described in this elegantly phrased remark by Father Le Mercier: 'The pleasantest days often have their clouds, and it is not God's will that our joys in this world should be quite free from shadows. The vessel that was returning to France, richly laden with the spoils of the Beavers of this country, was itself despoiled, falling into the hands of the English who were waiting for it in the Channel.'[294]

After 1640, escalating warfare completely disrupted the demographic map of northeastern North America. Epidemics and Iroquois raids caused such disarray among the Algonkins that, from then on, they took refuge either with the French, or in greater numbers with the Hurons.[295] Naturally, those who asked for protection from the French were forced to convert to Christianity. The Hurons then took over from the Algonkins and intensified their northern trade. They may have had difficulty getting a supply of furs from the north, however, and this may have forced them to escalate their military drive southward.

The Neutrals, one of the Hurons' fur-supplying allies, turned against the Algonkian-speaking 'Nation of fire' (or Assistaronon) to the south, who were reportedly more numerous than all the Neutrals, Hurons, and Iroquois put together.[296] The Neutrals took 800 captives, killed seventy warriors, and put out the eyes of the old men. Jérôme de Lalement wrote of them: 'Such is the scourge that depopulates all these countries; for their wars are but wars of extermination.'[297] In 1642, the Sauk people told the Jesuits that they had given shelter at Sault Sainte Marie to a 'more remote Nation whom they called Pouteatami [who] had abandoned their own Country and taken refuge with the Inhabitants of the Sault, in order to remove from some other hostile Nation who persecuted them with endless wars.'[298] Had the fur wars already reached this group living near Green Bay on Lake Michigan? It is very possible.

Relations between the two major fur trade middlemen had already been polarized before 1630, but after this date they began to look like all-out war. Gradually, the Iroquois recommenced their raids against the Hurons and Saint Lawrence valley Algonkins. Until 1640, the Iroquois were mainly interested in plundering the victims' possessions, but during the following decade they became more intent on exterminating the Hurons and Algonkins.

The Iroquois held a certain number of trump cards in this confrontation. In the first place, they had more advantageous trading terms than their adversaries. They had a greater range of European products at their disposal, including metal weapons and, after 1640, firearms. They also had a geographical advantage. The Mohawks were only obliged to cover about eighty kilometres, all within their own territory, to reach Fort Orange. The Hurons had to cover several hundred kilometres from Georgian Bay to Trois-Rivières, and were therefore more exposed to enemy raids. Lastly, the Iroquois did not have to face the internal tensions experienced by the Hurons as a result of the missionaries' presence in their midst.

All in all, the balance of power favoured the Iroquois. This made the Hurons more and more dependent on the French, in a military sense, and enabled the missionaries to 'sell' them Christian ideology in exchange for trade goods and weapons. The result was growing ideological dependence, which the Hurons themselves reinforced. Because they were anxious to maintain their status as primary middlemen to the French, to the exclusion of other allied tribes, they objected to the missionaries and company traders settling anywhere else.[299]

It was between these two great rival confederacies, the two major middlemen in the fur trade, that war was to be waged most fiercely. Not only did the Iroquois have the military advantage of firearms, but they began stepping up their raids, attacking Huron villages and trade routes at the same time.[300] This meant that women working in the fields at home and men travelling to Trois-Rivières were equally exposed to enemy fire. The Iroquois managed to reduce the flow of European trade goods into Huron territory by a considerable margin,[301] as well as disrupt commerce and drive their adversaries toward famine. It must also be remembered that the Hurons needed corn to trade for furs. Famine, which had been unknown in Huronia, occurred in 1643, then much more seriously in 1644, when there was 'universal' famine and the people lived on acorns and pumpkins. Moreover, the epidemics began again, and 'these Countries ... seem[ed] to be drawing near their ruin.'[302] During the same period, the Iroquois drove out numerous bands of

Algonkins and Montagnais from their homes and occupied their hunting grounds.[303] We know that this forced the Hurons to seek furs farther
north,[304] which in turn placed them in greater danger of attack. The
Hurons were under such pressure that they considered totally abandon-
ing their trade with the French.[305] In 1645, a short-lived peace was concluded among the belligerents: Hurons, Algonkins, Montagnais,
Attikamegues, Iroquois, and French.[306] It was mainly a question of
exchanging prisoners and reuniting families. This gave the Hurons a
breathing space. For the last time they had good trading relations, good
fishing, and a good harvest.[307] Then, in the fall of 1645, war broke out
again. Iroquois strategy remained the same, but the goal changed. Now
the Iroquois wanted territorial expansion and were prepared to wipe out
rival populations.

Goods were plentifully available during this period of free trade in
New Netherland, and competition among merchants was stiff. As a
result, furs were exchanged at high prices, especially after 1645 when the
scarcity of fur-bearing animals on Iroquois territory became obvious to
all. The Iroquois had never had such a favourable rate of exchange. Now,
more than ever, they wanted to increase their supply sources.

The Hurons, on the other hand, were deeply divided over what strategy to follow. Should they remain the allies of the French? Or should
they ally themselves with the Susquehannocks (the allies of the Swedes)
against the Iroquois?[308] Or should they even become the allies of the
Iroquois, and thus completely escape their total dependence on the
French? The Attignawantans or Bear Nation, which had suffered least
from Iroquois attack, were in favour of fighting the Iroquois. The
Arendarhonons, who had suffered severe losses at the hands of the
Iroquois, favoured peace.[309] Coincidentally, however, the Attignawantans
had more converts and the Jesuits favoured war. It was a struggle
between converts and traditionalists.[310] The latter felt that, between the
French and the Iroquois, the second of the two evils was preferable. It
would be better to cease being the privileged trading partner of the
French and to diversify sources of supply. When Iroquois pressure
increased, however, the Hurons became more and more dependent on
the French. In the 1647-48 period, 3,000 Hurons asked for protection and
food. The Jesuits took them into Sainte-Marie-among-the-Hurons in
return for conversion. By the summer of 1648, one in five Hurons was a

Christian. A few months later, half of them had been converted.[311]

The Iroquois, who were better armed than any other Amerindian group, destroyed a neutral Aondironnon village near Huronia.[312] In 1648, they took the Huron village of Teanaostaiaé and carried off 700 prisoners, mostly women and children.[313] Panic gripped the Hurons. They sowed no crops, and famine followed. In 1649, 'the Iroquois, enemies of the Hurons, to the number of about a thousand men, well furnished with weapons, – and mostly with firearms, which they obtained from the Dutch, their allies,' captured another important Huron village, Taenhatentaron (Saint-Ignace), then took Saint-Louis.[314] They pillaged, killed the old people, the sick, and the children as never before.[315] The *Jesuit Relations* described scenes resembling something from Dante's *Inferno*, 'where children were broiling beside their mothers; where a husband saw his wife roasting near him; where cruelty itself would have had compassion at a spectacle which had nothing human about it, except the innocence of those who were in torture, most of whom were Christians.'[316]

The Iroquois took two Jesuit missionaries prisoner. Jean de Brébeuf and Gabriel Lalement were tied to the stake and tortured according to the usual methods, with fire, hot coals, blows, cuts, fractures, and so on. The two victims resisted this torment with a stoic impassivity in keeping with Amerindian mores, which called for the prisoner to show courage and express his deepest convictions until death. It seems that it was not so much the Iroquois as the captive Hurons who conducted this rite of torturing the missionaries, whom they accused of being responsible for the destruction of Huronia. The torture took the form of a derisive baptism, with the victims being 'christened' with boiling water. The torturers said they were treating the missionaries as friends, and that they should be thanked for providing them with greater joy in heaven, since the more the victims suffered, the more their Christian God would reward them.[317]

What followed was a series of catastrophes that need not be given in detail here. All the Huron villages fell, and Huronia was no more. In 1649, the Jesuits burned their fortified village of Sainte-Marie-among-the-Hurons to prevent it falling into Iroquois hands.[318] Some Hurons migrated west onto the island of Gahoendoe (Christian Island). After a terrible famine during the course of the winter,[319] the Iroquois broke through in 1650 and massacred all these survivors.

In 1649-50, Huronia collapsed. Several thousand were dead and a great many had been taken captive. Some escaped to the Eries, the Petuns, and the Neutrals, but in the winter of 1650-51, the Neutral confederacy fell in turn.

> Great was the carnage, especially among the old people and the children, who would not have been able to follow the Iroquois into their country. The number of captives was exceedingly large, – especially of young women, whom they reserve, in order to keep up the population of their own villages. This loss was very great, and entailed the complete ruin and desolation of the Neutral nation; the inhabitants of their other villages, which were more distant from the enemy, took fright; abandoned their houses, their property, and their country; and condemned themselves to voluntary exile, to escape still further from the fury and cruelty of the conquerors. Famine pursues these poor fugitives everywhere, and compels them to scatter through the woods and over the more remote lakes and rivers, to find some relief from the misery that keeps pace with them and causes them to die.[320]

As the Neutrals had very few firearms, they fled in all directions, as the Hurons had done. It was a veritable chain reaction. Most of the Hurons had taken refuge with the Petuns, and some of them now went west with their host tribe. The Petun villages were also attacked, however, and they, too, succumbed to the Iroquois onslaught.[321] The Ottawas fled west to Green Bay on Lake Michigan, thereby escaping Iroquois raids that reached as far as Sault Sainte Marie and Michilimackinac.[322] Hurons and other refugees first established themselves at Michilimackinac, then migrated in 1653 to Green Bay on Lake Michigan, after which they moved to Black River in Wisconsin. Here, skirmishes with the Sioux drove them to settle on Lake Superior, where they became the Wyandots.[323]

Another group of Hurons went east. These were Christians who expected to be welcomed in Quebec according to the rules of hospitality that they themselves had practised vis-à-vis other refugee nations. French aid was meagre by comparison. Although the nuns took care of the young girls, some 200 Hurons 'were unable to find any help in the famine that pressed hard upon them, and followed them everywhere.'[324]

The Hurons settled temporarily near Quebec. In March 1651, they were given a parcel of land on the western tip of the Île d'Orléans, opposite Quebec. Some thirty families settled on tiny plots, the largest of which was no bigger than half an arpent.[325] They had possessed a homeland, and here they were, on a reserve. In 1653, some forty Huron canoes arrived. Their occupants had taken refuge on Manitoulin Island, trying to escape famine. By the end of the year both groups had cleared about 300 arpents, and this provided subsistence.[326] Like the Algonkins of Sillery, however, they were under the ideological thumb of the Jesuits. 'The Savages know very well that it is not a place that is open to Apostates from the Faith, or to those who live scandalously in sin ... The walls which had been built there were not for the purpose of sheltering vice, but of preventing it from entering.'[327]

In 1652, an Iroquois ambassador came to invite the Hurons in Quebec to join his people. The French persuaded the Hurons to kill the ambassador.[328] The following year, to everyone's surprise, the Iroquois came to propose peace to the French. The Jesuits, who had looked favourably on the war against the Iroquois, did a complete about-face. In view of the fact that their principal mission had disappeared with Huronia, they seriously considered settling among the Iroquois to continue their work. Most Iroquois were not opposed to the idea. (The Onondagas, for example, were particularly anxious to escape the burdensome Mohawk influence.)[329] The Iroquois now controlled an immense fur-supplying area as a result of military victories, and had acquired a virtual monopoly. They would have liked to place the French in competition with the Dutch, thus diversifying their source of supply for European goods. French help in repairing their guns would also have been welcome.[330]

This Iroquois interest in negotiating and trading with the French was partly the result of a particular occurrence. They had been trading their furs for high prices at Fort Orange since about 1643. In 1653-54, the direction of the wind changed. The Anglo-Dutch war of 1652-54, and in particular England's blockade of Holland, reduced international commerce and consequently the entry of trade goods into New Netherland. The prices of goods at Fort Orange climbed and the Iroquois received less for the same quantity of furs. Not understanding the mechanisms of price fluctuations in response to supply and demand, the Iroquois felt the Dutch were cheating them. They retaliated wrathfully by killing some cattle. To prevent a serious deterioration of relationships, the Dutch called the Iroquois to Fort Orange in a move to improve bilateral relations.[331] The end of the Anglo-Dutch war made things easier by increasing the volume of trade goods reaching Fort Orange. Prices dropped, and so did interest in a French alliance. Shortly afterward, the Iroquois resumed their attacks on the French and their allies. It seemed that the Iroquois wars were now keyed to price fluctuations on the Fort Orange market.

In the meantime, the Mohawks came down the Saint Lawrence in 1653 to seek the Île d'Orléans Hurons and integrate them into Iroquois society.[332] The French objected to this, but grudgingly negotiated. In May 1656, the Iroquois came downriver again, and 'under the cover of that very dark night,'[333] they passed in front of Quebec to reach the Île d'Orléans, where they surprised the Huron reserve, taking seventy-one prisoners away in their canoes, and passing Quebec once more on their way upriver. The French made no move to prevent them. A Jesuit met the captives at Trois-Rivières, but did nothing to free them.[334] The vanquished Hurons no longer represented anything – they had no military power, no economic power, not even any symbolic power, for they were already converts. Both merchants and missionaries were now more interested in the Iroquois.

For their part, the Iroquois looked to the east, having wiped out Huronia and all the tribes once part of the network of Huron alliances. The pressure was such that the Jesuits of Acadia sent an ambassador to New England to ask for help.[335] Then, in 1651, the Iroquois took on a last great rival, the Susquehannock tribe, suppliers of furs to the Swedes. According to Governor-General Kieft of New Netherland, writing in 1639, the Susquehannocks siphoned off furs to New Sweden valued at about 30,000 florins annually. In the approximate prices of 1639, this represented about 3,500 to 4,000 pelts, or more than half the furs traded by the Iroquois at Fort Orange (5,000 to 6,000 pelts).[336] Unlike other Iroquois enemies, the Susquehannocks resisted, as they were well armed by their Swedish allies. Arms traffic had been as brisk on the Susquehannock River as on the Hudson.

To neutralize this competition, the Dutch conquered New Sweden in September 1655. This event may have altered the balance of power among rival tribes, because in the following year the Iroquois successfully attacked the Eries, who were Susquehannock suppliers. About 1,200 Iroquois warriors bearing firearms crushed between 3,000 and 4,000 poorly armed Erie warriors, who had neither firearms nor powder.[337] 'This was their ruin; for, after most of the first fugitives had been killed, the others were surrounded by the Onnontaguehronnons [the Iroquois Onondaga tribe], who entered the fort and there wrought such carnage among the women and children, that blood was knee-deep in certain places.'[338] Like the Hurons and the Neutrals before them, the Eries disappeared as a nation.

One missionary's reaction to the Erie massacre provides a good illustration of the Jesuits' knack of turning everything to account. In Huronia's heyday, they had viewed the Iroquois as hellhounds of Satan and enemies of the faith. However, these same, now victorious, Iroquois were looked upon as a sign of Providence, once the Jesuits had established themselves in their midst. Some Iroquois who were in the process of being converted, and who had been welcomed by the missionary into his dwelling, told him 'that what made them believe [the missionary's religious message] was partly their last victory over the Cat Nation [the Eries], their enemies, when they were only twelve hundred against three or four thousand; and, as they had promised, before the battle, to embrace the Faith if they returned victorious, they could not now retract after so successful a triumph. This speech ended, the Father made them all pray to God; and one of the Deputies had the prayer repeated to him several times, that he might learn it by heart.'[339]

The Iroquois had conquered nearly all their enemies, which meant that they – and the missionaries – could now reach the Ohio tribes previously outside the fur trade network. 'For our Iroquois have discovered, beyond the Cat Nation, other and numerous Nations who speak the Algonquin language. There are more than thirty villages whose inhabitants have never had any knowledge of Europeans; they still use only stone hatchets and knives, and the other things that these Savages used before they began to trade with the French. Since the Iroquois carry fire and war thither, why should not we carry to them the fire and the peace that Jesus Christ has brought into the world?'[340]

In 1662, at the summit of their power, Iroquois bands extended the war as far as possible, travelling to the southeast and to a coast where something resembling palm trees grew. The Jesuits believed this to be the Virginia shore. Other bands brought back prisoners from the villages of the southwest. These villages were situated on 'a beautiful river [the Mississippi] which serves to carry the people down to the great Lake (for so they call the Sea), where they trade with Europeans who pray as we do, and use Rosaries, as well as Bells for calling to Prayers. According to the description given us, we judge them to be Spaniards.'[341]

The possession of firearms made the Iroquois victorious everywhere. Other raids took them to the upper Ottawa and even as far as Nekouba, north of Lac Saint-Jean.[342] At the same period, they also attacked the Illinois and drove them west of the Mississippi.[343] The only tribes to resist were their near neighbours, the Susquehannocks, and to a lesser degree the Mahicans, who had been forced to let the Iroquois take over their role as principal trading partners of the Dutch. Nevertheless, the Mahicans could still trade with the latter and acquire arms. In 1664, they successfully resisted an Iroquois attack on one of their villages. The Susquehannocks, on the other hand, had to conclude a peace treaty with the Iroquois after the fall of New Sweden. Nevertheless, these people were described by the Jesuits in 1664 as being 'very warlike, and better able than any others to exterminate the Hyroquois.'[344] When Iroquois warriors presented themselves at the gates of the village of Andastoé, 'planning, as is their wont, to sack the whole village and return home at the earliest moment, loaded with glory and with captives,'[345] they found themselves face to face with an enemy that was as well if not better armed. They also saw that the village was protected on one side by the river, and on the other by a double row of thick trees, with two European-style 'bastions' at each end, which were even equipped with several artillery pieces.[346]

Although the Susquehannocks' resistance shows to what extent the possession of arms was a determining factor,[347] it also says something about the trading strategies of various European powers. The Swedes produced the best iron in Europe, and theirs was the leading arms industry. Their prices were therefore competitive, and they had the means to assist their allies in controlling the western trade routes.[348]

From 1664 onward, the Iroquois were obliged to draw in their horns, so to speak. All these wars had caused severe losses, added to the fact that the epidemics were now beginning again.[349] Although the Iroquois controlled an immense area, it had become drastically depopulated.

Father Ragueneau, who accompanied several hundred Hurons as they fled to Quebec, described the desolation found between Huronia and Montreal following the Iroquois raids. Not only this small sector, but the entire northeast had been laid waste.

> By roads which covered a distance of about three hundred leagues we marched, upon our guard as in an enemy's country, – there not being any spot where the Iroquois is not to be feared, and where we did not see traces of his cruelty, or signs of his treachery. On one side we surveyed districts which, not ten years ago, I reckoned to contain eight or ten thousand men. For all that, there remains not one of them. Going on beyond, we coasted along shores but lately reddened with the blood of our Christians. On another side you might have seen the trail, quite recent, of those who had been taken captive. A little farther on, were but the shells of cabins abandoned to the fury of the enemy, – those who had dwelt in them having fled into the forest, and condemned themselves to a life which is but perpetual banishment. The Nipissirinien people, who speak the Algonquin tongue, had quite lately been massacred at their lake, – forty leagues in circumference, which formerly I had seen inhabited in almost the entire length of its coast; but which, now, is nothing but a solitude ... So we pursued our way. Alas, that those wretched Iroquois should have caused such desolation in all these regions! When I ascended the great River, only thirteen years ago, I had seen it bordered with large numbers of people of the Algonquin tongue, who knew no God. These, in the midst of their unbelief, looked upon themselves as the Gods of the earth, for the reason that nothing was lacking to them in the richness of their fisheries, their hunting-grounds, and the traffic which they carried on with allied nations; add to which, they were the terror of their enemies. Since they have embraced the faith, and adored the Cross of Jesus Christ, he has given them, as their lot, a portion of that Cross, – verily a heavy one, having made them a prey to miseries, torments, and cruel deaths; in a word, they are a people wiped off from the face of the earth. Our sole consolation is that, having died Christians, they have entered on the heritage of true children of God. *Flagellat Deus omnem filium quem recipit* [God punishes the Son He has chosen].[350]

Following this description of the country's desolation and of these peoples wiped from the face of the earth, Father Ragueneau notes one final consolation: that so many Christian dead have happily met again in heaven. This unique consolation was in fact the sole objective of Jesuit missionaries of the time. In 1652, Father Ragueneau took up the theme once again, attributing a providential meaning to the defeat of the Hurons and Algonkins:

> God's ways are none the less just for being hidden. He often humbles those whom he intends to exalt ... When the Hurons were in affluence, and the Algonquins in prosperity, they mocked at the Gospel, and tried to murder those who proclaimed it in their country ... And it seems to me, I can say, with a very great appearance of truth, that the Algonquins, and the Hurons, and numerous other Nations whom we have instructed, would have been lost if they had not been ruined; that the greater part of those who came in quest of baptism in affliction, would never have found it in prosperity; and that those who have found Paradise in the Hell of their torments, would have found the true Hell in their earthly Paradise. Let us say, then, that the Hiroquois have rendered men rich, thinking to make them poor; that they have made saints, thinking to make victims of wretchedness; in a word, that we owe to them ... the conversion and sanctification of many souls.[351]

The Jesuits took sincerity, courage, and self-abnegation to the point of being tortured at the stake in their pursuit of a single goal – that is, to pluck souls from the hands of Satan and send them to heaven. 'Let people lose their property, let them lose their lives, let them be killed, massacred, burnt, roasted, broiled, and eaten alive – patience! that matters not, so long as the Gospel takes its course, and God is known, and souls saved.'[352] When the Iroquois attacked the Hurons, the fathers made it their business to baptize as many as they could.[353] As the Amerindians had done for themselves, the Jesuits reinterpreted, according to the logic of their own ideology and culture, the terrifying unfolding of events. The far-reaching significance of these events inevitably went beyond the comprehension of all parties. It involved nothing less than the collapse of a civilization.

The effect of this catastrophe was already visible in 1660. The east had been laid waste by wars and disease. The entire Lake Michigan and

Lake Superior region to the west had become a refugee zone. Their presence in turn disrupted the population balance and led to further wars.[354] Confrontation was especially marked on the west coast of Lake Michigan, where the newly arrived horticultural peoples drove the hunters into Wisconsin.[355] The Jesuits, who at this period were moving into the area west of the Great Lakes, continually came upon the 'debris' or remnants of old nations that had once lived in the east. Sometimes refugees from various nations would regroup in one place.[356] Occasionally, they were taken in by sedentary peoples such as the Abimiouecs, a nation of sixty villages on the shores of the Mississippi.[357] At other times the refugees were forced to fight to carve out a place for themselves. This diaspora scattered refugees 'to the very end of that part of the world.'[358]

The Iroquois were the unchallenged masters of northeastern North America. Despite this fact, they could never make themselves commercial middlemen in the way the Hurons had done. They had neither the traditions, habits, or methods of diplomacy that the Hurons had acquired over several generations. When the fur wars ceased, it was the Dutch who emerged the victors. Moreover, their territory had been spared in the combat, whereas the allies of New France had been routed and the colony devastated. The real losers, however, were primarily the Amerindians. Inextricably involved in the vicious circle of unequal exchange, they had become the instruments of their own downfall.

The Disruption of Relationships with Nature

The race for European products resulted in the depletion of resources, as we have seen. It also altered the relationship between man and nature. The Amerindians intensified the hunt for fur-bearing animals in order to get European goods, which they themselves could not produce. Competition plus unequal exchange put enormous pressure on Amerindians to produce furs. As a result, stocks were depleted beyond the critical point for maintaining the species. Archaeological projects on Huron village sites reveal an initial period where the quantity of beaver bones was abnormally high (indicating intensive hunting at the beginning of the fur trade), followed by a second period, where beaver bones were significantly fewer (indicating a scarcity of beaver as the fur trade developed).[359] This confirms a comment by Father Le Jeune in 1635, to the effect that the beaver had completely disappeared from Huronia. 'These animals are more prolific than our sheep in France, the females bearing as many as five or six every year; but, when the Savages find a lodge of them, they kill all, great and small, male and female. There is danger that they will finally exterminate the species in this Region, as has happened among the Hurons, who have not a single Beaver, going elsewhere to buy the skins they bring to the storehouse of these Gentlemen.'[360]

Ten years later, the beaver disappeared from Iroquoia. Supplies had to come from ever farther afield, and yet the Amerindians' demand for European products was persistent and kept growing. Tribes therefore diversified their hunting. At Fort Orange, they exchanged deer for cloth worth six or seven florins, but in 1639, when the hunting was good, a deer was traded for a loaf of bread, a knife, or even a pipe.[361] In 1655, the Amerindians were selling turkeys for ten stuivers (ten cents) each.[362] Mercantile relationships were then extended to the gathering of wild plants. The Swedes gave a loaf of bread in exchange for thirty feet of Canadian hemp cord, which was stronger than their own manufactured cord, used for fishing nets.[363] The result of all this was that the Amerindians gradually altered the balance of nature by squandering the wealth of the country in order to acquire objects made elsewhere.

Losing Control of the Centres of Trade

Quebec, Montreal, and New Amsterdam had always been the places where Amerindian tribes met and exchanged goods among themselves. However, the establishment of Europeans at these centres was to have a long-term effect on the regionalization of tribes. For example, in New Netherland, the coastal and upper Hudson Amerindians gradually stopped trading among themselves. Each tribe dealt separately with the Dutch. The same was true of the Algonkians of Quebec after the fall of Huronia. For the Huron trading commodities of corn and tobacco, this group substituted flour, biscuit, and French provisions, and later added tobacco imported from the West Indies.[364]

Wealth for Some

Prior to 1629, it is difficult to evaluate, other than indirectly, the profits realized by fur-trading companies. La Chesnaye, writing of the early days of the trade, said that at this period 'the pelts of beaver and moose, which were much sought after and brought very high prices in Europe, could be had for a needle, a sleigh bell, or a cheap tin mirror.'[365] In the sixteenth century, Cartier traded 'knives and other things of little value' for furs.[366] According to Lescarbot, competition among traders made the purchase price of beaver from Amerindians rise during the first half of the seventeenth century. It rose from two cakes or two knives to fifteen or twenty.[367] Such an exchange ratio would inevitably produce large profits. These trading companies certainly didn't trade so avidly without good reason. The French nobles who received royalties accumulated considerable sums of money. In 1619, for example, the Duc de Condé ceded his rights as viceroy of New France to the Duc de Ventadour for the sum of 30,000 livres. In 1625, the latter resold them for 100,000 livres. In 1621, de Caën and his associates shared a profit of 119,546 livres. On the other hand, they declared a deficit of 7,654 livres the following year.[368] It hardly needs to be said that trading profits paid directly for the building of forts and maintenance of garrisons. De Caën spent 10,000 livres for the Habitation of Quebec and the maintenance of between forty and fifty people there annually.[369]

Without evaluating profits, we can get a good indication of the exchange ratio from the following figures. One beaver pelt was worth 4 livres, 10 sous in Paris in 1603, and 7 livres, 10 sous upon arrival at Dieppe in 1610. After 1618, one pelt averaged 10 livres, a price that remained stable for several decades.

Each year, de Caën sent two ships to Tadoussac loaded with trade goods worth a total of 4,800 livres.[370] If we estimate the annual volume of fur exports at 12,000 to 15,000 pelts,[371] at an average price of 10 livres per pelt, this represents a gross revenue of 120,000 to 150,000 livres. The exchange ratio therefore fluctuated between 24 and 30 to 1. However, large expenses had to be taken into account: wages, food, and defence for some fifty people wintering over and for fifty men on the two ships. De Caën estimated expenses at about 46,000 livres,[372] a sum that cannot be attributed to incidental expenses, since transport is a productive activity. Nevertheless, this still left a good profit margin – around 100,000 livres to be shared between old and new associates. If we compare this net profit with the value of goods delivered to the Amerindians, the result is still 20 to 1. Of course, this ratio cannot be applied generally throughout the period, nor does it have the reliability of accounting series; it simply shows that the exchange was unequal.

The Compagnie des Cent Associés acquired the trading monopoly in 1627. However, almost from the beginning, the English seizure of Quebec and of ships bound for it brought losses in the order of 400,000 livres. The company was forced to cede the monopoly between 1632 and 1637 to a special company made up of a group of shareholders of the Cent Associés. They did this in return for a third of the dividends. We have no record of this subsidiary's balance sheet. We do know, however, that in 1638 a new subcontractor, made up in part of the members of the preceding group, obtained the monopoly until 1642. It seems that the balance sheet was negative at the latter date, both for the special company, and for the Compagnie des Cent Associés.[373] In both cases, the interests of the Dieppe and Rouen merchants apparently prevailed.[374] We have no way of knowing whether the second subcontractor realized any profits. Nevertheless, with a deficit of 70,000 livres in 1641, the balance sheet is clearly negative for the Cent Associés. Between 1641 and 1645, therefore, the shareholders decided to reinvest 150,000 livres, or about 1,500 livres each, a sum that would bring large gross returns between 1645 and 1647 (320,000 livres in beaver pelts in 1646). However, as Marcel Trudel points out, once the company had paid the seigneurial rent, the administrative costs of the colony, the embarkation costs, the crews' salaries, interest on loans between 1645 and 1646 (at a high rate of 25 or 30 per cent), and the debts for the two years, there could not be much left.[375] After the destruction of Huronia in 1649, Holland held unquestioned hegemony in the North American fur trade. The net profits realized by the Dutch West India Company were greater than those in New France. Between 1655 and 1664, furs imported into Holland totalled 454,127 florins in value; it had cost the company 272,847 florins to keep the colony going, which represents a net profit of 181,280 florins, or an average of 75,512 florins per year.[376]

Despite these sometimes unreliable and very superficial accounting figures, we can plainly see that companies and merchants made money from the fur trade. They would have left North America, otherwise. If we posit the existence of profits, therefore, we admit that there was unequal exchange and a negative ratio unfavourable to the Amerindians. What can we say in cases where there were no profits, when the monopoly-holding company reported deficits? To find the answer, we need only look in the coffers of the moneylenders, the middlemen, the viceroy, and the government. Beaver paid all, it was said[377] – paid for building forts, maintaining garrisons, and keeping ships and crews in circulation. Beaver? The labour of the Amerindian paid all!

Impoverishment for Others

The Huron and Iroquois societies found themselves with a population that had been cut in half by epidemics, but which was working less and less for its own needs and more and more to obtain the surplus product needed to acquire European goods. On the one hand, the introduction of new tools made it easier to procure the surplus product, but on the other, intensive hunting made it more difficult, because the fur-bearing animal populations were driven below a critical point for maintenance of the species. This led to growing marginal costs. The sources of supply moved ever farther from the initial trapping areas, requiring more time for transportation; competition among Amerindian peoples became correspondingly more acute, and the human toll of war spiralled. Growth in productivity due to new arms and tools fell far short of compensating for the cost in human lives and labour time, the latter having increased because of the higher production volume coupled with the phenomenal extension of hunting grounds.

If we look at the most time-consuming activity, trapping, we find that actual work methods remained traditional. Surprising as it seems, metal traps only appeared at the end of the eighteenth century.[378] Although iron did indeed replace bone and stone for axes, ice picks, and harpoons, it did not revolutionize hunting habits or reduce labour time substantially, because it was the need to cover distances that took by far the most time. To begin with, the hunters had to get to the hunting ground. With the greater use of iron implements in hunting, Amerindians had to go farther and farther afield, because they had to hunt more animals so as to acquire more iron goods. Once they had reached their destination, the hunters first had to reconnoitre the territory, locating beaver dams on the territory's rivers and lakes. 'Most of the time, these places were at least a few miles away from the camp, which meant that the chase would take place after several hours of walking, involving at least an overnight expedition or longer.'[379] Hunters often took along a specially trained dog. They also profited from their walk through the forest to locate the trails of other animals to be hunted, either with snares or traps 'which are made to open, when a heavy piece of wood falls upon the animal and kills it.'[380] Once the beaver dwelling had been found, snow had to be cleared around the area, and the beavers' bolt holes found. These were passages used by the beaver to circulate under the ice from its house to various refuges consisting of air pockets. 'In the course of these comings and goings, [the beaver] gives off carbon dioxide bubbles that in time create a space under the ice, altering its composition. The hunter can discover these spaces by tapping the ice with a stick or branch and listening for the distinctive sound. The unique thing about these passages is that they are the only means of entry to the beaver's dwelling.'[381] Hunters would cut through the ice at these points and drop in nets or snares. Another technique was to destroy the beaver house and locate the air pockets under the ice. 'They cut the ice with their iron blade, looking to see if the water is stirred up by the movement or breathing of the Beaver. If the water moves, they have a curved stick which they thrust into the hole that they have just made; if they feel the beaver, they kill it with their big club, which they call *ca ouikachit.*'[382]

Such descriptions effectively show that the introduction of iron tools did not reduce labour time enormously. Firearms could not be used, since they damaged the pelts. As mentioned, metal traps did not exist at that time. It was the travelling and location of beaver sites that took up the most time.

Firearms were mainly acquired for warfare, but, nevertheless, they did improve hunting. The Amerindians quickly transferred their acquired bow-and-arrow skills to firearms, and became expert shots.[383] Although unable to make guns themselves, the Amerindians sought every possible means of reducing their dependence on the Europeans by learning how to repair them, interchanging pieces from discarded firearms and learning the art of the blacksmith. Such was the case with the Narragansetts, who boasted a qualified blacksmith and a forge.[384]

In New England, one Thomas Morton sold the Amerindians powder and lead, and taught them how to load a gun – how much powder to use, and the size of bullets for the animal hunted. He employed Amerindians to hunt for him. Soon, they were far more adroit in handling arms than most whites. Since they wanted to be as self-sufficient as possible, they acquired moulds and learned how to make bullets, and also used dies to make screws. Although the governor of Plymouth was horrified by the idea that these 'barbarians' could drive them into the sea, and had Morton deported to England, the Amerindians realized just how far they had been cheated in the exchange.[385] As they gradually benefitted from technological exchanges, the likelihood of profits for European merchants evaporated. Still, Amerindian societies could only go so far in acquiring European production techniques, and they could not escape their growing dependence, even if they resisted it. They were locked into a relationship of unequal exchange for the foreseeable future, and so worked harder and harder as they acquired more European goods, including firearms.

Throughout this whole period, the Amerindians never showed any interest in European methods of agriculture, which in their view imposed too many constraints.[386] In any case, sweet corn already provided them with a yield that completely outclassed European cereal production. In 1657, the Mohawks asked the Dutch to supply them with a few horses to haul logs for building palisades, in addition to three cannons to defend the village.[387] In the same year, the Onondagas requested that the Dutch bring them horses.[388] The Iroquois wanted horses in response to military pressure (the need to fortify villages with the trunks of large trees rather than stakes). There is nothing to show that horses were used in agriculture, nor is there anything to indicate the introduction of the plough or of domestic animals on a significant scale.

Although firearms permitted some reduction in labour time devoted to hunting, this was still a marginal activity among the Iroquoians and the Algonkian coastal societies. Horticulture continued to provide their material base, and horticultural methods remained traditional in nature. As a result of trade, however, there was increasing pressure for horticultural produce. Huronia, which had long been the granary of the Algonkians,[389] had to come up with increasing surpluses to exchange with the non-horticultural peoples of the north for furs. The Iroquois were equally affected. Although they were more inclined to steal furs than to trade for them, they still had to produce more food to feed the growing number of men who left the villages on long hunting or raiding expeditions. As in the period prior to 1630, the time gained through acquiring metal tools was lost because of the need to clear and cultivate more land. Indeed, we may well ask exactly how much easier it was to clear land with iron axes and knives. Although metal knives certainly reduced labour time when working with bones and wood, it was the introduction of iron axes to fell trees for horticultural purposes, or for construction and fortification, that really saved time. Still, flint axes were more effective than we might think. They were used in the traditional method of hitting the wood with small, rapid blows. Experiments have shown that an experienced user could cut down an oak of about thirty-five centimetres in diameter in less than half an hour. On the other hand, compared to modern tools, trade axes were made of inferior metal and lacked a heavy head; consequently, they were far less effective. The trade axe may have increased the rate of clearing by a factor of about two, which in itself is not negligible.[390]

Pressure from the fur trade also meant that Amerindians had to dry more fish, meat, and fruit for provisions when travelling. The women had to dress an ever-growing number of pelts.[391] The net result of having better tools was that the Hurons had to work as much if not more than before. As far as the men were concerned, what was gained in labour time (mainly in clearing land) was lost because trading required more men and more time while imposing a new constraint – the need to increase the agricultural production on which the growth of trade depended. Women most definitely had to work much more than in the past. They had to produce more, even though their tools had generally not changed. Exceptions were the metal cooking pot, and the trading axe that women used to cut firewood.[392] The question remains as to whether men, because they were the ones involved in the actual trading, replaced their own stone tools before doing the same for women? Did they only buy tools that would guarantee the greatest additional yield? For example, the men rarely replaced bone tools such as needles or arrowheads.[393] We know that traditional methods persisted in all women's agricultural work. However, there is nothing that says these women would not have considered it a priority to acquire iron tools for digging, turning, and breaking up the soil, had they been in a position to enter into direct contact with Europeans.

Looking back, we can see that the Huron confederacy never became markedly wealthier at any time during the historical period. Archaeological evidence tells us that during this period, common objects such as jewellery, combs, and pipes were generally made by the Hurons themselves,[394] and the same was true for the Iroquois. However, it may be less a question of increased wealth than of the development of commerce and the division of labour. Among the Hurons, we can observe a development of ceremonial functions, particularly for the Feast of the Dead. This was formerly a community feast, but later became an occasion for distribution. Huron and Algonkin tribes used this occasion to commemorate their alliance, and the chiefs showed that they belonged to an egalitarian community by sharing wealth acquired through trade. In fact, the development of ritualism appears less a question of demonstrating collective enrichment than the need for a growing recourse to the kind of social mechanisms that would keep the society whole, despite the new tensions. One indication of this is the fact that, despite considerably greater agricultural production, reserves for two or three years were not put aside for bad years, as had once been the case.[395] Famine, a virtually unknown phenomenon, struck several times after 1638.[396] During the historical period, reserves were sold, which explains the greater vulnerability of the Hurons when crop yields were low.

In the final analysis, the development of labour among the Hurons is the best evidence we have of unequal exchange between Amerindians and Europeans. Despite more efficient tools, which would normally either reduce labour time or add considerably to the wealth of a society, the Hurons had to work harder and harder, without getting any richer. In a word, the more efficient their tools, the harder they worked.

Huronia and Iroquoia

Epidemics, wars, dispossession, increased labour, dependency – all these factors characterized the process whereby Amerindian societies were integrated into the world market. Caught in the web of an unequal trading relationship, Amerindian civilization in northeastern North America disintegrated at the speed with which it became an integral part of this world market. In the short term, however, not all Amerindian societies experienced the same fate. Shifting alliances and the fortunes of war created winners and losers. The present chapter deals with the process of change in two Amerindian societies: the Huron and the Iroquois.

THE DESTRUCTION OF HURONIA: AN INSIDE VIEW

The Missionary Offensive

Between 1632 and 1649, the year of Huronia's destruction, the Hurons developed increasingly close trade relations with the French while becoming progressively dependent on them. During the same period, the Hurons had to withstand an unprecedented ideological offensive mounted by numbers of Jesuit missionaries and their helpers who settled in Huron territory. These missionaries played a definitive role in French-Huron relations. The Jesuits had powerful backing in the French court and had managed to link their fortunes to those of the Hurons by making sure that the Franco-Huron alliance turned on whether missionaries were admitted into Huron villages.[1] The Hurons were bound to comply with these terms in order to maintain their status as chief middlemen in the fur trade, and indeed they readily agreed. Several villages even competed for the privilege of welcoming the missionaries in their midst.[2] The Jesuits chose Ossossané, 'the most renowned Village of the Huron,' one in which 'all the Councils of the country are held for final action.'[3]

Missionaries began to settle among the Hurons in 1634. They already had a rudimentary knowledge of the Huron language, thanks to a vanguard of interpreters.[4] After spreading out among several villages, they learned to speak the language fluently and became familiar with the customs and habits of their hosts.[5] In 1640, the thirteen priests and fourteen helpers then living in Huronia built the fortified village of Sainte-Marie-among-the-Hurons for themselves and their converts. Gradually their numbers increased, until finally there were eighteen priests and forty-six helpers.[6]

The missionaries had settled in a society with a rudimentary division of labour. No one had an exclusive role in spiritual matters – that is, no one specialized in religious 'production.' In Europe, where a highly differentiated religious framework had developed, specialists monopolized religious production. In Huronia, however, and among Amerindians throughout northeastern North America generally, there existed what amounted to religious self-sufficiency.[7] By the simple process of familiarization, all members of Huron society acquired a working knowledge of sets of thoughts and actions which, taken as a whole, governed their relationship with spiritual life. This body of knowledge included, among other things, the creation myth, food taboos, and rituals for the dead and ailing. The Hurons did indeed have shamans – men and occasionally women who were better than others at interpreting dreams and recounting myths, who knew the ritual dances, and possessed greater knowledge or skill in treating the sick. Shamans, however, did not exercise exclusive religious functions. Any Huron man or woman could handle symbolic objects. Furthermore, the shaman was only called on from time to time for immediate needs such as curing a sick person or making rain,[8] usually in return for payment – perhaps a meal, wampum, or some other form of remuneration.[9]

The shaman's function was essentially different from that of the priest, who was a member of an initiated elite functioning on a permanent, continual, and routine basis. Unlike the shaman, the priest had no productive role within the community. Even in Huronia the Jesuits never shared in communal tasks. When they needed corn, they offered wampum in the form of porcelain beads in exchange. Indentured servants and devout lay workers called *donnés* saw to the priests' domestic needs, while donations by the readers of the *Jesuit Relations*, coupled with Huron hospitality, took care of the rest.[10] As a result, the Jesuits could devote all their time to their religious calling.

Unlike the priest, the shaman was paid for services rendered and had no ascetic vocation. The missionary, on the contrary, rejected both the economic and sexual benefits of this world (although with an objective goal in view) and thus reinforced his own and others' faith in his symbolic effectiveness.[11] The courage and sincerity involved in such rejection were undeniably persuasive traits; but behind this lay the evident masochism typical of the missionary personality. Take, for example, the practice of self-flagellation and the wearing of hair-shirts, or consider Father Lalemant's description of Jean de la Lande, a young donné tortured by the Iroquois:

> He was endowed with a humility altogether rare; he not only recognized his own lowliness, but he desired to be treated according to his nothingness. He approved from his youth those who chastised him, secretly kissing the rods and whips which were used for correcting him. Being in the country of the Hiroquois, he could not behold without joy the posts which supported the scaffold whereon he had suffered so much; he would go to kiss them and embrace them, – not only through a love for sufferings, but because they were, he said, the instruments of divine justice for his crimes.[12]

To establish a power base, a priest had to begin by appropriating and monopolizing the religious authority dispersed throughout the community at large. Contrary to the shaman, he had to put himself forward as the indispensable instrument of salvation. He, and no one else, had mastered the body of explicit knowledge and norms; he, and no other, had legitimate authority handed down by a bureaucratic institution, in other words, an organized church.[13] He alone was a specialist in 'symbolic labour.' Furthermore, in order to concentrate religious capital in his hands – capital that had hitherto been distributed among all members of the community – he had to employ both symbolic and material forces. On the symbolic level, the priest invoked eternal damnation,[14] dwelling on themes of sin, redemption, and humility. Such themes reflected a paradoxical conception of the world, totally at odds with the sentiments of dignity and pride characteristic of Iroquoian societies, and generally of all societies where division of labour is relatively simple and social classes nonexistent. For this reason, the missionary's message was unlikely to gain acceptance unless buttressed by strong material considerations.

The material force used by the Jesuits to acquire and legitimate their religious capital was simple: no trade unless missionaries were allowed into Huronia. With powerful friends at the court of France, the Jesuits were able to make themselves part and parcel of the Franco-Huron alliance, in addition to acquiring the right of free passage on ships. Moreover, their missionary work was financed by the 'pious donors' to whom the *Jesuit Relations* were destined. In order for the Jesuits' monopoly of religious functions to be socially recognized, their political supporters managed not only to exclude all heretics from the colony, but also to bar all rival Roman Catholic religious communities from areas destined for missionary work. They even succeeded in excluding all lay people from 'missionary country' other than those men (generally donnés) over whom they exercised absolute ideological control.[15] The aim of this exclusion was to keep Frenchmen who lived among the Hurons from adopting native manners and customs, thereby saving them from becoming 'savages,' as had happened prior to 1630.[16] All this meant that the Hurons were faced not only with a commercial monopoly, but with a religious monopoly as well. In fact, religious, economic, and political powers were indissolubly united – a phenomenon that the Jesuits openly referred to on numerous occasions. 'The great show of power made at first by the Portuguese in the East and West Indies,' states the writer of the 1634 *Jesuit Relations*, 'inspired profound admiration in the minds of the Indians, so that these people embraced, without any contradiction, the beliefs of those whom they admired. Now the following is, it seems to me, the way in which to acquire an ascendancy over our Savages.'[17]

As a means of gaining ascendancy over 'his Savages,' Father Le Jeune suggested founding a boys' seminary, restricting white travel among the Hurons, instilling fear into the Iroquois, and sending a few settlers to Huronia to teach the inhabitants about European agriculture[18] (although as far as the latter went, the Jesuits soon lost their illusions about turning Hurons into French peasants). The following year (1635), Father Le Jeune wrote in the same vein, 'Besides, if these Countries are peopled by our French, not only will this weaken the strength of the Foreigners ... but it will also strengthen France, for those who will be born in New France, will be French ... The more imposing the power of our French people is made in these Countries, the more easily they can make their belief received by these Barbarians, who are influenced even more through the senses, than through reason.'[19]

French settlement and French military might were inextricably entwined, constituting the 'foundation for the conversion of all these tribes.'[20] In fact, political and religious powers routinely worked together, quite aside from collaborating on ambitious imperialistic projects. In 1635, for example, as missionaries were embarking for Huronia, Governor Du Plessis marked their departure with 'several volleys, to recommend us still more to our Savages.'[21] The Jesuits also struck a deal with the Compagnie des Cents Associés whereby the latter's pricing policy for trade goods encouraged conversion to Christianity: Christians paid less, pagans paid more – a significant distinction. Converted Amerindians would receive more presents and be accorded the place of honour in all ceremonies.[22] The Jesuits also used guns to encourage conversion. The embargo on selling firearms to Amerindians remained in force until about 1640, giving the French a clear military advantage. For reasons already explained, restrictions were eased somewhat after 1640. Only Christians could obtain guns, however, and as a result Hurons could not get hold of firearms without agreeing to be baptized. Baptism also guaranteed them protection from their enemies, for only converted Amerindians were allowed into French forts.[23]

Finally, as proof of the superiority of Christian doctrine over Amerindian beliefs, the Jesuits brought to bear the full weight of developing European production forces. In 1634 the missionaries had noticed how the Amerindians marvelled at a clock. The following year they brought a series of European gadgets, as described in the *Jesuit Relations*:

> Speaking of their expressions of admiration, I might here set down several on the subject of the lodestone, into which they looked to see if there was some paste; and of a glass with eleven facets, which represented a single object as many times; of a little phial in which a flea appears as large as a beetle; of the prism, of the joiner's tools; but above

all of the writing, for they could not conceive how, what one of us, being in the village, had said to them, and put down at the same time in writing, another, who meanwhile was in a house far away, could say readily on seeing the writing. I believe they have made a hundred trials of it. All this serves to gain their affections, and to render them more docile when we introduce the admirable and incomprehensible mysteries of our Faith; for the belief they have in our intelligence and capacity causes them to accept without reply what we say to them.[24]

The Jesuits employed 'as much decoration and splendor as possible,' including quantities of candles that amazed the Amerindians.[25] Father Lalement mentions the use of pomp and ceremony as a means of exciting admiration while instilling the Amerindians with a sense of their own unworthiness:

> The outward splendor with which we endeavor to surround the Ceremonies of the Church; the beauty of our Chapel (which is looked upon in this Country as one of the Wonders of the World, although in France it would be considered but a poor affair); the Masses, Sermons, Vespers, Processions, and Benedictions of the Blessed Sacrament that are said and celebrated at such times, with a magnificence surpassing anything that the eyes of our Savages have ever beheld, – all these things produce an impression on their minds, and give them an idea of the Majesty of God, who, we tell them, is honored throughout the World by a worship a thousand times more imposing.[26]

When building Sainte-Marie in 1639, the French were motivated by a desire to impress the Amerindians with their technological superiority. They did everything possible to recreate an island of European culture, whether it involved buildings (chapel, hospital, and dwellings), artisanal trades (blacksmiths, masons, and carpenters), or the small farm (stocked with chickens, calves, and hogs) where wheat was grown.[27] The missionaries used the symbolic advantage of the written word to discredit oral tradition, for writing embodied the impressive power of being able to transmit messages that need not be spoken to be understood, messages that remained constant no matter when or where they were read, or by whom.[28] The art of printing provided missionaries with a ready supply of holy pictures, most often portraying heaven or hell,[29] that excited the curiosity and admiration of the Amerindians.

Missionaries also encouraged conversion by the use of scientific discoveries likely to amaze the 'Savages.' Discoveries such as the earth being round were put forward as a way of questioning native beliefs and substituting Christian precepts in their stead. 'At last, I told them that the Europeans navigated the whole world. I explained to them and made them see by a round figure what country it was where the sun sets according to their idea, assuring them that no one had ever found this great village, that all that was nothing but nonsense.'[30]

A little later the missionary informed the Hurons, who were intrigued by geography, 'As I am truthful in speaking about things of the earth, also thou shouldst persuade thyself that I am not lying when I speak to thee about the things of Heaven; and therefore thou oughtst believe what I have told thee about the other life.'[31] The same tactics were used in 1637, 1638, and 1646, when the Jesuits predicted an eclipse.[32]

The first Jesuits to penetrate Huronia were looked upon merely as 'black robes' whose behaviour, particularly their habit of celibacy, was a source of some surprise. Initially they had no religious hold over the Hurons, who respected individual differences and were free of the intolerance that comes with dogmatic thought. As far as the Hurons were concerned, the Jesuits were simply shamans – white shamans with their own special rituals, their own magic. To begin with, therefore, the Jesuits dealt with the shamans.[33] Confrontation was strictly ideological at first; two types of religious discourse were juxtaposed then placed in opposition to one another, as illustrated in this conversation between a Montagnais shaman and a missionary who was recounting the coming of 'the son of God upon earth:'

> 'Thy god,' he [the shaman] replied, 'has not come to our country, and that is why we do not believe in him; make me see him and I will believe in him.' 'Listen to me and thou wilt see him,' said I. 'We have two kinds of sight, the sight of the eyes of the body, and the sight of the eyes of the soul. What thou seest with the eyes of the soul may be just as true as what thou seest with the eyes of the body.' 'No,' said he, 'I see nothing except with the eyes of the body, save in sleeping, and thou dost not approve our dreams.'[34]

In order to undermine the shaman's authority, the missionary called
into question his ability to cure the sick with traditional medicine, claim-
ing that prayers and Catholic rites, including baptism, were more effective, even on the physical plane. The missionary thereby assumed the role
of shaman and threw down the gauntlet. For example, when an ailing
Amerindian beat the drum each night as a cure, the missionary explained
that there was no connection between the noise of the drum and a return
to health. To prove it, the missionary proposed a deal: the Amerindian
would keep on beating the drum for ten nights. If he were not cured, he
would stop for ten nights, whereupon the missionary would retire for
'three days to pray in a little cabin,'[35] asking his God to cure the Amerindian in body and soul. Should the Amerindian be cured, he would renounce
his magic and acknowledge the missionary's God as all-powerful.[36]

Missionaries in Huronia first baptized the sick and dying. The
Hurons accepted this initiative as an additional ritual for recovery.[37] The
missionaries, however, tried to counter the Hurons' 'relativism' by
denouncing their methods of seeking a cure, methods that they not only
considered ineffectual[38] but immoral. The most reprehensible of these
customary practices, the missionaries felt, was the sexually promiscuous
ceremony known as the *andacwander*.[39] Nevertheless, the Jesuits would
have had little chance of winning converts, either on medical or moral
grounds, had it not been for the epidemics that swept through Huronia
from 1634 on. Generally speaking, traditional Amerindian medicine probably worked better than the recognized medical practices of seventeenth-
century Europe, with its bloodletting, emetics, and purgatives. Native
practices included knowledge of the medicinal properties of a wide range
of plants, as well as numerous rituals that gave the sick person a sense of
community support, solidarity, and affection. If nothing else, the native
methods were undeniably more effective than those the missionaries
tried to put in their place.[40] The Hurons, however, knew nothing about
the new, epidemic, often fatal, diseases now afflicting them, and their
traditional medicine had no way of combating the effects.

The shaman (*arendwane*) fought epidemics by organizing 'eat-all
feasts' (*awataerohi*), dances, carnivals, and lacrosse matches, but his rituals achieved nothing,[41] for the Hurons perished, shamans included,
while the missionaries inevitably survived. The smallpox epidemic of
1639 spared the black robes; at most, they were affected by the influenza

of 1636-37. Among Amerindians, the epidemic was particularly hard on the older members of the community – the very people who acted as custodians of tradition. To the Jesuits it seemed as though the hand of God were sweeping aside their adversaries.[42]

Initially, the Jesuits were perceived by the Hurons as shamans endowed with superior powers. From this position of strength they asserted the effectiveness of their prayers, religious rites, and holy water, as well as their manner of treating the sick by bloodletting, keeping the patient away from noise and disturbance,[43] and so on. They rejected the songs and dances of shaman rituals but took a somewhat more lenient view of the shaman's medicinal ointments and teas.[44] Some Hurons, believing the Jesuits were sorcerers and remarking that a great many of the baptized children later died, began to wonder. Might the rite of baptism cause death? Why did the missionaries rush to the side of the sick? To make them die? What were the images the black robes set up in their cabins? And the litanies intoned in private?[45] In 1637 an old Huron man, to whose sickbed the Jesuits had hastened, angrily scorned their ministrations. 'It is you people who are making me die; since you set foot in this house, six days ago, I have eaten nothing; and I have seen you in a dream as persons who are bringing us misfortune; it is you who are making me die.'[46]

Father Le Jeune added to this account, 'Observe that among these peoples nothing more need be said for a man to have his head split.'[47] Behind the confrontation between priest and shaman, a struggle was going on between two modes of talking and acting. With the advent of epidemic disease, however, the priest began to gain acceptance at the shaman's expense.

The Montagnais and Hurons had already suffered extraordinary hardship from an epidemic that started before the Jesuits set off from Trois-Rivières for Huronia in 1634. Nevertheless, when a second pandemic struck in 1636-37, the Amerindians turned an accusatory eye on the missionaries. From then until the fall of Huronia, the Jesuits lived under the constant threat of death.[48] They were accused of witchcraft and brought before the grand council of the Huron confederacy in 1637. The Amerindians believed them responsible for 'the universal contagion.'[49] Witchcraft was usually punishable by death. Since the vast majority of Hurons considered that the Jesuits had caused the epidemic, the missionaries should have been executed – and yet they were not. The grand council resolved not to take any decision before the return of the 'bark flotilla' from Trois-Rivières. When the canoes did return, the members of the expedition opposed any repressive measures against the Jesuits and expressed doubts as to the missionaries' responsibility for the epidemic. The sickness probably originated on the coast, they felt, and was transmitted by the Susquehannocks and the Mohawks.[50] From a modern standpoint, it must be admitted that this was a plausible theory, even though it seems obvious that the native traders had a vested interest in establishing the Jesuits' innocence.

Although the missionaries believed that they were 'indebted ... after God to the most holy Virgin'[51] for their escape from death, it behooves us to look for another explanation. Two contradictory elements stand out in the oft-told story of Huron and missionary confrontation: on the one hand, the Hurons displayed aggressive behaviour and issued death threats, while, on the other, they sought an alliance and even showed a willingness to concede some authority to the Jesuits. In 1637, for example, although the majority was convinced of the missionaries' responsibility for the epidemic, individual Hurons were quick to seek renewed contact once the council had decided against the death sentence.[52] It seemed as though each wanted to forge a link with the missionaries while hoping that others would kill them. The Hurons were already heavily dependent on French trade goods, particularly as the exhausted beaver reserves forced them to go farther and farther afield in their search of furs. Under the circumstances, French military protection was as indispensable as French merchandise. This dependency is evident from the reported remarks of a chief to some of his peers, who each expressed a desire to 'split the head of the first Frenchman' he met if 'any one of those in his cabin should die.'

> Thereupon the Captain Aënons began to speak – at least, by his own account – and represented to them that they were speaking of a very dangerous matter, namely, of the destruction and ruin of the country; that, if they should remain two years without going down to Kebec to trade, they would find themselves reduced to such extremities that they might consider themselves fortunate to join with the Algonquins and to embark in their canoes. Relating this to the Father Superior, he added that after all that we should have no fear; and that if we would

settle down in his village, we should always be very welcome there.[53]

Only one village (possibly Contareia) severed relations entirely with the French and 'decided no longer to use French kettles, imagining that everything which came in any way from us was capable of communicating the disease to them.'[54]

The same ambivalence was evident in 1639 with the return of epidemic disease: the missionary-sorcerers must be killed,[55] but on the other hand, why jeopardize the French alliance when it was so vital, given the redoubled Iroquois offensive, and the fact that the latter now possessed firearms? With the fur wars heating up, Huron dependency increased and was further compounded by tribal rivalry within the wide network of alliances and trade relations centred on the French. The Hurons were the principal middlemen in this network. Their confederacy operated as a hegemony, but there was always the danger of the French sidestepping Huron middlemen to trade directly with other tribes or confederacies. This was precisely what the Hurons feared when missionaries visited the Petuns in the winter of 1639-40 and the Neutrals in the following winter.

When fathers Charles Garnier and Isaac Jogues reached the Petuns, an epidemic was already raging. Four hundred and fifty children alone had already died,[56] and women and children fled at the priests' approach.[57] The Petuns barred the missionaries from nearly all their dwellings. The Hurons turned these events to good account, it was noted. 'Some Hurons, who went thither from time to time to effect some trades, incensed minds against them [the missionaries], and even did their utmost to the end that they be got rid of as soon as possible.'[58]

Tension rose to such a pitch that the missionaries were forced to leave to escape being massacred by the Petuns,[59] yet paradoxically the Petun council decided to give the missionaries complete freedom of movement.[60] Why would such liberty be granted unless the Petuns wanted to develop direct commercial ties with the French? So reasoned the Jesuits, at any rate, when speaking of Huron attempts to prevent Father Brébeuf's journey to the Neutrals. 'This, joined to the evil tricks which were played on him then by the Hurons, – who feared the removal of their trade ... did not permit him in so short a time, to do what he had desired for the service of God.'[61] The Hurons terrified the Neutrals with warnings against the black-robed sorcerers.[62] Despite their fear, however, the Neutrals did not dare attack the missionaries. They probably hoped to use their contact with the Jesuits as a means of escaping Huron hegemony.

The Hurons were determined to retain their privileged trading status with the French, and this forced them not only to accept the presence of missionaries in their midst, but to try to keep the relationship exclusive. Furthermore, they contributed to their own increased dependency because of their desire for continued domination over various other Amerindian tribes. In 1642, for example, the Hurons forced the Jesuits to give up their missions among the Neutrals and the Petuns.[63] The Jesuits would return, stated the *Jesuit Relations*, once they had made 'a sufficient breach here among the Hurons.'[64]

The missionaries were trapped in the contradictory roles of potential victims on the one hand, and – given their virtual stranglehold on Huronia – of blackmailers, on the other. As missionary-entrepreneurs they therefore took steps to protect themselves physically, while creating a framework that would utilize the effects of dependency for purposes of conversion. This framework was exemplified by the fortified village of Sainte-Marie-among-the-Hurons, which the Jesuits built to shelter both themselves and their converts, noting that 'the insolence of the Savages obliged us to do so much sooner than on other accounts we have decided to.'[65] The buildings of Sainte-Marie were constructed so as to create a hierarchical segregation. The area reserved for Jesuits was the least accessible. Next on a descending scale was the space reserved for Europeans (workshops and living quarters for donnés), then the space for Amerindian converts, with its chapel and longhouses. Outside these areas, confined between two stockades, lay the 'pagan' space. Having thus made sure of their safety, the Jesuits proceeded to intensify their policy of discrimination, favouring converts over the unconverted in selling arms and in the pricing of trade goods generally.

Father Vimont drew a vivid picture in 1645 of the social relationships between Hurons and missionaries:

> Add to this the fury of a Hiroquois enemy who closes the way to us; who deprives us of the necessities of life, and of the help that may be sent us in a forsaken country; who kills and massacres those who come to our aid; whose insolence grows from year to year; who depopulates

the country, and makes our Hurons think of giving up the trade with the French, because they find that it costs them too dear, and they prefer to do without European goods rather than to expose themselves every year, not to a death that would be endurable, but to fires and flames, for which they have a thousand times greater horror.

Now therefore, what can we expect in the midst of a barbarous nation where we shall no longer have the necessaries of life; where they will no longer venture to send us the reinforcement of laborers that would be required here to promote the affairs of God; where all who shall remain will be abandoned to the fury of a desperate people, who will no longer be restrained from massacring us all by the fear of losing their trade with the French, – which they will find impossible to them, and which will be completely ruined, as far as they are concerned?[66]

We have identified the economic and military factors that forced the Hurons to maintain their alliance with the French. These 'objective' and 'rational' factors certainly influenced the course of events enormously. But there were also compelling considerations of a religious or mythical nature. For example, how did the Hurons view the severing of an alliance? Did it not constitute a refusal to give in return, to provide the traditional quid pro quo, therefore breaking the exchange cycle? Such rejection of a gift was not merely tantamount to a declaration of war; it also conferred magical powers on the giver, since the intended recipient thereby incurred a debt to the spirit of the donor. To sever the Franco-Huron alliance would endow the French with magical power, a hypothesis that is substantiated in the *Jesuit Relations* of 1633 and 1637. In order to understand the context, however, we must first look at the circumstances surrounding the death of Étienne Brûlé.

The interpreter Étienne Brûlé had worked with Champlain and had lived in Huronia since 1620. When the Kirke brothers took Quebec in 1629, he agreed to work for the English. Champlain viewed this as treason. Étienne Brûlé probably tried subsequently to establish an alliance with tribes other than the Hurons – possibly the Senecas.[67] The Hurons, however, were afraid of being ousted by their enemies, and in 1633 they decided to kill Brûlé, knowing Champlain considered him a traitor.[68] Even in these circumstances, such a killing was a matter of the utmost gravity in the Amerindian tradition of alliances. The people of the village where the murder occurred abandoned their homes to settle in two other localities.[69] That same year the Hurons went down to Quebec filled with apprehension,[70] a fact that did not go unnoticed by the Algonkins, whose 'design was to get all the merchandise from the Hurons at a very low price, in order afterwards to come themselves and trade it, with either the French or the English.'[71]

Champlain reassured his Huron allies by making it clear that they owed him no compensation for the death of a traitor. Nevertheless, all their fears resurfaced with the epidemic of 1636-37. 'Upon this occasion they [the Hurons] confessed to us the evil designs they had had this winter upon our lives, – having learned from a reliable source, as they thought, that the uncle of the late Étienne Brûlé, in revenge for the death of his nephew, for which no satisfaction had been obtained, had undertaken the ruin of the whole country, and had caused this contagious disease.'[72]

It was the Huron custom to compensate the family of a murder victim with generous gifts. In the case of Étienne Brûlé, however, 'no satisfaction had been obtained' by the French. Since the Hurons had taken a life without providing the customary compensation, Brûlé's family had therefore acquired magical power over them. The Algonkins, who themselves had suffered from epidemics and were jealous of the Hurons' privileged status in the French alliance, circulated a rumour blaming the French:

> Besides this, very recently a certain Algonquin captain has given our Hurons to understand that they were mistaken in thinking that the devils caused them to die, – that they should blame only the French for this; and that he had seen, as it were, a French woman who was infecting the whole country with her breath and her exhalations. Our Savages imagine that it is the sister of the late Étienne Brûlé, who is avenging her brother's death. This Sorcerer added that we, even we ourselves, meddle with sorcery; that for this purpose we employ the images of our saints, – that, when we show them, certain tainted influences issue therefrom which steal down into the chests of those who look at them, and therefore they need not be astonished if they afterwards find themselves assailed by the disease. The prominent and chief men of the country show us quite plainly that they do not share this belief, but nevertheless intimate that they fear some heedless fellow will commit some foul deed that will cause them to blush.[73]

Variations on the theme of this rumour asserted that 'Champlain had wished to ruin the country and drag it down to death with him,' or that 'the French had bewitched a cloak to cause their death.'[74] Actually, from the standpoint of those who believed in witchcraft, this was a logical interpretation of an epidemiological phenomenon that neither Amerindians or Europeans understood at the time. Current medical opinion holds that 'the wearing of European clothes was certainly a major vector of contagion, especially in cases of smallpox, where the virus remains active for as long as several months, even outside a living organism.'[75]

During trading at Trois-Rivières in 1637, one of the Huron chiefs offered his gifts to Bréhaut de l'Isle, the governor's lieutenant, accompanied by a speech that clearly demonstrated the mythical component of diplomatic and commercial relations:

'L'Isle' (it is thus these peoples call every thing, by its name, without other ceremony), 'you and your people are Okhi,' – that is to say, 'you are Demons, or extraordinary beings, and more than common men. Although our country is ruined, although pestilence and war are laying all waste, you attract us to you, making us surmount all sorts of difficulties to come and see you.' Then, showing us their presents, 'These tell but little; but then we are in small numbers, for they are all dying in our villages, and along the way; this does not prevent us from coming to confirm the peace and friendship which exists between us.'[76]

The French assured the Hurons of their friendship, denying that there was any foundation to the rumours and informing their trading partner of the existence of European epidemics. It was an ambiguous reply, nevertheless, as the French invited the Hurons to do as the missionaries did and pray to God 'to check these maladies.' Father Le Jeune then stepped forward.

Thereupon, [he wrote in the *Jesuit Relations*] I drew forth a beautiful picture of our Savior, Jesus Christ; I uncovered it, and placed it before their eyes. Then beginning to speak, I told them that we were not the masters of life and death; that he whose image they saw was [the] Son of the Almighty, – that he is good, that he loved men, that the demons who do so much harm were only his slaves. I said that when we offended this great Captain, son of God, either by stealing, or refusing to believe in and obey him, that he permitted the devils to afflict us; but that, when we had recourse to him, asking pardon for our offenses and promising to be faithful to him, he cured us of our ills and bound the hands of the evil spirits, so that they could no longer injure us.[77]

As their speeches show, both French and Hurons sought the origins of disease in the world of the supernatural. While the French declined all responsibility for the epidemics, they nevertheless stated that these diseases originated in their own pantheon (that is, in Christian devils), whereupon they put the ball squarely in the Huron court: you have only to believe in our God. What did this mode of speech convey to the Hurons? What did the Huron mode of speech convey to the French? Each side reacted in the light of what it considered the 'nature' of the other, and somehow the two sides established communication. The paradigm of this communication was to be seen in the lopsided nature of the balance of power between the two communities – biological power to begin with, as epidemics cut down Amerindians and spared Europeans; then economic power, involving the unequal development of production forces. Each side expressed the reality of the situation in symbolic language endowed with special meaning. The Hurons saw the French as formidable magicians. If they were capable of deploying such supernatural powers for the death of an inconsequential interpreter, what evil powers would they unleash if their missionaries were killed and/or the alliance broken? If the Algonkins threatened the Hurons, their allies and rivals, with French witchcraft, and if in turn the Hurons made the same threats to their allies and rivals, the Neutrals, it was because witchcraft inspired genuine fear. Consequently, the breaking of an alliance, with its implied defaulting on reciprocal gifts, would confer upon the French a horrifying, supernatural power of destruction.

The Process of Conversion

The faith must propagate itself as it has been planted, namely, in calamities.[78]

So true are those words, *Sanguis martyrum semen est Christianorum* – 'the blood of the Martyrs,' if they may be so named, 'is the seed and germ of Christians.'[79]

The missionaries had begun to baptize the dying as soon as they arrived in Huronia,[80] and, accordingly, the number of baptisms fluctuated with epidemics.[81] In 1638 only one family had converted to Christianity, but by the following year the Jesuits boasted 'fully 300 souls.'[82] Between 1639 and 1640 they baptized about a thousand people, although among them 'there [were] not twenty baptized ones out of danger of death.'[83] The year 1641 marked a turning point, however, for, despite much stricter standards in evaluating the genuine nature of professions of faith, the number of converts grew. The year 1642 saw 620 baptisms, with both men and women filling the chapels each morning.[84] 'The faith finds no distinction between the sexes,' noted the missionaries.[85]

Among the 250 Hurons of the bark flotilla that went down to Trois-Rivières in 1648, nearly half (120) were converts. They prayed twice a day and travelled together 'in the presence of the pagans.'[86] Between the *Jesuit Relations* of 1647 and that of 1648, the Jesuits baptized 'nearly thirteen hundred persons.'[87] Then came the final disaster, and conversions increased as Huron villages fell into the hands of the Iroquois. 'More than 1300 persons' were baptized between July 1648 and March 1649, and 'more than fourteen hundred' between March and August 1649.[88] 'Thus the Christian Church was increased by more than two thousand seven hundred souls in thirteen months, without counting those baptized at the Breach [the storming of the Huron villages], and those who were made Christians in other places.'[89]

For a time, the Jesuits had thought they would convert the Hurons by educating the offspring of sachem families and by systematically baptizing all children. However, such baptisms – often surreptitiously practised by means of a handkerchief or finger dipped in holy water – could not provide the foundation for a new, organized church.[90]

The Jesuits would have dearly liked to send a large number of Huron children to a residential school. This would not only win over children who might 'aspire to the highest positions'[91] in their native land; it would provide hostages to consolidate trade and ensure the safety of the French in Huronia. The Huron women always managed to scuttle such a project, however.[92] In 1636, only five of the twelve children destined for instruction at Quebec actually went. The venture was a fiasco: only two children displayed any pliancy, and these later died. The missionaries complained that the other three were incapable of submitting to the discipline of the

Jesuits. The young Hurons were taught how to perform 'neat courtesies' and greet 'our Frenchmen' by 'humbly ... touching their hats when meeting them.'[93] However, the three recalcitrants 'aimed at nothing but the enjoyment of their pleasures and the gratification of their senses.' They secretly got hold of 'a canoe-load of provisions ... and one fine morning they stole away, taking with them everything they could.'[94]

Efforts to educate Montagnais children were equally ill-fated. In 1636 the French governor reproached the Montagnais for refusing to entrust their children to the French, although they entrusted a certain number to Amerindian allies. To this the Montagnais sachem of Tadoussac replied:

> 'As to children, ... one does not see anything else but little Savages in the houses of the French; there are little boys there and little girls – what more do you want? I believe that some of these days you will be asking for our wives. You are continually asking us for our children, and you do not give yours; I do not know any family among us which keeps a Frenchman with it.' Monsieur the Governor, upon hearing this answer, said to me [Father Le Jeune], 'I do not know what a Roman Senator could have answered that would have been more appropriate to the subject under discussion.' I replied that in France our Savages were represented as far more obtuse than they are.[95]

By 1639 the Jesuits had virtually given up the idea of converting Huronia by teaching its children, and their seminary in Quebec was of no use in this respect. The Ursuline nuns of Quebec met with about as much success in their attempts to educate young Amerindian girls, although a few Montagnais families found it convenient to leave their daughters at the convent over the winter.[96] Several little girls were sent to France, where they were fashionable curiosities in aristocratic circles. Generally speaking, however, church authorities considered it impossible to 'train' the children.

> The freedom of the children in these countries is so great, and they prove so incapable of government and discipline, that, far from being able to hope for the conversion of the country through the instruction of the children, we must even despair of their instruction without the conversion of the parents. And consequently, all well considered, the first matter to which we should attend is the stability of the marriages

of our Christians, who give us children that may in good time be reared in the fear of God and of their parents. Behold the only means of furnishing the Seminaries with young plants.[97]

Such were the first in a series of repeated attempts at educating Amerindian children by both French and English throughout the seventeenth and eighteenth centuries. The results were always the same, and young Amerindians never adapted to the manners and discipline of European institutions. The reverse process – that is, the integration of young whites into Amerindian society – was usually successful.

The Jesuits' efforts prospered most in Ossossané, the principal village of the Attignawantans. In 1648, it outstripped all other villages in the number and zeal of its Christians,[98] and it therefore offers the best example for observing the process of conversion.

As mentioned earlier, the inhabitants of Ossossané had welcomed the missionaries with open arms from the beginning.[99] Initially, the missionary offensive consisted of merely baptizing 'children and elderly sick persons' as they lay dying.[100] The Amerindians did not consider baptism a sign of genuine conversion, but simply an additional ritual, accepted in a spirit of hospitality and tolerance. Even so, the missionaries did succeed in gaining a genuine convert – a thirty-five-year-old man named Chihwatenha, whom they christened Joseph. He seems to have been a fairly marginal individual, according to the Jesuits, although he was the nephew of a village chief.[101] 'He has been married since his youth, and has never had more than one wife, contrary to the ordinary practice of the Savages, who are accustomed at that age to change wives at almost every season of the year. He does not gamble, not even knowing how to handle the straws, which are the cards of the country. He does not use Tobacco, which is, as it were, the wine and the intoxication of the country ... He never indulged in the diabolical feasts.'[102]

The use of tobacco was actually more of a social activity than an individual habit. The surprising thing about Joseph Chihwatenha is his attitude of withdrawal and his refusal to join in play activities, factors that make him particularly marginal. The Jesuits interpreted these behavioural and personality traits according to their own logic, and believed them to be Christian ascetic values. In the context of two opposing value systems, that is, Amerindian tradition and Christian morality, it seemed that the exclusion from the first automatically implied inclusion in the other.

How much weight should we attach to this evidence? Might the Amerindian have hidden his true motives and adjusted his behaviour to meet the missionaries' expectations? This is not an implausible suggestion, considering that Joseph Chihwatenha was among the Huron traders going to Quebec.[103] He may have hoped to gain power and prestige by giving his allegiance to the missionaries, a goal he in fact achieved some years later.[104] One cannot help noticing his obsequious, servile attitude, quite at variance with the ways of his people,[105] or the fact that it worked to his advantage.

Joseph Chihwatenha turned his conversion to good account. If he visited his brother's home in a neighbouring village, for example, he would use his baptism as grounds for taking precedence over his older sibling, and treat him like a younger brother.[106] Moreover, conversion brought the privilege of accompanying missionaries on their travels to the Petuns and Neutrals.[107] Joseph played no political role in his community, yet there he was – the ambassador, the Amerindian herald of the Good Tidings who was nicknamed the 'Christian,' the spokesman and trusted agent of the Jesuits.[108] Joseph took it upon himself to interpret facts in a manner favourable to the missionaries. He informed Amerindians who 'maliciously complained that not one of the French had died during the contagion,' that the Frenchmen's remedy was 'to believe in him who made all; it only depends upon thee to avail thyself of this. We are under too great obligations to them for coming from so great a distance to give us the knowledge of this so salutary remedy, which, thank God, they have taught me; it is for me a great glory to believe the same as the French do.'[109]

Joseph Chihwatenha's response to his fellow Amerindians, who insisted on mutual respect of customs, is revealing. It indicates how the symbolic effects arising from the penetration of trade goods into the Amerindian community were employed for ideological ends – that is, to gain open recognition of the Roman Catholic faith.

> You are disheartened, my Brothers (he sometimes said to them), because the matters of your salvation that the French propose to you are new things, and customs of their own which overthrow ours. You tell them that every country has its own ways of doing things; that, as

you do not urge them to adopt ours, so you are surprised at their urging us to adopt theirs in this matter, and to acknowledge with them the same Creator of Heaven and of Earth, and the universal Lord of all things. I ask you, when at first you saw their hatchets and kettles, after having discovered that they were incomparably better and more convenient than our stone hatchets and our wooden and earthen vessels, did you reject their hatchets and kettles, because they were new things in your country, and because it was the custom of France to use them and not yours? Now if they urge us to believe what they believe, and to live conformably to this belief, we are under great obligations to them; for indeed, if what they say is true, as it is, we are the most miserable people in the world if we do not do as they tell us.[110]

Despite tensions, the Ossossané village council allowed the Jesuits to move about as they pleased. Although the missionaries aroused opposition, they also inspired respect because of their ability to write, their eloquence, confidence, courage, and, said the Amerindians, their aversion 'to all kinds of sensuality.'[111] Nevertheless, when the epidemic reappeared in 1639, most converts recanted, particularly as Christian dwellings were the most seriously affected.[112] The missionaries fled after an attempt on their lives.[113] Joseph Chihwatenha became the object of mounting hostility and was barred from council meetings by a shaman who undertook to free the land from pestilence. The ensuing failure demonstrated the powerlessness of traditional rituals,[114] a failure compounded by the fact that Joseph Chihwatenha, derisively nicknamed 'the Believer,'[115] journeyed to Quebec to trade[116] and got the best prices. Were traditional values outmoded in comparison to the values of the converts? Might not Joseph Chihwatenha, who was what we would now term acculturated,[117] be showing the way to acquire weapons and trade goods? The Hurons might well have asked themselves such questions, seeing how the once insignificant Joseph Chihwatenha had gained prestige. According to the Jesuits, 'This good man, until now, was not of much importance among those of his Tribe; but since he has become a Christian he has been looked upon in a very different light by the Captains themselves, and by the most influential men of his village, who have wished to employ him in public affairs.'[118]

Joseph Chihwatenha was killed in 1641, reportedly by the Iroquois.

His brother took his place and his daughter was entrusted to the Ursulines in Quebec. Half of his dwelling was turned into a chapel.[119]

After 1639 the Jesuits concentrated their efforts on converting council members, 'some Old Men, and the more prominent heads of families.'[120] The missionaries had remarked that 'one truly Christian Savage, who is zealous for the faith, accomplishes more among his people than do three Jesuits,'[121] and therefore felt that converting leaders would have a ripple effect. It is worth noting that the men generally won over the women and children.[122] The arguments given were the need to conform to the new morality and the desire to meet again in the afterlife. Nonetheless, their influence also indicated the growing power of men involved in trade over their wives and the community in general.

With an eye to winning over community leaders, the Jesuits tightened their grip on the sale of weapons and the price of trade goods. After 1642, the desire to own a firearm became a strong inducement to convert to Christianity. This was the year in which one Ahatsistari, reputed to be the bravest warrior of Huronia, was baptized. He had been asking for baptism for three years, but the Jesuits had hitherto refused because he could not 'make up his mind to abandon some Superstitious practices that are customary among the Infidels.'[123] Now at last he would be able to replace bow and arrow with firepower and confront the Iroquois on an equal footing. That same year, 'some Infidels, who were about to go to war ... began to think of their Souls as much as, if not more than, of their bodies.'[124] The following year, the missionaries wrote that 'the affairs of our Lord advance in proportion to the adversities which he sends us. Hardly could one find, hitherto, among our Christians two or three warriors; but, since the capture of that worthy Neophyte, named Eustache, the most valiant of all the Hurons, we have counted in a single band as many as twenty-two Believers – all men of courage, and mostly Captains or people of importance. The use of arquebuses, refused to the Infidels by Monsieur the Governor, and granted to the Christian Neophytes, is a powerful attraction to win them.'[125]

It is no surprise to find Jesuits succeeding in their efforts to convert the families and villages most involved in the fur trade, since the trading expeditions were what exposed the Hurons, more than anything else, to Iroquois guns. Ossossané was such a village. One of its traders went down to Quebec and had himself baptized there with great ceremony, even managing to have the governor stand as godfather.[126] However, although the Ossossané chapel was filled every day, the majority of the population and most of the sachems remained hostile to the new religion.[127] Yet despite the hostility, the Jesuits were soon able to write that 'among them it is now no longer a thing to be ashamed of to profess Christianity, to pray to God night and morning, even in the presence of infidels.'[128] The same phenomenon occurred in other villages where chiefs asked for baptism.[129]

Initially, the Jesuits' efforts at conversion had come up against the Hurons' fear of being separated from their relatives and ancestors in the other world. '"For my part, I have no desire to go to heaven," said one. "I have no acquaintances there."'[130] Dead relatives and friends had gone to the hunting and fishing grounds of the afterlife.[131] Once converts were sufficiently numerous, however, the process rapidly snowballed. The argument that had held people back now became an incentive to convert, and for some the fear of separation from their families was actually the prime reason.[132]

The year 1645 marked a watershed in Huronia. The following dialogue demonstrates the confrontation between converted and unconverted Huron chiefs. '"Then," said the Elders, "we must resign ourselves to seeing our Country ruined, since our chief Captains range themselves on the side of the Faith. How can we prevent this disorder?" "You are thinking of it too late," he replies; "you should have opposed the progress of the Faith before it had entered our hearts. Now it will reign there in spite of you; and it will be easier to tear our souls from our bodies than to remove from our minds the fear of Hell-fire, and the desire for the happiness that awaits us in Heaven."'[133]

The following year the Jesuits built a chapel in Ossossané, with a bell to mark the rhythm of the Christian day. The number and 'zeal' of the Christians grew, and 'three of the chief Captains and many persons of consideration, give an example by their lives that preaches more eloquently than our words.'[134]

By 1649 Ossossané was completely 'overthrown,' as the Hurons expressed it. They called it 'the Believing Village.'[135] Christians not only formed the majority and professed their faith publicly: they would not tolerate anything deemed pagan.[136]

The process of conversion may in part be accounted for by dependency and the multitude of constraints under which the Hurons lived. A firearm was worth a baptism, certainly, but this does not offer a satisfactory explanation of why a significant number of converts actually interiorized the new religion. Why, in the words of a converted chief to his peers, had the faith entered his heart?[137] What accounted for the proselytizing zeal of many converts?[138] Some of the answers can, it seems, be found by considering the question from two standpoints: one sociological, the other psychoanalytical.

In the first instance, might the blood of martyrs indeed be the seed of Christianity? In other words, might the sense of insecurity created by the accumulated disasters (epidemics and wars), as well as intensified labour, have provided fertile ground for Christian ideology? Since 1634, disease and war had been undermining native societies and endangering the whole of Amerindian civilization. The mechanisms for transmitting tradition had been dislocated and relations between tribes thrown into disarray. Furthermore, war had contributed to the displacement and marginalization of entire populations.[139] A closer look reveals that it was often the people who had lost or suffered most who were the most receptive to the evangelical message. In 1639, the missionaries reported nearly sixty converts in Ossossané, 'of whom many are Wenroronons from among those poor Strangers taking refuge in this country.'[140] This was a reference to a tribe of the Neutral confederacy that had been defeated by the Iroquois and forced to abandon its territory. Six hundred arrived in pitiable condition to seek refuge among the Hurons, who took them in.[141] Was there a connection between the rate of conversion at Ossossané and the number of refugees? There does seem to be a correlation between their presence and a willingness to welcome the missionaries.

In the same year, fathers Garnier and Jogues made their first journey to the Petuns. At this time all doors were closed to them through fear of witchcraft, except that of a 'stranger,' a former captive who had originally been a member of the 'nation which they call Atsistahronons, "Nation of fire."'[142] The fathers met with an equally frosty welcome on their first journey to the Neutrals in 1640-41, except for in one village where several Wenroronon refugees were lodged.[143] It would seem that the refugees, in other words the most deprived members of the community, were the most willing to listen to what the missionaries had to say. In earlier days refugees would have been integrated into the tribe. With the upheaval of traditional Huron values, however, integration was predominantly religious. In 1642, for example, when an Iroquois attack threatened to overthrow the country, even the unconverted Ossossané villagers asked the Jesuits to baptize everyone.[144] The seed of doubt was already sown. It would seem that recurrent epidemics, intensified warfare, and the process of Huronia's gradual strangulation created not only the material conditions, but the ideological base for conversion. In 1644 Father Lalemant wrote of the Hurons, 'As for the new Christians, their number has been much greater this year than in previous ones. Even the Infidels, who are humiliated and made more docile by affliction, seem to us to be less distant from God's Kingdom. Finally, the body of Christians, after heavy trials sent by Heaven, is becoming more considerable, and begins to be in the majority in some of the villages.'[145]

Also in 1644, Father Vimont described the Amerindians' general situation in more or less similar terms. 'Although there is not in the world a nation poorer than this one, nevertheless there is none prouder than they. When they were prosperous, we could hardly approach them; the French were dogs, and all that we preached them were fables. But since affliction has humiliated them, and necessity has made them more dependent upon the French, and has made them experience the effects of Christian charity, their eyes are opened; and they see more clearly than ever that there is no other Divinity than he whom we preach to them.'[146]

Several years later, in 1656, Father Chaumonot met some Hurons who had become Iroquois captives, about whom he had this to say: 'The Hurons of the Village of Contareia, who, because of their strong aversion to the Faith, never allowed themselves to be instructed, are already beginning to yield, lending an attentive ear to the Father's words. So true is it that *afflictio dat intellectum*.'[147]

Considering the degree to which Amerindian societies had become profoundly destabilized, could the traditional religious system have given meaning to the way of life their members were now facing? Dependency, tension, hierarchization, the establishment of a destructive relationship between man and nature, the crumbling of a civilization, dispossession – all these were realities that shook the old explanations of the world, engendering anomie (that is, the weakening of normative standards of conduct and belief) at the heart of Huron society, and what Pierre Bourdieu calls 'the expectation of a systematic message capable of

giving a unified meaning to life by offering its chosen recipients a consistent vision of the world and human existence, and by giving them the
means to integrate it systematically into their daily behaviour – a message therefore able to provide them with the justification to live as they
do, that is, in a defined social position.'[148]

Such an expectation can be divined from the changes taking place in
the Hurons' mythical universe. Thus, Aataentsic, the moon-mother goddess, changed herself into a vengeful goddess, sending fatal epidemics to
punish the Amerindians who for years had been waging war with
increasing frequency.[149] In the main, however, unlike Christianity, the
traditional systems of explanation could not, despite alterations, offer a
coherent vision of societies where oppression was the dominant factor.
The missionary offensive therefore took advantage (at least in the case of
the most deprived) of an ideological destabilization caused by the collapse of Amerindian societies. Pierre Bourdieu cites Max Weber on the
historical origin of religions, to the effect that all requests for salvation
are an expression of a 'need,' economic and social oppression being the
most important, but not the only instance of such a need.[150] It might be
said that, as of 1640, this request for salvation came as much from
within, instigated by the oppression to which Amerindians were subjected, as from without, in response to external pressure applied by the
missionaries. The missionaries' conversion strategies could not have succeeded without the Amerindians being socially predisposed to join the
faith. The evangelical message focused on themes of original sin, sins
committed, redemption, resignation (to hell on earth), and hope (for
heaven in the afterlife). It conformed to the world view then held by
many Amerindians who, as with all those who are 'disinherited by the
brutalities of society,' had developed an apocalyptic vision of history.[151]

Epidemics and wars marked the overturning of the Amerindian
world. The missionaries interpreted all the visible stigmata (disease and
suffering) as signs heralding 'divine election' and eternal bliss. In so
doing – that is, by promising 'posthumous subversion' of the social
order[152] – the missionaries forced the objective recognition that history
was irreversible and that European power had been legitimated. The
terms in which they spoke symbolically reinforced a world view where
subjugation was the norm, linked to 'the ethos of resignation and renun-
ciation instilled by the conditions of life.'[153] This meant legitimation of

the dependency of Amerindian societies and of the process whereby these societies were divided into classes. In fact, insofar as Amerindian societies were crumbling from within, the new religion was the answer both to those seeking compensation (the promise of salvation from suffering for the most deprived), and those seeking legitimation of the established order (the inculcation of a sense of dignity and rightful superiority among the dominant forces).[154]

The fur trade had changed the Hurons' manner of acquiring wealth. Sachems possessed the right to grant passage over trade routes and accorded these rights in exchange for gifts, as well as reserving for themselves a relatively large share of the trade goods. As it developed, the fur trade gave rise to an increasingly unequal acquisition of wealth, and fostered the appearance of a distinction between governed and governors, whereas they had previously been mingled in a collective 'we.'

> Formerly only worthy men were Captains, and so they were called *Enondecha*, the same name by which they call the Country, Nation, district, – as if a good Chief and the Country were one and the same thing. But today they do not pay so much attention to the selection of their captains; and so they no longer give them that name, although they still call them *atiwarontas, atiwanens, ondakhienhai*, 'big stones, the elders, the stay-at-homes.' However, those still hold, as I have said, the first rank as well in the special affairs of the Villages as of the whole Country, who are most highly esteemed and intellectually preëminent. Their relatives are like so many Lieutenants and Councilors.[155]

This dichotomy was not merely one of language; it reflected a socioeconomic reality. In 1636, for example, on the occasion of the great feast of the dead, the 'Old Men and the notables of the Country,' according to Father Brébeuf, 'took possession secretly of a considerable quantity' of beaver cloaks.[156] In 1644, the missionaries were congratulating themselves on having converted Barnabé Otsinonannhont, for 'this man has always been one of the leading personages of his tribe, on account of his birth (for they have their nobility here, as well as in France) and are as proud of it.'[157] Although the comparison is obviously exaggerated, it echoes another comment of 1648 about access to and symbolic value of curing rituals. 'When the prescription is given, the Captains of the village hold a council, as in a matter of public importance, and deliberate whether they will exert themselves for the patient. And, if there be a number of sick who are persons of note, it is impossible to conceive the ambition and intrigue displayed by their relatives and friends to obtain the preference for them, because the public cannot pay those honors to all.'[158]

Taken together, these comments are indicative of emerging class relations and clearly show that there was unequal access to material and symbolic goods. Hitherto, social relations within Huron society had been based on redistribution and sharing. With the advent of the fur trade, however, social relations based on redistribution developed at the expense of those based on sharing. We know that redistribution carries with it a specific tension, because it sets unequal acquisition against equal consumption. It is true that the function of many traditional rituals was to counteract unequal acquisition of wealth by guaranteeing redistribution of goods in the community. Should these redistribution mechanisms disappear, unequal consumption would follow, bringing with it new social relations – relations that had been latent from the beginning. The work of the missionaries helped create a framework for this new social relationship.

The missionaries urged the converts not to take part in the feast of the dead, curing rituals, banquets, and exchanges of goods organized in response to dreams.[159] For ideological and moral reasons, the Jesuits also asked the converts to live among themselves, apart from non-Christians. By doing this, the missionaries effectively severed the traditional bonds of solidarity within the community and cut converts off from the redistribution network. As 'the Feasts, which are the chief pleasure of the country, are so many sacrifices to the Devil,' all Christians had to shun them. This meant that those who were well off did not share their wealth, while for those without resources 'it requires a very ardent Faith to banish oneself from them.'[160] As can be seen, Christian precepts favoured the haves and penalized the have-nots. Moreover, some Amerindians quickly grasped the fact that Christianity cost them less and accordingly took advantage of it:

'The Demons,' said one of them, 'command us to do impossible things. They do not give us what is necessary for a feast, and they require us to make one. Sometimes they compel us, if we would avoid some great misfortune, to offer what we do not possess, and cannot get. Does not this show that they either trifle with us, or that they are pleased to see us miserable? But the God of the Christians commands them to do nothing that is impossible for them; and, if they fail, it is of their own will. It is by this,' he said, 'that I recognize that he alone is the Master of our lives, since he desires only our good.'[161]

Despite their special status, Christians could not easily escape the redistribution ceremonies. Any attempt to do so immediately led to charges of witchcraft by the unconverted,[162] charges that became more frequent after 1634.[163]

Christianity offered two concepts that legitimated such opting out. First, it introduced Amerindians to the idea that acts were private property, that is, the private concern of each individual: to each, in the afterlife, according to his or her works.[164] Then, on the symbolic level, it proposed the view of a world divided between the redeemed and the damned – a view expressed in terms of inclusion and exclusion, to which a social content could be easily added.[165] Christianity thus justified 'the big stones' in opting out of redistribution mechanisms, thereby legitimating inequality and privileged status. In fact, while the fur trade accentuated the relative importance of redistribution compared to reciprocity, the Christian religion effectively restricted redistribution of the social product.

In 1642, Father Jérôme Lalemant wrote that 'the grace of baptism works powerfully in a heart.'[166] Looking at individual behaviour, one is indeed struck by the profound effect of baptism, and the sometimes radical personality change in certain converts. Like the social structure, personality structure was equally affected by Christianity, and this made interiorization of the new religious values all the more effective. The new religion was thrust upon a society already in the process of destructuration – that is, the disintegration of social and cultural patterns of thought. This was aggravated by the society itself, and it touched individuals whose sense of security had been deeply shaken and whose personalities were undergoing a similar process. It was as though this religion were reprogramming and restructuring profoundly traumatized human beings. One cannot help drawing a parallel, hypothetically at least, with the methods of modern religious sects for converting individ-

uals who are either socially marginal or in a (temporary) state of psychological instability. We are familiar with the effects of personality restruc-
turation resulting from membership in an institution that provides the
double security of human and dogmatic support.

What stands out primarily is the intensity of religious practice.
Huron converts and the Christian Algonkins of Quebec and Miscou displayed an uncommon degree of zeal and fervour.[167] According to Marie
de l'Incarnation, it was beyond description.[168] The missionaries noted
that there was nothing half-hearted about the Amerindians' faith, and
neither cold nor ice nor distance could deter them.[169] The new Christians
were proselytizers as well, and despite all opposition worked ardently to
win over friends and relations. Often they had greater success than the
missionaries.[170]

The more active the converts, the more they opposed tradition; the
greater the aggressivity and hatred displayed by their traditionalist compatriots, the greater their own conviction about their role as 'public victims,' martyrs to the faith.[171] Their self-image as members of the chosen
few was strengthened by the many sufferings they were able to offer God
as a passport to heaven.[172] By implication, pleasure was forbidden in this
context of suffering. Take the case of the young girl who adopted a
melancholy air in public in order to avoid 'the licence which the young
men here assume ... "When I go anywhere" (she said), "I alter my appearance; I keep my eyes cast down, and my forehead wrinkled, and I try to
look sad so that no one is encouraged to accost me."'[173]

The new religion involved a highly negative self-image: that of the
sinner who must redeem himself or herself. The following reply by an
Attikamègue convert to Father Buteux offers convincing evidence of this:
'Question: "What thoughts hast thou about thyself?" Answer: "That I am
a dog, and less than a flea before God."'[174] The convert was afraid of himself, afraid of his thoughts and desires.[175]

In these circumstances, it comes as no surprise to find converts flog-
ging themselves to expiate their sins,[176] rolling in the snow to escape the
'infernal flames' of temptation,[177] or scorching themselves with live
coals.[178] It is true that traditional Huron civilization had forms of bodily
discipline and self-repressive behaviour. Children were trained from a
very young age, for example, to withstand the cold by being scantily
clad.[179] Hurons (and Amerindians in general) were very hardy in this

respect and always dressed less warmly than the French.[180] Boys were trained to hide their emotions. Men were expected to remain impassive in the face of pain or suffering,[181] to endure ritual fasting for a successful hunt, or to harden themselves to pain by applying brands to their bodies.[182] Such practices appear to have been the exception rather than the rule, however, and were intended to develop, rather than break down, bodily strength and resistance. Conversion, on the other hand, established conscious self-repression as a basic form of behaviour, accompanied by the massive introjection of the missionaries' directives.[183]

Guilt and self-conscious repression, combined with the ostentatious and proselytizing practice of their religion, epitomized the converts' behaviour. The evolution of the human animal to the human being (or *animal sapiens*) involves the conscious repression of basic instincts, beginning with a radical transformation of the original value system. According to Herbert Marcuse, this conversion of the pleasure principle to the reality principle can be defined as follows:[184]

FROM	TO
immediate satisfaction	delayed satisfaction
pleasure	restraint of pleasure
joy (play)	toil (work)
receptiveness	productiveness
absence of repression	security

Transformations within Huron society in the first half of the seventeenth century all resulted in the repression of the pleasure principle. Wars, disease, longer and more intensified labour, and finally the social division of labour, were all factors that brought new constraints and prepared the ground for establishing further controls that went beyond those traditionally required by Huron society. Christianity was to catalyze the need for an ideology and institutions to reinforce what Marcuse calls surplus repression. Theoretically, the inhibition of the pleasure principle in response to the imperatives of reality was aimed at guaranteeing greater individual security. The wars and epidemics that led to the disappearance of Huronia were accompanied by an observable inhibition of desire, a rise in surplus repression, and growing insecurity.

It is perhaps needless to add that constraints imposed in adulthood were not truly interiorized, the Huron super-ego having been formed in the context of the permissive upbringing characteristic of Amerindian civilizations.[185] However, the previously accepted instinctive tendencies were becoming increasingly incompatible with an ever more hostile reality. Although most constraints imposed on children were interiorized and belonged to the unconscious, among converts no prohibition imposed in adulthood could become an automatic, unconscious response. It could only give rise to a strong feeling of guilt accompanied by the need to adopt conspicuous forms of religious practice.

The concentration of religious capital in the hands of the missionaries brought about the correlative dispossession of the converted. The missionaries' conversion strategy aimed at removing the Amerindian's entire identity, so that 'being oneself' gave way to identification with another, to 'being like.'[186] The religious specialist's view of the convert established his or her identity. It was a view that both structured and destructured the personality. Unable to escape the eye of their religious mentors, the most credulous converts lived a life of pretence, mimicking the desired behaviour. They wore a mask and played a part. What the missionaries had once condemned, they now praised. Behaviour previously considered pagan was no longer associated with witchcraft. Thus the application of live brands to the body became a Christian purification practice – an act that, by the same token, embodied the recognition and legitimation of the missionary. Indeed, the influence of spells, associated with the privilege of being Christian, was now publicly recognized.

The Social Impact of Christianity

Previously, all social relationships in Huron society had been structured by the kinship system. Now, however, a new type of social relationship was developing outside kinship links.[187] Huron society already had some social relationships not based on kinship, such as shaman groupings for medical purposes, but these always fitted in harmoniously with the kinship system. Such was not the case with the type of social relationship produced by the combined effects of the fur trade and Christianity: that is, dominant/dominated or rich/poor. Equally discordant was the new social bipolarization between Christians and non-Christians. In its specific historic form, Christianity was incompatible with the Hurons' old social structure. A shift took place at the expense of kinship relationships. From 1640 on, the convert/traditionalist or Christian/non-

Christian polarity undermined Huron society. This meant that an antagonistic relationship had taken hold *within* Huron society, polarizing it into two camps at the very moment when another, exterior, antagonistic relationship – the war between the Huron and Iroquois confederacies – had reached its climax. Briefly put, the social impact of Christianity was not only a determining factor in the slow emergence of an initial class relationship within Huron society, but went far beyond this, as we shall see.

In order to entrench their authority, the Jesuits had to win over Hurons who recognized them as the sole custodians of religious power. Such converts were continually exposed to questions, jeers,[188] aggressive behaviour, and death threats.[189] The Jesuits therefore deemed it necessary to remove their converts from the influence of their fellows and to create conditions favourable to a new, Christian identity focus, thereby severing the traditional relationships of solidarity. Christians fraternized with one another and abstained as much as possible from taking part in the social activities of their village. When travelling, they stayed with other Christians rather than with clan relatives. If the men were setting off for Trois-Rivières, the Christians among them would form a separate group and use the same canoes, thus distinguishing themselves from the 'infidels.'[190] This exclusiveness was further emphasized by the fact that non-Christians were given lower prices for their furs. In everyday life, the distinction was marked by a whole range of symbolic acts, such as wearing a rosary around the neck[191] or placing small crosses in the corn fields.[192] Converts tended to substitute a new identity for the old, creating a breach in the traditional frontiers of Huron group identity – the collective 'we.' Christianity became the pole of fraternity. The old rules of solidarity were shaken: once a Huron was baptized, yesterday's enemy became today's brother, whereas the infidel – the brother of yesterday and member of the same tribe – became the enemy.[193] This phenomenon was explicit in the behaviour of Charles Tsondatsaa, an Ossossoné convert. He had lost a brother in an Iroquois raid during a trading expedition to Trois-Rivières. He sought consolation, not with the Hurons, but with his Christian brothers whose language he did not speak.[194] Similarly, in 1641 a Huron chief defined himself as being French and a convert, thus signifying his rejection of Huronia as his principal pole of identity. The Huron traditionalists spurned him as a result, and retorted, 'Go then, thou Frenchman, that is right, go away into thine own country.

Embark in the Ships, since thou art a Frenchman; cross the sea, and go to thine own land; thou hast for too long a time caused us to die here.'[195]

The Jesuits always gave Christian names to their converts, as well as French and Christian names to places. Ossossané became La Rochelle; Taenhatentaron, Saint-Ignace; Gahouendoe, Saint-Joseph; and so on.[196] These name changes symbolized dispossession of a tradition, an adherence, and an identity. The Jesuits, aspiring to exclusive religious control, had appropriated the power of naming.

This attack on traditional religion inevitably led to cultural erosion. Huron religion permeated every facet of existence, contrary to the view held by the first Jesuits,[197] who found no official creed or religious institution among the Hurons. As with all religions, it responded to existential angst, but in this case the response took forms that were specific to, and consistent with, an egalitarian, horticultural society (originally a society of hunter-gatherers). It provided an integrated system of appropriate beliefs and practices for interpreting dreams and the omens for a good hunt,[198] bringing rain, curing the sick,[199] or holding feasts. The Jesuits changed their views within a few years of their arrival, however, realizing the deep-rooted nature of the Huron religion. In their efforts to impose a Judeo-Christian creed based on original sin and the desire for redemption, they introduced an alien tradition[200] that had developed with the emergence of towns and social classes in the Middle East. Actually, the universal factor in all this was not the Jesuits' message, but the market economy that led the missionaries from the ports of France to the shores of Lake Huron. By subordinating Amerindian societies to the laws of accumulation of capital on a world scale, the market economy created economic and social conditions (subordination, destabilization, and anomie) that prepared these societies to receive the Christian message.

For converts, the immediate effect of conversion was to sever their ties with tradition and to reject their origins. The Huron elders held regular meetings at which they customarily recounted tales and myths handed down from their ancestors, 'so that the young people, who are present and hear them, may preserve the memory thereof, and relate them in their turn, when they shall have become old.' But in the winter of 1645, when an old Christian came to recount the creation myth, he began to tell it in Christian terms instead of Huron, speaking of angels, demons, and the Creator. The oldest chief immediately told him to be quiet, saying he was 'wrong to relate the stories of the French, and not those of the Hurons.' Instead, he himself would 'relate the pure truth, and how it has happened that the earth, which was submerged in the waters, has been pushed out of them by a certain Tortoise of prodigious size, which sustains it and which serves it for support.'[201] Huron converts became dependent on a clergy that held the monopoly on another tradition. Some stated they were more attached to the missionaries than to 'My Country' or kin.[202] Converts gradually relinquished their religious capital to a specialist, in this case, the missionary. From then on, the 'salvation' of the convert depended on the priest's absolution.[203] It is therefore not surprising that converts who had drunk brandy would wish to be punished by the priest. One Huron convert gave spontaneous expression to his dispossession with the remark, 'You my Father, who decide upon prayers and upon faults, order some needful remedy for bringing back sense to this girl.'[204] Three years later, it was not just one man, but a whole council (the Ossossané village council where converts were now in the majority)[205] that divested itself of authority in favour of the Jesuits.

> At the beginning of the Winter, these good Neophytes assembled a general Council, in order to confer upon means of strengthening the Faith among them. Their conclusion was that it was necessary to apply to the Father who was in charge of that Mission, that he might cut off, in their customs, those which are contrary to the Faith; that he should correct in others, unimportant in themselves, all evil which might in any way corrupt the use of them; and that they would obey him in every point, and would regard him as bearing the word of God, – and, hereafter, as the chief of their Captains. The best is, that they have kept their word in that; and that in the slightest doubts which could arise, the Captains themselves came to the Father to receive and execute his orders.[206]

This Christian majority not only abstained from traditional Huron rituals, but succeeded in preventing them from taking place.[207] In this way, the people of Ossossané, the principal village of the Attignawantans, were dispossessed of their powers for the benefit of a new clergy. Everything that constituted the Huron identity was forbidden. The great Huron democracy was dying.

The importance of celebrations in the Huron culture is well known. They were the occasion for dancing, feasting, exchanging gifts, and hold-

ing carnivals and games. Equally well known is the importance accorded
the body. The Hurons respected keenness in the five senses and the
search for sensual pleasure. They painted their bodies and paid careful
attention to dreams. The Jesuits, however, did not develop a philosophy
of cultural relativism in this respect, despite the fact that they recorded
an enormous number of cultural differences between Amerindian civilization and their own. 'Verily, God alone is constant; he alone is
unchangeable; he alone varies not, and to him we must hold fast, to
avoid change and inconstancy.'[208] They therefore saw in Huron mores the
omnipresent influence of Satan. Furthermore, such mores – apart from
their 'scandalous' and unacceptable nature in terms of Christian morality – inevitably awakened all the impulses that the missionaries themselves had been obliged to repress and sublimate. Indeed, their writings
reveal an association of words and images strongly indicative of the
dichotomy between Faith and Nature in the Jesuit view:

> With them, to conquer one's passions is considered a great joke, while
> to give free rein to the senses is a lofty Philosophy. The Law of our
> Lord is far removed from this dissoluteness; it gives us boundaries and
> prescribes limits, outside of which we cannot step without offending
> God and reason. Now it is very hard to place this yoke, although it is
> very mild and easy, upon the necks of people who make a profession of
> not submitting to anything, either in heaven or upon earth.[209]

> Their minds, for the most part, are weak in the extreme in conceiving
> and apprehending things that they do not see, and in sustaining them-
> selves in these attacks, by the spirit of the faith, in the hope of the
> future. And their hearts seem incapable of resisting the assaults of the
> affection of corrupted nature for kindred, and for the comforts and
> conveniences of this life, in which so long they have placed their
> supreme good.[210]

> René counts as many as eleven dead in his cabin; the good Anne sees
> herself robbed of all her children, the sole support of her old age, –
> whereas minds rebellious against God, and those which have always
> leagued themselves against the faith, boast to see their whole family in
> health, and that, in spite of heaven, they are happy in this world.[211]

But what has most delighted me is to see that the sentiments of the

Faith have so far entered these hearts, which we formerly called Barbarian, that I may truthfully say that grace has stifled in many of them the fears, the desires, the joys, and the feelings of Nature.[212]

The murderers of the Preachers of the Gospel – those ravenous wolves that had vented their fury on the fold of Jesus Christ with greater rage and more atrocious tortures than any Nero or Diocletian – now embrace our holy Religion with more fervor than those whom they have exterminated, and assume the yoke of the same faith of which they were, some years ago, the Oppressors.[213]

If we put the oppositional words and key images in separate columns, we get the following:

FAITH	NATURE
conquer	passions
law	senses
boundaries	free rein
limits	dissoluteness
prescribes	
yoke	
limits	not submitting
sustaining themselves in these attacks	minds ... weak
in the hope of the future	comforts and conveniences of life
resisting the assaults	corrupted nature
the good Anne robbed	minds rebellious
	leagued against
	boast
	in health
	happy in this world
truthfully	barbarian
grace	fears
	desires
	joys
	feelings

preachers	murderers
fold	ravenous wolves
holy religion	rage
yoke	fury
	atrocious tortures
	oppressors

The repressive nature of the new religion is apparent in all these opposites: self-control/desire, constraint/freedom, deferred pleasure/present pleasure, resignation/group resistance, stifle/listen, reason/emotion. Faith is associated with truth, saintliness, goodness, and the fold or chosen of God, whereas nature evokes images of rebellion, pride, barbarity, murder, savagery, oppression, and horrible torture. Christianity, as presented to seventeenth-century Hurons, built up an objective ideology of surplus repression. It introduced a whole series of new constraints that would previously have had no purpose. This phenomenon was not entirely due to the missionary offensive, however. Additional controls were in fact required for the transition from an egalitarian, independent society to one that was stratified and dependent. Whereas Hurons had previously worked at a comfortable rate in an economy geared to the satisfaction of needs, now they had to work at an accelerated pace in an economy with a goal (worldwide accumulation of capital) that escaped them. Poverty, war, and disease were everywhere. In this context, adherence to Christianity was for some the bitter pill to be swallowed in adapting to an overwhelming present and the disintegration of the fairly unrepressive, matrilinear society of tradition.[214] Adherence brought a sense of guilt, accompanied by self-repression and rejection of pleasure.

Carnivals, the feast of fools (ononharoia),[215] dancing and feasting, and all such rejoicing was denounced by the Jesuits. They did so, not only because they viewed these as communications with the devil – a phenomenon they saw everywhere – but because the celebration of the feast itself disgusted them. A convert stated that he had 'abandoned all the dances, wherein you know what power I had. I afterward deprived myself of attending most of the feasts of the Country. If any woman were to accost me now, she would receive nothing but blows.'[216]

Among the Hurons, almost all rituals were the occasion for feasting.[217] Take, for example, the March fishing ritual of Algonkin origin, which consecrated the marriage of the spirit of the fishing net to two little girls of four or five. In 1639, the missionaries advised the Christian parents of a little girl chosen for this ritual to refuse, 'but lo, there ensued a grievance. For, as the whole family profit considerably from such a marriage, – part of the fish caught reverting to them in the year when it takes place, and being then due and appropriated to them, in consideration of such an alliance, – to refuse their consent to such a marriage is to deprive and defraud an entire family of the greatest pleasure and the best opportunity that can be found in the country.'[218]

Traditionally, sexuality in Huronia was not relegated merely to the *sexuality* function of reproduction. Sensual pleasure was clearly a factor in the sexual freedom of young people, the free choice of spouses, and the place accorded sexuality in festivals and carnivals. In many rituals, especially the *andacwander* ceremonies, sexuality clearly fulfilled the function of bringing comfort and solidarity. It was also manifest in what Herbert Marcuse calls the eroticizing of the body, in this case through body painting (for converts flagellation would be the substitute),[219] and the importance attached to the 'proximity senses' (smell, taste, touch).[220] The missionaries strove to 'de-eroticize' social relationships and to channel sexuality into reproductive goals within the monogamous and patriarchal unit.

The Jesuits had no particular need to interfere with the Hurons on the score of modesty. It was rather the Algonkian Ottawas, who went about naked all summer long, that aroused their scandalized disapproval.[221] The missionaries were nevertheless shocked by the habitual nakedness of Huron children, the women's scanty clothing, and what they considered the immodesty of undressing before people of the same sex.[222]

In attempting to inculcate sexual repression, the missionaries also taught submission to authority.[223] This encouraged the development of class relations and a hierarchical social structure. However, replacing the clan organization with the monogamous family unit had a profoundly disruptive effect on Huron society. The clan was the keystone of the social structure: housing units, the election of sachems, redistribution, and the rules governing solidarity, mutual aid, and hospitality were all based on the clan. Insofar as kinship formed the backbone of social relations, to undermine the existing form of marriage amounted to disrupting the society as a whole. Furthermore, prohibiting divorce meant forbidding all sexual relations following separation. Then how was marriage between Christian and pagan possible? Such was the anxiety expressed by a convert, who feared his spouse would leave him if she did not also submit to the new restraints:

> One day, in speaking with his companion upon the indissolubility of marriage, when he observed the great difficulties in regard to this among the people of his nation, he showed himself much concerned thereat. 'For we shall either marry, or we shall not,' said he. 'If we take a wife, at the first whim that seizes her, she will at once leave us; and then we are reduced to a wretched life, seeing that it is the women in our country who sow, plant, and cultivate the land, and prepare food for their husbands. To forego marriage among the Hurons is something which requires a chastity our country has never known. What shall we do then? As for me,' said this worthy young man, 'I will never take a Huron woman, if I do not see in her extraordinary constancy; I will try to find a French woman. If I am refused, I am resolved to live and die in chastity.'[224]

Jesuits urged Christians to marry among themselves,[225] so that the tenets of Roman Catholic conjugal morality would be respected. The aim and effect of this was to eliminate conflict between two irreconcilable concepts of marriage. Since Huron society accepted divorce initiated by women, and because 'the Church has in this case no sword'[226] – that is, because the church could not yet rely on repressive institutions to impose its values in Huronia – the Jesuits used economic means to reduce the number of divorces among converts. They obtained gifts from the readers of the *Jesuit Relations* in order to assist converted couples economically,[227] since the principal reason for divorce was the husband's inability as a provider. Nevertheless, according to the Jesuits, divorce and 'dreams' were the main obstacles to conversion[228] – witness the case of a woman who refused baptism in order to keep her right to divorce.[229] In fact, the Jesuits were attempting to dispossess the Hurons of the Amerindian sexual code in order to impose their own. Prior to 1630, Frenchmen living in Huronia were free to marry Huron women, in accordance with local custom. In 1637, Father Brébeuf asked a sachem to hold a council meeting to debate, among other things, the question of marriages between Frenchmen and Huron women. In the ensuing discussion, the sachem stated that

> concerning the marriages, it was not necessary to go through so many
> ceremonies, that those Frenchmen who had resolved to marry were
> free to take wives where it seemed good to them; that those who had
> married in the past had not demanded a general council for that pur-
> pose, but that they had taken them in whatever way they had desired.
> The Father replied to this that it was very true that the Frenchmen who
> had hitherto married in the country had not made such a stir about it,
> but also that their intentions were far removed from ours, that their
> purpose had been to become barbarians, and to render themselves
> exactly like them. He said that we, on the contrary, aimed by this
> alliance to make them like us, to give them the knowledge of the true
> God, and to teach them to keep his holy commandments, and that the
> marriages of which we were speaking were to be stable and perpetual;
> and he laid before them all the other advantages they would derive
> therefrom. These brutal minds gave but little heed to the spiritual con-
> siderations; the temporal were more to their taste, and of these they
> wished to have very definite assurances.[230]

As I emphasized earlier, a new social relation had been set in place
alongside the old kinship system. Although parallel, the two were incompatible and placed converts and traditionalists in opposition to one
another.

The Jesuits took a firm stand against sexual freedom among Hurons
in general, and among young people in particular. The traditionalists, on
the other hand, considered the new restrictions an aberration, and
incited young girls to seduce Christian youths.[231] They ridiculed the converts' aversion to sex[232] and their fear of women:[233]

> From that time, this new Christian has had many violent attacks.
> Frequent attempts have been made to draw him into the superstitions
> of the Country, but he has always resisted. So far, even, have these
> efforts gone, that when one of his sons fell ill, and when he refused ever
> to allow recourse to be had, in his Cabin, to such diabolical remedies,
> his wife left him, carried the child away from him, and took another
> husband. His chastity was exposed to equally violent assaults. In a

Country where women and girls have nothing to restrain them; where the modesty which nature has given them as a protection for their sex passes for a disgrace; where for honor's sake they are compelled to dishonor themselves; it is very difficult for a young Man who has been engaged in such affairs all his life, to parry these blows when he wishes to effect a retreat. But the fear of God was his sole defense. In vain did they solicit him; he refused presents, and trembled with fear, as he had said, when he fled from the danger of losing what Faith alone had taught him to cherish above pleasure and above life. 'I walk through the village,' he has sometimes said, speaking even to Infidels, 'as in an enemy's country. I dread meeting women as I would an Iroquois. Even an enemy would cause me less fear, for I can look at him boldly; but I dare not lift my eyes when a Woman approaches me.'[234]

Sexual freedom acted as a kind of social cement, bonding men and women of the same community. It was linked to the rules of hospitality, and also to relations between men and women of allied tribes.[235] Once conversion began, two networks of sexual exchange coexisted: the Christian network, inflexible and restrictive, and the traditional network, open and relatively free. Not only did Christians refuse to participate in community rituals that included sexual activity;[236] they denied themselves all sexual contact and/or marriage with the unconverted.[237]

The recognition and respect accorded desire was one trait of Huron and northeastern Amerindian civilization that literally horrified the missionaries. It was expressed in many forms – both in ritual and daily life. To begin with, it could be seen in the rearing of children, where love and attention were more important than discipline. Of the love of fathers for their children, Sagard wrote, 'But I can assure you yet again that they hold them [children] so dear, & make such a fuss about them that they have no judgment in the matter, but give them all the freedom they want and never discipline them for any fault, for punishment is a thing they never mention.'[238] This observer also associated the non-repressive education of children with freedom: 'There is no punishment for any fault whatsoever; this is why everyone lives in freedom, and each does as he desires.'[239]

By introducing notions of sin and guilt, repression of desires, and bodily self-control, Christianity applied an education model that was clearly more repressive than the Amerindian tradition. Surplus repression affected child-rearing in the way missionaries wanted.[240] Inevitably, converts projected their self-repressive behaviour onto their children. Converted mothers would take their children to watch beatings of converts who had decided to expiate their sin (alcohol consumption) publicly. 'The women showed this sight to their children. "How now?" said they, "will you be naughty? will you ever lie? See how they treat the disobedient."'[241]

According to custom, Hurons could change their names at different *names* stages of life – childhood, adolescence, adulthood, and old age – according to how they wished to be identified, or even according to their fantasies.[242] A man might take the name of a deceased relative or friend and assume all that person's family responsibilities. The dead man's wife and children would henceforth consider the bearer of his name as spouse and father. The same behaviour occurred in cases of adoption: 'Mothers or other relatives who love a son, or a daughter, or any of their kindred, cause such persons to be resuscitated, through a desire to see them close by them, transferring the affection that they felt for the deceased to the persons who take their names. This ceremony takes place at a solemn feast in the presence of many guests.'[243] Converts broke with tradition in renouncing their Huron given names for Christian ones – a phenomenon that held true for their children as well. In this way the convert gave up the power to name himself, and the choice of names would henceforth be based on models from an alien tradition.

'Belief in dreams is incompatible with the Faith,'[244] said the mission- *dreams* aries. Hurons paid close attention to dreams, recounting them and trying to interpret their meaning so as to determine future behaviour.[245] Dreams were also a guarantee of the legitimacy of desires. When it came to curing the sick, the wish to satisfy desires took on a truly psychotherapeutic function. The sick man or woman expressed what the Hurons called *ondinonc*,[246] that is, all his or her desires, whatever their nature, for gifts, feasts, dances, the *andacwander*, and so on. The sachems would then inform the people of the village, who would all try to find the means of fulfilling the sick person's wishes. The *Jesuit Relations* of 1639 gives a detailed account of one of these ceremonies.[247]

In this case, a woman said she had had a dream in which she saw the moon bearing down upon her while she held her small daughter in her arms. The moon seemed to be a tall and beautiful lady holding a little

girl resembling the dreamer's. The lady ordered the woman to ask for
presents and to clothe herself in fire. 'This poor creature returned to her
cabin, and no sooner had she reached it than behold her prostrated with
a giddiness in the head and a contraction of the muscles.'[248] She asked
that a celebration be held for her. The council met and decided to give
her what she asked. Some thirty dancing and chanting people carried the
woman, dressed entirely in red, to the feast. The principal sachem made
a speech asking the Jesuits to show discretion. The sick woman then
requested 'that they should send her two men and two girls arrayed in
robes and collars of such and such a fashion, with certain fish and presents in their hands, – and this, in order to learn from her own lips her
desires and what was necessary for her recovery. No sooner proposed,
than executed.'[249] She asked for twenty-two gifts, including a blue blanket
belonging to a Frenchman. The chiefs asked everyone to satisfy the sick
person's desires, and they all complied – except for the Jesuits, who
refused to obey Satan. The gifts were taken to the sick woman, and that
evening she visited the hearths of all the longhouses. She had asked that
the fires be 'as large and bright as possible,'[250] and proceeded to walk
through the middle of them. That night a carnival took place, accompanied by body-painting, masquerades, and generally free behaviour, 'the
point being that, the more noise and uproar one makes, the more relief
the sick person will experience.'[251] Next morning everyone went the rounds
of the hearths visited by the sick woman and told of his or her desires as
revealed in dreams. Everyone tried to interpret these dreams, and as soon
as some enigma was resolved, the joyful event was marked with noise-
making. The carnival and guessing games lasted three days. On the final
day, the sick woman again made the rounds of the longhouses to announce
her 'last and principal desire.' Those who accompanied her wore sad and
afflicted expressions. The sick woman told of 'her troubles in a plaintive
and languishing voice ... Those who are attending the sick woman collect
all these things and go out burdened with kettles, pots, skins, robes,
blankets, cloaks, necklaces, belts, leggings, shoes, corn, fish, – in short,
everything that is used by the Savages, and which they have been able to
think of, to attain the satisfaction of the sick woman's desire.'[252]

General rejoicing followed the resolution of the sick person's
enigma. After the patient had made a third tour of the longhouses, a
council was held to take stock; although comforted, the sick woman was

unfortunately not completely cured, a circumstance explained by the fact that the Jesuits had refused to give a woollen blanket.[253]

The missionaries considered dreams to be absolute nonsense and the temptations of Satan. They would not hear of converts giving them any credence. However, in doing as the Jesuits wished, the converts placed themselves on the horns of a dilemma: to ignore the dream was to run the risk of some misfortune, while to take account of it was to fall into Satan's clutches.[254]

The new diseases and pandemics carried off a significant portion of Huron society and undermined the collective confidence. As we have seen, disease not only struck relentlessly, but traditional medicine was plainly powerless to deal with it. In this context, the presence of the missionaries made the Hurons feel doubly insecure. Were they not the most terrible of sorcerers? Disease went wherever the missionaries travelled, but they themselves did not succumb, a circumstance that both attracted and repelled the Amerindians.

Initially, the Hurons called simultaneously on the old medicine and that of the black-robed sorcerers for help, but it soon became clear that the latter intended to exercise a monopoly in this matter. The missionaries opposed all the old rituals, which in their view were defiled by Satanic practices. This led to the medical (and religious) practices of the two camps becoming competitive rather than complementary. Disease was now a far greater calamity, for instead of being the occasion for providing support and security, and granting the patient's wishes, disease itself became a source of individual and social tension.

It would have been impossible to amalgamate the two traditions, because the attitude toward disease in each civilization was diametrically opposed. Differences in caring for the sick were especially significant in this regard. The Amerindians surrounded the patient with a continual round of dancing, music, raucous noise, and visits, whereas the Jesuits insisted on isolation, silence, decorum, and reserve, leading to a sense of alienation. The Amerindians stuffed their sick with food, whereas the Jesuit fathers gave them clear soups. Instead of pure water and meat, the Jesuits gave wine and light, seasoned foods. Basically, the Amerindians considered that unsatisfied desires were the cause of disease. The solution was therefore to satisfy the desires of all senses in profusion. The missionaries, on the other hand, considered that disease was caused by this very attention to desires. One was sick from having had too much, and so less must be given, the patient must be deprived. This view of illness had its roots in two dichotomies: pagan/Christian (with paganism denoting sin and the supremacy of the body), and barbarity/civilization. At a deeper level, it was a conflict of nature against culture. This was why the Jesuits cared for their patients with the remedies of the civilized, Christian world: baptism, sugar and dried fruits from Europe, imported spices, all aimed at the soul rather than the body.[255]

First let us look at the individual tension created by this dichotomy. Which tradition should one adhere to? In Ossossoné, a sixty-year-old convert named René Tsondihouane had a dream in his youth 'in which he was forbidden ever to make a dog feast, or to permit that any one should make one for him, or else misfortune would happen to him.' He had never taken part in such a feast until just after his conversion. He was visiting a friend in another village. The friend offered him a dog feast. 'He immediately remembered his dream; nevertheless, thinking at the same time that he was a Christian and that his dreams ought no longer to be important to him, he accepted the feast. He had no sooner returned to his house than he found one of his daughters and one of his sons sick, who afterward died. This stroke unsettled him, and caused him to make a false step ... but having recovered from his fall at the end of a few days ... here is an occasion upon which he wholly repaired the error of his fall by the firmness of his faith.'[256]

What was the sin here? To have abjured the Roman Catholic religion or to have denied his traditions? Either way, René Tsondihouane felt guilty: guilty of the death of near relatives for having rejected his traditions, and equally guilty for not having withstood the test and for having abjured his faith.

In Ossossoné a two-day curing ritual was held during the winter of 1641-42. It had no effect, and the shaman in charge complained about the Christians who did not participate in 'such a public feast.' The Christians were in the minority at this time, but scrupulously respected the Jesuits' veto of 'these diabolical superstitions.' A council was held to discuss an affair deemed important, and three sachems were sent to the home of Charles Tsondatsaa, the leader of the Christians, to invite the latter to participate. Tsondatsaa called the emissaries slaves of Satan and categorically declined all participation. One of the sachems was insistent:

'My brother,' said he, 'I do not come here alone, or of my own accord. The Council has sent us to say a word to thee, but I dare not speak. No, it is not I who speak, but all the Cabins. Hast thou seen that sick woman who languishes? She is exhausted, and her voice has but strength enough to say to thee: "Tsondatsaa, have pity on me!" All the People have striven for her during the past two days, but our remedies are without effect, not being animated by thy voice. Such a one desires that thou shouldst be the one to preside with him at the ceremony. Do not refuse the People that favor, for a single day.'[257]

'Death before sin,' was Charles Tsondatsaa's terse answer. Tempers began to flare. 'At the same time, a Captain, more impetuous than they, had entered the Cabin of some other Christians. Addressing the youngest, he said to him in a fiendish voice, "My nephew, make a truce for one day with the Faith. Our Country is going to ruin; the sick are dying. Whither can we flee to avoid death? Why do you keep away from our dances? Why do you refuse to do this act of kindness to the People? It is the Christians who kill us, since they will not help us."'[258] The conflict spread beyond the longhouse to the whole village. The Jesuits noted that there was not a single dwelling in which a Christian lived that did not prove that the Faith was stronger than the power of all the 'captains.'[259]

In the summer, Charles Tsondatsaa went down to Quebec where he managed to be baptized. Governor Montmagny was his godfather. When he returned to his village, one of his nieces fell ill. 'It is rumored that this illness is of the sort caused by a certain Demon, who is never appeased until homage has been paid to him in a dance, of which this new Christian had been the Leader before he was baptized. "But," said he, "let her die, rather than that I should have recourse to the assistance of a sworn enemy of God."'[260] The Amerindians were shocked by this refusal of a gift, but that was not all. 'The Savages know not what it is to refuse what another has dreamed ought to be done for his health.'[261] Furthermore, this refusal was evidence of the profound social division that grew up around Christianity. From now on, Christians and traditionalists would each have their own rituals. By taking the converts into their Sainte-Marie hospital,[262] the Jesuits managed to detach their flock from traditional medicine. The same thing occurred for other rituals, such as those for the sick or for procuring good harvests.[263]

Peace of mind, sympathy, mutual aid, and solidarity provided support for the sick person under the traditional system. With the onset of
Christianity, illness brought tension, anomie, and rejection. Instead of
being listened to, the patient was treated to a sermon, and a terrifying
one at that. Heaven and hell were the central themes.[264] According to the
Jesuits, the torments of hell were comparable to the most excruciating
tortures inflicted on captives, with this difference: hell was for eternity.
The comparison was a telling one, for the Hurons knew all about torture. The missionary offensive was achieving results: why would parents
condemn their dying children to eternal fire when the Jesuits could make
them angels in heaven? Harassed on their deathbeds, several adults
agreed to baptism, knowing they could recant if they recovered. Not all
gave in to this form of blackmail, however.

> Finally, there are some hearts so hardened in their impiety, that,
> although they are unable to resist the truth of what they acknowledge,
> instead of submitting to God, they become furious, and refuse to listen
> to what they would be very glad not to fear. 'If thou wishest to speak to
> me of Hell,' they sometimes say, 'go out of my Cabin at once. Such
> thoughts disturb my rest, and cause me uneasiness amid my pleasures.'
> 'I see very well that there is a God,' another will say; 'but I cannot
> endure that he should punish our crimes.' A certain man, who one day
> found himself pressed too hard, said to him who came to instruct him:
> 'I am content to be damned,' while dealing him a blow with a knife,
> which, however, merely cut his cassock. In another Village, a woman
> who would not listen to God's word, and had closed her ears, threw
> live coals in the face of one of our Fathers who spoke to her, calling out
> that she became crazy when she heard his discourse. 'No,' said an
> impious man, whose relatives had seized him when he tried to kill one
> of our Fathers, who had gone into his Cabin to hear the Confession of
> a sick woman, – 'no, I will not listen to what they preach to us about
> Hell. It is these impostors who, because they have no other defense in
> this Country than the fear of an imaginary fire of Hell, intimidate us by
> such penalties, in order to save their own lives, and to arrest the blow
> that we would already have struck, had we any resolution.'[265]

In fact, for the missionaries, medicine was merely a means of imple-
menting a conversion strategy. Consequently, they considered it less

important to cure bodies than souls. In 1639, they wrote, concerning a sick child whom they had secretly baptized, 'This poor little girl died happily, some time afterward.'[266] Happily? Yes, because here a victim was snatched from Satan's hands. Death with the promise of heaven was worth more than life at the risk of going to hell. For the Jesuits, death took priority; for the Hurons, life.

> On one occasion, a Savage told the Father Superior that they were not very well pleased when we asked the sick 'where they wished to go after death, to heaven or to hell?' 'That is not right,' said he, 'we people do not ask such questions, for we always hope that they will not die, and that they will recover their health.' Another one said, 'For my part, I have no desire to go to heaven; I have no acquaintances there, and the French who are there would not care to give me anything to eat.' For the most part, they think of nothing but their stomachs, and of means for prolonging this miserable life.[267]

The missionaries went after the sick and dying relentlessly, threatening them with eternal suffering. They denounced curing rituals and forbad converts to participate in them. All these factors both increased stress on the sick and deprived them of the psychotherapeutic effects of the old rituals, which provided moral support from the community.[268] In a sense, one might say that the missionary made people die.

The Jesuits were strongly opposed to torture as practised by the Amerindians, declaring that it was inhuman and barbarous. They were in the habit of comforting torture victims by proposing baptism, promising escape from continued torture in eternity. The missionaries felt justified in intervening because of the profound conviction that 'God was God of the Iroquois as well as of the Hurons, and of all men who are upon the earth.'[269] The 1637 *Jesuit Relations* cites a conversation between a missionary and a Huron to this effect:

> 'Why art thou sorry,' added some one, 'that we tormented him?' 'I do not disapprove of your killing him, but of your treating him in that way.' 'What then! how do you French people do? Do you not kill men?' 'Yes, indeed; we kill them, but not with this cruelty.' 'What! do you never burn any?' 'Not often,' said the Father, 'and even then fire is only for enormous crimes, and there is only one person to whom this kind of

execution belongs by right; and besides, they are not made to linger so long – often they are first strangled, and generally they are thrown at once into the fire, where they are immediately smothered and consumed.'[270]

We saw earlier that the length, refinement, and intensity of torture were comparable in terms of cruelty on both continents. The missionary was therefore misleading his Huron interlocutor. There is still the question, however, of why Jesuits, who never opposed torture in Europe, protested against it in America. What was it that aroused their indignation? Not the fact of torture itself, evidently. As mentioned in Chapter 2, only the state could legitimately inflict torture in Europe. Was it therefore the collective appropriation of violence in Huronia that shocked the missionaries? Such violence was acceptable when monopolized by the sovereign. In Huronia, however, where it reinforced no authority, this kind of violence was equated by the missionaries with needless suffering. It was all the more gratuitous because the victim did not fulfil the conditions that justified torture in Europe. In Huronia, he personified the strength that his torturers wished to appropriate for themselves. In Europe, the victim embodied an evil to be crushed. The missionaries could not understand the respect and attention that the Hurons gave their victim before and during the ordeal. The torturers would encourage the victim to suffer stoically, to keep on singing and not lose heart. In this context, one is not surprised to find a sachem speaking to a Seneca victim thus: 'Come then, my nephew, be of good courage; prepare thyself for this evening, and do not allow thyself to be cast down through fear of the tortures.'[271] The prisoner was then given his farewell feast:

> About noon he made his Astataion, that is, his farewell feast, according to the custom of those who are about to die. No special invitations were given, every one being free to come; the people were there in crowds. Before the feast began, he walked through the middle of the cabin and said in a loud and confident voice, 'My brothers, I am going to die; amuse yourselves boldly around me, I fear neither tortures nor death.' He straightway began to sing and dance through the whole length of the cabin; some of the others sang also and danced in their turn. Then food was given those who had plates, and those who had none watched the others eat. We were of the latter, since we were not there to eat. The feast over, he was taken back to Arontaen, to die there.[272]

Once the victim had been put to death, his body was cut up and eaten.[273] Must one not respect the victim in order to talk to him and encourage him to sing? And to incorporate the victim into one's own body by devouring him, must one not 'love him a little?'[274] In the European tradition, the victim was an object of loathing. He was guilty, a blasphemer, sin and evil incarnate. His torturers therefore proceeded to annihilate him physically and morally. However, cannibalism and imperialism are mutually exclusive phenomena. The missionaries were shocked at the respect paid to the victim, for how could one respect that which was despicable? In Europe, disorder and revolt were punished. In Huronia, the torturers respected the courage of the victim and wished to appropriate it for themselves.

Why, we may ask, did the missionaries reject certain forms of torture while accepting others? To the extent that it was an identification ritual, a means of establishing oneself through opposition, torture sustained the structure of the 'we' – the collective identity. The Huron 'we' was unacceptable to the Jesuits. On the other hand, how did the missionaries define their own collective identity? To find the answer, one must ascertain who was the 'other,' the enemy of the missionary. At first glance, it would appear that this 'other' was the unbeliever, representing all barbarians to be subjugated by the faith. However, the 'other' was also someone not subject to the king of France: 'The strength of the French would be the support of the new Churches that we endeavor to beget to Jesus Christ at this extremity of the World.'[275] In 1646, the Jesuits in Quebec received 'a magnificent Portrait of the King, the Queen, and of Monsieur [Louis xiv's brother].'[276] The missionary who showed it to the Amerindians gave this brief homily: "I am only the voice," he said to them, "of those whom you see depicted with so much grace and majesty in this rich Picture.'"[277] The 'other' was therefore someone who had not submitted to the Catholic Church as well as to the king of France. Might it not also be simply one who had not submitted at all? Or the part of the individual that, in each of us, is free? The 'corrupt nature'[278] that is endlessly surfacing in dreams and desires? What internal enemy was the missionary combating when he desired his own martyrdom[279] or indulged in self-flagellation and wore hair shirts, thus torturing his own body? Had not the body itself, with all its urges, become the most subversive, the most dangerous of enemies? The body must be subjugated before anything else. The masochism of converts would seem to confirm this hypothesis. The missionaries' 'we' was therefore the product of a trinity of polarities: believer/unbeliever, subjugated/free, Thanatos/Eros. This new focus of identity was to destroy not only the 'subject,' but the whole of Huron society.

On the one hand, conversion to Christianity triggered disintegration of the Hurons' traditional political structure, while on the other, it set up the conditions for the creation and development of institutions for surplus repression.

How could a Christian fulfil political functions within a society where all was diabolical superstition? 'To be a Captain among them and to be a Christian, is to unite fire and water, as almost the entire occupation of the Captains consists in obeying the Devil, in presiding over Hellish Ceremonies, in exhorting young people to dances, to feasts, to nudity, and to most infamous lewdness.'[280] In some cases, converted sachems resigned from their posts,[281] in others, an attempt was made to distinguish between what was 'pagan' and what was not.[282] Later, the sachems would give up their power to the Jesuits.[283] This is what happened in Ossossané once the majority of the population and the council had become Christian. However, the crisis in the Huron political system arose less from the difficulty of recruiting sachems to replace converts, than from the disintegration of kinship relations. We have seen how clan organization, which was the foundation of Huron democracy, was destabilized by the convert/non-convert split.

Christianity had introduced the notion that acts were private property,[284] at the same time imposing a whole series of new constraints and restrictions. Concurrently, class relationships and the social division of labour were developing. In these circumstances, it is not surprising to find the missionaries wishing for a sword[285] to support the church in its endeavours and favouring the establishment of repressive institutions. Here is what Father Jérôme Lalemant had to say in this regard:

> But to return to our subject, and to tell your Reverence my sentiments
> respecting the conversion of this country, I may frankly confess that, if
> we had to judge the establishment of the Faith in these countries from
> the standpoint of human prudence, I could hardly believe that there is
> any place in the world more difficult to subject to the Laws of Jesus

Christ. Not only because they have no knowledge of letters, no Historical monuments, and no idea of a Divinity who has created the world and who governs it; but, above all, because I do not believe that there is any people on earth freer than they, and less able to allow the subjection of their wills to any power whatever – so much so that Fathers here have no control over their children, or Captains over their subjects, or the Laws of the country over any of them, except in so far as each is pleased to submit to them. There is no punishment which is inflicted on the guilty, and no criminal who is not sure that his life and property are in no danger, even if he were convicted of three or four murders, of having received a reward from the enemy for betraying his country, or breaking off by his own act a peace, that is decided upon by the general consent of the whole country. These are crimes that I have seen committed, the authors whereof have gloried in them and have boasted that the wars that they had aroused would make their names immortal. It is not because there are no Laws or punishments proportionate to the crimes, but it is not the guilty who suffer the penalty. It is the public that must make amends for the offenses of individuals; so that, if a Huron has killed an Algonquin or another Huron, the whole country assembles; and they come to an agreement respecting the number of presents to be given to the Tribe or to the relatives of him who has been killed, to stay the vengeance that they might take. The Captains urge their subjects to provide what is needed; no one is compelled to it, but those who are willing bring publicly what they wish to contribute; it seems as if they vied with one another according to the amount of their wealth, and as the desire of glory and of appearing solicitous for the public welfare urges them to do on like occasions. Now although this form of justice restrains all these peoples, and seems more effectually to repress disorders than the personal punishment of criminals does in France, it is nevertheless a very mild proceeding, which leaves individuals in such a spirit of liberty that they never submit to any Laws and obey no other impulse than that of their own will. This, without doubt, is a disposition quite contrary to the spirit of the Faith, which requires us to submit not only our wills, but our minds, our judgments, and all the sentiments of man to a power unknown to our senses, to a Law that is not of earth, and that is entirely opposed to the laws and sentiments of corrupt nature.

Add to this that the laws of the Country, which to them seem most just, attack the purity of the Christian life in a thousand ways, especially as regards their marriages, the dissolution of which, with freedom to seek another consort, is more frequent and easy here than it is in France for a master to take another servant, when the one he has does not please him. The result is, truth to tell, that, in the closest of their marriages, and those which they consider most conformable to reason, the faith that they pledge each other is nothing more than a conditional promise to live together so long as each shall continue to render the services that they mutually expect from each other, and shall not in any way wound the affection that they owe each other. If this fail, divorce is considered reasonable on the part of the injured one, although the other party who has given occasion for it is blamed.

But the greatest opposition that we meet in these Countries to the spirit of the Faith consists in the fact that their remedies for diseases; their greatest amusements when in good health; their fishing, their hunting, and their trading; the success of their crops, of their wars, and of their councils, – almost all abound in diabolical ceremonies. So that, as superstition has contaminated nearly all the actions of their lives, it would seem that to be a Christian, one must deprive himself not only of pastimes which elsewhere are wholly innocent, and of the dearest pleasures of life, but even of the most necessary things, and, in a word, die to the world at the very moment that one wishes to assume the life of a Christian.

Not that, after examining their superstitions more closely, we find that the Devil interferes and gives them any help beyond the operation of nature; but nevertheless they have recourse to him; they believe that he speaks to them in dreams; they invoke his aid; they make presents and sacrifices to him, sometimes to appease him and sometimes to render him favorable to them; they attribute to him their health, their cures, and all the happiness of their lives. In this, they are all the more miserable that they are slaves of the Devil, without gaining anything in his service, not even in this world, of which he is called the Prince, and wherein he seems to have some power.

If lesser difficulties have caused trouble in converting civilized Nations, and if it has taken entire centuries to implant the Faith in them, though God then assisted those who preached his word, with a multitude of miracles, – with the gift of cures, the gift of tongues, of prophecies, and everything that can astonish nature and make even the most impious acknowledge the power and majesty of him whose greatness they proclaimed, – what can be expected from these barbarous nations when it has not pleased God to bless us with frequent miracles, and to make the Faith more agreeable to them by the pleasant things that it would cause Heaven to shower, even in this life, on those who should submit to his Laws; and when we have not here even such temporal aids as the succor, the benefits, and the gifts which have been employed with the Savages in the other countries of the World to procure their conversion? Finally, we cannot here have force at hand, and the support of that sharp sword which serves the Church in so holy a manner to give authority to her Decrees, to maintain Justice, and curb the insolence of those who trample under foot the holiness of her Mysteries.[286]

In 1637, in the middle of an epidemic, the Huron sachems met in council and asked the Jesuits what they must do 'that God might have compassion on them.'[287] 'The principal thing was to believe in him [God], and to be firmly resolved to keep his commandments,' replied the Jesuit superior, who took this unlooked for opportunity to outline the following ambitious program: 'He proposed to them that ... they should henceforth give up their belief in their dreams; 2nd, that their marriages should be binding and for life, and that they should observe conjugal chastity; 3rd, he gave them to understand that God forbade vomiting [eat-all] feasts; 4th, those shameless assemblies of men and women (I would blush to speak more clearly); 5th, eating human flesh; 6th, those feasts they call Aoutaerohi, – which they make, they say, to appease a certain little demon to whom they give this name.'[288] After hearing the magnitude of these suggested 'reforms,' an old sachem replied: 'We have our own ways of doing things, and you yours, as well as other nations. When you speak to us about obeying and acknowledging as our master him whom you say has made Heaven and earth, I imagine you are talking of overthrowing the country.'[289] Overthrowing the country was exactly what this was all about. In fact, very few aspects of Huron society escaped the undermining effects of the Jesuits' work – 'superstition [having] contaminated nearly all the actions' of their lives.[290]

In earlier times, the feast of the dead, a major ritual, symbolized the unity of Huronia. It will be remembered that initial burial places were temporary. When the time came to move the village, bodies would be dug up to be reburied in a huge common grave. Champlain indicated the significance of this in unmistakable terms: 'By means of these ceremonies, as with dances, feasts, and assemblies similarly carried out, they renew their pledge of friendship among themselves, saying that the bones of their relatives & friends are all to be placed together, creating one form, that everything, including their bones, is assembled and united in the same place, just as, during their lives, they must be united by friendship and concord, as relatives and friends, unable to separate.'[291] From now on, however, there would be two burial grounds, and Christians would not mingle their bones with those of pagans. Huronia was divided for eternity.

Christianity spared nothing. It affected every aspect of life: kinship relations and everything that this implied (relations between men and women, marriage, sexuality, family and clan, children, the rules of hospitality and mutual aid, and political organization); the rituals connected with sickness, fishing, hunting, horticulture, death, war, and diplomacy; and finally, the mechanisms for sharing and redistribution (including their system of giving). In a society like the Hurons', where social relations were forged and maintained by the symbolism of the gift and the requisite counter-gift, to break the rules of exchange was to deal a blow to the basic social structure. Not only was the collective aspect of Huron life affected, but the personalities of Huronia's men and women were destabilized. A nation, an identity, and a civilization were crippled.

By the time the Iroquois had mounted their major offensive against the Hurons, the latter's once-unified society was already a house divided. Unlike members of Montagnais society, the Hurons did not fall prey to the disintegrating effects of alcoholism.[292] The Jesuits had successfully forbidden trafficking in alcohol in Huronia. Although the Hurons obtained alcohol during their trips to Trois-Rivières,[293] its consumption did not have a destructive effect and in no way contributed to the crisis in Huron society. Rather, it was the antagonism between converts and traditionalists that shook the foundations of Huron society, and, as we have seen, this antagonism was expressed at all levels of society. The tolerant Hurons, who were accustomed to respect individual differences, had allowed an intolerant clergy to establish itself in their midst.

The Jesuits were first accepted as magicians, then in 1639 they built Sainte-Marie-among-the-Hurons, a fortified European village that was self-sufficient from an agricultural and military standpoint. Christians now had a place of their own in the heart of Huronia. They were few in number to begin with – individual converts were called 'the Christian'[294] – and led a marginal life in their society, refusing to participate in almost all religious and cultural activities. As their numbers increased, however, tension mounted within lineages, a grandmother objecting to a daughter and son-in-law having her grandchild baptized,[295] for example, or a woman evicting her converted husband from her longhouse.[296] The missionaries and their neophytes were the targets of snowballs, clubs, and cornstalks.[297] The traditionalists, ridiculing the act of baptism, threw water over the Christians.[298] They treated them as 'Marian in mockery, because they frequently heard the Name of the most Blessed Virgin repeated in their Prayers.'[299] Death threats became more frequent.[300] Epidemics and the refusal of Christians to take part in any ritual (harvest rituals, for example)[301] fanned the embers of threatened massacre, which were soon smouldering in earnest, ready to burst into flame at any moment. The Jesuits, for their part, always rejoiced at the death of 'renegades.'[302] The traditionalist camp wanted the converts to leave for France.[303] Their opponents wanted to do away with paganism and impose Christian rituals to the exclusion of all else. It was to be a fight to the finish, with no middle ground.[304]

As the converts became increasingly cut off from their community, they developed a correspondingly greater attachment to the Jesuits than to their own nation.[305] Their obsession with escaping 'paganism' and distinguishing themselves from their pagan brothers at all costs led to disaster. Should a shaman, guided by ritual divination, predict an Iroquois attack from the south, the converts, determined to escape his 'satanic' influence, would wait for the enemy on the west. As a result, the pagan Hurons confronted the enemy and were beaten, while to the west, the Christian Hurons waited in vain.[306]

The traditionalists began to draw their own conclusions. Since the arrival of the missionaries in their midst, famine, sickness, and war had rained down upon them, while their Iroquois enemies prospered because they had a horror of prayer.

Since we have published the law of Jesus Christ in these regions, plagues have rushed in as in a throng. Contagious diseases, war, famine, – these are the tyrants that have sought to wrest the faith from the faithful, and that have caused it to be hated by the infidels. How many times have we been reproached that, wherever we set foot, death came in with us! How many times have they told us that they had never seen calamities like those which have appeared since we speak of Jesus Christ! 'You tell us' (exclaim some) 'that God is full of goodness; and then, when we give ourselves up to him, he massacres us. The Iroquois, our mortal enemies, do not believe in God, they do not love the prayers, they are more wicked than the Demons, and yet they prosper; and since we have forsaken the usages of our ancestors, they kill us, they massacre us, they burn us, they exterminate us, root and branch. What profit can there come to us from lending ear to the Gospel, since death and the faith nearly always march in company?' There are Christians who generously answer these complaints: 'Though the faith should cause us to lose life, is it a great misfortune to leave the earth in order to be blest in Heaven? If death and war slaughter the Christians, no more do they spare the infidels.' 'Yes, but,' answer the others, 'the Iroquois do not die, and yet they hold prayer in abomination. Before these innovations appeared in these regions, we lived as long as the Iroquois; but, since some have accepted prayer, one sees no more white heads – we die at half age.'[307]

An Algonkin chief agreed, telling the Hurons with whom he had overwintered, 'Your village is moved by the discourses of the black gowns ... We [the Algonkins] were the terror of our enemies. Now we are reduced to nothing ... It is the Faith that brings these misfortunes upon us ... But since those who refuse to worship him are happier than those who are his subjects ... choose with me to consider him rather as an enemy than as a friend.'[308]

After about 1645, converts became sufficiently influential in some villages to abstain from traditionalist rituals and to practise their own in public (religious processions, for example).[309] They were even strong enough to prohibit pagan rituals. Faced with this rising power, the traditionalists spontaneously developed an ideology of resistance, so that the sachems 'traversed the streets, shouting in loud voices that pity be taken on a country which is going to ruin because the old customs are neglected; that the faith is too rigorous, in never granting dispensation from its laws.'[310]

People reported having all kinds of dreams showing the wrath of the betrayed gods and the urgency of getting rid of the new clergy. One such dream involved a ghost appearing amid dreadful scenes of war, announcing that he was leaving Huronia, where he was refused honours, and going to Agnée, the Mohawk country. There he would be honoured and would bring victory to the Mohawks, leaving 'terror and fear in the hearts of the Hurons.'[311] A dream incited one warrior to 'a kind of martial fury' during which he broke in the church door and tore down the Frenchmen's bell.[312]

There were also all sorts of rumours and stories about the treachery of the French[313] and the need to return to ancient ways. The existence of heaven and hell was denied, or else heaven was described as a place of torture where Hurons would be slaves of the French. Contrasted to this was the belief in a place of delight in the afterlife, a valley where only Hurons who had respected tradition would go. In addition, the Algonkins were rumoured to have wandered into lands where they had recently discovered 'very populous cities, inhabited only by the souls.'[314] These souls, after living a life in the Huron manner, were reportedly reincarnated in a second, more vigorous, body in a happier country. They had confirmed the fact that neither heaven nor hell existed. Another marvellous account, using the myth of the origin of man, tried to recover a Huron identity that was being taken away:

At other times there have come, it is said, certain news that there has appeared in the woods a phantom of prodigious size, who bears in one hand ears of Indian corn, and, in the other, a great abundance of fish; who says that it is he alone who has created men, who has taught them to till the earth, and who has stocked all the lakes and the seas with fish, so that nothing might fail for the livelihood of men. These he recognized as children, although they did not yet recognize him as their father, – just like an infant in the cradle, who has not firm enough judgment to recognize those to whom he owes all that he is, and all the support of his life. But this phantom added, they said, that our souls, being separated from our bodies, would then have a greater knowledge; that they would see that it is from him that they hold life; and that then, upon rendering him the honors which he deserves, he would increase both his love and his cares for them, – that he would do good to them all. He also said that to believe that any one of them was destined to a place of torments and to the fires, which are not beneath the earth, were false notions, with which, nevertheless, we treacherously strive to terrify them.[315]

The most widespread of all these rumours concerned the resurrection of a converted Huron woman who had been buried in the Christian cemetery. She had indeed gone to heaven and was therefore the only person able to describe it accurately. According to some, the Christians of the village of Saint-Michel had discovered the secret, but refused to talk of it. They had been persuaded to keep silent by gifts from the Jesuits, said some. Still, it was known that the resurrected woman

had said that the French were impostors; that her soul, having left the body, had actually been taken to Heaven; that the French had welcomed it there, but in the manner in which an Iroquois captive is received at the entrance to their Villages, with firebrands and burning torches, with cruelties and torments inconceivable. She had related that all Heaven is nothing but fire, and that there the satisfaction of the French is to burn now some, now others; and that, in order to possess many of these captive souls, which are the object of their pleasures, they cross the seas, and come into these regions as into a land of conquest, just as a Huron exposes himself with joy to the fatigues and all the dangers of war, in the hope of bringing back some captive. It was further said that those who are thus burned in heaven, as captives of war, are the Huron, Algonquin, and Montagnais Christians, and that those who have not been willing in this world to render themselves slaves of the French, or to receive their laws, go after this life into a place of delights, where everything good abounds, and whence all evil is banished.

This risen woman added, they said, that, after having been thus tormented in Heaven a whole day, – which seemed to her longer than our years, – the night having come, she had felt herself roused, near the beginning of her sleep; that a certain person, moved with compassion for her, had broken her bonds and chains, and had shown her, at one side, a deep valley which descended into the earth, and which led into that place of delights whither the souls of the infidel Hurons go; that from afar she had seen their villages and their fields, and had heard their voices as of people who dance and who are feasting. But she had chosen to return into her body, as long as was necessary to warn those who were there present of such terrible news, and of that great misfortune which awaited them at death, if they continued to believe in the impostures of the French.[316]

Despite numerous death threats, the Jesuits were never directly attacked. In 1648, the tension reached a climax. A young French servant was murdered. The Jesuits knew that the killing had been fomented by 'Captains, who are not among the least notable of the country, [and who] have always declared themselves hostile to the Faith.'[317] The day after the murder, Christians from neighbouring villages took refuge in Sainte-Marie. The affair was debated in the grand council. The traditionalists, said the missionaries, insisted 'that the doors of their villages should be closed to us, and that we should be driven from the country. Some even added that all the Christians should be banished from it, and their number be prevented from increasing.'[318] The Christians maintained, on the contrary, that the traditionalists were in the pay of the Iroquois.[319] The *Jesuit Relations* do not say so explicitly, but it is probable that when the traditionalists proposed breaking with the French, they also suggested an alliance with the Iroquois. In the event, the Christians made a convincing case for maintaining a military and economic alliance with the French, and it was decided that the Jesuits would receive substantial reparations for the murder of their servant.

The possibility of an alliance with the Iroquois as an alternative to that with the French had been broached as far back as 1636. In that year, a sachem by the name of Oumasasikweie, who was an influential member of the Island Algonkins or Kichesipirini (one of the Hurons' trading allies) had visited the Iroquois for the purpose of concluding a peace treaty and directing Huron trade toward the Dutch. However, he had been murdered by the Iroquois.[320]

In summary, the dependency of the Huron confederacy within the Franco-Huron alliance enabled missionaries and converts to maintain their position, despite a great deal of hostility. On the eve of the massive

Iroquois offensive, the Huron confederacy was already divided in every respect. A few years later, after the fall of Huronia, there were Huron captives who stated that, 'the moment the Hurons received the Faith and abandoned their dreams, their ruin began, and their whole Country has ever since been declining to its final total destruction.'[321]

IROQUOIA IN TRANSITION TOWARD A CLASS SOCIETY

The Iroquois emerged as 'victors' of the intertribal wars over control of the fur trade. Nevertheless, although they had not been driven from their territory or exterminated, their society had suffered internal injury, so to speak. How could it be otherwise in the circumstances? Relationships between man and nature had undergone a tremendous upheaval. The Iroquois had fought an intensive war such as never before. Furthermore, every traditional form of labour organization had undergone profound change. As a final disruption, the Iroquois had integrated a multitude of captives into their society.

Intertribal Tension

The integration of several previously autonomous tribes into a single, fur-trading economy had prompted the development of hierarchical intertribal relationships. We have seen how the Iroquois collected tribute from the tribes of the New Amsterdam region. Similarly, unequal access to trade goods by different Iroquois tribes gave rise to domination relationships within their confederacy. This confederacy consisted of five tribes – Oneidas, Onondagas, Cayugas, Senecas, and Mohawks.[322] These were equal in principle, and all were represented on the confederacy council. However, the Mohawks had the advantage of being near Fort Orange and so became the principal middlemen in dealing with the Dutch. Among the Iroquois, this tribe soon had the best supply of lead, powder, and firearms.[323] This privileged relationship with the Dutch appears to have ensured the Mohawks' hegemony within the confederacy.

In 1654, in response to an invitation by the Onondaga tribe, the Jesuits sent Father Simon Le Moyne to them. The Mohawks feared an alliance between the French and the Onondagas that might threaten their hegemony. Accordingly, they addressed the French governor as follows:

'We, the five Iroquois Nations, compose but one cabin; we maintain but one fire; and we have, from time immemorial, dwelt under one and the same roof.' In fact, from the earliest times, these five Iroquois Nations have been called in their own language, which is Huron, *Hotinnonchiendi* – that is, 'the completed Cabin,' as if to express that they constituted but one family. 'Well, then,' he continued, 'will you not enter the cabin by the door, which is at the ground floor of the house? It is with us Anniehronnons [Mohawks], that you should begin; whereas you, by beginning with the Onnontaehronnons [Onondagas], try to enter by the roof and through the chimney. Have you no fear that the smoke may blind you, our fire not being extinguished, and that you may fall from the top to the bottom, having nothing solid on which to plant your feet?'[324]

In 1655, the Mohawks murdered two French ambassadors and a Seneca chief, at the risk of causing 'war between those two Iroquois Nations.'[325] The French and the Senecas had wanted to establish trade relations – the Senecas hoping thereby to escape the Mohawks' hold over them.[326] In 1657, the Onondagas in turn tried to establish trade relations with the French for the same reason: 'They [the Onondagas] desired [the presence of] some of the French for the sake of obtaining firearms from them, and having them mend such as should be broken. Furthermore, as the Agnieronnons [Mohawks] sometimes treated them rather roughly when they passed through their Villages to go and trade with the Dutch, they wished to free themselves from this dependence by opening commerce with the French.'[327]

The Captives

In the *Jesuit Relations* of 1652-53, Bressani, the Italian Jesuit, gave an account of a visit to the Iroquois. After a few remarks on the lack of comfort (they had no beds, benches, or tables), he added, 'But, in this almost unexampled poverty, there are nevertheless among them both poor and rich, noble and plebeian.'[328] In the past, travellers and missionaries had noted the egalitarian nature of Iroquoian societies. Who, therefore, were these poor people, these 'plebeians'?

This newly observed element in Iroquois society was made up of captives and 'prisoners of war.' Epidemics and constant warfare had decimated the Iroquois tribes. To replace those lost, the Iroquois adopted prisoners. This was a customary phenomenon, but now it took on a new dimension. In view of the high number of people lost and the upsurge in intertribal rivalry, it became necessary to adopt and assimilate prisoners on an unprecedented scale. According to the Jesuits, prisoners came from within a radius of 400 leagues and spoke all sorts of languages.[329] Perhaps they were even in the majority: 'If anyone should compute the number of pure-blooded Iroquois, he would have difficulty in finding more than twelve hundred of them in all the five Nations, since these are, for the most part, only aggregations of different tribes whom they have conquered ... who, utter Foreigners although they are, form without doubt the largest and best part of the Iroquois.'[330]

Prisoners were spread out through several villages, irrespective of their nuclear families or clans. One village was the exception to this rule, however. Gandougarae was entirely made up 'of the remnants of three different Nations' – Onnontiogas, Neutrals, and Hurons.[331] Here, the conquered groups retained their customs and even a certain amount of autonomy,[332] although they did not have the right to be represented on the confederacy council.[333] The adopting families had the right of life and death over the prisoners, a right they often exercised. The adopted prisoner might be old, weak, or unpleasing in his behaviour, or the family might wish to revenge itself for the death of one of its own. The Jesuits reported an extreme case in which a chief, who wished to avenge the death of his brother, killed eighty prisoners.[334] Strangers who had voluntarily become part of the Iroquois ranks received lenient treatment, but life was harsh for prisoners of war. Nearly all men underwent torture to some degree and those women who did not marry became servants.

> The Iroquois have three classes of captives. The first are those who, having willingly submitted to the yoke of the conquerors and elected to remain among them, have become heads of families after the deaths of their Masters, or have married. Although they lead a tolerably easy life, they are looked upon as slaves, and have no voice, either active or passive, in the public Councils. The second class are those who have fallen into slavery after having been the richest and the most esteemed in their own villages, and who receive no other reward from their Masters, in exchange for their ceaseless labor and sweat, than food and

shelter. But the fate of the third class is much more deplorable; it consists chiefly of young women or girls, who, because they have not yet found a husband among the Iroquois, are constantly exposed to the danger of losing their honors or their lives through the brutal lechery or cruelty of their Masters or Mistresses. Every moment is one of dread for them; their rest is never free from anxiety and danger; the only punishment for even their slightest faults is death; and their most harmless and most holy actions may be considered as faults.[335]

The technique for a prisoner's acculturation was based on constant threats of death and torture and on the valorization of the attachment to his new family and tribe.[336] The participation of captives in Iroquois wars, including those against the captives' own people, was a testing-ground for their new loyalty.[337] They were forced to do the hardest work, and, in particular, carry the heaviest loads. Recalcitrants were killed on the spot. As for their bodies, 'It is a dead dog; there is nothing to be done but to cast it upon the dunghill.'[338] If captive children hampered their new mother's work, they were eliminated.[339] An oft-told account concerned a 'captive girl' of the Cat Nation (Eries). Her mistress was displeased 'by her occasional obstinacy' and 'commissioned a young man to kill her.' The missionaries noted that 'this murder did not startle the children playing near by, or even divert them from their game, so accustomed are they to the sight of these poor captives' blood.'[340]

At night the prisoners were tied up to prevent escape.[341] When the chiefs travelled, they had their captives in tow. As far as the missionaries were concerned, the captives were veritable slaves.[342] Generally speaking, the fate reserved for Algonkins was harsher than that meted out to Hurons, who were culturally nearer to the Iroquois. All this is evidence of a dominated class in Iroquois society – that is, one that assumes the heaviest burden of labour and for which life depends on the good will of the 'masters.' In this society, where social relations were formerly based on kinship, a new social relationship now developed between native Iroquois and their captives – a relation that marked the social division of labour. In the long term, this relationship disappeared because the mechanisms for social control were not designed to turn the conquered people into a dominated group in a permanent way, but to assimilate and integrate them into Iroquois society. Interethnic marriages contributed to achieving this goal, and births that occurred in Iroquois country even more so. The native/captive relationship did not survive for more than one generation, and kinship relations once more prevailed. The captives adopted by Iroquois families then became eligible for positions appropriate to their adopted family line.[343] Some even occupied political positions. After 1659, the Mohawks invited Algonkin and Huron captives to accompany them on trade journeys to Quebec City.[344] They prohibited the latter from putting their commercial talents to use, however, fearing a rise in Huron leadership.[345]

The Role of Women

It is interesting to observe what part Iroquois women played in the process of change in their society. On the one hand, it was mainly women who implemented the policy of assimilation. This was a role of great importance since revolt was a constant threat and Iroquois men were often absent on trading or war parties. As a result, women's power grew. In the opinion of Bruce Trigger, women's right to forbid men to wage war when community interests were at stake can be dated from this period.[346] Running parallel to this growing power was a tendency among Iroquois men to marry Huron women, thus avoiding the social obligations of sharing imposed by the matrilinear kinship system.[347] Are we looking at a change (albeit temporary) in kinship relations and an evolution toward the nuclear family? It appears that the emergence of classes in Iroquois society reinforced the relative position of women. Yet, at the same time, men were trying to escape redistribution obligations and possibly a confrontation by choosing female captives over native Iroquois women.

Birth of a State?

During this period, there was one significant change in the political structure that was indicative of social upheaval and transition. This was the growing power of the war chiefs. In Mesoamerican cultures, military and civil positions were traditionally separate. Pre-Columbian war chiefs were chosen as needed for frontier raids, the best warriors being most often the best hunters. With the fur wars, in addition to the sachems (peace chiefs), each lineage named a war chief. According to Lewis H. Morgan, two further posts were created for coordinating military activity, although the incumbents could not be considered generals since they had no coercive power over the Iroquois people. These two posts were hereditary, handed down from uncle to nephew. Again according to Morgan, assistant sachems were also named. However, these posts were not hereditary and could vary in number. They tended to multiply, and this contributed to the gradual ousting of the sachems.[348] It could be suggested that this rise in the power of assistant sachems was evidence of increasingly weak links between the kinship and political structures, although we have too little information to corroborate such an assumption. Nevertheless, various circumstances clearly made it necessary to enlarge the political infrastructure – circumstances such as the growing number of wars, the establishment of relationships of domination over allied tribes, and the exercise of coercive force over a large number of captives who were in the process of being integrated and assimilated. This enlarged political apparatus performed the two obvious functions of coordination and repression. It would seem that the victorious Iroquois confederacy was on the verge of developing the political structures of an embryo state.

The Secular Nature of New Netherland

The Iroquois was a proud individual who considered himself in no way inferior to the European.[349] He saw himself as a member of a sovereign people, the ally of the Dutch, noting regretfully that the Dutchman's primary considerations were commercial. As the Dutch trade offensive was not accompanied by an ideological attack,[350] Iroquois society was able to retain its cultural and religious distinctiveness. Proof of this is the Iroquois' disdainful attitude toward Christianity and their criticism of European mores, as revealed by the pastor Johannes Megapolensis:

> When we pray they laugh at us. Some of them despise it entirely; and some, when we tell them what we do when we pray, stand astonished. When we deliver a sermon, sometimes ten or twelve of them, more or less, will attend, each having a long tobacco pipe, made by himself, in his mouth, and will stand awhile and look, and afterwards ask me what I am doing and what I want, that I stand there alone and make so many words, while none of the rest may speak. I tell them that I am admonishing the Christians, that they must not steal, nor commit lewdness, nor get drunk, nor commit murder, and that they ought not to do

these things; and that I intend in process of time to preach the same to
them and come to them in their own country and castles (about three
days' journey from here, further inland), when I am acquainted with
their language. Then they say I do well to teach the Christians; but
immediately add, *Diatennon jawij Assirioni, hagiouisk*, that is, 'Why do
so many Christians do these things?'[351]

In his book of 1655, *Beschriivinge van Nieuw-Nederlant*, Adriaen Van
der Donck remarked that he knew of only one native convert and
reported the following Amerindian comments. Observe how a Roman
Catholic ritual, originally performed exclusively by a religious specialist,
has been reappropriated by the community:

> Their common answer is, 'We do not know that God, we have never
> seen him, we know not who he is – if you know him and fear him, as
> you say you do, how does it then happen that so many thieves, drunk-
> ards, and evil-doers are found among you? Certainly that God will
> punish you severely, because he has warned you to beware of those
> deeds, which he has never done to us. We know nothing about it, and
> therefore we do not deserve such punishment.' Very seldom do they
> adopt our religion, nor have there been any political measures taken
> for their conversion ... The Jesuits have taken great pains and trouble
> in Canada to convert the Indians to the Roman Church, and outwardly
> many profess that religion; but inasmuch as they are not well
> instructed in its fundamental principles, they fall off lightly and make
> sport of the subject and its doctrine.
>
> In the year 1639, when a certain merchant, who is still living with
> us, went into that country to trade with an Indian chief who spoke good
> French, after he had drank two or three glasses of wine, they began to
> converse on the subject of religion. The chief said that he had been
> instructed so far that he often said mass among the Indians, and that
> on a certain occasion the place where the altar stood caught fire by
> accident, and our people made preparations to put out the fire, which
> he forbade them to do, saying that God, who stands there, is almighty,
> and he will put out the fire himself; and we waited with great attention,
> but the fire continued till all was burned up, with your almighty God
> himself and with all the fine things about him. Since that time I have
> never held to that religion, but regard the sun and moon much more,

as being better than all your Gods are; for they warm the earth and cause the fruits to grow, when your lovely Gods cannot preserve themselves from the fire. In the whole country I know no more than one Indian who is firm in his religious profession, nor can any change be expected among them, as long as matters are permitted to remain as heretofore.[352]

Huron captives in Iroquois country were quick to note the difference between French and Dutch attitudes in their relationships with Amerindians. Many of the captives believed that the Jesuits had caused their downfall, whereas the Iroquois' Dutch ally had let them live in the traditional way, an advantage that had ensured victory. When the Jesuits began to come among the Iroquois in the 1650s, traditionalist Hurons lost no time in warning the Iroquois about the danger involved. The missionaries recorded their dismay at this turn of events:

We have not so much trouble to clear ourselves of such ridiculous reproaches, as we have to disabuse the people of the rumors spread by some Huron Apostates, who attribute to the Faith all the wars, diseases, and calamities of the country. They allege their own experience in confirmation of their imposture; they assert that their change of Religion has caused their change of fortune; and that their Baptism was at once followed by every possible misfortune. The Dutch, they say, have preserved the Iroquois by allowing them to live in their own fashion, just as the black Gowns have ruined the Hurons by preaching the faith to them.[353]

Radisson was of a similar opinion when he denounced the moral control exercised by the Jesuits over the private lives of Frenchmen living in Huronia. The long and short of it was, said he, that while the Dutch sold weapons, the Jesuits were busy with morals.

The Dutch settled in Manhattan and equipped this nation [the Iroquois] with weapons, which enabled it to become a victor. The French colonists of New France went to live among the [Huron] nation. They stayed several years. In their ambition, and in order to bend everything to their own ends, the Jesuit fathers objected to having French families settle there. They acted in this way on the pretext of preventing the young men from frequenting the Indian women, for this bad example would have been harmful in establishing Christianity.

But the time came when they were caught in their own toils. After a
while, the Iroquois – seven hundred of them – came over the snow in
early spring and carried out a cruel massacre, as in past years. On this
occasion, several of the fathers, brothers, or their domestics were taken
prisoner or even burned.[354]

The Jesuit Offensive

In the month of September of last year, 1655, two of our Fathers went
up to the country of the Onontaeronon Iroquois, to start a new
Mission among people who, after killing, slaughtering, burning, and
eating us, came to solicit our services.[355]

As in the past, the missionaries continued to act as go-betweens in
trade relations between the Amerindians and the French. The Iroquois
were allies of the Dutch and had been informed by the Hurons of all the
rumours of witchcraft that held the Jesuits responsible for the epidemics
and the disappearance of Huronia.[356] Why, then, did the Iroquois invite
the Jesuits to live among them?

The Iroquois probably intended to reduce their dependence on the
Dutch, having crushed the great rival confederacy of Huronia. In fact,
this was almost certainly the case, since the Anglo-Dutch war of 1653-54
had reduced imports of trade goods and pushed up prices sharply at Fort
Orange.[357] Furthermore, the rivalry between the Iroquois and the tribes
of the Swedish network (Susquehannocks and Eries) for access to western furs was heating up. Although the war against the Hurons had united
the Iroquois confederacy, dissension resurfaced once victory had been
gained.[358] The four so-called upper Iroquois tribes (Oneidas, Onondagas,
Cayugas, and Senecas) feared the growth of Mohawk power. The latter
were the privileged allies of the Dutch and had used their position as
middlemen to make sure they had more firearms than the other tribes of
the confederacy. Moreover, they limited the other tribes' access to
firearms. However, rivalry between Iroquois tribes was not only based on
arms control. The Huron refugees at Quebec were also a factor. Every
tribe wanted to integrate these refugees, whether they came willingly or
by force, and thus increase its complement of warriors.[359] The upper
Iroquois were afraid that if the Mohawks got hold of the refugees, the
balance of power within the confederacy would be irreversibly altered.[360]

Geographically speaking, trade with the French would be easier. The upper Iroquois villages lay near Lake Ontario, and the journey to Montreal could be done entirely by canoe, whereas the Dutch had to be reached on foot.[361] Furthermore, the French had reduced restrictions on the sale of arms since the fall of Huronia.[362] They still sold firearms to converts only, but – to paraphrase Henri IV – was not a gun worth a mass? Firearms would enable the upper Iroquois to conquer the Eries[363] and put an end, once and for all, to Mohawk 'ascendancy' inside the confederacy and Susquehannock 'arrogance' outside it.

In 1654 the Onondagas wanted to conclude a peace treaty with the French. They welcomed Father Simon Le Moyne as an ambassador negotiating with the four upper Iroquois tribes. In the autumn of the same year,[364] he returned to Quebec where negotiations continued. In September 1655, two other missionaries, Father Chaumonot and Father D'Ablon, travelled to Onondaga, the main village of the Onondagas.[365] They spent the winter there, settling on the shores of Lake Gannentaa (today Lake Onondaga). 'This is the site chosen for the French settlement, on account of its central position among the four Iroquois Nations – being accessible to them by canoe, over Rivers and Lakes which make communication free and very easy.'[366] According to Amerindian custom, the fathers negotiated by offering gifts, in this case porcelain beads (wampum).[367] However, in line with missionary strategy, they soon combined their diplomatic and religious objectives. 'Although the two Fathers who passed the winter at Onnontaghé [Onondaga] in the year 1656 had gone there as Ambassadors rather than as Preachers of the Gospel, they did not fail from that very moment to sow the divine seed in those uncultivated lands, and to dispose them to make peace with God by inducing them to become reconciled with men.'[368]

The Onondaga council gave permission for the construction of 'a Chapel for the Believers,'[369] and the missionaries began their work of conversion, aided by holy pictures.[370] Their success with the Onondagas was in marked contrast to the meagre results of Father Le Moyne's diplomatic mission to the Mohawks in 1636, when he narrowly escaped being murdered.[371] The Mohawks were opposed to French penetration, perceiving it as a threat to their hegemony within the confederacy.[372]

Five ecclesiastics and some fifty Frenchmen left Quebec for Onondaga on 17 May 1656. Because of the many rapids upstream from Montreal, they had to abandon their chaloupes. On 8 June they set off again in twenty canoes. One month later, they were paddling on Lake Gannentaa.[373] The Onondagas welcomed them in traditional Iroquois fashion with canoes laden with sacks of corn and large, freshly cooked salmon.[374]

In keeping with the missionaries' basic conversion strategy of impressive display, the French responded to the Onondagas' show of hospitality with a demonstration of exceptional military pomp. Drums rolled, accompanied by a salvo of five small canon and all the muskets in the expedition,[375] and numerous gifts were presented to the Onondagas: 'It will not be out of place to observe in passing, that these presents consist entirely of porcelain collars, beads, arquebuses, powder and lead, coats, hatchets, kettles, and other similar articles. These are purchased from the Merchants with beaver-skins, which are the money that they demand in payment for their wares.'[376]

The small French colony settled on a bluff and built the European-style village of Sainte-Marie of Gannentaa.[377] The missionaries used it as a base for travelling to each of the four upper Iroquois tribes.[378] The Jesuits established themselves and concluded secure alliances. Then, in the summer of 1657, they began a systematic program of conversion and 'openly declared war against Paganism.'[379]

The missionaries used the same apostolic approach as in Huronia, denouncing the 'immorality' of attending to dreams,[380] of the right of divorce,[381] sexual freedom,[382] carnivals, and feasts such as the *Honnonovaroria*, which was 'a special festival to the Demon of dreams. This festival might be called the festival of fools, or the Carnival of wicked Christians.'[383]

The missionaries preached in the Iroquois language to captives from 'sixteen or seventeen Nations.'[384] A good many of them, particularly the women, were very receptive to the Jesuits' message. Former converts, for whom 'disaster has not extinguished the Faith in their hearts,'[385] lived in the Iroquois villages. They came to the priest for confession, a sure sign that they recognized the missionaries' legitimate role as exclusive holders of religious power.[386] A note of 1664 actually mentions the existence of a clandestine church among the Mohawks:

> For among the Iroquois the life of a captive is valued no more than that of a dog, and it needs only a slight disobedience on his part to merit a hatchet-stroke.

As for the Hurons who are in captivity, they are also in the same dangers, and some of their number bravely preserve their faith amid so many storms. There are in Agnie some Huron Matrons who constitute flying and hidden Churches, and who assemble either in the thickness of the Forests or in some out-of-the-way Cabins, in order to recite there what prayers they know.[387]

Would not a message in the name of God and 'the freedom of his children'[388] have touched a responsive chord in these captives – people who had been taken from their homelands, mothers whose children had been killed,[389] or men who had been put to torture?[390] Christianity focused on fear and a theology in which the message of Good Friday predominated – that is, a theology of pain and suffering, of death and redemption. It might well have provided a construct that, more than any other, adequately reflected the experiences of these captives, victims of every conceivable calamity. To put it another way, did Christianity respond to a need for compensation, in the Weberian sense of the term, in either Huronia or Iroquoia? Christianity was based on an institutionalized body of specialists, on the transmutation of gods into ethical powers that gave good and evil their just reward, on the development of a sense of sin, and on the desire for salvation. These are characteristics typical of religions in societies undergoing a process of division of labour – societies in which there is an urban/rural dichotomy and where hierarchical relationships and social classes are taking shape.[391]

During the period in which a class structure was developing in Amerindian societies, Christianity may have penetrated certain facets of social life so deeply that its values were fully interiorized, thereby becoming a reality of native life. Part of the Jesuits' strategy had always been to convert leaders, banking on the supposition that the rest of the population would follow. Contrary to expectations, however, the first to convert were the most deprived members of society. Was this because Christian ideology offered defeated people a world vision that could give meaning to their objective situation? On another level, Christianity may have become a focus of social identity for the underdog, especially for women. This would have given symbolic expression to the latent tendency of Iroquois society to view native Iroquois and their captives as opposites. Such a hypothesis is at least permissible when we find the Jesuits reporting that 'Huron women, who form the greater part of those that have been reared in the Faith, are keeping it inviolate, and making public profession of prayer, despite all the ridicule and scorn heaped upon it by those Infidels. He [their informant] adds that one of these women takes care to mark the Sundays, in order to observe them in so far as their captive condition will admit; and that, after whole years, she has not been found to be a single day in error in her reckoning.'[392]

On the whole, the missionaries were very satisfied with the results of their preaching, not only among Huron captives, but among the Iroquois themselves. The Jesuits were welcomed in all dwellings, religious services were well attended,[393] and chapels were built in several villages.[394] They were well aware that it suited the Iroquois' 'temporal interest,'[395] and this was precisely what they counted on. It clearly suited the Onondagas, the tribe most keen to have a French presence in its midst. These people showed a 'greater leaning toward Christianity'[396] and stated that all of them were 'Believers.'[397] Nevertheless, illness and epidemics were to revive the rumours continuously circulated by resolutely anti-Jesuit Huron captives. The daughter of a chief had only to fall ill in Onondaga for a missionary to be at her bedside. Rumour was already rife, however: the 'black Gown would accomplish her death.'[398] Death threats and accusations of witchcraft resurfaced with the winter epidemic of 1656-57.[399] Several Iroquois refused baptism, such as this woman on her deathbed:

> While endeavoring to prepare for Baptism and for death, that poor Pagan woman, whose jaw was dislocated ... fell into a swoon, and, on recovering consciousness soon after, she related news of the other world. She had been taken, she said, to the land where the souls of the French go; but, as she was preparing to enter, she saw a bluish smoke rising from the center of Paradise, which caused her to mistrust what was going on. Then at two different times, she looked more attentively, and saw several of her countrymen being burned by the French amid loud shouting. This had induced her to escape from the hands of those who were leading her to heaven, and to return to life, in order to avoid similar treatment, and to warn the public of the danger that lay in believing the French.[400]

Only economic and military considerations now protected the Jesuits from danger. This barrier was to disappear, first with the end of the Anglo-Dutch war, which brought down the price of trade goods at Fort Orange, then with the Onondagas' victory over the Eries, whom they had previously feared.[401] The anti-French party rallied the council and on 20 March 1658 the French, who were warned, had barely time to make a furtive escape.[402] Thereupon, war broke out afresh between the French and the Iroquois. The latter cut off the French from their fur suppliers[403] and brought New France to the brink of total ruin.[404] In 1661, a brief period of calm occurred, and the Onondagas asked for 'a black robe.' Father Simon Le Moyne responded to the call. Disease was on the rise again, however, and with this new pandemic, Father Le Moyne became a hostage. 'He was driven out of the cabin' and it was said that 'the faith is only fitted to kill people.'[405] Circumstances had changed, moreover. It was no longer of much interest to maintain trade relations with the French, since in 1660 the Senecas had persuaded the Dutch to trade directly with them,[406] thus breaking the Mohawk monopoly. For their part, the Dutch no longer wished to save the missionaries, 'as it costs them too dearly.'[407]

On the whole, the Iroquois were impervious to Christianity, even though in Onondaga, a social divide persisted between 'persecutors' and 'Preachers,'[408] and captives in the various tribes remained true to the missionaries' teachings. Faced with the failure of their conversion strategy and the Iroquois threat to New France's very survival, the missionaries incited the Algonkins on the Sillery reserve to wage a 'holy war'[409] against the Iroquois. They also urged Louis XIV to consider that he was 'a great King, who, while making Europe tremble, ought not to be held in contempt in America.'[410] In response to this appeal, France sent over the Carignan regiment to burn the Mohawk villages,[411] a move intended to 'pacify' the country.

Conquer America and
Conquer the Atlantic

5

This book began with Europe and a brief outline of the three main powers battling for control of the world market. The power of Holland, Great Britain, and France was, we noted, in inverse proportion to their respective populations. The transition to capitalism within Dutch, and later British, social structures was what enabled these two countries to play a central role in amassing capital on a world-wide scale. Conversely, it was the persistence of feudal structures in France that accounted for its difficulties in entering the race to accumulate capital and in developing the corresponding economic and military systems to provide the material base for a colonial empire.

We then looked at northeastern North America – the people who inhabited it and its rich resources – and observed what happened after contact with the outside world or, more specifically, after the integration-subordination of North America to the world market. Our analysis focused on the fur trade because the unequal exchange between Europeans and Amerindians revolved mainly around this aspect of contact. It was the development of trade between the two continents that brought North America into the world microbial network and exposed it to pandemics. Unequal exchange also generated more and bloodier wars, resulting in the tragic depopulation of the entire northeastern region of the continent.

It is now time to turn our attention to the rivalry between the Dutch, British, and French for control of the Atlantic economy. Given the context of American depopulation, demographics were to play a major role in this rivalry. Unlike the trade offensive in the Indian and Pacific oceans, it would take more than capital and ships to capture the Atlantic economy: it would take settlers – a great many settlers.

THE DUTCH HEGEMONY

Holland, the major power of the seventeenth century, had built up an excellent trading position on the North Atlantic and within the new peripheral area of northeastern North America. Initially, three commodities were involved: fish, furs, and lumber.

The Dutch had managed to acquire a considerable slice of the profits from the Newfoundland fisheries without being directly involved in production. They outfitted the fishermen of other countries and bought their catch, shipping it back to Europe faster than anyone else and thus getting the best prices.[1] Similarly, the Dutch became major players in the fur economy. Despite the disadvantage of being relative latecomers (because their Amerindian allies were not significant middlemen in the fur trade), they succeeded in garnering a growing share of American furs. Furthermore, their presence and intervention were determining factors in destroying the great Huron confederacy – the Hurons being the allies of their rivals, the French traders. Basically, no matter who controlled the North American fur trade, the product always moved toward Muscovy and the workshops of Russian artisans who specialized in treating pelts and making fur felt.[2] The Dutch controlled access to Muscovy through their virtual monopoly of Baltic trade. They also controlled the northern European trade networks, and this gave them preferential access to the forests of Scandinavia and Russia. The virgin forests of North America were of little interest in Europe because the cost of transporting the lumber was prohibitive.

THE LOSER'S REVENGE

At the beginning of the seventeenth century, England was economically dependent on Holland. The latter dominated the world market and had monopolized the most profitable production, shunting the intensive labour sector to the periphery or semi-periphery. In this division of labour, England provided wool – a crucial raw material for the Dutch textile industry. The English raised the sheep, spun the wool, and wove it into lengths (sheets or *draps*, hence the drapery trade). The semi-finished, unbleached or bleached fabric was then exported to Holland. Dyeing and finishing, complex operations that represented nearly half of the added value, were done in Holland.

The Cokayne plan[3] of 1614-17 was an initial attempt by the English to free themselves from foreign domination. Protectionist measures were designed to establish the whole process of textile production on English shores. The plan was doomed to failure, however, because the English lacked a qualified work force. Their economy was still reeling from the failure of the Cokayne plan when a crisis occurred that sent the textile trade into a major slump until about 1630. The outbreak of the Thirty Years' War in 1618 reduced the possibility of finding northern outlets. This was a serious matter in a country with an export trade almost totally dependent on cloth. At the same time, sizeable monetary fluctuations helped push up the relative value of English currency and, consequently, the price of English textiles on foreign markets.[4] The more competitive Dutch, in contrast, were able to maintain and even increase their share of the market. Once again, Holland had successfully exported economic depression, this time to England, a country on the semi-periphery.

The depression drove large numbers of English workers into unemployment or emigration, and forced England to abandon completely its most profitable industrial sector, the production of the old-style fine broadcloths made of short staple wool.[5] The English responded by using coarser wool with a longer thread to produce a new type of fabric ('the new draperies')[6] destined for Mediterranean and American markets. Unable to challenge Dutch competition for the fine wool market, the English drapery sector now moved from town to country in search of workers who had been reduced to poverty by the enclosure system. English textile production was reorganized on a new basis – that of 'putting out,' commonly referred to as the cottage industry.

The English government stepped in with a new series of protectionist measures,[7] again aimed at establishing the entire textile manufacturing process within the British Isles. These measures led to a marked reduction in wool exports to Holland, forcing the latter to turn to Spain, even though Spanish wool prices were higher. Meanwhile, the English had created a captive market in Ireland, which was forced to deliver its raw wool to England.

A number of conditions now enabled England to become a major power, at the same time engendering a relatively high surplus population that in turn led to poverty, unemployment, and emigration. These conditions included depression, the reorganization of the textile industry on the cottage industry system, the resumption of enclosure and the resulting peasant evictions, the introduction of protectionist measures, and the establishment of Ireland as a vassal state. Between 1620 and 1642, tens of thousands of men, women, and children crossed the Atlantic to North America.[8] Emigration slowed to a trickle for a short time after Cromwell's revolution brought hope to the peasantry. But it resumed in greater numbers than ever, now swollen by religious dissenters and disappointed democrats who had been silenced by the Restoration army for supporting the republic and advocating much wider suffrage.[9]

England had reorganized its economy and forced large numbers to emigrate – two determining factors in the successful penetration of the North Atlantic market. Later, the Navigation Acts were to complete the arsenal of measures designed to dislodge Holland from its hegemony.

THREE TYPES OF MIGRATION

In order to understand the migratory process, it is important to bear in mind that eviction and expulsion were implicit in the English mode of development at the time. Emigrants to North America were pushed by a less-than-nurturing mother country rather than attracted by the somewhat inhospitable shores of New England.

In striking contrast, Holland attracted people rather than expelling them, and its economic model was based on the prosperity rather than the poverty of the peasantry. It was certainly true that the Dutch economy could not maintain its growth rate without creating relative overpopulation and the poverty of an urban sub-proletariat. Nevertheless, poverty at the very heart of the European economic world-system never reached the proportions it assumed on the semi-periphery (England, Poland, and so on) or on the periphery (such as the Bolivian silver mines of Potosi).

France, incontestably on the semi-periphery and burdened with an outdated economy, had as yet little real involvement in the economic world-system. The French countryside was more self-sufficient than elsewhere, and its inertia reduced the effect of the violent swings in the

world market. Whereas social relationships in rural England were geared
to a market economy and took on a definite capitalistic aspect, rural
France was still dominated by feudal relationships, and society remained
fairly stationary. The fact that the French rural population was undoubt-
edly too large did not lead to a violent upheaval of traditional ways, as
had occurred in England. French rural overpopulation had been a factor
in feudal relationships for centuries and therefore must have been considered normal and in the nature of things. Despite sporadic revolts,
migration from France was in fact a matter of individuals moving one by
one in search of work, mainly toward Spain and, later, in far fewer numbers, toward the West Indies.

In the British Isles, however, the more concentrated aggression
toward the peasants appears to have made them aware of their collective
situation. This awareness was probably reflected in the burgeoning religious sects. These groups represented the resistance of the lower orders
to social and economic changes for which they were paying the price.
They were also instrumental in establishing minimal organization of the
poor and the dispossessed as well as in fostering the search for collective
solutions such as emigration – not in an individual, serial fashion but in
a collective, organized manner. This was the case with the Puritans, who
emigrated first to Holland to escape persecution, then to New England
to escape the corrupting secularism of Holland. They crossed the
Atlantic to find religious freedom and land that they could own.[10]

MIGRATIONS TO NORTH AMERICA

Settlement and the Fur Trade

In the first half of the seventeenth century, very few Europeans would
have risked their lives crossing the Atlantic if the only issue had been to
settle (and in fact to repopulate) northeastern North America.
Settlement and the fur trade were incompatible activities, as we know.
Apart from a small farming population to provide sustenance for traders
and their agents, any increase in the European population meant possibly increasing the number of middlemen, thereby altering the terms of
trade and consequently the profits, to the detriment of a company
monopoly. All trading companies understood this rule. That is why they
did not repopulate the new territories with white settlers, despite being
forced to acknowledge their obligation to do so by various European

states. Proof of this can be seen in the fact that New France had a population of little over 200 Europeans in 1640, and New Netherland had about 1,000 during the same period (see table).

Population of European origin in northeastern North America, 1608-65

	New France	New Netherland	New England
1608	28		
1620	60		
1625		200	
1628	76	270	
1629	117	300	
1630		500	2,300
1640		1,000	13,700
1641	240		
1643		3,000	
1650	657	3,000	22,300
1653	2,000		
1660			33,000
1663	3,035		
1664		8,000	
1665	3,215		

The Tide of Migration from the British Isles

It was the English, Irish, and Scottish who radically altered the situation. At the beginning of the seventeenth century, British merchants in west coast ports dreamed of making their fortunes in America. In 1606, several of them formed the Plymouth Company, which opened a trading post in New England comparable to the trading stations of Asia, in order to obtain all sorts of exotic products from the interior of the continent. There was, however, 'no returne to satisfy the expectation of the Adventurers.'[11] Other, similar enterprises, such as the New Plymouth and the Dorchester companies, met with an equal lack of success. It took large-scale expulsions from the British Isles to launch European settlement on the Atlantic seaboard of North America.[12]

After 1620, emigrants came in the tens of thousands. Some went to the Caribbean where centres of permanent settlement had begun to develop after this date in Saint Kitts, Nevis, and Barbados. By 1640, the latter had 10,000 inhabitants, the majority of them Irish. By 1660, there were 40,000 inhabitants on the island of Barbados, although half were slaves.[13] Others went to Virginia. Between November 1619 and February 1625,[14] 4,800 emigrants settled there. By 1640, their numbers had risen to 8,000 and, by 1660, to 33,000. Emigration represented a veritable human tide that completely upset the existing balance of power in North America.

The Dutch Counter-offensive

By the 1630s, the Dutch realized that the sharp rise in emigration from the British Isles to North America might cost them everything. In 1629, the Dutch West India Company had become resigned to the fact that, in order to encourage European settlement of its territories, it must allow an initial breach in its patroon-based monopoly. In April 1638, the states-general of Holland adopted a resolution to speed up settlement in New Netherland:

> [Whereas] their High Mightinesses receive additional information that the population of New Netherland not only does not increase as it ought, but even that the population which had been commenced is decreasing, and appears to be neglected by the West India Company, so that the inhabitants of foreign princes and potentates are endeavoring to incorporate New Netherland, and if not seasonably attended to, will at once entirely overrun it ... Their Mightinesses have resolved and concluded ... that [their] deputies shall assist in making and enacting such effectual order regarding the population of New Netherland, providing all needed incentives for colonists, so that this State may not be deprived of the aforesaid New Netherland.[15]

Shortly afterward, the Dutch West India Company opened the fur trade to all and opted for settlement.[16] This decision was a veritable about-face. The economic objectives of the colony were made clear: priority would shift from the fur trade to making the colony the breadbasket of the Atlantic empire (Curaçao, Bonaire, Aruba, and Brazil). The company would assume the cost of free transport for immigrants to the colony and would supply them with the necessary equipment for getting settled, clearing the land, and starting farming operations.[17] In return, the settlers were to pay the company 10 per cent of their production after four or ten years, depending on circumstances.[18] The company must have invested large sums in this project because within twenty years the population rose from 1,000 (1640) to 7,000 or 8,000.

These efforts to colonize New Netherland did not, however, stem the tide of British immigrants. For example, in the Connecticut River valley (an area considered by the Dutch as falling within their jurisdiction), the five or six Dutch settlers were overwhelmed by the 2,000 British settlers present in 1642.[19] The same phenomenon occurred in Long Island, where British settlers soon occupied two thirds of the territory. In addition to the efforts of the Dutch West India Company, the city of Amsterdam also intervened directly to encourage settlement. Between 1659 and 1662, it invested nearly 44,000 florins to develop New Amstel, a settlement located on the Delaware River.[20] New Netherland was open to all, irrespective of religion or nationality,[21] and settlers did indeed come from everywhere. Father Jogues remarked in 1643 that 'eighteen different languages' were spoken in New Amsterdam.[22]

In 1659, Director-General Stuyvesant planned to contain British settlers on the upper Hudson River by bringing in dispossessed peasants. 'Some homeless *Polish, Lithuanian, Prussian, Jutlandish* or *Flemish* farmers (who, we trust, are soon and easily to be found during this Eastern and Northern war) may be sent over by the first ships.'[23]

The British Outstrip the Dutch
The Dutch had traditionally gained the upper hand in their enterprises. Now, however, they found themselves on the losing end of things. Paradoxically, the basis of their economic success became a disadvantage in North America. Holland was a rich and tolerant country with a prosperous peasant class. Furthermore, it was the pivot of the world economy and controlled the major trade networks on the Baltic Sea as well as on the Arctic, Indian, and Pacific oceans (Java in 1619 and Japan in 1641). The Dutch had operated within these trade networks. Becoming the major power in the Atlantic economy proved more difficult. It was no longer enough to control enormous accumulations of capital or to possess the largest fleet. To take over the Atlantic economy, it was necessary to repopulate North America, where the native inhabitants were dying

out. Holland, however, had to pay to transport and settle people in North America, whereas the same process cost Great Britain nothing.

As we have seen, in the British Isles, a number of circumstances combined to cause an exodus toward the North American colonies. These included economic depression between 1615 and 1630, the colonization of Ireland, cumulative hardships imposed on the peasantry by enclosure (beginning in the 1620s), religious persecution, and the introduction of the new draperies sector with its attendant cottage industry system. There was no need to finance settlement out of public funds. Emigrants went of their own accord. Although these settlers were indigent and therefore could not pay for their passage or for the cost of getting established in North America, credit was advanced. This came from trading companies interested in American investment and sympathetic to religious dissenters. For example, the New England Company, born in 1628 from the ashes of the Dorchester Company, had both religious and commercial objectives. The refugees (individuals, families, and whole villages) set off in fishing and trading vessels as well as in specially chartered ships.[24] Some embarked as indentured servants to be sold by contract by ships' captains on American shores, usually for three to seven years' labour. The colonies were thus settled as a result of poverty, without either government or companies having to invest large sums of money. By 1660, there were 100,000 British settlers in New England, Virginia, and the West Indies, compared to 8,000 in New Netherland.

Lack of French Settlement

Before 1630, there were barely a hundred settlers in New France. The French government had tried to remedy the situation by sending out a few hundred settlers in 1627, but British pirates successfully foiled this attempt. In 1632, following the capture of Quebec, the whole process had to begin again. In 1635, Father Le Jeune expressed his anxiety about France's slowness in founding colonies:

> Shall the French, alone of all the Nations of the earth, be deprived of the honor of expanding and spreading over this New World? Shall France, much more populous than all the other Kingdoms, have Inhabitants only for itself? or, when her children leave her, shall they go here and there and lose the name of Frenchmen among Foreigners?

Geographers, Historians, and experience itself, show us that every year a great many people leave France who go to enroll themselves elsewhere. For, although the Soil of our country is very fertile, the French women have this blessing, that they are still more so; and thence it happens that our ancient Gauls, in want of land, went to seek it in different parts of Europe ... At present, our French people are no less numerous than our old Gauls; but they do not go forth in bands, but separately, some going in one direction, some in another, to make their fortunes among Strangers. Would it not be better to empty Old France into New, by means of Colonies which could be sent there, than to people Foreign countries?[25]

French emigration remained minimal throughout this period, with 296 colonists reaching New France between 1608 and 1639, and 964 between 1640 and 1659.[26] A good number of these individuals came in response 'to hearsay and the fine accounts that the Jesuit fathers ... took great care to print and distribute every year.'[27] After 1650, the Compagnie des Habitants took several steps to encourage settlement. Ships had to bring to Quebec one man for every sixteen gross tons.[28] In a survey of seventeenth-century contracts for indentured servants in La Rochelle, Gabriel Debien has shown that, between 1655 and 1660, 250 were destined for Canada. Most settlers going out to Canada were indentured servants.[29] Very few financed themselves. However, the majority of indentured servants were embarking in a steady stream for the West Indies, although even this movement never reached the extent of the immigration from the British Isles.

In 1663, there were 3,035 French living in the Saint Lawrence valley. This number was nearly a third of the New Netherland figure and one-twentieth of the population in the British colonies on the Atlantic seaboard. Although France had a high rate of emigration in the sixteenth and seventeenth centuries, most of it was in the direction of Spain. Nevertheless, a good number set off to settle on the other side of the Atlantic. The question is, why did so few of them land at Quebec?

New France was as much a missionary as a commercial venture. After 1632, only Roman Catholics were allowed to come to the colony. This meant that the large numbers of Huguenots who embarked on a transatlantic passage went to British or Dutch colonies, although it is impossible to

estimate just how many. Fort Orange was first settled by Protestant Walloons. There were fifteen French settlers among the 200 people in the Jamestown colony.[30] New Netherland archives reveal many French Huguenot
names: De Lancey, Forest, Vassar, Gallaudet, and Delano (De La Noye),
among others.[31] New England also had its share of French Huguenots.
The exclusion of Protestants from New France was not so much an error
in colonial strategy as an indication of France's backward and feudal
society and the marginal, peripheral nature of this colony's economy.

The state of permanent war counted for much in New France's poor
reputation. Traditionally, nations had gone to war outside their own
borders. However, the fur wars occurred in the heart of New France, not
in New Netherland. Between 1640 and 1667, the French colony lived in
constant fear of Iroquois raids. Not only did the Iroquois cause the
colony's economic strangulation by cutting off its fur supply; they
threatened to burn the little 'city' of Quebec.[32]

All in all, there was not much hope of white settlement in the French
colony, given its geographical position in the Saint Lawrence valley
beyond all trade circuits except that of the beaver, its inability to admit
any but practising Roman Catholics 'of good morals,' and the on-going
fur wars that threatened its very existence. Any development of an internal market[33] was a mere pipe-dream. In this context, New France was
doomed to failure.

A DEMOGRAPHIC INVESTMENT

> We could spare from the Netherlands thousands from year to year,
> and send them abroad without injury; and if ever there should happen
> to be any defect in our population, this would be supplied from the
> neighbouring countries. At a word, we could use those people and
> make them Netherlanders. Our neighbours must put up with it, and
> the people who now go to the New Netherlands are not lost or
> destroyed, but are as if they were placed at interest, for we know how
> fast the population increases ... Hence I conclude that out of this coun-
> try we can send as many colonial settlers as Spain can, and one-half
> more, without missing any man out from the Netherlands. We could
> increase our strength by so doing; for they who are colonists in the
> New Netherlands become Netherlanders as well as they do who
> become burghers here, and remain devoted to us.[34]

According to Van der Donck, colonization offered two advantages. On the one hand, the settlers would become Dutchmen and create a sort of second Holland. On the other – and it is this aspect that concerns us – repopulating northeastern North America represented an extremely profitable demographic investment, the results of which would effectively change the balance of power among colonial empires.

Some Statistics

Let us take a look at the figures underlying Van der Donck's central demographic statement. Statistics show the extent of the gap between total population growth in Europe and North America. Between 1500 and 1750, the annual growth rate in Europe was 0.17 per cent,[35] whereas white population growth in northeastern North America in the eighteenth century was 2.5 per cent, or fifteen times greater.[36] The latter rate was even higher in the seventeenth century, when immigration was correspondingly larger. In New England between 1650 and 1660, as a result of the combined effects of natural growth and immigration, the white population had an average annual growth rate of 4.51 per cent (other estimates put it at 6.88 per cent).[37] I stipulate white population because, as we know, the fate of Amerindians and blacks was very different. To realize the relative significance of these figures, consider that the population of seventeenth-century France was 20 million, compared to something under 60 million today – that is, the population has risen by a coefficient of less than three. By contrast, the 10,000 immigrants who settled in New France have an estimated 10 million descendants scattered throughout North America – that is, a growth coefficient of 1,000.

What accounts for this enormous disparity in demographic development? Why did the slow-growing European population increase so rapidly once it was transferred to North American soil?

At first glance, one might think that settlers in North America produced more children, but this was not the case. The crucial difference lay in the fact that the survival rate was higher. In Europe, the birth and death rates were fairly even – forty per one thousand – thus keeping population numbers fairly steady. In North America, however, the spectre of death for whites did not loom so large. Settlers had just as many children, but infant mortality was not so drastic, and people generally lived longer.[38]

In London during 1662, for example, 10 out of 100 children reached the age of five, and the survivors had a life expectancy of 17.5 years.[39] In New France, 82 out of 100 children reached the age of five.[40] This comparison is not entirely satisfactory, however, since death rates have always been higher in urban areas.[41] Take, instead, a figure from rural France. Pierre Goubert's demographic survey of an eighteenth-century village (Saint-Laurent-des-Eaux) establishes an infant mortality rate (under one year) of 32.6 per cent and a juvenile rate (one to four years) of 22.4 per cent – that is, 55 per cent mortality under five years of age.[42] In seventeenth-century Andover, Massachusetts, the life expectancy of a twenty-one-year-old man was 64.2 years, compared to 59.8 years in England. In comparing seventeenth-century New England and nineteenth-century England, it is noted that women had the same life expectancy, although men lived an average of 12.6 years longer in the former.[43]

Phase A of a Malthusian Cycle

Why was the survival rate higher in North America? It could be suggested that initially the ocean crossings resulted in a cruelly effective selection of the fittest. But, more significantly, white immigrants found themselves in an environment where humans had become rare and land was abundant. Moreover, this environment was unspoiled. Two aspects of the immigrants' new situation contributed to their well-being. The first of these was social. Wage-earners were now scarce and could demand higher wages,[44] and peasants, now equally scarce, could use their rarity as a bargaining tool in preventing the development of crush- ing social relationships. The second aspect was ecological: Europeans profited from the accumulated benefits of the respect for nature practised by Amerindian populations over past millennia. This Malthusian phase A applied only to European settlers, for Amerindian populations in the same environment melted away like ice on a summer day, and black slaves suffered exploitive conditions that made any sharp population growth impossible.

This is not to say that living conditions were especially easy for European newcomers. Indentured servants toiled long, hard hours for their masters. Settlers had to build basic shelters as soon as they arrived. Some 'simply dug a ditch ... [and] covered it with the trunks of small trees.'[45] Others built a cabin with upright stakes and filled in the chinks.

Marie de l'Incarnation referred to these dwellings as 'houses with half-timbered, stone-filled walls.'[46] The floors were simply packed earth, which was no worse than in the dwellings of the poor in Europe. With the abundance of wood and stone, these cabins soon became houses. The significant difference, however, was that people did not die of cold in their dwellings. The various reports are unanimous on this point. Pierre Boucher writes: 'The houses are well-warmed, as wood costs nothing but the effort of cutting and carrying it to the fire. Oxen are used for carting it on machines called *traines* [toboggans].'[47] The *Jesuit Relations* noted that 'the Winter – of which so much is said in Europe, because of its severity and length – seemed to me more endurable than in Paris. Wood costs nothing but the cutting, for those who own land, which is given freely to such as ask for it, and are willing to cultivate it. Some may receive four or five hundred arpents, and others more.'[48] Van der Donck stated that 'there is everywhere fuel in abundance, and to be obtained for the expense of cutting and procuring the same. The super-abundance of this country is not equalled by any other in the world.'[49]

Another determining social factor in population growth was the ease of access to land. The British peasants who were evicted following enclosure of land for grazing were able to recover their principal means of production, the soil. In Massachusetts, a settler had an average of 150 acres.[50] In New France, a settler cleared an arpent of land per year and, by his death, would have cleared about thirty.[51] The soil, rich from thousands of years of forest growth, was incredibly productive. Numerous documents contain remarks on the high yields, but I will limit myself to citing two. The 1633 *Jesuit Relations* state that, 'as to the soil, I send you some of its fruits; they are heads of wheat, of rye, and of barley, that we planted near our little house. We gathered last year a few wisps of rye that we found here and there among the peas; I counted in some of them 60 kernels, in others 80, in others 112.'[52] De Vries notes in 1639 that, 'as to what the land produces, the soil ... in the low plains, often clay-ground is very fertile, as Brand-pylen told me that he had produced wheat on this island [near Fort Orange] for twelve years successively without its lying fallow.'[53] And further that 'I have begun to take hold of Vriessendale, as it was a fine place, situated along the river, under the mountains ... I have sown wheat which grew higher than the tallest man in the country.'[54]

Often, settlers would start cultivating abandoned Amerindian fields, as Champlain noted in Montreal in 1611: 'And near the said Place Royale is a little river that flows fairly far inland, and all along it lie more than sixty arpents of abandoned land resembling meadows, where one could sow seed and plant gardens. In the past, the savages worked this soil, but they left in pursuit of their usual wars.'[55] Father Jogues also remarked on this practice in New Netherland: 'The first comers found lands fit for use, deserted by the savages, who formerly had fields here. Those who came later have cleared the woods, which are mostly oak. The soil is good.'[56] Similarly, Plymouth settlers cultivated the fields of the Pokanokets, who had been decimated by an epidemic in 1617.[57]

The settlers also raised hogs and allowed them to run free. The animals ate what the forest produced and, unlike their brethren in Europe, did not need to be fattened on grain, peas, or broad beans. The cost of meat production was therefore low, and herds of swine increased rapidly.[58] The rich plant life and plentiful wild game were an important food source. 'Game is abundant, and there is no lack of Moose-hunting. But the eel constitutes a manna exceeding all belief.'[59] It was eaten boiled, roasted, smoked, and salted, as were pigeons. These birds were so plentiful that the settlers even fed them to their pigs.

> Among the birds of every variety to be found here, it is to be noted that Pigeons abound in such numbers that this year one man killed a hundred and thirty-two at a single shot. They passed continually in flocks so dense, and so near the ground, that sometimes they were struck down with oars. This season they attacked the grain fields, where they made great havoc, after stripping the woods and fields of strawberries and raspberries, which grow here everywhere underfoot. But when these Pigeons were taken in requital, they were made to pay the cost very heavily; for the Farmers, besides having plenty of them for home use, and giving them to their servants, and even to their dogs and pigs, salted caskfuls of them for the winter.[60]

All European settlements were located on the seaboard or along the shores of rivers leading to the ocean. Everyone therefore had access to marine life. No seigneurial or property rights interfered with such access as long as it was not used for commercial purposes. 'Salmon and Sturgeon are very plentiful in their seasons; to tell the truth, this country is the Kingdom of water and of fish.'[61]

In New Netherland, turkeys, pigeons, and partridge formed a significant part of the settlers' diet. They could be caught in nets, in snares, with guns, or with dogs.[62] Large game was also abundant, particularly deer.

During times when food was scarce, the Europeans could always count on Amerindian agricultural produce. The Dutch bought 'corn and beans, of which we obtain whole cargoes in sloops and galleys in trade.'[63] Throughout the seaboard areas, Amerindians provided food for the newly arrived settlers and enabled them to survive the difficult early stages. The Powhatans gave wood and food to the Jamestown colonists in 1607. Without the help of the Pemaquids and the Wampanoags, who shared their corn, the pilgrims would probably have starved to death.[64] In 1643, after the Dutch had slaughtered his people, an Amerindian orator recalled the hospitality with which those same people had welcomed the newcomers.[65]

Letting the Records Speak

The growth rate of European populations in North America was fifteen times greater than in Europe. This phenomenon is easily explained by the circumstances: free access to land, higher agricultural yields from virgin soil, availability of land already cleared by the Amerindians, high wages, help from the Amerindians (including the purchase of staples), rapid increase of domestic animals living off forest produce, and fabulously rich hunting and fishing resources. This growth in population could also be seen as a reliable indicator of the quality of life on a material and social level, much like we now consider the rate of infant mortality to be the best mark of a population's socio-economic health. The material conditions of the first few generations of settlers are described in the accounts of Father Menard and the Swedish botanist Pehr Kalm. First, let us hear what Father Menard has to say:

> It must be admitted that, in spite of this, the prospects of our French colonies would be excellent if the fear of the Iroquois did not render their stay dangerous. The soil is very productive; and, if the husbandman who cultivates it only labors with diligence, in a few years he will see himself not merely out of need, but at his ease, – he, his wife, and his children. We see many such men who, having received a grant, – which can here be had for the asking, – in less than five or six years

harvest enough grain to feed themselves with all their family, and even
to sell some. They are furnished with all the conveniences of a farm-
yard, and soon find themselves rich in live stock, so that they can lead a
life free from hardship and full of happiness.

In a few years the families increase; for, as the air of this country is
very salubrious, one sees few children die in the cradle. Though the
winters are long, and snow covers the earth for five whole months to
the depth of three, four, or five feet, yet I can affirm that the cold often
seems more endurable here than in France – whether because the winters are not rainy here, and the days are always pleasant, or because we
have wood at our doors. Moreover, the greater the fire one keeps, day
and night, to combat the cold, the more does he fell the neighboring
forest, and make himself new lands to till and sow, which yield good
harvests of grain, and enrich their Owners. Often one has fishing in
plenty, before his own door, chiefly of eels, which are very excellent in
this country, not being muddy as they are in France, because they swim
in the vast waters of our river St. Lawrence. In the months of
September and October, this eel-fishing is so productive that many a
man will catch for his portion, forty, fifty, sixty, and seventy thousand.
And the great advantage is that we have found means of salting them
conveniently, and thus preserving them untainted. They constitute a
wonderful manna for this country, and one that costs nothing beyond
the catching, and ordinarily carries with it all its own seasoning.
During the winter, Moose are hunted on the snow; and many of our
Frenchmen have killed thirty or forty apiece. Their flesh is easily preserved by freezing, and serves as provision throughout the winter,
while their skins are still more valuable. Formerly, the hunting of them
appeared to our Frenchmen an impossibility, and now it serves them
as recreation. They have also adapted themselves to the hunting of the
beaver, which forms one of this country's great sources of wealth.[66]

In 1749, when Pehr Kalm was travelling through Pennsylvania (formerly New Sweden), he carried out a brief ethnographic inquiry, asking
two old Swedes to talk of their childhood and that of their parents.
Through oral tradition, he was able to go back to the earliest days of New
Sweden. The first Swede, Nils Gustafson, was a hale nonagenarian who
remembered the Dutch regime and the time when a great forest grew on

the site of Philadelphia. His father had come from Sweden to settle there. This unique account is worth citing at length:

Query, Whence did the Swedes, who first came hither, get their cattle? The old man answered, that when he was a boy, his father and other people had told him that the Swedes brought their horses, cows and oxen, sheep, hogs, geese and ducks, over with them. There were but few of a kind at first, but they multiplied greatly here afterwards. He said that Maryland, New York, New England, and Virginia, had been earlier inhabited by Europeans than this part of the country; but he did not know whether the Swedes ever got cattle of any kind from any of these provinces, except from New York. While he was yet very young, the Swedes, as far as he could remember, had already a sufficient stock of all these animals. The hogs had propagated so much at that time, there being so great a plenty of food for them, that they ran about wild in the woods, and that the people were obliged to shoot them when they wanted them. The old man likewise recollected, that horses ran wild in the woods, in some places; but he could not tell whether any other kind of cattle turned wild. He thought that the cattle grew as big at present as they did when he was a boy, provided they received as much food as they needed. For in his younger years food for all kinds of cattle was so plentiful and abundant that the cattle were extremely fat. A cow at that time gave more milk than three or four do at present; but she got more and better food at that time than three or four get now; and, as the old man said, the scanty allowance of grass which the cattle get in summer is really very pitiful ...

Query, Whence did the English in Pennsylvania and New Jersey get their cattle? They bought them chiefly from the Swedes and Dutch who lived here, and a small number were brought over from Old England. The physical form of the cattle and the unanimous accounts of the English here confirmed what the old man had said.

Query, Whence did the Swedes here settled get their several sorts of grain and likewise their fruit trees and kitchen herbs? The old man told me that he had frequently heard when he was young, that the Swedes had brought all kinds of grain and fruits and herbs or seeds of them with them. For as far as he could recollect, the Swedes here were plentifully provided with wheat, rye, barley and oats. The Swedes, at that time, brewed all their beer of malt made of barley, and likewise made good strong beer. They had already got distilling apparatus, and when they intended to distil they lent their apparatus to one another. At first they were forced to buy corn of the Indians, both for sowing and eating. But after continuing for some years in this country, they extended their corn plantations so much that the Indians were obliged some time after to buy corn of the Swedes. The old man likewise assured me that the Indians formerly, and about the time of the first settling of the Swedes, were more industrious, but that now they had become very lazy in comparison. When he was young the Swedes had a great quantity of very good white cabbage. Winter cabbage, or kale, which was left on the ground during winter, was also abundant. They were likewise well provided with turnips ... The Swedes likewise cultivated carrots, in the old man's younger years. Among the fruit trees were apple trees. They were not numerous, and only some of the Swedes had little orchards of them, while others had not a single tree. None of the Swedes made cider, for it had come into use but lately. The Swedes brewed beer and that was their common drink. But at present there are very few who brew beer, for they commonly make cider. Cherry trees were abundant when Nils Gustafson was a boy. Peach trees were at that time more numerous than at present and the Swedes brewed beer of the fruit. The old man could not tell from whence the Swedes first of all got the peach trees ...

At the time when the Swedes arrived, they bought land at a very small price. For a piece of baize, or a pot full of brandy or the like, they could get a piece of ground, which at present would be worth more than four hundred pounds, Pennsylvania currency.[67]

Pehr Kalm interviewed another Swede, Åke Helm, who was in his seventies:

[He] assured me that in his lifetime there had been no failure of crops but that the people had always had plenty. It is likewise to be observed that the people eat their bread or corn, rye, or wheat, quite pure and free from chaff and other impurities. Many aged Swedes and Englishmen confirmed this account, and said that they could not remember any crop so bad as to make the people suffer in the least, much less that anybody had starved to death, while they were in America. Sometimes the price of grain rose higher in one year than in another, on account of a great drought or bad weather, but still there was always sufficient for the consumption of the inhabitants. Nor is it likely that any great famine can happen in this country, unless it please God to afflict it with extraordinary punishments. The weather is well known from more than sixty years experience. Here are no nights cold enough to hurt the seeds. The rainy periods are of short duration and the drought is seldom or never severe. But the chief thing is a great variety of grain. The people sow the different kinds, at different times and seasons, and though one crop turns out bad, yet another succeeds. The summer is so long that of some species of grain they may get two crops. There is hardly a month from May to October or November, inclusive, in which the people do not reap some kind of cereal, or gather some sort of fruit. It would indeed be a very great misfortune if a bad crop should happen; for here, as in many other places, they lay up no stores, and are contented with living from hand to mouth, as the saying goes.[68]

The Comparison with Europe

Apart from the peculiarities of New Sweden, climate included, it is clear from these accounts that European colonists did not die of hunger and even lived well – a basic reality in North America in striking contrast to Europe. There, except for the rich, people ate very little meat. Europeans lived mostly on bread, gruel, and cooked roots and tubers. How could it be otherwise? In France (although the figures are for 1780), meat and saltwater fish cost respectively eleven and sixty-six times more than bread.[69] The peasant sold his best wheat and never ate whole wheat bread himself, making do with a loaf made from wheat mixed with some other grain, such as rye or barley.[70] In the Paris of 1780, average calorie consumption was 2,000 per day,[71] compared to about 4,000 per day in seventeenth-century New France.[72] Furthermore, the water in Europe was usually polluted, especially in the cities, whereas it was still pure on the other side of the Atlantic. The well-nourished European in North America could withstand epidemics. Briefly put, in North American colonies, subsistence was not a source of social crisis.

In France during the same period, huge demographic crises were decimating the population. These occurred in 1630, 1648 to 1653, 1661 to 1662, 1693 to 1694, 1709 to 1710, and 1741 to 1742. 'These dates,' says Pierre Goubert, 'correspond exactly to great economic crises triggered by a considerable cyclical rise in the price of wheat.'[73] Other epidemics, not linked to severe fluctuations in wheat prices, struck in 1625, 1637, 1638, 1668, 1701, and 1719. Plague raged several times in Rouen, Amiens, and Beauvais during the first half of the seventeenth century. It recurred annually in Amsterdam between 1622 and 1628 (leaving 35,000 dead); in Paris in 1612, 1619, 1631, 1638, 1662, and 1668; and in London, where it reputedly claimed 156,463 victims between 1593 and 1665.[74] No such calamities occurred among Europeans in North America. Their numbers grew apace, while epidemics ravaged the Amerindians.

RIVALRIES IN THE RACE TO CONTROL THE ATLANTIC ECONOMY

At the outset of the seventeenth century, Great Britain, Holland, and France began to rival each other in the race to accumulate capital in North America. They were attracted principally by furs but also by wood and fish. The Dutch had the initial advantage with their large fleet and capital resources. However, the balance of power shifted when England began to expel masses of poor people, dissenters, and evicted peasants. Whereas the French who emigrated to Spain became Spaniards, and the thousands of Dutch sailors who travelled the seven seas were never anything but an immense ship's company, in North America the new arrivals became colonists. They put down roots in a continent where the original inhabitants were dying out – a continent with tremendous natural wealth. The colonial population grew rapidly to become New Englanders, New Netherlanders, and New Frenchmen, so to speak. Their demographic strength was also a military asset as well as providing a market and forming the basis of a colonial empire. Among the three competing powers, Great Britain would eventually profit most, since it had made the biggest demographic investment.

The British Breakthrough

In Virginia and New England, immigration was almost the only force driving the economy. During the 1620s, less than 500 immigrants settled in New England. This was not much, but it was enough to build an initial infrastructure for receiving newcomers. During the next decade, immigrants arrived at a rate of 2,000 per year.[75] Small villages gradually appeared all along the coast of Massachusetts, Rhode Island, New Hampshire, and up the Connecticut River. These were populated by religious dissenters for the most part, although there were a great many Anglicans north of the Merrimack River.[76] The process of homesteading required all these new arrivals to clear, build, farm, make clothing, and provide themselves with tools and other equipment. In the beginning, self-sufficiency could only be a dream for the future. For the present they had to buy what they needed, and it was precisely this demand for goods, created year after year by waves of settlement, that kept the economy rolling. British and Dutch ships arrived laden with immigrants and merchandise – clothing, iron tools, nails, powder, vinegar, salt, candles, and so on. The immigrants themselves often owned some of these goods, which they would exchange on arrival for cattle, corn, and wood.[77] To be able to buy, however, the colonist had to produce – supplies for the latest settlers, to begin with, and, more notably, products to fill the holds of ships sailing back to Europe. The colonists had only one major resource: the forest. At first they hunted the beaver, this being the principal, if not the only, export product in the early days. The Pilgrim Fathers repaid the debts contracted for the cost of settlement with beaver pelts. Soon small trading posts had sprung up at all strategic localities in New England. Wampum was used as a means of exchange. Trade reached a peak in the 1630s and remained stable until after 1637, when excessive hunting brought about a quick drop in the number of pelts. By 1640, it was no longer possible to trade for beaver. Without a large river basin as a means of contact with more distant regions, this initial trading phase came to an end.[78]

The flora remained a resource, however. The magnificent virgin forest was filled with giant trees, far taller than anything now growing in the same regions – mature pine standing 45 to 60 metres high, with trunks 1 to 1.25 metres thick, and mature oak 30 metres tall and 6 metres around,[79] not to mention elm, maple, walnut, and others. The colonists were quick to exploit this rich resource. Ships were loaded with cargoes of wood, mainly masts for ship-building in Britain and oak staves for the manufacture of wine barrels in the Azores, the Canary Islands, and Madeira. Attempts were also made in New England to develop other economic activities such as salt production, but these came to nothing. Ocean fishing brought in very little, because the colonists had almost no experience. Prior to 1640, they bought most of their fish from fishermen who hailed from the west coast of England.[80] Ultimately however, although the soil produced high yields at the outset, it could not support continued intensive farming. After turning first to the fur trade, settlers established a lumber-based economy, building saw mills and making an initial attempt to develop shipbuilding.

In 1640, the flow of migration slowed to a trickle, and New England's emerging economy entered its first depression. The price of wood, food, and domestic animals fell with a drop in demand by the few new arrivals. For example, the price of a cow declined from twenty to four or five pounds sterling.[81] Established settlers were unable to sell their produce at good prices and therefore had difficulty buying British merchandise. They got around this predicament by doubling their forest exploitation since the demand for wood continued to rise in the Atlantic economy.

One possible solution to New England's problem was to redress its high-deficit trade balance with Great Britain by exporting more wood to the mother country. This was the first route taken. The great forests of England had disappeared in the fifteenth century, and wood had become increasingly scarce while the demand was constantly growing. Wood was used for domestic and commercial construction as well as for shipbuilding. It was the fuel for heating houses and for making glass, iron, bricks, pottery, alcohol, and the potash needed in the manufacture of soap,[82] gunpowder, and glass.

Since the sixteenth century, Britain had imported its wood and potash in enormous amounts from the Baltic region. It became even more dependent on this source between 1600 and 1640 – a further reflection of how the whole British economy, including shipbuilding, was dependent on Holland, which controlled access to the Baltic market. In 1649, the Russian tsar forbad the sale of potash to the British as a sanction in response to the death sentence passed on Charles I. The measure caused a sudden crisis in the British textile industry. In 1651, Holland obtained from Denmark the right to collect taxes in the Sund, and this enabled it to block British ships from entering the Baltic in wartime.[83] Given this context, access to the North American lumber market became necessary in order to escape total dependence on a foreign power.

However, there were other, more technical, reasons which favoured the American market. New England pine may have been more costly and less enduring than the fir from Riga, but a single great pine could serve as a mainmast in place of two Riga firs.[84] Masts made of one tree were more flexible and allowed for greater speed.[85] Furthermore, some parts of a ship's hull had to be built of oak pieces with a specific natural curve. Such pieces were rare, but could be supplied by American colonists. Although the British shipyards continued to buy large quantities of wood from the Baltic because it was significantly cheaper,[86] they always had the foresight to buy at least part of their supply from New England.

New England's most profitable lumber trade, however, was not with the mother country, but with Spain, Portugal, the Canary Islands, the Azores, and Madeira. Spain and Portugal imported wood from the Baltic because their forests had long since disappeared. Likewise, the forest covering the above-mentioned islands had been cut down to make room for growing sugar cane. This activity was later ruined by Brazilian sugar production, and the islands turned to the production of grapes for wine.[87] As wine production increased, however, so did the demand for barrels – and not just any barrels. They had to be made of wood that did not alter the taste of the wine and that remained watertight while allowing enough air through to oxygenate the contents. Only white oak, which grew abundantly in New England, fulfilled all these requirements. The British colonists were thus able to gain a foothold in the wine business by producing white oak staves by the thousands. The stave trade stimulated other activities. Small shipyards sprang up in Boston, Salem, and Charlestown. Organized fishing then got under way, for the wine producers were also in the market for fish. Although they considered the quality of New England fish unsatisfactory, they were obliged to use this source because their usual supplier, England, was embroiled in both civil war[88] and the Anglo-Dutch war. It is interesting to note that even in these early days, European wars were stimulating American growth!

New England settlers also looked to the West Indies for trade. Between 1640 and 1650, there were more British in Barbados than in New England. There, as elsewhere in the West Indies, the newcomers cut down almost all the trees in order to grow cash crops such as tobacco, sweet corn, indigo, and tapioca. After 1640, the economic and human configuration of these islands changed totally. Slave labour replaced the small independent producer, and almost all land was given over to sugar cane. By 1660, the Barbadian forests had disappeared and half the island's 40,000 inhabitants were slaves – a proportion that rose to two-thirds in the next twenty years. The planters needed white oak staves for rum, red oak staves for sugar and tobacco, and cedar and pine for construction. With the specialization of production, the islands became dependent on offshore sources for food. They imported farm produce such as peas, corn, cheese, biscuit, salt beef, salt pork, and poor quality fish for slaves. New England fishermen worked off their own shores and even off Newfoundland, where they sold all kinds of products purchased elsewhere, in addition to lumber from New England forests. The forests of Newfoundland had shrunk toward the interior as a result of excessive cutting by thousands of European fishermen.

Gradually, the entire New England economy (lumbering, fishing, farming, and even iron production)[89] was integrated into the Atlantic economy, where labour was in the process of being divided on a regional basis. The New England colonists found themselves learning the Atlantic shipping business. As Charles F. Carroll notes in his book, *The Timber Economy of Puritan New England*, 40 per cent of the tonnage of Boston exports in 1661 was bound for wine-producing areas, 30 per cent for the West Indies, 18 per cent for London, 9 per cent for other North American colonies, and 3 per cent for Newfoundland.[90] In 1643, at least five ships set sail from New England for various Atlantic destinations. This was only a beginning, however. Twenty years later, the Boston fleet alone numbered about 300 ships.[91] Little by little, New England's expanding trade helped integrate the various parts of an Atlantic empire within which New England occupied a semi-peripheral or sub-imperial status. The Navigation Acts, which made the hitherto ignored colonies the pivot of imperial policy, brought political weight into an equation where demographic and economic forces were already important factors. The Acts were aimed at Holland, Britain's main rival in the Atlantic market, as well as in the textile and shipbuilding sectors. Great Britain was about to make use of a new, unexpected strength, created on the islands and shores of the North Atlantic by those same people whom it had expelled and who had taken refuge across the sea.

Holland's Failed Offensive

New Netherland formed a very small part of the Dutch commercial empire. Even the relative strength of the entire Atlantic economy was of secondary importance in the Dutch trading network. Holland had its own 'America' within arm's reach – the Baltic and the North Sea regions and Russia via the port of Archangel.[92] Holland could draw on these sources for its wood and wood derivatives as well as for grain, flax, hemp, iron, and fish. In a sense, the Baltic was the heart of the Dutch empire.[93] In 1666, three-quarters of the capital circulating on the Amsterdam Exchange was involved in the Baltic. Moreover, Dutch merchants were able to counter the initial imbalance in this trade, for at first they had little to export and everything to import. To do this, they had to maintain their Spanish connection, despite the war, in order to acquire gold and silver with which to pay for their purchases. After 1640, Amsterdam completely surpassed London and Genoa by gaining control of monetary circulation in Northern Europe. Then the Dutch succeeded in diversifying and increasing the merchandise offered by their ships on the Baltic, which meant plying the seven seas, particularly in the direction of Asia, in order to get spices, sugar, tea, and tobacco. Around 1660, they were exporting 14.5 million pounds of colonial products to the Baltic and had succeeded in stabilizing their balance of trade with this region.[94]

After their northern trade offensive (and because of it), the Dutch turned their attention to the east. They were able to benefit from Portugal's loss of military strength and established a new, highly profitable, trade route that complemented their existing network. This eastern thrust demanded immense financial and human resources. The Dutch East India Company was created in 1602 with six and a half million florins in capital, or ten times the sum invested by the British East India Company established two years earlier. The Dutch set up trading posts in the Moluccas (the Spice Islands) in 1605, in Batavia in 1619, in Formosa in 1624, in Japan in 1634, in Mauritius in 1638, in Malacca and the Cape of Good Hope in 1652, in Ceylon in 1656, and then went on to India. Between 1600 and 1620, an average of twenty-five ships left Europe annually for Asia. During the 1650s and 1660s, the average rose to forty ships and at least half of these were Dutch.[95] If we estimate an average crew of fifty sailors per ship,[96] this means that about 1,000 Dutchmen embarked each year for the East Indies. To this we must add the forty men-of-war (2,000 sailors) commissioned to watch over Dutch interests in the event of a conflict as well as the garrisons established alongside the trading posts.

Since Europe had very little to offer Asia, it developed a deficit trade balance. Holland therefore set up intra-Asiatic trade to reduce shipments of gold and silver to the Orient.[97] The Dutch bought calico (Indian cotton fabric) in India, elephants in Ceylon, and copper in Japan, which they then sold to the Moluccas and Java.[98] The volume of the trade within Asia forced the Dutch to use more boats and men. In addition to the ships plying between Europe and Asia, the Dutch East India Company maintained eighty-five ships (4,250 sailors) in the trade within Asia alone during the 1640s. The number increased from one decade to the next.[99] In the course of the company's two-hundred-year history, a million people were in transit aboard these boats, an average of 5,000 per year. The round trip took five years and claimed the lives of two out of three men, so that only a third saw their homeland again.[100] The human cost was enormous, but this did not weigh very heavily in comparison to an average annual profit of 20 to 22 per cent between 1605 and 1720.[101] In this way, tiny Holland, with two million inhabitants, took over the Asian world-economy – a considerable accomplishment!

There was still the Atlantic economy to the west, however. When shareholders founded the Dutch West India Company in 1621, they had in mind the same aims as in the east. The initial capital input was equally great – seven million florins.[102] Investors were mainly counting on profits from intercepting the fleet of Spanish galleons laden with precious metals, a coup that they successfully managed off Havana in 1629.[103] Their second endeavour, similar to that in the Indian Ocean, was to attack Portugal, a weak link in the chain of European occupation. Seen in this context, New Netherland, situated on the shores of the Hudson River, remained a marginal and expensive enterprise. Between 1626 and 1654, it lost more than half a million florins.[104] Furthermore, it became obvious at the outset that taking over the Atlantic economy would be a harder task than capturing the Asian market. In the Orient, superabundant manpower was never lacking; in America, however, it had become rare, following the disastrous population losses suffered by the Amerindians during the sixteenth and early seventeenth centuries. Not only was greater capital investment needed to create a commercial empire, but the project had to cope with the scarcity of manpower. Large numbers of Dutch were already involved in developing Holland's northern European and Oriental trade. Would it be possible to increase these numbers even more in order to develop western trade? There was no problem with financial investment, but demographic investment was another matter, and it is probable that a population of two million had reached its capacity in this regard. Such is the opinion of Fernand Braudel in his conclusion to a chapter on the failure of the Dutch in the New World: 'Perhaps it is only reasonable to suppose ... that tiny Holland was not big enough to swallow the Indian Ocean, the Brazilian forest, and a sizeable chunk of Africa all at once.'[105]

In order to establish the Dutch West India Company's Atlantic trade empire, Dutch boats first attacked Brazil, which they had blithely pillaged early in the century and where they had gained control of between half and two-thirds of the trade by about 1620. In 1622, Amsterdam already had at least twenty-five sugar refineries. Taking over Brazil would give the Dutch control of the entire sugar production industry. The Dutch believed that the cost of capturing Brazil could be amortized merely by seizing the wealth of the king of Spain, the clergy, and merchants residing in Portugal. They were also counting on support from the Jews in Brazil, sworn enemies of the Spanish Inquisition.[106] They therefore opened their offensive by taking San Salvador (Bahia), the capital of Brazil, in 1624. They lost it the following year, only to recapture it in 1630, after which they occupied the towns of the Nordeste sugar region – Recife, Olinda, and Paraiba. The area was indeed the richest in Brazil, but since the Dutch occupation was confined to the coast, they acquired only partial control. The Luso-Brazilians (Portuguese Brazilians) waged a long war against the Dutch, forcing them to remain in the towns and import supplies by sea, rather than using produce from the surrounding countryside.[107]

With a toehold in Brazil, the Dutch now tried to integrate the Atlantic world-system into their trading network. On 5 July 1638, the agenda for the Dutch West India Company board meeting called for discussion of New Netherland, Curaçao, Cape Verde, Senegal, Sierra Leone, Brazil, and other colonies on Atlantic coasts.[108] Brazil would continue to be used for sugar production, but for this, slaves were considered 'necessary.' The Dutch would therefore dislodge the Portuguese from the coast of Africa and take over the slave trade, using their own ships for transport. In 1640, the Portuguese gained independence (Portugal had been under Spanish rule since 1584), and Spain withdrew its *asiento* – that is, Portugal lost its exclusive right to sell slaves in the Spanish colonies. The Dutch stepped into this convenient vacuum.

It was at this juncture that the Dutch decided to change the economic vocation of New Netherland. Instead of being a source of furs, as in the past, it would become the forest and garden for Curaçao, Bonaire, Aruba, and Brazil.[109] This was the only way to make the colony profitable while peopling it with settlers whose presence would keep the territory from being taken over by the British. As the colony on the Hudson took this new direction, exports gradually increased in volume. These included tobacco, cereals, fish, salt beef, horses, pine, and oak staves.[110] Shipbuilding also began at this time.[111] Although New Netherland possessed the same resources as the Baltic area (wood, wood by-products, and cereals), it could not compete as a supplier to the mother country since the cost of transport from Holland to its colony was three times that from Holland to the Baltic.[112] Conversely, the colony's products became competitive as a result of the shorter distances between New Netherland and the West Indies or Brazil.

Between 1637 and 1645, Dutch merchants transported over 23,000 slaves to Brazil. Business was good. Between 1640 and 1644, they transported 6,500 slaves to Barbados,[113] where they encouraged colonists to grow sugar rather than tobacco, since the latter was very difficult to sell.[114] But now, for the first time, Dutch merchants suffered a serious setback: a Portuguese uprising in Brazil in 1645 ousted the Dutch from the principal sugar-growing regions.

Losing Brazil meant losing the main slave market in one blow. An underground war continued in Brazil, and the Dutch had to withdraw completely in 1654, at the very moment when Holland was confronting England in the first Anglo-Dutch war. The Portuguese would soon recover most of their lost trading posts on the African coast.[115] With the loss of their principal outlet for slave labour, the Dutch fell back on Curaçao, transforming it into a trans-shipping port and an island depot for slaves. These slaves were subsequently resold to Barbados (about 6,000 between 1645 and 1672),[116] to the Spanish colonies, and to the French West Indies, where a good many Dutch refugees from Brazil had settled. Meanwhile, Holland had numerous sugar refineries (sixty-one in Amsterdam in 1650) that it wanted to keep profitable. Consequently, the Dutch resumed their war with the Portuguese in 1657 – a ruinous war with astronomical costs that the Dutch West India Company was unable to bear for long. In 1661, the two countries signed a treaty. Portugal recognized Dutch conquests of its Asian possessions but was firm about holding onto Brazil. As compensation, it agreed to sell its salt to the Dutch at a reduced price. In other words, the latter sacrificed Brazil and its sugar in exchange for a guaranteed cheap salt supply.[117] This treaty marked the end of the rise of Dutch power.

In order to forestall further Dutch aggression and prevent its empire from collapsing, Portugal had no choice but to enter into an alliance with Britain. With circumstances clearly in Britain's favour, Portugal opened wide the doors of its American, African, and Asian colonies in exchange for British naval protection. The negotiations played a part in bringing about the marriage of Charles II and Catherine of Braganza, the Portuguese *infanta*. Her dowry 'brought him Bombay and direct trading rights with Portuguese West Africa, a source of slaves, and Brazil, a source of sugar (some of which was re-exported) and gold. Another plum in her trousseau was Tangier, which thus became Britain's first Mediterranean port.'[118] Briefly put, the declining power, Portugal, allied itself to the rising power, Great Britain, in order to check the hegemony of Holland. For the British, it meant the opening of an important export market, especially for its new draperies, as well as access to Portuguese wines, the acquisition of its first important base in Asia, and finally – an essential condition for any power aspiring to Atlantic domination – access to the slave trade. Furthermore, Britain became a dangerous rival for Holland after it took Jamaica from Spain in 1655.

During this time, the Dutch West India Company brought in virtually no profits, and by 1674 it was bankrupt. Holland now lost its uncontested hegemony in the Atlantic. It was still powerful enough to keep control of the Asian economy (at Portugal's expense) as well as the North Sea fisheries (aided by a guaranteed supply of Portuguese salt), but the Atlantic economy was beginning to slip from its grasp. Although unable to secure a firm foothold and to populate its territory,[119] Holland was still in a position to carry merchandise back and forth across the ocean. Nevertheless, from this time forward, settlers in the American colonies came from European countries other than Holland. With the Dutch concentrating exclusively on carrying merchandise, it now became possible to challenge their control of Atlantic trade. The first effort to dislodge the Dutch was the passage of the British Navigation Acts, followed by Colbert's protectionist measures in France. The fact remained, however, that transportation costs on Dutch ships heading for the American colonies were 33 to 50 per cent lower than competitors' rates.[120] The Dutch also continued to be the main suppliers to West Indian planters.[121] Despite the numerous protectionist barriers raised against them, they remained the main buyers of West Indian tobacco and sugar throughout the seventeenth century. They were also able to maintain their favoured position in the Spanish colonies.

New Netherland merchants developed an important coastal trade that attracted colonial North American products – mainly Virginia tobacco – to New Amsterdam, where Dutch ships bound for Europe took on freight.[122] These merchants used the company ships to export food supplies, horses, beer, and wood to the West Indies.[123] The Dutch colonists, however, did not develop a trade triangle in the way the New England colonists had, because metropolitan Holland had already monopolized this area of activity.

The Navigation Acts, promulgated in 1651, were the first shot in an offensive designed to counteract Dutch supremacy as Atlantic carriers. In a 1651 petition to the states-general, several Dutch merchants protested against protectionist measures that excluded them from a trade they had carried on for over twenty years with the Caribbean Islands and Virginia, from which they had realized considerable profits. According to the petition:

> Independent of the profit accruing from shipbuilding and what is connected therewith, our cargoes, which are exported thither to the value yearly of several millions, consist, not of gold, silver, or any description of coin, but exclusively of all sorts of domestic manufactures, brewed beer, linen cloth, brandies, or other distilled liquors, duffels, coarse cloth, and other articles suitable for food and raiment for the people inhabiting those places, in return for which are imported all sorts of eastern commodities, as from Virginia, beavers and other eastern furs, considerable tobacco, and from the Caribbean islands a large quantity of sugars, tobacco, indigo, ginger, cotton, and divers sorts of valuable wood, affording extensive trade by the exportation of said wares to countries and places far and near; contributing to the support of several thousand people independent of the profit of common stock.[124]

The states-general decided not to defer to the Navigation Acts.[125] In fact these remained almost unenforceable in the West Indies mainly because the British navy could not supply enough slaves.[126] As a result, Dutch merchants kept up a busy trade. The situation was identical in Maryland and Virginia – planters needed slaves. Nevertheless, when the Acts were renewed in 1661, along with more stringent enforcement, New Amsterdam warehouses were considerably affected.

The tighter protectionist measures decreed by the new Navigation Acts struck at the heart of the competition. By closing the British colonial network to foreign commerce, Britain challenged Holland as a major warehouser and carrier. In 1664, the second Dutch-Anglo war broke out. It lasted three years.

Charles II dispatched four warships to besiege New Amsterdam. The presence of this Dutch colony in the middle of the British colonies hindered the application of the Navigation Acts. In any case, its capture represented an important prize in terms of furs, foodstores, and wood. The siege lasted from 28 August to 5 September 1664. The town lacked enough gunpowder to defend itself and surrendered without a shot being fired. The British started their siege at a time of year when trade was heaviest at Fort Orange. As gunpowder was the principal trading commodity, the Dutch had transported almost all their stock to Fort Orange, leaving New Amsterdam defenceless.[127] Charles II ceded the colony to his brother, the Duke of York, a member of the Company of Royal Adventurers into Africa. This impressive title was a euphemism for a group of slave traders. With the signing of the Peace of Breda in 1667, Holland obtained Surinam (Dutch Guiana) as compensation for the loss of its northern colony. Did the Dutch prefer the highly profitable sugar plantations of Surinam to the northern fur trade? Did they cede New Netherland in exchange for the easing of the Navigation Acts, as obtained in the peace treaty?[128] However that may be, a good number of Dutch merchants, distinctly disappointed by the outcome of the war, applied pressure for the defence of Dutch interests in the Atlantic during the peace negotiations. Seventy of them addressed a petition to the Dutch states-general in March 1667 pointing out the size of their losses, denouncing the damage caused by protectionism, demanding the return of New Netherland, and underscoring the primary importance of maintaining Dutch hegemony in the west:

To the High and Mighty Lords States-General of the United

Netherlands. Respectfully and humbly represent[:]

The undersigned persons, all traders beyond the seas, proprietors of ships and inhabitants of this State. That these Netherlands having always from ancient times had their foundations on trade and navigation by ships to all countries of the world, have arrived ... at such prosperity and success, that other Kings, Princes and Republics whose countries also border on the sea, have become ... not only jealous and envious, but have invented and set on foot all means and practices to put a stop to the further progress of this country in trade and navigation ... and, if possible, to divert the same, each in his Kingdom and country; having, to that end, erected Commercial Companies to attract all trade to themselves ... and to prohibit trade and commerce to their Islands, Colonies and Plantations situate beyond Europe; also seriously to burthen and overcharge the goods belonging to the inhabitants of this country with customs, tolls, tonnage, beyond those of their own subjects. In the same manner, also, as your Mightinesses' subjects were by those of Portugal on frivolous and impertinent pretexts prevented and hindered to trade and carry on business from Portugal and its dependencies to Brazil and back from Brazil to Portugal, pursuant to the 3rd article of the Treaty and Alliance concluded between the Kingdom of Portugal and your High Mightinesses on the 6th August, 1661; which trade, in case it were permitted, might otherwise be of considerable profit and importance, it having been, in former times, whilst it belonged to this State, of such importance that more than 25,000 seamen were employed on that coast. In addition to this, it has come to pass that other countries have not scrupled to take from ours, by force and violence, many and divers forts on the coast of Africa, viz.: Cape Verde, although it was afterwards again recovered by our men of war. *Item:* the trade and commerce to the River Gambia and Fort St. Andrew, and Cape Cors, in Guinea, together with Isyquepe, Tobago, Eustatia, Taba, Verges and other places in America and the seas thereunto belonging, and principally the whole of New Netherland, being a country not only possessed for nearly half a century by your High Mightinesses and your subjects, by a just and indisputable title, but, in addition, of such importance that from it could be brought, in time of need ... an abundant quantity of grain, hemp, flax, pork, tar, oak and pine timber fit for the construction of large ships and houses, masts of

30 palms or more, lumber for staves, wainscoting, salts (*weedasch*) and potash, besides all other descriptions of merchandise which were procured and laden by us in the Baltic. Moreover, it is a healthy and fertile country ... inhabited by more than 8,000 souls, consisting of about 1,500 families ... [We could export] linen and woolen cloths and stuffs which are manufactured here and can be disposed of and sold there. *Item:* wines, brandies, and other goods, which amounted, heretofore, to many shiploads annually ... bringing back of merchandise and returns grown there, which, exclusive of the wares and fruits hereinbefore specified, consist principally of peltries, beavers, otters and such like skins, whereby many tons of gold were circulated yearly ... [We are] humbly requesting ... that for reasons aforesaid and many others, said places, countries and islands, and especially New Netherland, which is the most populous and considerable of your High Mightinesses' Colonies, may, by the treaty be recovered from the English and restored to our nation. Especially, the rather on account that in case the aforesaid country be left to, and remain in the power and hands of the English nation, it could gain and obtain therefrom, in time of war, considerable advantage over this State and its inhabitants, as well on account that it will be able to draw and receive thence, and therefore from its own lands and Colonies, almost all the wares, which, being necessary for its equipments, it hitherto has been obliged to obtain from the Baltic; that, whenever it will possess and be master of nearly the entire Northern part of America (for the French will be illy able to hold Canada against that Nation) it can, without people here in Europe having the least knowledge of the circumstance, fit out a considerable fleet of large and small ships there (among the rest a frigate of 30 guns is built there), and with such fleet, in a season of misunderstanding, difference, or war, easily and unexpectedly fall on the ships which come from the West, be it from the islands, the East Indies, yea, from Russia, and will sail North around Scotland, the distance not being very great, and, consequently, can be sailed in a short time; whereby said English Nation then would found and extend considerably its pretended dominion over the sea.[129]

The petitioners, however, failed to gain their point. Holland found its ability to circulate limited, especially on the Atlantic where it had let

Brazil and a strategic bit of North America slip through its fingers. Its commerce was condemned to gradual suffocation, due to the determined protectionism of the major European powers who were now increasing their colonial populations. These considerations aside, the fact that Holland gave up its claims in North America made it possible for Britain to dispense with the Baltic as a supply area, and, in the long run, with the Dutch as middlemen. As the signatories clearly saw, it meant handing over to its most dangerous rival the means of building an Atlantic empire. Although in the short term, Holland had only sacrificed what was least profitable, it had already lost its grip on the future. The Dutch had had their day. Furthermore, the 1660s were accompanied by a minor slump in the Dutch economy, as demonstrated by several economic indicators: a drop in the import-export trade, fewer ferry passengers after 1661-62, lower textile production in Leiden, and the plague in 1664-65.[130] It was also no coincidence that around 1660 serious difficulties confronted the most productive Dutch industry – textiles – centred in Haarlem since the beginning of the century. It could not compete with English production and the low prices resulting from the combined effect of subjugating Ireland, enclosure, the creation of a vast internal market, and the opening of new external markets. The Dutch gradually returned to making luxury fabrics, renouncing the new draperies – a mass production sector of the textile industry in which the accelerated division of labour was now a major factor.

In other words, if I may be permitted to take a slightly teleological point of view, the new draperies sector of the industry sowed the seed of industrial revolution. In the 1660s, it became evident that Britain would assume the control and organization of the Atlantic economy. All the conditions for establishing a hegemony were there. Several indicators confirm Britain's role in this respect, quite apart from the capitalist organization of its internal production. First, it had developed a technically advanced sector with potential (the new draperies) which expanded under protectionist measures. It also possessed the largest internal market plus a rapidly growing external market in America, where the flood of immigrants swelled a peasant class of prosperous small producers. Finally, dispossessed peasants and religious dissenters from Britain populated the sugar islands of the Caribbean, gained access to the Portuguese colonial market, became involved in the 'noble' slave trade, and penetrated the Asian economic world-system.

Despite all this, Holland was still a force to reckon with in the 1660s. However, its three wars against Britain (1652-54, 1664-67, 1672-74) and its success in repelling Louis XIV's invading army exacted a toll comparatively greater than the cost to its adversaries. After all, Holland had one tenth the population of France and a third that of Britain. It nevertheless kept the upper hand in the lucrative Asian trade. At the end of the century, it still carried half of all European tonnage, double that of Britain and eight or nine times that of France.[131] The Navigation Acts failed to oust Holland from its role as middleman, even within Britain. Despite the protectionist measures imposed by France since Colbert, Holland continued to dominate the French economy.[132] It still controlled the northern fishing industry and the Baltic economy. The centre of the economic world-system may have moved to London, but all the large Dutch houses had subsidiaries there that conducted profitable business. In London, several English firms used Dutch as the language of business in their correspondence.[133] Dutch shipyards remained the most prosperous, and the British continued to buy a large number of ships from the Dutch throughout the seventeenth century because of the low prices. In 1667, the Dutch attracted about 3,000 Scottish and English sailors to its fleet,[134] not counting the even greater numbers of Scandinavians, Germans, French, and others. Moreover, colonial products shipped to London were bought by Dutch merchants at auction for resale all over the world. It may well be that Dutch merchants, at least until 1730, realized more profit from the British colonies than did British merchants at home.[135]

The commercial success of the Dutch was the reason for their loss of the Atlantic economy. The thousands of Dutch who left their country (50,000 sailors in 1670) stayed on their boats and did not put down roots in foreign lands. As the major economic power of the seventeenth century, Holland got the greatest prize – that is the most profitable. As we have seen, it took over the Asian economic world-system by dislodging the Portuguese. Britain, close behind, had to make do with the Atlantic, but this disadvantage was to become an advantage. Asia imported almost nothing from Europe, while Europe, on the contrary, imported a great number of products from Asia, for which it payed in precious metals. North America, however, had a great need for products manufactured in Europe. In terms of national manufacturing development, Britain, as the centre of the Atlantic world-system, was in a better position to satisfy this need than Holland, centre of the Asian world-system. Apart from this, Britain's more advanced division of labour and stronger demographic growth meant that the Atlantic economy would expand faster than its Asian counterpart. In this context, it is not surprising that the Industrial Revolution took place in Britain rather than Holland.

France's Marginality

As we have seen, at the beginning of the seventeenth century, Holland possessed a powerful fleet and a large amount of capital, hence its hegemony in the Atlantic. In Britain, however, the bourgeoisie was about to succeed in its bid for power, and the country's subsequent mode of development was to lead to the expulsion of a great number of its inhabitants. This exodus provided the settlers who were needed to farm, fish, and cut wood in the colonies, thus enabling Britain to dislodge Holland and replace it as the major Atlantic power. France, by comparison, had very few assets with which to offset the domination of the other major powers: an anemic fleet, not much capital, a trickle of emigrants crossing the Atlantic – and among these few, only Roman Catholics were selected for New France.

The French fleet was something of a joke. The fact was, most French sailors were in the Dutch fleet. The Dutch commercial empire controlled virtually all of France and particularly the west coast. Among other sectors, it dominated the entire wine industry.[136] Of the western seaports such as La Rochelle, Bordeaux, and Nantes, perhaps only Saint-Malo was relatively less controlled by Dutch traders, but even so it was not 'French.' Its commerce depended on Britain, on whose behalf it resold merchandise.[137] There were plenty of French ships plying the Atlantic, however, and they had long been present at the fishing grounds of the Gulf of Saint Lawrence. In the second half of the seventeenth century, French fishing off Newfoundland began to expand once more. Several dozen Frenchmen settled in Placentia on the Avalon peninsula. Others went to the West Indies, where there were enough settlers to establish a base at Santo Domingo and from there to develop the French West Indies. On the whole, however, French maritime activity on the Atlantic remained marginal and failed to create the nucleus of what could be called an integrated commercial empire.

French merchants had opened trading posts here and there (in Quebec, Acadia, and the West Indies), but no commercial network was established between these points. Quebec supplied furs and nothing else. On average, only four boats per year came from France between 1632 and 1669.[138] Often, these would fall into the hands of the British or Spanish on the return voyage.[139] Acadia, with barely 500 French inhabitants in 1670, had already been taken three times by the British (1613, 1629, and 1654) and was simply a periphery of Boston, economically speaking. French colonists in the West Indies depended mainly on the Dutch navy. As W.T. Easterbrook and H.G.J. Aitken pointed out in their *Canadian Economic History* (and the remark is as valid for the seventeenth as for the eighteenth century), the French Atlantic empire developed in a centrifugal manner, contrary to Britain with its intensive intercolonial trade.[140] This phenomenon is explained by the low rate of French emigration across the Atlantic, the absence of a big enough fleet to control the seas, and geographical considerations.

Initially, French ships were at a disadvantage since they were forced to fall back on the Gulf of Saint Lawrence as a fishing ground. This became an advantage, however, as it provided access to an immense fur trading basin in a cold region. Nevertheless, this in turn became a disadvantage when it came to integrating the Saint Lawrence valley into the Atlantic economy because the river was frozen for four months of the year.

Unlike Boston and the other New England ports, the St. Lawrence was closed to shipping during the winter months because of ice. During the summer months of July, August, and September, on the other hand, the West Indies were highly dangerous for small sailing-ships because of hurricanes. A ship which left the St. Lawrence as soon as the river was free from ice (the end of April at the earliest) could barely reach the West Indies before the hurricane season began. Sailings from Quebec during the fall months were less hazardous, but likely to encounter many delays. Ordinarily no cargoes of sugar were available in the West Indies until the end of February. A ship which left the St. Lawrence in the late fall, just before the ice formed, would reach the West Indies about the end of December or early January. There it would have to wait idle for six or eight weeks before loading its cargo of sugar for France. With luck and good management it might be able to return to the St. Lawrence toward the end of summer, so that one round trip annually was the most it could make. Alternatively it might leave Quebec in the late summer and arrive in the West Indies about the middle of October, in which case it might reach France in January and return to Quebec in the spring; but the late summer was the worst time for securing cargoes of dried fish in New France and October was not a good month to get a price for such a cargo in the West Indies.

In short, whatever arrangements were devised, the three-cornered voyage between New France, the West Indies, and France was slow and expensive. New England ships, in contrast, could make two voyages a year to the West Indies during the winter season and occupy themselves in the off-shore fisheries during the summer. New France, handicapped by distance and climate, could not compete with New England as a supply base for the West Indies. The situation might have been different if a shipping and trading centre had been developed in Nova Scotia or Cape Breton, but as we have seen this was not done.[141]

In these circumstances, how could New France provide food for the West Indies, keep ships at sea, and sell lumber? It was impossible. Furs were the only exploitable commodity. Marie de l'Incarnation stated in a letter of 1660 that 'without the trade [in furs] the country has nothing material to offer. It could do without France for food, but it depends entirely on the mother country for clothing, tools, wine, spirits, and for an infinity of small commodities, and all this only comes to us through trade.'[142]

A triangular commercial network was scarcely feasible since the policy of selective immigration made it difficult to establish an economy, and the only way of amassing capital was through the fur trade. But how were the French to compete with low Dutch prices for trade goods? How were they to deal with the successful alliance of Dutch capitalism and Iroquois arms? What could they do after the total defeat of their allies, the Hurons? 'Trade with the South is almost wiped out, [leaving only] the North,' wrote Marie de l'Incarnation in 1652.[143] Only territorial expansion to the west and north could offset Dutch competition. The quest for furs had to be extended to ever more distant tribes so as to take advantage of both their inexperience in European commerce and the distance separating these tribes from the Dutch.

In 1634, the interpreter Jean Nicollet had already reached the

Winnebagos of Green Bay on Lake Michigan in order to conclude a treaty, imagining, as the following remark indicates, that after travelling so many leagues by water, he had perhaps reached China: 'He wore a grand robe of China damask, all strewn with flowers and birds of many colors.'[144]

After the fall of Huronia, the pressure to find new sources for furs reached its height. In the spring of 1653, the arrival of three canoes at Trois-Rivières, heralding the willingness of the peoples of Lake Michigan and Lake Superior to trade with the French, stimulated much interest. 'Moreover, all our young Frenchmen are planning to go on a trading expedition, to find the Nations that are scattered here and there; and they hope to come back laden with the Beaver-skins of several years' accumulation.'[145] The following year, Jean Bourdon went up the rivers north of the Gulf to reach Labrador through the interior and perhaps Hudson Bay.[146] In 1656, some thirty canoes left Trois-Rivières for the west, but inexperience and Iroquois raids forced them to turn back.[147] That same year, Desgroseilliers came back from the west laden with furs.[148] In 1659, he left with Radisson for Lake Superior and Hudson Bay. They brought back pelts worth 200,000 livres.[149]

Three events occurred that were to reduce the severity and frequency of Iroquois raids on the Ottawas, thereby reopening the passage west. In 1660, Dollard des Ormeaux, at the head of a group of Frenchmen and Amerindian allies, confronted a group of Iroquois hunters at Long Sault on the Ottawa River. The Iroquois were returning from trading upriver. The battle effectively diverted a planned Iroquois attack on Quebec. A group of Iroquois coming down the Richelieu and heading for Quebec were to provide reinforcements for their compatriots on the Ottawa River.[150] Two years later, Iroquoia was to be struck by an epidemic. Finally, in 1665, the Carignan regiment would land in New France.

The commercial strategy of the French in North America during the following century was already evident. To offset Dutch, and subsequently British, competition, they had to push farther and farther into the interior (west as far as the Rocky Mountains, south as far as Louisiana) to find new tribes, then build a network of forts right across the continent to prevent the Amerindians from trading directly with their rivals.

Unequal Development

New Netherland and New France were both born out of the fur trade. However, whereas integration into the Atlantic economy encouraged diversification of the New Netherland economy, the peripheral nature of New France condemned the latter colony to a single-staple system.

Quebec, Trois-Rivières, and Montreal were merely fur-trading posts, with food provided by farming nearby land. Neither agriculture nor lumbering were carried on for export. In 1664, there was not a single horse in New France,[151] yet New Netherland was raising horses for export to the West Indies. At every level in New France, one finds evidence of total dependence on a single staple (furs). This phenomenon accounted for the lack of diversification in the economy, its marginality in relation to Atlantic trade, the difficulties and delays in getting a market economy moving, and the continued reliance on subsistence farming.

The economic picture was entirely different in the colonies along the eastern seaboard. Virginia, of course, had completely dissimilar climate and resources. For example, on 22 October 1643, De Vries counted some thirty British and Dutch ships in the process of loading tobacco.[152] When we look at the northern colonies where natural resources were comparable to those of the Saint Lawrence valley, we find that agricultural and forest products for export in these colonies developed along with the Atlantic economy, and that their frontiers pushed westward in response to the rate of trade with the West Indies. Very soon, therefore, the economy became diversified and grew in tandem with maritime traffic. 'We begin to supply provisions and drink ... to the West Indies and the Caribbee Islands,' wrote Van der Donck in 1653.[153] Windmills were needed for this and they were built.[154]

Soon, a trading location had to be organized in New Amsterdam. In 1641, the government passed initial laws for fairs: there would be two per year, one for cattle on 15 October and one for swine on 1 November.[155] In 1648, a ten-day fair was set up for domestic products.[156] Then it was noted that settlers and Amerindians had become accustomed to coming to Manhattan at any time to buy or sell, which was becoming inconvenient. It had been all right to begin with because one simply went to the Dutch West India Company store. Gradually, however, commercial activity spilled over into the town, involving the entire population. There was a gradual passage from a trading post economy to a colonial economy. Accordingly, laws were passed in 1648 fixing Monday as market day. In 1656, this was changed to Saturday to give butchers time to prepare meat for the Sunday holiday. The market place was also moved to a more central location. Two years later, a special market was set up for meat and small livestock.[157] Commerce then took another leap forward with the opening of shops. Twelve butchers in New Amsterdam obtained a monopoly for slaughtering cattle in the town. The milling and bakery trades also acquired monopolies. After 1650, laws were passed governing weights and measures as well as the quality of bread. After 1660, a permit was needed to be a baker. After 1665, bread could no longer be sold from door to door but only in a licensed shop.[158]

In New France, the restrictions imposed on free trade and the lack of overseas market outlets for products other than furs considerably hampered economic growth. The presence of a company monopoly hindered all economic activity for quite some time. It was not until 1648 to 1655 that the Compagnie des Habitants got rid of its shops, bakery, brewery, and forge in Quebec's Lower Town.[159] Little by little, these activities passed into private hands, independent of the company. Even so, there were few independent merchants in Quebec, only a handful of accredited bakers and just four butchers in 1706.[160] The Montreal fur fair did not get going until after 1660 and was slow to develop. In fact, there was no true market until the eighteenth century. In Quebec, the inhabitants exchanged produce and provisions on the beach or even in their canoes. It was not until 1708 that fixed market days and hours were established by ordinance on Tuesdays and Fridays as well as a fixed market place in the Lower Town.[161]

Another unmistakable indication of the deep-rooted qualitative difference between the emerging economies of New France and New Netherland was the growing use of coinage in internal trade relationships. This was at best a slow and difficult process. All the colonies of North America faced the same problem of vanishing specie. The deficit trade balance with their mother countries was the cause, and this imbalance greatly stimulated trading ventures along the coast and in the West Indies – this being the colonies' only way of acquiring coinage. What was an initial disadvantage contributed in the long run to New England's wealth. New Netherland worked at developing this kind of trade, but for New France it was almost impossible.

New France's only currency at the time was the beaver, the general equivalent.[162] Wampum had no value in the colony except for trading with Amerindians.[163] A 1661 ordinance inflated the value of French currency by 60 per cent, which was readjusted to 33 per cent in 1662.[164] These measures had little effect as French merchants dared not take the risk of carrying precious metals across the ocean. Consequently, barter was the prevailing form of exchange. Beaver skins were also used, but this was a most inconvenient form of currency for small purchases. A good quality pelt was worth ten livres on average, whereas a man earned one or one and a half livres per day.[165] The basic monetary unit (one pelt) therefore represented one or two weeks' labour. This was hardly suitable for everyday commercial transactions. How could a market economy develop in such conditions?

New Netherland acquired currency other than beaver pelts by developing its coastal and West Indian commerce and by re-exporting Virginia tobacco. It also used wampum, the Amerindian currency, for small trading. 'This is the only article of moneyed medium among the natives, with which any traffic can be driven; and it is also common with us in purchasing necessaries and carrying on our trade; many thousand strings are exchanged every year for peltries near the seashores where the wampum is only made, and where the peltries are brought for sale. Among the Netherlanders gold and silver begin to increase and are current, but still the amount differs much from that of the Netherlands.'[166]

The functioning of a market economy depends not only on the volume of money circulating but also on the existence of small denominations that can accommodate minor trading. Wampum, despite the vagaries of numerous and successive devaluations, fulfilled this latter role. With it, people could pay cash in the marketplace for fresh (not salted) meat, butter, cheese, vegetables, straw, and so on.[167] Barter did not disappear, however, since the volume of money in circulation was still insufficient – witness, for example, Director-General Stuyvesant's measure, somewhat late in the day, of raising the local value of Dutch money by 25 per cent in order to keep it in the colony.[168] A number of transactions were carried out partly with money, partly in kind. Teachers were frequently paid with a mixture of money, beaver, and wheat.[169] On Long Island, 'the town of Hempstead ... allowed six bushels of corn for killing a wolf,'[170] and many contracts for the sale of land were payable in kind. Throughout the seventeenth century, currency in various forms was indeed scarce, but even so it could be found everywhere – less in the outlying regions, more in New Amsterdam.

Unlike Quebec, which was both a trading post and a mission, New Amsterdam, with slightly over 2,000 inhabitants in 1664, already displayed urban traits – for example, brick was gradually supplanting wood as the main construction material.[171] It was a cosmopolitan town from the start. In 1654, twenty-three Marrano (Christianized) Jews, who had been expelled from Brazil after the Dutch defeat, settled there – a sure sign of economic growth. A merchant class was beginning to take shape, and its members were stimulating business. This class defended its privileges, although it was unable to exclude itinerant traders. In New Amsterdam, where the skyline was dominated by windmills and the warehouses of the Dutch West India Company, there was no church of any size, whereas the town of Quebec bristled with convents and churches.[172]

LAND USE: CONFLICTING TRADITIONS

As we have seen, the North American continent was already populated before Europeans settled there. As time went by, a network of relations developed among fur traders and Amerindians, its main features being unequal exchange and war over furs. Initially, war involved tribes fighting for the role of middleman to gain access to, and control of, trade merchandise. In reality, the tribes were acting as intermediaries in the confrontation between the French commercial empire in Quebec and the Dutch commercial empire in Fort Orange. This first type of war continued until French power was eliminated in North America in 1760.

There was, however, a second form of confrontation: the colonial, or more accurately, colonizing wars. These enabled a population of European origin to dislodge indigenous societies. This second type of war did not take place in New France, since the Saint Lawrence valley below Montreal had already lost its population of aboriginal farmers during the second half of the sixteenth century as a result of the combined effects of intertribal warfare, cooling of the climate, and epidemics. The French settled in a part of the continent where there were no competing Amerindian farmers (although hunter-gatherers were still present). The opposite, however, was the case for the Dutch and the

British. These newcomers found themselves in an area with a high density of sedentary peoples and a low density of hunter-gatherers. Before the arrival of the Dutch and British, trade between Europeans and Amerindians had occurred mainly along the Gulf of Saint Lawrence, leaving the Atlantic coast relatively isolated from commercial activity and also from the resulting epidemics and fur wars. The principal characteristic of the colonizing wars, which went on until the end of the nineteenth century with the conquest of the west, was that societies based on collective ownership were driven back by a society based on private ownership.

The Destruction of the Wilderness

The settlers arrived, installed themselves on the land, cleared and stacked the wood in huge piles, and set fire to them.[173] They cut more wood for the emerging towns, for export, and for shipbuilding. A single warship of the time required over 2,000 oak trees, many of them from 100 to 150 years old and measuring more than fifty centimetres in diameter.[174] White cedar, white pine, oak, elm, and maple – there was so much, why spare the axe? Wasn't the best way to gather walnuts simply to cut down the tree?[175] Within a very short time, the entire ecosystem was affected. Historian C.F. Carroll has pointed out that 'when trees are destroyed en masse – the term used by foresters is "clear-cutting" – the severe and sudden change affects all living things in the forest. Shade-loving plants die, food chains are interrupted, birds and animals migrate, and the new microbes and insects invade. The relation of sun, land, vegetation, and fauna is drastically changed, and in the struggle for existence only those things that can adapt to the new environment will survive.'[176]

The practice of setting bush fires to create burnt-over land must have done immense damage to the forest. It was the current practice in New Netherland where the settlers learned it from the Amerindians. Very probably, major forest fires resulted from the increase in the number of fires actively set (the easiest way of preparing a field for cultivation), coupled with the settlers' inexperience, although Van der Donck says this was not the case:

> The Indians have a yearly custom (which some of our Christians have
> also adopted) of burning the woods, plains and meadows in the fall of

the year, when the leaves have fallen, and when the grass and vegetable substances are dry. Those places which are then passed over are fired in the spring in April. This practice is named by us and the Indians, 'bush-burning' ...

The bush burning presents a grand and sublime appearance. On seeing it from without, we would imagine that not only the dry leaves, vegetables and limbs would be burnt, but that the whole woods would be consumed where the fire passes, for it frequently spreads and rages with such violence, that it is awful to behold; and when the fire approaches houses, gardens, and wooden enclosures, then great care and vigilance are necessary for their preservation, for I have seen several houses which have recently been destroyed, before the owners were apprized of their danger.

Notwithstanding the apparent danger of the entire destruction of the woodlands by the burning, still the green trees do not suffer. The outside bark is scorched three or four feet high, which does them no injury, for the trees are not killed ... Frequently great injuries are done by such fires, but the burning down of entire woods never happens. I have seen many instances of wood-burning in the colony of Rensselaerwyck, where there is much pine wood. Those fires appear grand at night from the passing vessels in the river, when the woods are burning on both sides of the same. Then we can see a great distance by the light of the blazing trees, the flames being driven by the wind, and fed by the tops of the trees. But the dead and dying trees remain burning in their standing positions, which appear sublime and beautiful when seen at a distance.[177]

In one way or another, the forest retreated as the farming and wood-cutting settlers advanced. The salt marshes and coastal estuaries, havens where fish and migrating birds could feed and mate, also retreated. Dikes could be built with a minimum of effort, holding back the sea to create arable land.[178] The Acadians used a system of sluice-gates for the same purpose. Increased cultivation meant decreased wildlife. Hunting, as mentioned earlier, also played a part. Hunters showed no moderation. One wonders why – did settlers think the game would never be exhausted? That the multitude of swans, for example, would always justify the name Swaanendael given to the little coastal village of New

Netherland? Who would have thought that the passenger pigeons whose flight literally darkened the skies would become extinct?[179] Did it automatically follow that a civilization based on agriculture and husbandry would destroy wildlife to save its cereals and lambs? Europeans came from a continent where nature had been tamed and domesticated, where forests belonged to seigneurs and kings. Were they overtaken by wholesale madness now that they found themselves in an Eden of hunting and fishing? Or, to paraphrase Herbert Marcuse, do humans necessarily regard nature as an object of domination and exploitation, to the extent that repressive relationships exist between themselves? Marcuse cites the Arapesh of New Guinea, for whom nature is a vast garden that enables men to grow.[180] This attitude was equally true of the northeastern Amerindian civilizations, who lived in harmony with nature. Clearly, the civilization now conquering the continent was in disharmony with nature. Ecology had no place in its value system. In earlier times, this negation of nature had cost Islam its forest resources,[181] turned its land into deserts, and brought about its downfall. Did Europeans exhibit this same suicidal disharmony with nature? Their excessive hunting and fishing went beyond the capacities of species to reproduce themselves. Wildlife began to diminish as a result of their killing turkeys by the dozen[182] and pigeons by the hundreds, of their slaughtering wild ducks in their migrating habitats, and of their keeping open season on deer, caribou, and wapiti. In 1664, Pierre Boucher was already writing on this subject: 'The hunt is not as abundant now around Quebec as it once was. Game has retreated by ten or twelve leagues. Only turtledoves and passenger pigeons remain in plenty each summer.'[183]

Van der Donck estimated that, in the previous twenty-five years, 80,000 beaver had been killed annually in New Netherland, not to mention moose, bear, otter, deer, and other species. He noted that there were those who thought that all would disappear at this rate, although he himself did not agree.[184]

Although hunting and gathering were secondary activities among the horticultural Amerindian tribes along the Atlantic seaboard, these activities were still a fairly significant part of community life. The European's destructive relationship with nature and with the flora and fauna of the region was bound to have a damaging effect on the Amerindians.

A Hog War: Private versus Public Property

A second type of conflict of interest arose with the juxtaposition of horticulture on the one hand and mixed farming on the other. The coastal tribes based their economy on growing corn in unfenced fields.[185] They also kept half-wild dogs. The Dutch and British, by contrast, cultivated fields and raised herds of domestic animals. In no time at all, Amerindian dogs were molesting the European livestock, and cattle were roaming through the Amerindians' cornfields.

Hog raising was by far the greatest bone of contention. Swine reproduce faster than any other farm animal. The settlers allowed their hogs to run free instead of keeping them in piggeries or fenced yards.[186] The animals ran half wild, proliferating and feeding off the forest at no cost to the settlers, thus providing a practically free source of meat. Amerindians who encountered pigs in the woods or in their cornfields considered them as game and killed them accordingly. But hogs were a very special breed of animal with an inherent characteristic that distinguished them from all other forest fauna. Hogs were *private property*. When Europeans settled in the Amerindians' territory, they chopped down the trees and killed the animals found there. Since these were collective property, however, no more was said on the subject. The Amerindians, seeing the forest retreating and the fauna diminishing, looked for other game. If there were no more deer, there were still hogs. But it seemed these particular animals were not to be touched.

Gathering was subject to the same principle. The Europeans cleared the land, sowed crops, and planted fruit trees.[187] Soon orchards replaced the forest where the Amerindians had gathered fruit. When, however, they gathered apples and pears instead of the customary cherries, wild grapes, highbush cranberries, or blackberries, they discovered that they were stealing! Like hogs, these new fruits possessed an inborn characteristic that made them totally different from everything that grew around them – they, too, were private property. 'After the Swedes had settled here and planted apple trees and peach trees, the Indians, and especially their women, sometimes stole the fruit in great quantity; but when the Swedes caught them, they gave them a severe drubbing, took the fruit from them, and often their clothes too. In the same manner it happened sometimes that as the Swedes had a great increase of hogs, and they ran about in the woods, the Indians killed some of them privately and ate them.'[188]

Above and beyond the conflict between horticultural/hunting peoples and European farmers, we are clearly looking at a conflict between two forms of ownership – collective and private – that were mutually exclusive, with the latter always (or should we say already?) at odds with ecological concerns.[189]

War

War broke out after a long series of confrontations. In New England after 1622, settlement by English colonists at Wessagusset gave rise to serious skirmishes with the Massachusetts, who appear to have formed an alliance to expel the new arrivals. The Puritans of Plymouth, upon learning of this, carried out a successful raid against the natives and killed their most important sachem, Obtakiest, and several of his closest allies.[190] In 1637, the English attacked and massacred the Pequots, taking advantage of the tragic depopulation of Amerindian villages following the smallpox epidemic of 1633 as well as the assistance of the Narragansetts and Mahicans, who wanted to throw off the Pequot yoke.[191] Once the Pequots were defeated, the Narragansetts turned on the Mahicans. The latter, however, were able to resist attack. They captured the Narragansett chief and handed him over to the English, who secretly executed him despite his having been their ally.[192] Although this was a perfidious act, it averted intertribal rivalry. In 1621, shortly after the Puritans had landed in Plymouth, a Pokanoket (Wampanoag) chief named Massasoit concluded a friendship treaty with the whites. The hospitality shown by Massasoit enabled the Puritans to surmount the harsh difficulties facing them after their arrival, but his generosity was not without motive. He counted on their aid to repulse the attacks of his traditional enemies to the west, the Narragansetts. Massasoit's younger son, Matacomet, known as 'King Philip,' comprehended the larger significance of the European conquest of the American continent and its corollary, the dispossession of native peoples. In 1675-76, he took the initiative in organizing a common Amerindian front from Rhode Island to Vermont and New Hampshire. This desperate attempt, known as 'King Philip's War,' ended in the defeat and extermination of the Pokanokets. Even the Narragansetts, who had refused to join the common front, were decimated by the English and their survivors condemned to become domestics for white families.[193] In the final analysis, the British and other

European groups were able to divide and conquer as a result of pandemics, intertribal wars (which predated the Europeans' arrival), and the military advantage of firearms.

In New Netherland, the reality of conquest began to penetrate the legal fiction of executing contracts with the Amerindians for the sale of land – a procedure that extinguished all right of ownership or usufruct prior to European occupation.[194] The most violent confrontations took place during the mandate of Director-General Kieft, who was particularly inept in his dealings with the Amerindians. The source of conflict, however, went far deeper than the individual administrator. The Raritans had long been complaining about the large-scale damage to their fields caused by Dutch domestic animals.[195] In 1639, the Raritans slaughtered the Staten Island hogs belonging to settlers and the Dutch West India Company and killed other animals including horses. Cornelis Van Thienhoven, secretary-general of New Netherland, went to the Staten Island area at the head of about a hundred armed men. Several Amerindians were killed, and the Dutch captured the chief's brother and applied torture to his genitalia. The Amerindians responded by killing a few whites and burning houses. Tension mounted further as the director-general attempted to levy a tax on Amerindians, payable in corn. The Amerindians refused. At Tapaen, on 20 October 1639, the natives expressed their surprise to De Vries: 'They said ... they were very much surprised that the Sachem [the director], who was now at the Fort [New Amsterdam], dare exact it, and he must be a very mean fellow to come to this country without being invited by them, and now wish to compel them to give him their corn for nothing.'[196]

New skirmishes between Raritans and settlers occurred in the Staten Island region during 1641-42, a result of further damage to crops caused by the settlers' herds.[197] That year, the Amerindians even tried to establish an alliance against the Europeans: 'A few weeks after this Miantonimo [a Narragansett from New England], principal sachem of Sloops Bay, came here [to New Amsterdam] with one hundred men, passing through all the Indian villages soliciting them to a general war against both the English and the Dutch, whereupon some of the neighboring Indians attempted to set our powder on fire and to poison the Director [Kieft] or to inchant him by their devilry.'[198] This project failed, as did several other similar attempts.[199] The Amerindians could never surmount the deep intertribal divisions that existed, and nothing else could have effectively blocked European military superiority.

The next phase in the escalating tension offered a tragic illustration of how European powers, Dutch, in this instance, took advantage of tribal rivalry and dissension to establish their own might. In February of 1643, eighty or ninety Mohawk warriors, each shouldering a gun, came down to the mouth of the Hudson River to gather tribute from the Raritans of Wickquasyeck, Tapaen, and nearby villages. The Raritans had no firearms. They panicked and fled, four or five hundred of them taking refuge in De Vries's house at Pavonia on Staten Island, where they asked for asylum and protection. De Vries had little choice and therefore decided to fetch arms from the fort at New Amsterdam. Director-General Kieft, learning of what was afoot, decided to take advantage of the Raritans' entrapment in a house to massacre them. De Vries, who objected to this, reported what he saw and heard on the night of 24 February and the following day:

> About midnight, I heard a great shrieking, and I ran to the ramparts of the fort, and looked over to Pavonia. Saw nothing but firing, and heard the shrieks of the Indians murdered in their sleep ... When it was day the soldiers returned to the fort, having massacred or murdered eighty Indians, and considering they had done a deed of Roman valour, in murdering so many in their sleep; where infants were torn from their mother's breasts, and hacked to pieces in the presence of the parents, and the pieces thrown into the fire and in the water, and other sucklings were bound to small boards, and then cut, stuck, and pierced, and miserably massacred in a manner to move a heart of stone. Some were thrown into the river, and when the fathers and mothers endeavoured to save them, the soldiers would not let them come on land, but made both parents and children drown, – children from five to six years of age, and also some old and decrepit persons. Many fled from this scene, and concealed themselves in the neighbouring sedge, and when it was morning, came out to beg a piece of bread, and to be permitted to warm themselves; but they were murdered in cold blood and tossed into the water. Some came by our lands in the country with their hands, some with their legs cut off, and some holding their entrails in their arms, and others had such horrible cuts, and gashes, that worse

than they were could never happen. And these poor simple creatures, as also many of our own people, did not know any better than that they had been attacked by a party of other Indians, – the Maquas [Mohawks]. After this exploit, the soldiers were rewarded for their services, and Director Kieft thanked them by taking them by the hand and congratulating them. At another place, on the same night at Corler's Hook on Corler's plantation, forty Indians were in the same manner attacked in their sleep, and massacred there in the same manner as the Duke of Alva did in the Netherlands, but more cruelly. This is indeed a disgrace to our nation, who have so generous a governor in our Fatherland as the Prince of Orange, who has always endeavoured in his wars to spill as little blood as possible. As soon as the Indians understood that the Swannekens had so treated them, all the men whom they could surprise on the farm-lands, they killed; but we have never heard that they have ever permitted women or children to be killed. They burned all the houses, farms, barns, grain, haystacks, and destroyed everything they could get hold of.[200]

When peace negotiations began, an Amerindian orator expressed the grievances of his people to De Vries, who had been chosen as ambassador:

There was one among them [the Raritans] who had a small bundle of sticks, and was the best speaker, who began his oration in Indian. He told how we first came upon their coast; that we sometimes had no victuals; they gave us their Turkish beans and Turkish wheat, they helped us with oysters and fish to eat, and now for a reward we had killed their people. Then he laid down one of the sticks, which was one point. He related also that at the beginning of our voyaging there, we left our people behind with the goods to trade, until the ships should come back; they had preserved these people like the apple of their eye; yea, they had given them their daughters to sleep with, by whom they had begotten children, and there roved many an Indian who was begotten by a Swanneken, but now our people had become so villainous as to kill their own blood.[201]

The legitimacy and justice of these complaints did not weigh very heavily on the Dutch. The Amerindians were weak, poor, and warring against one another. In their relations with this implacable force, the Raritan men were pitted not so much against the whites as against the underlying social relationships that accompanied the latter's arrival in the New World. These relationships, polarized by the workings of capital accumulation, lay behind the practice of genocide in America and the importation of slave labour from Africa crammed between the decks of slave ships.

War resumed in the fall of 1643 and continued through 1644, along with genocide. In a letter of protest addressed to company directors in Amsterdam,[202] eight Manhattan colonists denounced this destructive war that had laid waste to the country. All the Amerindian crops for fifteen or twenty miles around had been destroyed, they said. Soldiers had been given Amerindian prisoners as gifts and had been allowed to take them to Holland. Others had been shipped off to the English governor of the Bermudas as a present. Under Dutch rule, there were three other wars against Amerindian tribes: in 1655, 1656, and 1663[203] coupled with a series of epidemics between 1658 and 1666.[204] Although the details of these later wars are less well known, the general tenor was similar to that of 1642-44, except that the theatre of 'operations' moved away from New Amsterdam.

These wars were costly, and occasioned deficits for the Dutch West India Company.[205] In this respect, it might seem at first glance that the lack of profits during these years created an unequal exchange between the Dutch and the Amerindians. It must not be forgotten, however, that unequal exchange can exist without a net profit to the dominant partner. In this case, the company had to reinvest a large part of its gross earnings in military activities, thereby wiping out its net profit. All in all, profits realized from one group of Amerindians in the fur trade were used to finance war against others. In the final analysis, the Amerindians financed a war that was turned against themselves, thus contributing to the gradual shift in the balance of power in favour of the Europeans.

THE RESERVATION

In a sense, these wars involving furs and colonization were the first stage in the 'solution' to the Amerindian 'problem.' Ironically, although the Amerindians had inhabited the North American continent for thousands of years, it was they, not the invaders, who were suddenly a 'problem.' The French in the Saint Lawrence valley, or more precisely the French administrators and the Jesuits, were to develop a second 'solution' to the 'problem' – the reservation.

The Jesuits obtained generous support from a donor and built a chapel at Sillery along with houses and other buildings.[206] They hired some twenty indentured servants to clear and till the soil. Two Algonkin families, totalling about twenty people, settled there in 1635. By 1639, there were fifty-six and by 1645, 167, all of whom were Christian converts. Conversion to an agricultural way of life, however, did not work. Harvests were bad and hunting expeditions got longer and longer. By 1649, only two inhabitants were left at Sillery, and they were white. The Jesuits altered their strategy the following year, this time trying to start a seigneury at Sillery and transform the Amerindians into censitaires – that is, roughly the equivalent of tenant farmers. However, these Amerindians could not dispose of, cede, sell, or leave their land without the good fathers' permission. Under the circumstances, this was easier said than done. With the forest on their doorstep, it was about as feasible to prevent birds from flying as to stop nomads from moving on. If and when the Jesuits did succeed in keeping Amerindians in Sillery, disease and drunkenness finished them off. After this period, attempts to tame the barbarians, so to speak, led to idleness and alcoholism.[207] In 1660, the land was ceded to French settlers due to the lack of Amerindians. The Jesuits had slightly more success with the Hurons who were accustomed to a sedentary life. The latter settled on the Île d'Orléans, then at Sillery, and finally on the reservation at Ancienne-Lorette, where they remained permanently in what amounted to a refugee camp.

Why Reservations?

In the seventeenth century, the French used the word *réduction* rather than *réserve* when speaking of the reservation. The expression was highly evocative, implying that the object of the exercise was to cage individuals, reduce their space, diminish, and in fact subjugate them. This new offensive was inspired by models used in South America and particularly in Paraguay, where, wrote Father Paul Le Jeune, 'our Fathers worked more than forty years to subdue them.'[208]

Prior to 1640, the English took few steps to actually convert Amerindians. In their opinion, the natives had to become civilized before being Christianized, and the best way of converting the Amerindians was to employ the women and children as domestic servants.[209] Nevertheless, John Elliot translated the Bible into the Massachusetts' language. The Society for the Propagation of the Gospel, created in 1649, acquired land in order to found 'praying towns' for converts, who would receive daily instruction.[210] These towns consisted principally of the survivors of epidemics and wars. The Dutch, on the other hand, took no such initiative during that period – a further example of the fact that there was no single North American model for the way in which whites and Amerindians met and confronted one another. Emerging relationships between various native and European groups were strongly marked by their respective antecedents, history, and individual characteristics.

Why did the French opt for the reservation? Marie de l'Incarnation noted that it was a question of protecting the converts from the perverting influence of some of the French. 'For the rest,' she wrote, 'some Savages are more devout than others, as with Frenchmen, but generally speaking the Savages are more so than the French, and that is why we do not let them mix with each other, but put them in a separate village, for fear they might copy the behaviour of some. It is not that the French are not fairly well-behaved in this country, but that the Savages, although well-meaning, are not capable of handling the freedom of the French.'[211]

Apart from this attestation to the intensity of religious practice on the part of the converts, the striking thing about this citation is the idea of the Amerindian being incapable of handling freedom and requiring isolation and protection. Although this opinion accurately reflects the dominant view of the reservation, the real situation was very different. Whom did the reservation protect? The very existence of Amerindian civilization posed a threat to European society. Was the latter not trying to ward off this danger by confining Amerindians and reducing them to a state of powerlessness?

According to the Jesuits: 'The Savages are scantily grateful in their natural state, especially toward the Europeans; Christianity trains them, little by little in this virtue.'[212] The task of bringing about this delicate 'conversion' fell to the missionary. There is no need for us to ask who benefitted from all this. As long as Amerindian societies kept their own way of life, they would not allow themselves to be confined to reservations. It was only when epidemics and wars had wiped out numerous Amerindian societies that the reservation became an alternative, and then as a form of refugee camp. At last the missionaries would realize their long-sought dream of wielding exclusive religious power over a population reduced to material dependency – a state of affairs that suited the colonial authorities as well. In 1637, Father Le Jeune envisaged setting up a reservation at Quebec. Let us see who was afraid of whom:

> First, in a few years there would be a village of Christian Hurons, who would help in no slight degree to bring their compatriots to the faith, through commerce with each other; and our wandering Montagnez would, little by little, become stationary through their example and through alliance with them. Secondly, Messieurs the Directors and Associations would have hostages here to assure the lives of our French in the country of the Hurons, and to maintain the commerce they have with all the more distant peoples and nations.[213]

A Totalitarian Environment

The reservation was a truly totalitarian institution. The Jesuits had complete authority, including the power to impose punishment on those who contravened 'the Laws of Jesus Christ and of his Church.'[214] Only the most fervent converts came or were accepted. The rest excluded themselves or were excluded. 'Anyone who acted against the Christian faith or morals,' wrote Marie de l'Incarnation, 'would leave, banishing himself of his own accord, knowing full well that whatever happened he would be forced to do penance or suffer the humiliation of being driven from the village.'[215]

The following anecdote illustrates the climate of constraint that prevailed on the Sillery reservation in 1651. Public control over private lives is amply revealed:

> The Savages know very well that it is not a place that is open to Apostates from the Faith, or to those who live scandalously in sin. Noël Tekouerimat, their Captain, gave them clearly to understand that the walls which had been built there were not for the purpose of sheltering vice, but of preventing it from entering. A young Algonquin woman, who had been baptized some months before at three Rivers, and who had not led there a life in conformity with the promises of her baptism,

came down to Sillery with that bad reputation. 'My daughter,' the
Captain said to her on her arrival, 'you must either alter your mode of
living, or you must change your residence.' Some days afterward, as
she had been a cause of gossip, he spoke more plainly to her: 'Go away
from here,' he said. 'The fort of Sillery is not for dogs, but for those
who manifest their faith by the purity of their lives.' She had to obey at
once. Thanks be to God, vice finds no support among the Christians.[216]

Jesuits living within Amerindian communities had been hampered
by the fierce and manifold resistance of traditionalists. On the reservation they were now rid of such opposition and could step up their drive
to acculturate the Amerindians. It was not merely a question of imposing meatless days every Friday and throughout Lent on Montagnais
hunters,[217] but of crushing a culture. This can be seen from the remarks
of one of the 'principal Christians,' conversing with a new arrival at
Sillery: 'What they teach us is of importance; they forbid us everything
that is bad, – the feasts where all the food is eaten [eat-all feasts], the
invocation of evil spirits, the belief in dreams, the multiplicity of wives in
marriage, and in a word, all our wicked customs which betray us and
cast us into a fire after death.'[218]

For some converts, life on the reservation intensified various personality traits already described: excessive self-control, a sense of guilt and
humiliation, masochistic behaviour, obsequious devotion, and an exag-
geratedly repressive super ego. Their dwellings in Sillery were known as
'the Cabins of those who pray.'[219] A despairing mother, seeing her son
gravely ill, cried through her sobs, 'I am making my son die. My sins are
taking away his life.'[220]

Reservation Amerindians were few in number, dependent, and
stripped of all power other than their capacity to run away. Their behaviour and personalities reflected the integration of values transmitted by the
practice and ideology of surplus repression prevalent in French society.
This could be seen from the advent of prisons and, in some instances,
from spontaneous changes in their attitude toward child-rearing.

Traditionally, Amerindian adults treated children kindly, paying
great attention to them, allowing them to run free, and training them
without corporal punishment. Now the children had to learn to fear God
and their parents.[221] The sight of an Amerindian woman beating her

four-year-old child would have been absolutely unthinkable in earlier days.[222] Resignation, a subjective characteristic of this new relationship with reality, was transmitted as a way of life to the children:

> The manner of raising her children adopted by this good Huron woman is extremely wonderful. When her little son, only two or three years old, has been beaten by his little comrades, and comes back into the Cabin weeping, she does not set about soothing him, wiping away his tears, and caressing him, as other mothers ordinarily do; on the contrary, she teaches him to make an offering to God of his little sufferings. 'Be quiet,' she says, 'be quiet; thou art crying, instead of offering up to God the pain which thou feelest. Make haste; down on thy knees, and make an offering to God of the injury thou hast received. Pray for those who have hurt thee, in order that their sense may return to them, and they may abstain in the future from ill-treating others.' And then this poor little one kneels down, and repeats what his mother prompts him; and when the prayer is done, lo! he feels perfectly well again.[223]

In 1643, the Sillery reservation became the site of the first prison in an Amerindian community. One is struck by two aspects of this event. First, it was the Amerindians themselves who asked for the prison. In sociological terms, they had clearly integrated their oppression and even amplified it. Second, it was a woman who was to be imprisoned and men who wished to punish her in order to make her obedient. As we know, women in northeastern Amerindian societies possessed considerable freedom. Their sexual freedom and right to divorce, however, were incompatible with a patriarchal society. The first instance of imprisonment reflected the need to set an example for women:

> The stability of marriage is one of the most perplexing questions in the conversion and settlement of the Savages; we have much difficulty in obtaining and in maintaining it. A young woman wishing to leave her husband without just cause, the principal and most zealous Savages assembled, and begged Monsieur the Governor to allow them to make a little prison at Sillery, and there to lock up this woman for some time, and bring her to her duty. Estienne Pigarouich undertakes this commission, and has her seized; and as she was at the door of the prison, he addressed her as follows: 'My niece, pray earnestly to God all night,

thou wilt have leisure; ask him that thou mayst become sensible, and
that thou mayst no longer be self-willed. Endure this prison for thy
sins. Take courage; if thou wilt be obedient, thou wilt not stay there
long.' She entered very peaceably, suffering herself to be led like a
lamb, and stayed there all night, flat on the ground, without fire and
without covering; it was the second day of January, at the severest season of the winter. The next morning, Father de Quen went with
Estienne to visit her, and saw to it that she was given a little bread, and
some straw to rest on. The Father wished to have her go forth a little
while, to warm herself in a neighboring room, then to put her back in
her cell; but the Savage told him that she ought to endure that for her
faults, and he himself encouraged her to bear this penance patiently.
Toward evening, nevertheless, they Judged it proper to release her; it
was enough for inspiring terror in this poor creature, and was a little
beginning of government for these new Christians, – moreover, melancholy fixing itself in the mind of a Savage, he comes to great extremi-
ties therein, and often to a violent death. The punishment sufficed for
this young woman, and for several others.[224]

In this totalitarian environment, it comes as no surprise to find people dying of 'melancholy.' The following idyllic view would have us
believe that the new value system had simply replaced the old in the
Amerindian imagination: 'Formerly their dreams were the God of their
hearts, but now God is in their dreams; for the greater number dream
only of God, Paradise, or Hell, and of the Angels, who in their sleep
invite them to come to them in heaven.'[225] On the contrary, the new
value system had pushed aside the old, but ever-present, system. Each
individual therefore experienced the inner contradiction between the
freedom of the past and the surplus repression of the present. For some,
the strain was unbearable. If, as is said in the *Jesuit Relations*, heavenly
grace had 'stifled in many of them the fears, the desires, the joys, and the
feelings of Nature,'[226] it is not surprising to find a convert like Jacques
Atohonchioanne, a noted warrior, suffocating in his nightmares,
'sigh[ing] for [God] alone,' and dying in a religious delirium. Brought
up a Christian from childhood, and now about thirty, 'the profligacy of
youth had caused him to fall into evil ways.' After a Jesuit father had
threatened him with hell, he had terrible nightmares and a vision of a

'frightful specter,' and was stricken with a lengthy illness accompanied by 'extreme pain.' He lost interest in everything except praying, eschewing all worldly things including the subsistence of his needy mother. He died haunted by the fear of hell, in the throes of violent convulsions.[227]

For many, alcohol provided a safety valve. It allowed them to escape, but it also compounded their sense of powerlessness, humiliation, and guilt. Those who drank were convinced that they were 'wicked and had sinned.'[228] Nevertheless, although the reservation suited a European strategy of containment and subjugation (the effects of which could be seen in the native people), it also provided dispossessed Amerindians with a strategy for maximizing cultural barriers, thereby maintaining an identity that was a source of collective and individual security.[229] Which Amerindians moved to the reservations? In New England as in New France, they were the survivors of peoples who had been decimated and defeated: the Pequots and the Hurons. For the Hurons, the reservation guaranteed shelter, food, and a place where their specificity and their identity had significance. Reservation meant preservation.

An 'Angel from Paradise'

As might be expected, Amerindian specificity and identity played no visible part on great and solemn occasions. In 1659, Monseigneur de Laval, the first bishop of Quebec, was received with much ceremony. Father Lalemant wrote that the bishop, 'in pontifical vestments,' appeared 'like an Angel of Paradise' to 'our Savages.' During a service sung in four languages, the bishop confirmed 'all the elite' of 'two Churches, Algonkin and Huron.'[230] Afterward, according to the custom of the country, a 'solemn feast' was held. On this occasion a Huron made the following speech, as reported in the *Jesuit Relations*:

> The first who harangued was one of the oldest Hurons. He expatiated quite amply upon the praises of the Faith, which causes the greatest men in the world to cross the seas, and makes them incur a thousand dangers and experience a thousand fatigues, in order to come and seek wretches. 'We are now nothing,' he said, 'O Hariouaouagui,' – this is the name which they give Monseigneur, and which signifies in their language 'the man of the great work,' – 'we are now nothing but the fragments of a once flourishing nation, which was formerly the terror of the Iroquois, and which possessed every kind of riches. What thou

seest is only the skeleton of a great people, from which the Iroquois has gnawed off all the flesh, and which he is striving to suck out to the very marrow. What attractions canst thou find in our miseries? How canst thou be charmed by this remnant of living carrion, to come from so far and join us in the so pitiful condition in which thou seest us? It must needs be that the Faith, which works these marvels, is such as they have announced to us for more than thirty years. Thy presence alone, although thou shouldst say not a word to us, speaks to us quite audibly in its behalf, and confirms us in the opinion that we hold of it.

'But, if thou wilt have a Christian people, the infidel must be destroyed; and know that, if thou canst obtain from France armed forces to humble the Iroquois, who comes to us with yawning jaws to swallow up the remnant of thy people, as in a deep chasm, know, I say, that by the destruction of two or three of these enemies' villages thou wilt make for thyself a great highway to vast lands and to many nations, who extend their arms to thee and yearn only for the light of the Faith. Courage, then, Hariouaouagui; give life to thy poor children, who are at bay! On our life depends that of countless peoples; but our life depends on the death of the Iroquois.'[231]

This speech exemplifies the two great functions of Christianity: compensation and legitimation. It says, quite literally, we were a flourishing nation, we are now nothing; we are fragments, a skeleton, carrion, but faith can work marvels. This is the compensation. Further, the Christian people must destroy the infidel, that is, the Iroquois, after which we will go to those peoples who extend their arms and yearn only for the light of the Faith. That is the legitimation of colonialism, of the French seen as Roman Catholic saviours, and of the transformation of converted tribes into links in the chain of empire.

The Final Solution
The very existence of Amerindian societies was a threat to their European counterparts. The egalitarian nature of Amerindian relationships was antagonistic to the complex hierarchies of class societies. Clan organization was also incompatible with an organization along patriarchal family lines. Furthermore, freedom of the individual and willingness to recognize desire ran counter to a system of discipline and self-repression. Historians have had a general tendency to reduce the

conquest of America, and the ousting and extermination of its first peoples, to a harmonious model demonstrating the creation of new societies. Within these new groups, each ethnic community supposedly contributed in its own way to the creation of a great Canadian or American whole. Thus the Amerindian 'contribution' to 'our' history has been reduced to a few technical devices such as snowshoes, canoes, toboggans, hooped fishing nets, or produce such as sweet corn. At best, Amerindians are conceded to have handed on a certain folkloric knowledge of geography, flora, and fauna. This is a vision that conceals the dynamics of social relationships. It was the very existence of these relatively egalitarian societies, so different in their structure and social relationships from those of Europe, that exercised the greatest influence on the newcomers and, at the same time, repelled them most. We must remember that these people came from a Europe where the existence of poverty and wealth side by side was an accepted fact of life. In this respect, let us look at the parallel comments of Sagard on the Hurons and Ragueneau on the Iroquois:

> [Sagard:] For it is their custom to help passers-by, and receive with courtesy anyone among them who is not an enemy: and more especially those of their own nation, who make hospitality reciprocal and are so helpful to one another that they provide for the needs of all, so that there are no poor beggars in any of their towns and villages, and they felt it was a very bad thing when they heard that in France there are a great many beggars and needy people, being of the opinion that this was the result of a lack of charity on our part, and they blamed us greatly.[232]

> [Ragueneau:] However, amid so many defects due to their blindness and to their barbarous training, they still possess virtues which might cause shame to most Christians. No Hospitals are needed among them, because there are neither mendicants nor paupers as long as there are any rich people among them. Their kindness, humanity, and courtesy not only make them liberal with what they have, but cause them to possess hardly anything except in common. A whole village must be without corn, before any individual can be obliged to endure privation. They divide the produce of their fisheries equally with all who come; and the only reproach they address to us is our hesitation to send to them oftener for our supply of provisions.[233]

One can imagine the impact of native societies on coureurs de bois, sons of indentured servants, domestics, censitaires, and slaves, and what it meant to encounter cultures whose members did not know what it was to be waited on and where everyone served themselves.[234] According to French and Dutch observers, Amerindians were 'contented with a mere living, [and] not one of them gives himself to the Devil to acquire wealth,'[235] and they did not understand 'why one man should be so much higher than another as we represent them to be.'[236] At the same time, it is even easier to imagine the threat posed by the very existence of these classless cultures to the dominant classes of European societies – societies where everything was shared unequally, both materially and symbolically. In Europe, beggars were hanged and the jobless condemned to the galleys. Quarrels over precedence typified relationships between nobles, the latter never having lowered themselves to work with their hands so that they required an army of people to work in order that they be fed, housed, and clothed.

A symbiosis of Amerindian cultures and the cultures of the European popular classes was not impossible, as illustrated by the multitude of coureurs de bois, voyageurs, and adventurers who became integrated into Amerindian societies after 1660. Their descendants eventually created the Métis society of the Canadian west, the only society in which whites and Amerindians succeeded in living together, teaching each other to hunt and to farm, and peopling the world of their imagination with Indo-European and Amerindian tales. Because of its remote location, Métis society gained a temporary reprieve from the fate reserved for other native groups. In the nineteenth century, however, it was to be destroyed by the Canadian political establishment, for which it represented the very antithesis. The coexistence of the first peoples of northeastern North America and European settlements was bound to have a corrosive effect on the latter and to subvert their political and social organization. This is why, as the seventeenth century moved into its last three decades, the final solution to the Amerindian 'problem' had already been put in place. It was to be genocide and/or the reservation.

THE REBIRTH OF EUROPEAN SOCIETIES IN NORTH AMERICA

In this final chapter, we will look at European societies transplanted to North America and how they took shape, particularly with respect to the access to land and labour control as well as to social and institutional relationships.

As we know, seventeenth-century North America bore very little resemblance to Europe. Labour was scarce, the white population was armed, including indentured servants[1] (something that would have been inconceivable in Europe at that time), and the forest was close at hand for anyone who wished to take refuge there. These were certainly not propitious circumstances for re-establishing the structures and hierarchies of the old Europe, yet it happened. How did these societies manage to replicate themselves in a new environment?

There were other variables to consider in the equation. To begin with, these European societies had differing origins – the home countries of some were modern and capitalist in nature, others were archaic and feudal. Specific social relationships developed when they reached North American shores, especially given the lack of available workers. Finally, each of these societies occupied a different position in the Atlantic economy. All in all, the relative weight of these variables has yet to be evaluated.

FROM TRADING POST TO COLONY

When Quebec was founded in 1608, Trois-Rivières in 1634, Fort Nassau in 1614, and New Amsterdam in 1624, there was no question of colonizing the land or creating new societies. In the beginning, the companies who came to trade for furs limited their activity to setting up a few trading posts. Their aim was to reap maximum profit from the fur trade. The white population of these trading posts, barricaded behind fortified walls, was small, transitory, and largely male. Only one institution existed in the trading post and that was the company, with its administrative hierarchy as the only social structure.[2] It is true that Champlain had a few dreams of grandeur for New France and that the court of France harboured some large-scale settlement plans, while the clergy dreamed of a (Roman Catholic) City of God that would gather in the Amerindians. Nevertheless, New France prior to 1660 was essentially little more than a fur-trading post.

The transition from trading post to colony, although perceptible after 1650, did not really take hold until after 1660.[3] Transition, in this case, means the shift to a permanently installed European society that had moved beyond the trading posts, become self-subsistent through farming, and re-established the balance of the sexes. New France was a good twenty years behind New Netherland in this respect, although the latter was founded later. It was the threat of settlement in the English colonies to the north and south that had forced the states-general of Holland as well as the Dutch West India Company to sacrifice profits from the fur trade (an activity that was incompatible with settlement) for the greater interests of the Dutch empire in the Atlantic, and to encourage colonization in as large numbers as possible. In New France, political intervention in support of colonization did not occur until 1663.

Hitherto, the Roman Catholic church, principally through the agency of the Jesuits, had taken the initiative in colonization to further its missionary goals. The Société Notre-Dame de Montréal, the devotional organization that founded Ville-Marie (Montreal) in 1642, recruited indentured servants from France, cleared land, and put up buildings during the period of the Iroquois wars. It also fell to religious communities other than the Jesuits, all with a missionary vocation, to import workers for clearing, building, and maintenance.[4] These included the Hospitalières de Dieppe who founded the Hôtel-Dieu in Quebec in 1639,[5] and the Ursulines who founded a school in Quebec.[6] It goes without saying that the moral character of the new arrivals had to be exemplary — that is, they had to be good Catholics. In 1658, Governor d'Argençon sent back to France an unwed mother who had arrived on a ship from La Rochelle. The merchant who brought her was fined 150 livres, the governor remarking, 'This will give our country a reputation similar to that of the Îles Saint-Christophe [St. Kitts] and keep merchants from taking on this kind of cattle.'[7] Convicts were equally excluded from emigrating to New France.

UNEQUAL ACCESS TO LAND

Once indentured servants and settlers had established themselves, the company hierarchy no longer provided an adequate structure for social relationships. European newcomers were part of a class society and their numbers included nobles, senior administrators, officers, tradespeople, indentured servants, and slaves. They did not find egalitarian relationships awaiting them on the North American side of the Atlantic. In fact, the old hierarchies tended to be self-perpetuating. Apart from the fur trade, to which access was variously forbidden, limited, or controlled by monopoly-holding companies, the major source of social and economic disparity was unequal access to land.

In New France, some individuals were destined to have seigneuries, some a portion of land, and some to be indentured servants. As a matter of course, the seigneurial system was transplanted to the shores of the Saint Lawrence in 1623. Companies with fur-trading monopolies obtained seigneurial rights to their territories at this time.[8] These were soon divided into seigneuries (about seventy prior to 1664), then ceded to persons of note and to religious communities.

Take, for example, the case of Jean de Lauson, intendant of the Compagnie des Cent Associés. In 1636, he arranged for himself and his sons to be granted, either directly or under dummy names, a domain covering nearly the entire south shore of the Saint Lawrence between Quebec and Montreal, reserving for himself the exclusive monopoly on fishing and navigation, among other things.[9] Seigneuries gradually covered the whole territory. All the religious communities possessed at least one seigneury, as did newly arrived members of the minor nobility such as Jacques Leneuf de la Poterie and the brothers Pierre Legardeur de Repentigny and Charles Legardeur de Tilly, the latter two being admiral and ship's captain respectively.[10]

These seigneuries brought in no revenue in the beginning and would

not do so until peopled with censitaires. Nevertheless, the formation of
seigneuries and the transplantation of social relationships inherent in
the seigneurial system were guarantees of future prosperity for families
of 'notables.' The rules had been set, and new arrivals had no choice in
the matter. Those who thereby acquired land for nothing proceeded to
develop it with the labour of others – indentured servants to clear the
forest and construct buildings on the seigneury, settlers to develop the
value of the land held *en censive*. Historian Marcel Trudel[11] estimates the
gross total revenue of all seigneuries in 1662 at 2,889 livres – this income
being drawn from over 400 parcels of land, giving an average of 7 livres
per parcel. This was less than a labourer's weekly wage (1.5 livres per day
as opposed to 2.5 livres for an artisan).[12] Trudel's list of 27 seigneuries
shows 14 earning less than 100 livres per year. Heading the list were the
Jesuits with 375 livres, then Jean de Lauson, the Compagnie des Cent
Associés, Charles Aubert de la Chesnaye, Bishop Laval, and so on. In
other words, the largest annual seigneurial income was less than the
annual wage of a labourer or an artisan.

Although 'these first generation seigneurs were not yet living on
their rents,'[13] a social relationship had been established on the basis of
land. In fact, a seigneurial régime was reappearing in New France. The
religious communities and families that would form the dominant class
of the emerging society were already identifiable. Although settlers had
access to free land, they were not actually landowners. They were obliged
to sign a contract with the seigneur recognizing his rights over them and
providing for payment of *cens et rentes*.[14] The cens, a form of symbolic
annual tax (generally less than two livres per parcel of land), marked the
landholder's subjection to the seigneur. The rente was an annual ground
rent, usually payable partly in kind and partly in money, which in 1662
averaged a little over five livres per parcel. Another tax outlined in the
contract was the *lods et vente*, which equalled the twelfth part of the sale
price of a parcel of land and was payable by the buyer to the seigneur. In
addition, the seigneur had the right of veto over all transactions and a
right of *retrait du seigneur* (right of preemption), which gave him a prior
option to recover land at the price paid by another buyer within forty
days after the sale. The contract also provided for collecting a *droit de
banalité du moulin* – that is, a milling tax. The seigneur had a monopoly
on the seigneurial mill and the habitants were obliged to have their grain

milled there and to leave one fourteenth of the grain at the mill. The seigneur also held the monopoly on commercial fishing which he could cede in return for royalties. In certain cases, the contract stipulated a corvée of two or three days per year (days of unpaid labour) and occasionally mentioned the payment of the *dîme* or tithe to the curé. The censitaire was also obliged to clear his land and to inhabit it; failure to do so could result in the land being seized by the seigneur.

By no stretch of the imagination can the settlers along the shores of the Saint Lawrence be called a free peasant class, although the exploitation of Canadian censitaires was in no way comparable to that of their French counterparts. However, it is more the social relationship than the degree of exploitation that defines a social structure. What emerged in rural New France was not a mode of production based on small commercial production behind a seigneurial façade, but a genuine seigneurial regime in which the extortion of surplus labour was limited by the difficulties of settlement and, above all, by the scarcity of workers (and consequently the need to attract them).[15]

New Netherland, like New France, also had a history of unequal access to land but in markedly more varied forms. Possibly because of pressure from the English and the strategic need to populate its territory, settlement in New Netherland took on all the aspects of a seigneurial system, even though Holland itself was a capitalist country. The differences between France and Holland seem to have become blurred in their respective North American colonies.

Like French companies, the Dutch West India Company asked for and obtained the exclusive right to distribute land in the area that it had carved out for itself. Similarly, several of its major shareholders used their influence to acquire huge land grants for themselves. The 1629 charter of freedoms and exemptions (*Vryheden ende Exemptien*) authorized the company to settle the land in its fur-trading territory, either with free colonists or by setting up 'patroonships' – settlement ventures that were a form of seigneury identical in all respects to the settlement ventures already undertaken in Guiana. In actual fact, the fur-trading interests retained a virtual monopoly, and it was through this trade that the various means of access to land were developed. Resistance by a large faction of shareholders hampered – or at least failed to stimulate – immigration of independent settlers who would become small landholders.[16] Nevertheless, the several patroonships that were established got their impetus from fur-trade profits. In any case, the salient feature of this development was that certain 'ordinary' settlers had the right to a piece of 'ordinary' land that they would clear themselves, while others, either financiers or shareholders, built themselves small empires in which indentured servants and tenant-métayers (the term sharecropper is perhaps more evocative) developed the land and made it profitable for the original investors.

The patroonships consisted of about twenty-five kilometres of shore frontage or the same figure divided in half along both sides of a river. The depth of the holding could be as much as the holder desired. The patroons had to bring over at least fifty adult male settlers at their own cost and establish them on their holdings. Between 1630 and 1646, Van Rensselaer brought over 216 settlers for his domain, a large number of whom went back when their contract ran out.[17] Several specialized workmen also came as indentured servants to construct buildings, including a flour mill and a saw mill. When the settlers arrived, they signed a contract leasing (not buying) the land from the patroon. The latter continued to own the land while supplying the newcomer with basics – tools and animals. The sharecropper was free to leave at the end of the lease or to sign a second contract of lease for a period of between three and twelve years. The rate of payment varied between a third and half of the produce. Historian Clarence W. Rife showed how the patroon system worked by giving examples of a few successive leases:

> On September 7, 1646, one Thomas Chambers, who was evidently an English carpenter, obtained this desirable tract on a five-year contract beginning in November, 1647. As there were no buildings on the land at that time, the patroon's representatives arranged to have the tenant supply them. Chambers was induced to erect, at his own expense, a house and barn of specified sizes and types. The patroon delivered into his charge two mares, two stallions, and four milch cows. The tenant agreed to surrender the buildings, at the expiration of his term, in lieu of rent, but was permitted to retain half the increase of the animals. From the proceeds of his crops, however, he was required to pay tenths, and, 'as an acknowledgement five and twenty pounds of butter' yearly. This last charge, called *toepacht*, was more precisely a quit-rent

than the tenth, and it was usually payable in kind. Chambers alone was responsible for the safety of the buildings and fences; but, in case Indian disorders should oblige him to flee, his term was to be extended so as to make up the time lost. At the expiration of his lease, as it turned out, he remained for a further term of two years, and as the buildings were then no longer free, paid 500 guilders annually in addition to tenths. Upon his withdrawal, the farm was leased to Jan Barentsz Wemp. By this time the bouwerie had reached a flourishing state of development so that the director of the colony was able to drive a more remunerative bargain. The buildings were to be duly appraised and the risk borne equally by patroon and tenant. The lessee was given four mares, one stallion, and four cows which he was to return at the end of his term; but half the increase, he might retain. The annual rental was increased to 600 guilders and he paid in addition the customary tenth and *toepacht*.[18]

It was an odd system – this métayage with a distinctly capitalist bent discernible in the size of capital involved, the patroon's private ownership of the means of production, and the dispossession of the sharecroppers who were reduced to the position of quasi-wage-earning tenants. Equally curious were its feudal aspects – family production units, the cens, the tithe, the seigneurial mill, and the establishment of a seigneurial court to settle rent disputes.

The specific forms of land holding in New Netherland can best be understood by observing the relationships between the patroonship system and the fur trade. The patroonships owed their creation less to a desire to invest in land than an attempt by some shareholders to steal a march on the company and trade on their own account. These shareholders played a dual role, acting as a Trojan Horse, first introducing patroons into the Dutch territories, then exercising complete control over the labour force. By a strange coincidence, it was only in the trading areas that an attempt was made to establish a few patroonships. Only one survived – Rensselaerwyck near Fort Orange which was by far the most important trading post. The shareholders of the Dutch West India Company who opposed the creation of patroonships feared the patroons would turn the company's trading network to their own advantage. How right they were! Rensselaerwyck, which completely encircled Fort

Orange, quickly became a virtual business operation with a patroon at its head. Van Rensselaer's agents supplied their sharecroppers with trade goods, which the latter in turn traded on behalf of the patroon, although this was illegal before 1640.[19] The patroon's sharecroppers were in fact his employees, a state of affairs that gave rise to the remark, in 1638, that 'the inhabitants of Rensselaerswyck ... were as many traders as persons.'[20] These sharecroppers were definitely captive workers, a labour force made up of dispossessed persons. The success of Rensselaerwyck was therefore explained by the fact that Van Rensselaer was able to finance his domain with capital drawn from the fur trade and also because the sharecroppers were willing to submit to a particularly disadvantageous land-holding system without any hope of profiting from this same trade.

Looking beyond New Netherland's peculiarities, it is difficult not to be struck by the fact that seigneurial regimes were established in precisely the two colonies where the northeastern fur trade was mainly carried out. The seigneurial system was a normal outgrowth of the existing French social fabric, but the same cannot be said of Holland. The patroonship system only took root around the Dutch trading posts; elsewhere in New Netherland, small independent holdings were the general rule. There was, therefore, a structural link between the fur trade and the seigneurial system – a link based, in my opinion, on the need to keep the work force securely in place.

As we have seen, the logic of unequal exchange argued that settlement and the fur trade were incompatible activities. More settlers meant less profit. Rivalry among imperial powers drove them to populate their territories. This could only be effective if settlers stayed on their land so that participation in (or exclusion from) the fur trade would not threaten existing relationships of unequal exchange between Europeans and Amerindians. In both colonies, for example, undeveloped land was taken away from the settler. At best, this form of land holding would attract a relatively small number of settlers. Why would anyone leave Europe to become locked into a seigneurial regime, unable to enjoy the freedom sought in the New World? What Dutch peasant would leave his wholly-owned land, unencumbered by seigneurial constraints, to become a sharecropper? The patroons' aspirations struck a snag: few settlers came, few stayed, and labour was therefore scarce. Among those who did come, more than half were not even Dutch. Those who had dreamed of castles in America could not find enough manpower to build them. As the 1630s drew to a close, it became evident that the colony must be populated as quickly as possible. The only way to achieve this was to offer advantageous conditions to *coloniers* – that is, to free colonists.

During early Dutch settlement in North America, there was in fact no free access to land. It is true that the thirty Protestant Walloon families who formed the nucleus of Dutch settlement in 1624 were brought out for nothing by the company and had acquired full ownership of their land. However, this system of land tenure based on small production was subsequently replaced by patroonships.

After 1638, the Dutch West India Company seriously wanted to populate its land, but once again it took a niggardly approach. It offered a free parcel of land to immigrants who paid their passage, and it provided an advance of equipment and animals to get farms started. In return, however, it demanded payment of a cens representing 10 per cent of the value of the settler's land after four years.[21] In 1640, the company made fresh efforts to encourage settlement, this time offering a liberal stimulus: all immigrants would have their passage paid, excluding food costs. The settler paid nothing for his land and acquired full ownership of it; he was also given the necessary equipment. In addition, the deadline for the cens was moved to ten years, the size of patroonships was reduced, and provision was made for organizing and regrouping settlers on a municipal basis. These measures came into force at the beginning of the wars against the Amerindians and had little effect until they were over. After 1644, most of the new arrivals in New Netherland settled there on this basis. In 1650, further changes were introduced. The deadline for the cens was now delayed by a year per child. Of course, settlers were still offered a choice between owning land and seigneurial tenure. They were guaranteed free access to the forest with the reminder that they must extinguish Amerindian rights to the land in question by a contract of sale.[22] Apart from independent settlers, who formed the largest group, and sharecroppers, who probably formed the smallest, there were three other groups: wage labourers (*bouwelieden*),[23] indentured servants, and slaves. These three groups were hardly ever found on settlers' land nor, as in New France, on the estates of religious communities, the latter being nonexistent in Protestant New Netherland. Instead, they worked on the company farms (*bouwerijn* or bouweries). In 1630, the company had eight farms concentrated in the Manhattan region.

The peasant class was not a homogenous group, as in Holland. Instead, it included sharecroppers, indentured servants, farm labourers, and slaves, although, in fact, the labour shortage had made most of them farmer-owners. As in New France, they cleared long, narrow strips of land running back from the river frontage. The settlers built their home-steads close to waterways and established communities that formed long ribbon developments along both banks. Unlike New England, where set-tlement was frequently undertaken on a community basis, the colonizing patterns of New France and New Netherland were influenced by geogra-phy (the rivers) as much as by the phenomenon of individual settlement. With farmer-owners came the beginnings of a freer society, and the framework it adopted was not seigneurial, but municipal.

The uncompromising religious severity of New England led groups of English colonists to settle in New Netherland.[24] Land was granted freely, settlers were given the power to elect civic administrators and law officers, and, as was the case in New England, the municipal council had the power to oversee the distribution of land.[25] As a result, two types of municipal government were established in New Netherland. The first was modelled on the municipalities of Holland. It was slower to get going and less independent of the central power. The second type was mod-elled on the villages of New England. This was adopted by the minority English communities on eastern Long Island. It was more independent and more aggressive because it involved a founding community rather than a conglomeration of colonists. All in all, Dutch municipalities were not as autonomous as their English counterparts, and the central power retained sole right to distribute land, except in the very last years of the regime.[26] The Dutch municipalities also took longer to get organized. The colony's director and the company board named the mayor (*schout*) and the three councillors (*schepens*). In total, seventeen municipalities were formed during the last twenty years of the Dutch regime.

These municipal organizations gradually took on the role of orga-nizing and integrating rural dwellers – a role assumed by the seigneurial regime in New France and in Rensselaerwyck. The very existence of these forms of municipal organization illustrates the extent to which settlers could organize themselves outside of the seigneurial system, and to what degree the latter – far from being a form of mutual social aid developed into a system[27] – was a form of exploitation by no means essential to the colonization process.

In 1752, the organization of the village of Fort Orange into a municipality named Beverwyck enabled its inhabitants to escape the constraints of Rensselaerwyck. A new, municipal court was created. The incumbent company officer was automatically named president, and the court was empowered to distribute lots. Shortly after a municipal government was instituted in New Amsterdam in 1653, its burgomasters convoked the representatives of several municipalities. They agreed to denounce 'the exclusion of the people from all share in legislation – against the operation of old and obsolete laws – against withholding grants of land to settlers, and making extravagant grants to particular individuals – against the appointment of magistrates without the consent of the people, and against the neglect of effectual provision for the defence of the country.'[28]

Although nothing came of this reprimand, it serves to remind us of the existence of an authoritarian, arbitrary power as well as of the dubious practices that permitted speculation, hoarding, and exclusion. On the other hand, these very practices spurred people on to organize in order to demand bourgeois freedoms.

FORMS OF LABOUR CONTROL

The striking thing about the repopulation of northeastern North America by European colonies was the continuing tension between constraint and freedom. Often emigration was the result of poverty, the difficulty of subsisting, or even expropriation. A growing number of emigrants in the second half of the seventeenth century left Europe because of outright deportation, being what English judges called 'undesirables.' People also emigrated in the hope of acquiring land and a better life, enabling them to eat their fill and keep warm in winter, as well as in the hope of escaping the shackles of the seigneurial system.

On the other hand, the empire builders – the trading companies and governments – had schemes, investments, and businesses to be developed and made profitable, and such plans had little in common with the immigrants' preoccupations. The abundance of available land following the shrinking of the Amerindian population enhanced the worth of the individual. Independence was assured by easy access to land and the unheard-of environmental wealth of the flora and fauna. Why should people work themselves to death for others when they could work for themselves and live well? Such freedom, however, was a threat to the dominant classes, who were obliged to resort to force in all forms to keep the ordinary people in line and make sure they were tied to their jobs. The social makeup of the colonies therefore included not only the free settlers of Breukelen or Greewyck, but the donnés of the Jesuits at Quebec; the indentured servants attached to religious orders, seigneurs, or the Dutch West India Company; the wage-earners (more rarely) who were attached to the fur-trading companies; the censitaires of New France; the boer-métayers or sharecroppers of Rensselaerwyck; the black slaves who worked on a Dutch West India Company bouwerie on Manhattan Island (or even the slaves sold on 31 May 1664 as part of a contract to purchase 600 pounds of beef at four stuivers a pound and 600 pounds of pork at five stuivers a pound, payable in blacks, beaver, or goods evaluated in terms of beaver pelts);[29] and finally the Amerindian domestics taken 'into service.'[30] America offered freedom, but it also imposed chains.[31]

All forms of labour control and subjection existed throughout the Americas. Slavery became the predominant form of labour organization in the southern colonies. In Virginia, the labour force for a time consisted mainly of indentured servants. Further north, free settlers and censitaires formed the major labour force. Why did different methods of labour control emerge in various areas? Why should slavery not predominate in the north and small independent producers prevail in the Brazilian northeast? The answer is that labour organization in any given area is not just the result of deliberate planning by dominant classes or of the pressures of an expanding world economy (the latter stimulates a social division of labour). Labour organization also emerges as a result of class resistance and struggle in an expanding economic world-system.

Early in the seventeenth century, northeastern North America offered the following production sectors: fishing, lumbering, agriculture (cereals, fruits, and vegetables), and livestock raising. These are all activities that can only be accomplished with initiative, knowledge, skill, and a minimum of autonomy on the part of the worker. By contrast, mining or the production of sugar cane are intensive forms of economic activity that demand a large number of unskilled workers. Only in this type of economy is slavery possible.

There is no form of slavery that does not involve the fierce, daily, manifold, and unremitting opposition of those who are enslaved. They will seek every means to free themselves, flee, and revolt.[32] They will sabotage the work. If animals are entrusted to their care, they will maltreat them as soon as their master's back is turned. Give them a tool of any complexity and they will take advantage of the first opportunity to break it. If a black female slave becomes pregnant, she may try to abort her child to spare it a life of slavery and deny her master a free slave. All labour based on slavery requires considerable repressive force – constant armed surveillance, brutality, and capital punishment. In Mississippi, it was calculated that closely watched slaves picked cotton three times faster.[33] The relative significance of non-productive costs in the slavery system was therefore enormous. The slave could only be given work that was regular, repetitive, compartmentalized, monotonous, and unskilled, so that it could be measured – work that would leave the least possible opportunity for resistance. Conversely, free time, training, and education were politically dangerous. Teams of slaves that were organized to fish off Newfoundland would mutiny at the first opportunity and head for free territory, as did the Acadian Beausoleil-Broussard. Slaves had been brought across the Atlantic in chains. If given an axe and told to clear land for a master, a slave would build himself a cabin in some distant place. Let a northern master attempt to develop a large seigneury for growing wheat, barley, and rye, where the soil must be tilled, the crops reaped, the wood hewn, and the livestock cared for – if his slaves were in the least numerous, they would remind him of their condition by various acts of vandalism that would ruin the venture. There is no oppression without resistance. Slavery as the major form of labour organization in northern colonies was not effective and had to be abandoned.

We should remember that Christopher Columbus wrote that the Amerindians would make good servants when he first met them on 12 October 1492.[34] Why, in that case, shouldn't all these barbarous peoples be used as slaves in some great production enterprise? Since when has the central business world cared about working conditions on the periphery? Was it not the Amerindians who laboured to build the wealth of Spain and Portugal before being almost entirely wiped out?

In territories where fur trading was the main activity, Europeans could not do without Amerindian tribes. Total subordination or entire destruction was therefore out of the question. In situations where

Europeans sought to take over the territory or the work force, there was a far greater incentive to expropriate land or instigate slavery. Nevertheless, these economic factors, however fundamental, do not explain everything. If we take another approach, we see that institutionalized slavery did not exist in northeastern Amerindian societies. Actually, there was a form of 'proto-slavery' in which captives were forcibly integrated into the society of their masters – but in terms of kinship rather than class relationships. These captives were kept under surveillance, it is true, and subjected to a great deal of symbolic violence that forced them to relinquish their identities. Nevertheless, it was understood that they were taking the places of people who had died, and their children were treated no differently from other members of the society. North America was not Africa, as Fernand Braudel has pointed out: 'There was a slave trade in Africa because Europeans wanted and imposed it, but also because Africans had already contracted the bad habit of practising slavery well before the advent of the Europeans. Slaves were traded to the regions of Islam, the Mediterranean, and the Indian Ocean. Slavery in Africa was endemic, an institutionalized part of everyday life. It would be interesting to know more about the existing social framework.'[35]

All attempts to establish slavery in northeastern North America met with resistance and outright refusal. For example, the Virginia Company tried to make tribes pay a tax in the form of goods and labour. When the tribes revolted in 1622, the company adopted a policy of extermination.[36] Without Amerindians it had to rely on indentured servants.

The Americas were equally unlike Africa in microbial terms. Generally speaking, Africa belonged to the same bacterial universe as the Eurasian continent. The western hemisphere had been isolated from this world and had paid an enormous price for coming into contact with it. As became evident in South America, Amerindian slaves were less biologically resistant than black slaves; where the former died, the latter took their places and survived.

The northeastern Amerindians had not developed the class divisions present in most societies of South America and Africa. Hunter-gatherers occupied the northern reaches of the territory, while the remaining area was populated by horticultural peoples. These societies were all unaccustomed to the harsh and regular work of agriculture and knew nothing of rigid hierarchical distinctions. As we noted earlier, Van der Donck observed differences in status among the Amerindians but not to the degree that existed among Europeans, and he noted that the former were puzzled as to why one man should be ranked so much higher than another.[37]

It requires a great deal of training to turn humans into sedentary beings, to subject them to authoritarian social structures, unremitting labour, a repetitive daily routine, and, in short, to subject their activity to a measure of time calculated in terms of hours and days. Even in our own day, companies in the Canadian North have difficulty imposing fixed timetables on Amerindian and Inuit peoples. It would have been virtually impossible to turn a seventeenth-century Iroquois or Algonkin into a wage-earner. The first flight of wild geese and they would be off, leaving the field half mowed. And in any case, working in the fields was traditionally women's work among the Amerindians. The Amsterdam Exchange already had the habit of calculating almost everything – rates of interest, depreciation, travel risks, costs – but the contingencies of wild geese and caribou were a bit beyond its scope. The idea of turning an Iroquois or Algonkin into a slave was never even raised. Whereas the blacks in North America were at a loss in a strange environment, the Amerindian was on home ground and had no fear of the forest. Amerindians working for whites were few and far between in any of the new societies of North America except on a casual basis. In New Netherland, for example, Amerindians were hired to build forts at half the wage given to a white worker.[38] The Dutch also took in Amerindian children to be trained as domestic servants. These were probably the children of conquered peoples. Van der Donck was one of the first in a series of commentators who noted that as soon as these children grew up they went back to their own people, forgot what they had learned among the whites, and were reintegrated into their own culture.[39]

The history of slavery in New Netherland[40] illustrates how the labour shortage forced the Dutch to rely on slaves and how the latter, profiting from their bargaining power as moderately qualified workers, were able to better themselves. The Dutch were very active in the seventeenth-century Atlantic slave trade and, between 1645 and 1675, were the major traders. They could therefore transport captive workers to New Netherland on their own ships. In 1626, the Dutch West India Company began using slaves to build warehouses and forts and later used them on its bouweries. After 1648, the company allowed the colony's merchants to import slaves directly from Angola. The experiment was short-lived as slaves from the West Indies who were already 'seasoned' (second genera-tion) were preferred to the 'proud and treacherous' Angolans.[41] The patroons bought slaves, and the company had some in its service. The demand for slaves grew, as did prices. A slave was worth 100 florins in 1636, 300 in 1646, 450 in 1660, and 600 in 1664. Those owned by the com-pany were not expensive to maintain as they kept their own gardens. Thus, the annual wage of a free worker, about 280 florins, excluding room and board, represented the purchase price of a slave in 1630, and, by 1664, it represented about half the price.

It is difficult to estimate the colony's black population. We know that Director-General Stuyvesant bought forty slaves at once in Curaçao, and one of his lieutenants bought twenty. In 1664, a ship delivered 300 black slaves. It may be that slaves exceeded 10 per cent of the colony's popula-tion. The independent type of work entrusted to them, as well as the growing number of fugitives (who often got help from the white set-tlers), forced the company to make considerable concessions and to bring the status of slaves closer to that of indentured servants or censi-taires by conferring on them, as a form of reward, a status of 'half-free-dom.' Any slave could buy this status in return for a 'typical' annual payment to the company of 'thirty schepels of maize or wheat and one fat hog' and the obligation to take part in certain corvées which were mainly for 'fortifications and other public works.' Blacks were otherwise free, except that their children were considered slaves. 'Although the company never attempted to enslave such children,' their parents 'bom-barded the company with petitions for guarantees of freedom for their children' – petitions supported by Dutch settlers in the name of 'the law of every people.' It was noted that, although some blacks were freed after long service, 'children of manumitted slaves were retained in slavery, contrary to all public law.'[42]

Slavery in the Dutch colony illustrates both the power of the Dutch West India Company and the close ties that bound the colony to the Atlantic economy. We should add that at the same period, there were very few slaves in New England and none in New France (with the excep-tion of a young black who was brought by the Kirke brothers to Quebec in 1629 and who died in 1654).[43]

The labour shortage continued. Unable to hire or enslave the

Amerindians, unable to develop slavery on a large scale or bring in as many settlers as wanted, and unable, above all, to easily reduce settlers to the status of wage-earners, the various colonizing agents had to fall back on indentured servants (*engagés* in French, *hirelings* in Dutch). The system of indentured servants was marginal in New Netherland and New England, whereas in New France it formed the bulk of the small stream of migration before 1663. Pierre Boucher wrote in 1644, 'Most of our *habitants* are people who come as servants, & after serving a master for three years they work for themselves.'[44]

The indentured servant became a kind of slave for a limited time. In Europe, the same man generally lived in poverty or in a country at war. This made him an ideal candidate for labour recruiters who combed the ports and surrounding countryside on behalf of prominent merchants. This was actually a trade in labour. It cost about 100 livres to recruit an indentured servant in France, have the notarial contract signed, and pay the costs of lodging at an inn and the ship's passage. Most indentured servants were taken to the West Indies, and a lesser number to Canada. They were then resold at a profit, for a price that was as high as the wages stipulated in the notarial contract were low. Recruiters frequently had a list of Canadian buyers so that the indentured servant knew before embarking who his master would be.[45] Recruitment for Canada was mainly for woodsmen, sailors, and various workmen and day-labourers needed to clear and build.[46] Their wages averaged about 100 livres per year, rising a little higher around 1640 but dropping to about 70 livres per year after 1655.[47]

While immigrants to Canada were generally 'free,' that is, economically motivated, direct constraint still existed. In 1653, Jérôme Le Royer de La Dauversière, a district tax collector in Laflèche, had 119 indenture contracts. Recruitment for Canada was facilitated by rising wheat prices and the poverty that followed in the wake of the Fronde.[48] At boarding time, several failed to show up, at which point others were hastily taken on in the port. The men were closely watched. They were put aboard a first ship that proved to be leaky. The recruits mutinied and the ship was forced to return. Weapon in hand, Maisonneuve, the 're-founder' of Montreal, forced his human merchandise to embark for his 'city of Mary.'[49] Although recruits were also rounded up in the poor neighbourhoods of Paris, Bordeaux, and La Rochelle, it seems that these captives were shipped to the West Indies rather than to Canada, where the clergy carried enough weight to insist that recruits be screened in France for good morals by parish priests.[50] In researching seventeenth-century notarial records of La Rochelle, Gabriel Debien found 830 names of indentured servants bound for Canada.[51] Of these, 250 dated from 1655 to 1665, an average of twenty-five per year. This was a small but steady flow, although far lower than migration to Santo Domingo.[52] The Caribbean trade was directed by major Protestant traders, whereas it was the less prominent Catholic merchants who recruited for New France.

These numbers, however, amounted to relatively little beside British emigration figures. But the reasons for this imbalance may have been as much political as economic. Prior to 1624, large numbers of convicts were deported to Virginia. In 1617, poor London children were sold to Virginia as apprentices and bound to work until the age of twenty-one. In 1619, Virginia planters offered the equivalent of 500 pounds sterling in tobacco for fifty boys.[53] Finally, under Cromwell, huge numbers of Irish and Scottish prisoners were sent across the Atlantic as indentured servants.

Sold into service, the indentured servant had only one rule to follow: submit to his master to whom he owed absolute obedience. The master was entitled to inflict corporal punishment. Repression was greatest in Virginia, where indentured servants were very numerous. They could be executed for stealing company goods, for unauthorized trading with Amerindians, and for slaughtering domestic animals. If their work was unsatisfactory, they might be forced to wear an iron collar, beaten, or condemned to the galleys for a year.[54] When De Vries passed through Virginia, he saw masters betting their indentured servants at cards.[55] In New France, an indentured servant had to compensate for one day of flight with twenty days of labour. Although most decided to stay when their contract ran out (figures vary between 50 and 75 per cent per year in the seventeenth century),[56] some tried to escape and return to France. In 1658, the governor published a decree forbidding any habitant of the colony from leaving without permission signed by himself: 'Several French habitants of the country, especially servants and farm labourers working for wages, have attempted to return to France without their masters' knowledge, embarking at night in chaloupes in which they descended the length of the Saint Lawrence River as far as the aforementioned *île percée* and other places where they met French fishing boats, secretly carrying off pelts which they traded.'[57]

The same 'problem' developed in New Netherland, where colonists accused the English of giving asylum to fugitive company workers.[58] In reality, it was the slaves of New Netherland and the indentured servants of New France and New England who 'opened up the country,' cleared the land, and built the forts. They also built the first warehouses, stores, convents, seminaries, and chapels of Canada. Once the infrastructure was in place, their role became less important in an agricultural economy based on the family farm. Even so, in 1666, there were still 350 indentured servants under contract in New France – over a quarter of the male population over fifteen years of age.[59]

Once a contract had run out, the indentured servant could plan his own future. He could leave or, as was more often the case, settle on a parcel of land to which his three years of service gave him free access. With an axe, he could build a cabin and clear land. In New France, unlike in New Netherland, the settler had no yoke of oxen to haul tree trunks. He sowed his first seed in the fall and continued cutting for part of the winter. In spring, he sowed sweet corn, broad beans, and pumpkins between the trunks and stumps[60] in the Amerindian fashion. It took time for the stumps to rot, oxen were scarce, and ploughs were not used until a later date. While waiting for the stumps to rot, the settler tilled the earth with spades, mattocks, and hoes.[61] Pierre Boucher describes this process in somewhat idyllic terms: 'Before they have done a year's work, the land is cleared & they harvest more grain than they need to feed themselves. When they first begin working for themselves, they usually possess very little and marry a woman who has not much more; however, if they are the least inclined to work, in less than four or five years you see them at their ease, & well off for people of their condition. All the poor people do much better here than in France, provided they are not lazy.'[62]

In New Netherland, it was considered that at least two or three years were needed before a settler was self-sufficient.[63] On virgin land, the yield was higher than anything previously known. The land was worked for several years without lying fallow[64] or being fertilized, and the harvest was still abundant. River and forest supplied the rest. The work was hard, but at least there was work and it provided a living.

The labour shortage gave the artisan the same advantage as the peasant. Artisans commanded good wages. Concessions had to be made in order to attract workers; consequently New France and New Netherland had neither guild-masters nor mastership requirements.[65] Legally, nothing prevented a day-labourer in either colony from becoming an artisan. It was the market that decided. In New France, only a few religious brotherhoods based on the guild trades were re-established, but their role was purely symbolic. After 1627, any artisan who had practised his trade for six years in the colony was deemed to be a master in France.[66] New Amsterdam required anyone seeking the right to open a shop or exercise an artisanal trade to obtain a *burgerrecht* or freedom of the city officially recognizing him as a permanent resident.[67]

REPRODUCTION OF SOCIAL RELATIONSHIPS

If the seigneurial regime imposed in New France had subjugated the peasant class as much as it did in France, indentured servants would have certainly shipped out as soon as their contracts ended. To attract settlers, it was therefore necessary to reduce the degree of feudal exploitation. The fifty or sixty families of Walloons and French Lutherans who wanted to escape seigneurial oppression were well aware of this when they requested permission from Sir Dudley Carleton to settle a Virginia concession

> sixteen miles in diameter, which they could cultivate as fields, meadows, vineyards, and in other ways ... and [asked] whether those amongst them who could live as nobles would not be permitted to declare themselves such ... [Also] whether they might not hunt in said countries all game whether furred or feathered ... fish in the seas and rivers, cut trees of lofty and other growth both for navigation and other purposes according to their pleasure; in fine, make use of every thing under and above ground at their pleasure and will, (royalties excepted) and trade in all with those permitted them.[68]

European social relations were demonstrably not reproduced in their entirety on the North American side of the Atlantic. Karl Marx, in his chapter on the modern theory of colonization in *Capital: A Critique of Political Economy*, remarks with satirical emphasis that a certain Mr. Peel 'took with him from England to Swan River, West Australia, means of subsistence and of production to the amount of £50,000. Mr. Peel had the foresight to bring with him, besides, 3,000 persons of the working class, men, women, and children. Once arrived at his destination [and here Marx quotes E.G. Wakefield's *England and America*], "Mr. Peel was left without a servant to make his bed or fetch him water from the river."[69] The scarcity of workers was the main stumbling block in re-establishing European social relationships in North America. The north-eastern population was very small, and the various work methods employed in the emerging economy made it impossible to reduce the labour force to a state of slavery, given the fact that these methods required considerable independence on the part of the worker. The worker's worth increased as a result. He was in a better position to resist exploitation and earned a wage higher than in Europe, whatever his trade.

The result was a freer society with an improved quality of life – a little like fifteenth-century Europe where workers became scarce following the great plagues of the preceding century. Free, however, did not mean equal. The frontier myth, in which social barriers dropped for a time as men worked shoulder to shoulder, should be viewed as just that – a myth. In these colonies, the weight of the past influenced the social division of labour as much as the scarcity of workers – a past filled with oppression, social inequality based on birth, and unequal access to land and trade.

Originally, labour was centred on the fur trade and subsistence farming. As tension slowly mounted in the Atlantic trade network, the Dutch and English coastal economies made a qualitative leap in their division of labour. The economy of New France was too distant to be similarly affected and remained marginal.

The main social categories in New France consisted of fur traders, missionaries, seigneurs, censitaires, and indentured servants. By comparison, New Netherland was an urban microcosm, teeming with activity. New Amsterdam boasted no less than seventeen taverns.[70] People circulated news and made deals while chatting about the tide. Shops sprang up, the number and type of artisans grew – blacksmiths, nailsmiths, shoemakers, carpenters, and others whose work gradually became linked to the coastal trading pattern. A merchant class, conscious of its strength, was already trying to monopolize trade, and, by 1664, it had achieved its aim. As early as 1638, it was already asking that commerce in the colony be restricted to residents. After 1648, the town's shopkeepers and traders had to be residents with a capital of 2,000 to 3,000 florins.[71]

After 1657, anyone wishing to engage in trade or the import business had to purchase a *burgerrecht*. By paying slightly more (fifty florins instead of twenty), residents gained the right to occupy municipal posts.[72] Basically, the local bourgeoisie was defending itself against outsiders – itinerant traders and the lower orders (killing two birds with one stone). Possibly, there was also a developing sense of independence from the mother country. We are looking at a well-established merchant class, independent of the state in the sense that it did not depend on government contracts for its livelihood, but rather on trade. It would not be seriously affected by a change in regime or swept away by the English takeover.

The market economy extended its ramifications to the villages, and agriculture expanded with a market that, since its inception, had gone beyond merely supplying provisions to fur-trading posts. 'Plantations' – fields set aside for commercial growing – produced tobacco and cereals for export. A portion of the horses and cattle raised was intended for export to the West Indies. Given the context, it is not surprising to find public primary schools in most villages of any size.[73]

In northeastern North America, as elsewhere, most immigrants came from the dominated classes or the lower end of the dominant classes. Each individual hoped to improve his social status.[74] It took some time for the rules of the game to be set and for the social hierarchy to become fixed. Yet, while social relationships may have been similar to those in Europe, the dice were loaded, so to speak. Privilege engendered privilege, and poverty did likewise. Nevertheless, some flexibility did exist. The combination of environmental and socio-economic conditions brought failure to some and success to others.

Trading posts were embryo societies. The first arrivals, even though they might be of modest origins, had opportunities for upward social mobility that would not be present later on. It was they who had the chance to fill the openings in the emerging economy – and once these were filled, all the best positions had been taken. Pierre Boucher, for example, was a domestic servant employed by the Jesuits in Huronia in 1637. He subsequently became an interpreter and clerk in Trois-Rivières, then a senior clerk, a seigneur, and finally governor of Trois-Rivières. In 1661, he was raised to the status of *écuyer* – a distinction equivalent to 'esquire' or gentleman. Charles Lemoyne, also a Jesuit servant in Huronia, became an interpreter and rose to be one of the colony's prominent merchants. Others, such as Jacques Le Ber and Claude Robutel de La Noue, were equally successful.[75] Although of humble origins, they found themselves in the right place at the right time and were able to take advantage of the fur trade, which was the colony's economic pivot. When Jean de Lauson became governor, he did not have the same social code as his noble contemporaries who could not live without being surrounded by domestics. Charles Aubert de la Chesnaye wrote that 'I only saw him for two years in Canada, where he was not much liked because of his carelessness about upholding his position. He had no servants, and lived on lard and peas like some artisan or village yokel.'[76] There was a considerable amount of elbowing for position before a pecking order was firmly established. 'Pretention insinuated itself everywhere, it seemed, with the faithful arguing over precedence in handing around the holy bread, each having a higher opinion of himself than his circumstances warranted.'[77]

With some adjustments and various dizzying rises and falls, a new hierarchy settled into place. It differed from the company hierarchy in that it was more firmly rooted in the social division of labour which was then developing in the colonies. In New Netherland in 1646, a bailiff (*schout*) asked the burgher court what he should do about confining "persons of quality, or of good name and character," and was instructed to carry them to a tavern if they were willing to pay, otherwise, to the gaol at the Stadt Huys.'[78] An agreement between the Dutch West India Company and the burgomasters of Amsterdam provided that a municipal government in New Netherland must include 'three Burgomasters, to be chosen by the common burghers from the honestest, richest, and most capable men.'[79]

Thus far I have emphasized the external constraints influencing who occupied what position in the social hierarchy. There is, however, the possibility that those who were dominated accepted their domination as legitimate.[80] The significance of this should not be minimized. In a very enlightening study on the early stages of Montreal between 1642 and 1663, Marcel Trudel reports that during the Iroquois war this small society decided to organize its inhabitants into a militia and to elect a leader for each section.[81] The three nobles who, like everyone else, were eligible for this position, were elected. A similar phenomenon occurred in New England, where merchants from England almost always assumed leadership in local affairs.[82]

Trudel also reports that nobles were much in demand as witnesses or godparents at weddings and baptisms. A study of eighty-five marriages shows that none were interracial and that seventy-nine of them were socially endogamous – that is, between people of the same class. Interestingly enough, of the seventy-nine couples whose native provinces can be determined, only fourteen had spouses that came from the same province.[83] It is difficult to avoid the conclusion that, in New France, there was a fair amount of intermixing of regional and ethnic origins (in the sense that there are several ethnic groups in France) but very little mixing among social levels.

Social structure, after all, resembles material life or the characteristics of the society as a whole. The general tendency is for social patterns to reproduce themselves. Needless to say, these European emigrants were not coming to North America to provide a labour force for Amerindian societies nor to integrate with them; they came to build a New Europe. Some sought better surroundings, a little more space, and a decent food supply; others came to make their fortunes. Carried on the wave of European expansionism, these colonists created New England, New Netherland, New France, and New Sweden. Place names and street names almost always recalled Old Europe. The use of a European vocabulary to describe places, fauna, and flora also indicated a desire to take symbolic possession of the new land – to ward off the unknown, the stranger. Van der Donck recalled a scene from the colony's early days, when Christians went fishing for the first time in New Netherland, 'Then every one was desirous to see the fishes which were caught for the purpose of discovering whether the same were known to them, and if they did not know the fish, then they gave it a name.'[84] This practice was far more current than using Amerindian words. It conceals the fact that the Amerindians occupied the continent before the Europeans and shows the process of conquest at the linguistic level. It should be remembered that in New Netherland, an Amerindian who could not speak Dutch was described as a 'dumb savage.'

If we turn to architecture, we find the styles and methods of construction were those used in England, Holland, France, and Sweden. Once settlers had acquired a certain material ease, they would build a house in the Breton or Norman style if they inhabited the Île d'Orléans. It was only with years of collective experimentation that they learned to dig a more suitable foundation, raise the gallery, and take note of the best direction in which to face. The same attitude was evident in New Netherland barns. They were simpler versions but definitely Dutch, except that they were always detached from the dwelling, unlike those in Europe. This was probably because wood for heating was plentiful and because, when Amerindian wars broke out, only a few small buildings could be surrounded by stockades.[85] And can one imagine a Dutch city without canals? New Amsterdam was traversed by one canal, the Heeregraft, which became Broad Street.[86]

It was the same for the colonials' mental universe. The settlers retained their folklore, legends, manners, and cooking. After all, the Santa Claus of the present-day United States and Père Noël of French Canada both owe their existence to the Dutch legend of *Sint Nicolaas* or *Sinterklaas*.[87] Despite borrowings, variants, and adjustments, the basis of this mental universe remained the same with almost no shift in its deep-rooted structures. In the same way, these new arrivals all shared a common general perception of the social hierarchy: of the naturally unequal distribution of wealth, power, and symbolic status; of what was and was not respectable; of what was unique and distinguished as opposed to what was common and banal. Their view embraced all the dichotomies based on the 'principle of opposition between the "elite" of the dominant groups and the "masses" of the dominated.'[88] These included the initial economic 'inequalities,' the relationships of domination present at the 'birth' of European societies in North America which led to the reappearance of class structure in the very first trading posts and villages. But beyond this, there existed a subjective acceptance (which took specific forms in the various social classes) of what was considered a natural hierarchy and a recognition of what, to all appearances, seemed the innate superiority of the members of the various elites. Coercion aside, this attitude had the particular effect of preventing ordinary settlers from imagining that a member of the nobility, even minor nobility, could be a mere militiaman under the orders of a commoner captain.

As I mentioned earlier, it is hardly necessary to point out that close contact with Amerindian societies was extremely dangerous to the continued existence of this mental universe. As Pierre Bourdieu has shown[89] (admittedly in another context), all the European forms of classification, all the mind sets produced by the objective division of society into classes (according to age, sex, and social position) were generally shared by those who were to help reproduce them in the New World. Such classifications and outlooks were not and could not be shared by the Amerindians. By their very existence, these dissimilar societies illustrated the arbitrary and historical nature of the principles of division, hierarchization, and domination adhered to by European societies. For those who held political power in these new European societies, the only possible response to this threat was genocide and the reserve.

REPRODUCTION OF INSTITUTIONS

Apart from the most obvious differences between New France and New Netherland, the relative influence of their religious institutions can be seen in the profoundly different nature of these two societies. In preceding chapters, we have seen to what extent they did or did not affect the fur trade and, more generally, how they determined the types of relationships that were established between Europeans and Amerindians. The phenomenon of unequal exchange shaped the meetings of the two civilizations, although in different forms depending on the characteristics of the colonizing country. The Dutch strategy was essentially based on prices, whereas France was concerned with offsetting the economic disadvantage of overly high prices with a missionary offensive.

Religious Institutions

The powerful Dutch capitalist economy, allied to the Iroquois federation, succeeded in overthrowing the great Huron confederation, which was a partner in the French feudal economy. Religion was as much a factor in French colonial society as in French commerce. Conversely, we might also say that the absence of religion in the Dutch fur trade equalled (or almost equalled) its relative lack of influence or restrictive power in Dutch colonial society. Let us see what our two privileged observers, De Vries and Van der Donck, had to say on the subject. De Vries travelled to New England in January 1639. After interceding with a parson who wanted to beat his drunken indentured servant, he recorded a further incident:

> Whilst I happened here, another farce was played. There was a young man, who had been married two months, who was complained of before the consistory, by his brother, that he had slept with his wife before

they were married; whereupon they were both taken and whipped, and separated from each other six weeks. These people [in New England] give out that they are Israelites, and that we at our colony [New Netherland] are Egyptians ... I frequently told the [English] governor that it would be impossible for them to keep the people so strict, as they had come from so luxurious a country as England.[90]

Van der Donck commented that

until now few people of property have emigrated to the country. All who went over would gain much and bring nothing, except the merchants, who brought something, but carried much more away, which is common. Thus in new countries at the first, there are few churchmasters but persons who anoint their own breast, and are careless about the means and the latter end, and regardless of the common good, worthy citizens not included.[91]

New Amsterdam, for example, was known for its drunkenness. There were plenty of taverns, and its motley population had a reputation for brawling.[92] In both the long and short term, the Dutch West India Company's business interests took priority in New Netherland. There were no plans to build a City of God.

The charter of freedoms instituted the Dutch Reformed church as the official church. It also recognized freedom of conscience, with the proviso that other religious sects could not hold public meetings. There were few pastors of the Dutch Reformed church in the colony, however, and those who came did not assume responsibility for converting the Amerindians, teaching, charitable works, or hospitals – these last three services being under municipal jurisdiction. The company did not defray the clergy's expenses or grant it land, deeming that transporting settlers had already cost it enough.[93] In 1650, the colony had only one Dutch Reformed pastor and two more were to be sent for.[94] A chapel was not built until the end of the 1640s. De Vries noted indignantly that New Amsterdam 'had a fine inn, built of stone, in order to accommodate the English who daily passed with their vessels from New England to Virginia' but 'only a mean barn' for Dutch Reformed services.[95] Several observers testified that tolerance was the de facto policy. The Jesuit Father Jogues noted that, apart from the Calvinists, New Amsterdam included English Puritans, Roman Catholics, Lutherans, and Anabaptists.[96] The Dutch Reformed pastor Megapolensis, somewhat overwhelmed by the situation, added 'Atheists and various other servants of Baal' to this list, remarking that 'it would create still further confusion, if the obstinate and immovable Jews came to settle here.'[97] These dissenting groups, aware of their strength in numbers, demanded the right to hold public meetings. The Lutherans were the first to protest. They brought over a pastor, but he was sent back after pressure from the Dutch Reformed church. The company directors criticized this action when they heard of it.[98] The Calvinists, Presbyterians, and Congregationalists of New England[99] succeeded in keeping the pastors who had accompanied them to the New World, and the conquered Swedes to the south kept their Lutheran pastor. In 1654, Jews from Brazil arrived in a relatively hostile community but were able to settle permanently despite the strong anti-semitic prejudices of Director-General Stuyvesant.[100] In order to finance the Dutch Reformed church, he tried to impose a tithe on the lands and crops of all settlers but met with little success. His last demonstration of intolerance occurred with the arrival of 157 Quakers, whose sermons were enthusiastically received in several Long Island municipalities. Stuyvesant imposed fines, made arrests, and deported one of the Quaker leaders. This occasioned the signing of the Flushing Remonstrance by twenty-six settlers of various religions, insisting on freedom of conscience and worship. The company directors in Amsterdam once again condemned Stuyvesant's repressive policy, telling him: 'You may therefore shut your eyes, at least not force people's consciences, but allow everyone to have his own belief, as long as he behaves quietly and legally, gives no offence to his neighbors and does not oppose the government.'[101]

What a contrast with New France! Here, a single church was permitted to the exclusion of all others. Between 1632 and 1639, only one religious order, the Jesuits, was allowed into the Saint Lawrence valley. In 1639, nuns of the Ursuline and Hospitalière orders arrived in Quebec, followed in 1657 by the Sulpician fathers in Montreal. By the end of the 1650s, there were some fifty priests and nuns for a population of 675.[102]

The goal of all these religious communities was primarily evangelical.[103] When the Amerindians stopped coming to Quebec after the destruction of Huronia, the Hospitalières and Ursulines thought of returning to France. They could no longer do missionary work, and their hospital and school had been intended as much for the Amerindians as for the settlers, if not more.[104] They had followed in the footsteps of the Jesuits, who had founded a school in Quebec in 1635, and had intended mainly to convert Amerindian youths to Christianity and French culture – an aim that required the presence of French children. The Roman Catholic clergy assumed responsibility for teaching, hospitals, diplomatic relations with the Amerindians, and the religious and moral screening of immigrants.[105] Furthermore, the clergy was responsible for hiring a good half of the indentured servants. On the other hand, it received annual financial aid of 5,000 livres a year from the Compagnie des Cent Associés as well as acquiring seigneuries as a guarantee of its future security. However, the company subsidies were far from sufficient to finance works of such great scope. To augment their income, therefore, the clergy, mainly the Jesuits, financed themselves with the help of donations gathered from well-wishers, principally readers of the *Jesuit Relations*.

New France's missionary enterprise also had close links with a secret society, the Compagnie du Saint-Sacrement-de-l'Autel, founded by the Duc de Ventadour. The objective of this society, apart from holding religious meetings, insuring the 'sanctification of its members,' and managing charitable institutions, included combating the perils of prostitution, Protestants, Jews, duels, and the theatre.[106] It was an important agency for providing funds and also organized the Société Notre-Dame de Montréal, which led to the founding of that city. Needless to say, taverns were a rarity on the shores of the Saint Lawrence. The rigid moral framework imposed on the population was indeed effective. Only two illegitimate births were noted in the colony before 1691.[107] After 1663, the increasing presence of a civil government and the expansion of the fur trade put an end to this emerging theocracy.

Educational Institutions

In New Netherland, schools were usually founded when municipalities were incorporated. Education was a matter for secular authorities, except in New Amsterdam, where it was administered by the company and the Dutch Reformed church. The existence of a rural school system indicates both a move toward division of labour and the penetration of a market economy in rural areas. Municipalities raised a tax to cover part of the teachers' salaries, the rest being paid for by school fees (120 to 240 stuivers per year).[108] These schools accepted poor children free of charge; nevertheless, in addition to their teaching functions, they acted from their inception as agents of social reproduction. By comparison, the Latin school of New Amsterdam created a privileged network within the social framework; it was more expensive, had a well-off clientele, and enabled students to go on to secondary education. Alongside the public schools, which taught children to read and count, alternative schools existed in which the colony's future elite were brought together. Pupils in these alternative schools were separated from the general populace at the learning stage and acquired a knowledge of Latin – a code for distinguishing the educated from the uneducated. A final point: schools in New Netherland had no missionary function, and there is no evidence of Amerindian children having attended them.

New France had three schools during the comparable period: the Jesuit school (1633) intended initially for converting young Amerindian boys, the Ursuline convent (1639) for young girls, and later Marguerite Bourgeoys's primary school in Montreal. Three schools may not seem like much, but, in 1663, this represented one school for every thousand inhabitants, a higher rate than in France at that time. There were no country schools until the eighteenth century. As in France, schools were geared to the requirements of the Roman Catholic church and the monarchy, but in New France they became institutions working specifically against Amerindian civilization. These schools accepted Amerindian children in order to produce little French Catholics while working at the same time to eradicate the 'destructive' influence of the 'Savages' and to teach white children to submit to the French social order. Marie de l'Incarnation, for example, wrote in 1653, 'Without the education that we give our French girls who are old enough, in about the space of six months they would be worse brutes than the Savages.'[109]

Illiteracy decreased as a network of schools became established. If we take as a criterion of literacy the ability to sign one's name instead of making a mark, figures for the early seventeenth century show a rate of less than 40 per cent for men in England and slightly higher than 60 per cent for men in New England.[110] Between 1653 and 1656 in the Massachusetts county of Suffolk (Boston), the figures are 89 per cent for men and 42 per cent for women. Between 1654 and 1657 in New

Netherland, 79 per cent of the men in Fort Orange could sign their names (out of a sample of 360) and 40 per cent of women (based on a group of small samplings totalling 154 individuals).[111] In New France in 1663, 59.4 per cent of men could sign (out of a sample of 887) and 46.2 per cent of women (out of a sample of 357)[112] – figures comparable to those of New England. We know that at the same period, only 15 per cent of the Languedoc peasantry could sign their names and that the average for France was about 21 per cent.[113] The higher rates for North America over Europe and for New Netherland over neighbouring colonies has been explained in a study by François Furet and Jacques Ozouf.[114] They show that literacy in France was the result of several factors: the Protestant movement, which created competition among clergies and put the faithful in a position to choose; the desire of the lower classes to learn to write; and finally 'the market economy, which developed a division of labour and spread written communication from top to bottom of the social scale.'[115]

Political Institutions

Comparing the nature and role of government in New France and New Netherland offers a further opportunity for observing the fundamental difference between the two colonies. In Quebec, no real government existed before 1663. Until 1647, there was only a council made up of the governor general, the Jesuit superior, and the governor of Montreal.[116] The following year, the council was enlarged to seven members by adding the governor of Trois-Rivières, the former governor general, and, depending on whether the latter was available or not, two or three residents elected by town officials (who themselves were elected by landowning residents).[117] In 1657, the council was again changed, henceforth to be made up of the governor general, a director named by the Compagnie des Cent Associés, and four councillors elected by the Communauté des Habitants. Although the composition of the council changed, its main function remained the same throughout: to regulate and monitor the fur trade. This council was officially known as the Conseil de traite – the Trade Council.[118] Monseigneur Laval, who arrived in Quebec in 1659,[119] became a member in 1661. He opposed Governor d'Avaugour in the matter of selling brandy to the Amerindians and managed to have him recalled to France before the end of his term. The bishop even selected a successor, the 'very pious and very wise' Saffray de Mézy.'[120] In 1663, the French government took over the administration of the colony. The king set up a sovereign council composed of governor and bishop. Together they chose five other members. Throughout all these changes we can see the major role played by the most prominent actors in New France: the merchant and the missionary. The other two, the settler and the Amerindian, remained behind the scenes.

The political history of the Dutch colony gives us a glimpse of the development of civil authority alongside company rule. Municipal incorporation was a sure sign of this phenomenon. In 1641, Director-General Kieft asked the heads of families to elect twelve men to form a consultative council on the question of the Amerindian war. Once elected, the councillors quickly exceeded their narrow mandate. They were dismissed, but they promptly signed a petition. Kieft began again with eight fresh councillors but with the same result. The new council sent two letters of protest to Holland. Both councils had complained about the autocratic mode of government, the obligation to billet soldiers, the war tax,[121] and the war itself. A similar scenario occurred under Stuyvesant, who deported two of his councillors, Melyn and Kuyter. They returned after successfully appealing their deportation. In 1647, the first permanent council was created, made up of nine men including three merchants, three burghers, and three farmers. Six of them retired each year to be replaced by co-opted members. The conflict between this local power and the director recommenced, resulting in petitions, imprisonments, and remonstrances[122] to which were added the petitions of religious groups seeking freedom and the demands of municipalities seeking greater power and better management of land surveys. The British takeover of New Netherland put a halt to this evolving power struggle. Nevertheless, we can see that all the elements were present for constituting a local power, independent of church or state – one that defined itself by opposing the autocratic power of the company.

CONCLUSION

Our journey is nearly done, and we have stopped at the head of the rapids. The river of history could carry us much further, but – to extend the metaphor – we would have to undertake a long portage. The years 1663 and 1664 marked a turning point. The great recession of the seventeenth century began to ease, and the centre of the Atlantic economy moved to London. England established itself as a great naval power, and the Dutch presence in northeastern North America was eliminated. These years also saw the beginnings of large-scale intervention by the French and English governments as colonial rivals. Nevertheless, even without continuing our journey, we can see where it would lead us. The die had been cast and the basic structures of future development set firmly in place.

As we have seen, the race to accumulate capital drove European ships to the shores of northeastern North America, bringing into contact two civilizations – one on the brink of the Industrial Revolution, the other still in the Stone Age. The relationships that developed between them were based on unequal exchange, and it was this that would shape the future course of these two civilizations.

As Amerindian societies became increasingly involved in the exchange centred around the fur trade, they also worked longer hours despite the acquisition of more efficient tools. At the same time, they were unable to reproduce European goods locally because productive forces – that is, labour power and the means of production – developed in a way that made this impossible. The Amerindians were dependent on the Europeans as a result, and this phenomenon of dependency provided the underlying motif in the formation and growth of their commercial relations.

Unequal exchange caused a permanent transfer of wealth from the economic periphery to the centre. Natural resources such as the beaver were exploited with ever-increasing intensity, and this altered the ancient balance that had united Amerindian societies and nature. The depletion of resources in turn led to the enlargement of hunting grounds and finally to war. Of course, wars were nothing new. The peoples of America had fought wars from time immemorial but never with such intensity. Now, however, these wars, coupled with widespread epidemics, profoundly disrupted the human geography of the North American northeast. Entire peoples had vanished by 1660. The western Great Lakes region became a land of refugees. Subordinative relationships developed among allied tribes. In varying degrees, these tribes had become the links in several European imperialistic chains. Nevertheless, these wars and subordinative relationships could not have happened without a certain compliance on the part of the dominated parties – Amerindians who profited in the short term by the destruction of their fellow tribesmen, members of other tribes, and long-time hereditary enemies.

As Amerindian societies became integrated into the world market, an inner disintegration set in. The fur trade encouraged relationships based on redistribution rather than sharing. Redistribution brought tension because it was based on unequal appropriation of wealth. The fur trade also affected relations between men and women by altering the power and economic role of both sexes. In addition to all these stresses, however, Amerindian societies, in which almost half the population had been wiped out by terrible pandemics, were forced to produce between two and three times as many pelts for trade, so that the relative burden of trading increased fourfold and possibly even sixfold. The time for games and feasting had vanished, and pleasure had perforce to be postponed.

In these circumstances, the Jesuits' missionary offensive found fertile ground among Amerindians, for with the growing disintegration of their societies, the old explanations of the world could no longer offer them reassurance or comfort in their anguish. In 1637, the missionaries noted that there were Hurons who wished for an afterlife that resembled their everyday life on earth: 'You find some of them who renounce Heaven when you tell them there are no fields and no grain there; that people do not go trading, nor fishing there; and that they do not marry. Another one told us one day that he thought it was wrong that they should not work in Heaven, that it was not well to be idle; and for this reason he had no desire to go there.'[1]

As time passed, Amerindians found themselves facing the increased risk of falling into enemy hands on trading expeditions, the obligation to work ever harder for the benefit of fewer people, and the threat of death lurking everywhere. A growing number began to dream of a Christian heaven, particularly if they were refugees or prisoners. Some who were involved in trading found it worth their while to embrace a religion that relegated a just distribution to the hereafter.

To write a history of Amerindian societies on the basis of missionary accounts involves the risk of exaggerating the importance of the latter's role. The evangelical offensive was an undeniable factor in dispossessing the Amerindians of their culture (including their religion), dismantling the kinship relations on which native societies were based, and introducing antagonistic relationships. Nevertheless, we should be very clear about the fact that the ground had already been well prepared by the involvement of these societies in the worldwide process of accumulation of capital. It is certain that the missionaries themselves were largely unaware of the reasons for conversion. They thanked heaven for giving them the chance to trade weapons for a baptism, but there is nothing that prevents us from finding another explanation.

Why did the Huron trader convert to Christianity? Possibly the answer lies in the economic crisis in England, provoked by Holland between 1614 and 1630. After all, this crisis was responsible for the sizeable wave of British immigration to North American shores. The Dutch, now faced with the threat of this great flow of people into the North American northeast, were in turn obliged to encourage settlement in their own colony and give up their monopolistic hold on the fur trade. As settlers increased in number, so did traders, to the point where the fur trade became competitive. At Fort Orange, the Dutch began selling their trade goods and firearms to the Iroquois at low prices. Iroquois and particularly Mohawk access to arms completely altered the balance of power between the two rival confederacies, Iroquois and Huron. The Hurons in turn wanted firearms, and the missionaries took advantage of the

Hurons' dependence on the French for these weapons to impose a religious condition: conversion. This condition was unavoidable in any case. The missionary offensive in Huronia, coupled with epidemics, had raised tensions to such a pitch that the missionaries could only allow firearms to be given to men who were totally under their ideological control.

Although unequal exchange was the basic pattern in the encounter of different civilizations in the North American northeast in the seventeenth century, there were variations. The pattern was specifically influenced by differences among Europeans, depending on whether they came from feudal or capitalist societies and on their position in the Atlantic world-system. It was also influenced by differences among Amerindians, depending on whether they were horticulturalists or nomads and on their position in the pre-Columbian economy of the North American northeast. In this study, we have dealt mainly with the encounter between European societies and Amerindian horticultural societies. The study of contacts between Europeans and the nomad Algonkian societies in the same period has yet to be done.

To analyze the differences in colonial strategy among Europeans, it was first necessary to evaluate the exchange – a difficult operation since all the accounting archives that could have been used in researching the comparative history of prices have disappeared. In any event, I decided to evaluate the penetration of trade merchandise among the tribes allied to the French and Dutch. It transpired that the Iroquois were better off in the exchange relationships that were established by the Dutch (although these were necessarily unequal), than the Hurons in similar dealings with their French trading partners. In other words, with fewer furs, the Iroquois obtained more trade goods than the Hurons. The Dutch prices were competitive, whereas the French prices were not. This operated in North America in exactly the same way it would have elsewhere on the world market. Dutch shipping costs were lower than anyone else's, and their production methods the most advanced. This initial advantage was enhanced by the competitive pressure of the English and Swedes in the fur trade as well as by the rapid introduction of free trade. The Dutch strategy for accumulating capital was therefore based on low-priced goods and to some extent on the sale of firearms.

The French were unable to challenge Dutch commercial supremacy despite being allied to the Huron confederacy – the Hurons being the major middlemen in the northeastern fur trade at the beginning of the century. Instead, the French had to rely more on diplomacy, making use of missionaries and constantly pushing north and west in search of new tribes. The Dutch successfully eliminated almost all tribes allied to the French and siphoned off the greatest quantity of furs in the continent. They managed to do this despite having arrived rather late in the day and even though their allies, the Iroquois, were certainly no more powerful than the Hurons at the outset. In the final analysis, the explanation of the Iroquois victory over the Hurons must be sought on the Amsterdam Exchange. Similarly, the explanation of the difference between interracial relations established in North America by the Dutch and French must be looked for in the dynamism of the Dutch economy and in the outmoded nature of the French economy, still dominated by the feudal structures of a semi-peripheral France.

Fishing, commerce, wood, land, religious freedom – these were all aspects that could have motivated the emigrant. The newcomers eventually put down roots. Often the Amerindians helped them get through the first winter and taught them about the resources of the new land. Subsequently, the newcomers cleared the forest, often by ecologically wasteful means, or simply cultivated the fields abandoned by the Amerindians. Finally, they built houses and formed herds of domestic animals.

The new arrivals grew in number as quickly as the original inhabitants had been decimated by war and sickness. There was plenty of available land, teeming with plants and wildlife of all kinds. European societies transported to North America retained their typical notions of private property and their will to dominate nature, divide society into classes, and accumulate capital. Could they coexist with native societies who lived according to a system of social equality and collective ownership – a system that featured a harmonious relationship with nature, a great deal of individual freedom, and an absence of surplus repression? The answer to this question may be seen in the fact that the European newcomers progressively profited from their military superiority and the rivalries of warring tribes to occupy all the available space. To do this, it was necessary either to resort to genocide or to expropriate the land of the original inhabitants and confine them to reserves. Actually by 1660, the two possible forms of the 'final solution' to the Amerindian 'question' were already in place – that is, genocide and/or the reserve.

At no time were the Amerindians able to surmount their own divisions and unite to push the invaders back into the sea. The few attempts to do so failed. In trying to take advantage of their European allies in order to vanquish rival tribes, each tribe objectively transformed itself into a link in the chain of empire, and into cannon fodder. The Iroquois who, in 1660, came close to forcing the French to abandon the country, were not fighting the European invasion; they were fighting the Dutchmen's war.

Throughout this journey we have seen the land – and what a marvel it was! Majestic trees, clear waters teeming with fish, pigeons darkening the sky, pure air, and prodigious herds of wild animals were but a few of its wonders. At a time when the results of the ecological abuse perpetrated by our society are proliferating at an alarming rate, how can we avoid asking some soul-searching questions about the relationship of man to nature? In the seventeenth century, man was already involved in a destructive relationship with nature. Islam collapsed with the deforestation and desertification of its territory. In the headlong rush of great civilizations constantly seeking new peripheries because they had devastated the land in the centre, it was now Europe's turn to venture far afield in search of the wood, furs, and fish that it could no longer provide for itself. First the forests of the Atlantic seaboard, then those of the Pacific, then the Amazon, and then – what? Will all this struggle 'against nature' have achieved nothing more than merely replacing tens of millions of bison with an equal number of beef cattle?

The end justifies the means – such is the implacable law governing interimperial rivalry and the accumulation of capital. The toll was high – the natives of the West Indies wiped out and replaced with slaves so that these islands might sweeten European tongues; Huronia destroyed and the fauna of a whole continent decimated in order to get beaver pelts; hatmakers struck down by Minamata disease[2] as a result of the mercury process used in making felt: all this to enable a noble or a merchant to wear a beaver felt hat in the latest fashion. The civilization of rising capitalism was as destructive to man as to nature.

Northeastern North America was an economic unit and, as such, became integrated into the Atlantic economy. To study it properly, therefore, we must see it as a whole rather than divided by the artificial European frontiers established on the new continent. In other words, it has been necessary to sketch the entire picture of interimperial rivalries in the northeast. The outcome of these rivalries depended on the nature of the national economies striving to be the centre of a world-system: Holland, small and capitalist, Britain, far larger and also (with a little delay) capitalist, France, gigantic for the period and feudal. Each gained the place its strength made possible. Capitalist countries – in this case Holland and Britain – held up best in the economic slump of the seventeenth century. Holland, which led the competition, retained control of the main sources of accumulation: the Baltic trade network and the Asian economic world-system. Britain, because of its ability to provide settlers, won the Atlantic economy as a consolation prize. Unexpectedly, this turned out to be an advantage, because the Atlantic economy experienced greater expansion than any other, due partly to the galloping population growth of the white settlers. Britain was thus able to free itself from Holland's hegemony.

Shortage of labour was the central problem in the development of the Atlantic economy. How could an economy be organized with an Amerindian population that was dying out and which, in any case, refused to perform servile labour? It would require more than capital to take over the Atlantic economy. It would take settlers, and Britain was the country with the best combination of emigrants and capital.

The scarcity of workers was also the main stumbling block in the overseas reproduction of European social relations. Normally, hierarchies tended to reproduce themselves spontaneously, but the labour shortage enabled workers to negotiate their wages, working conditions, and access to land. The dominant classes had to make concessions. They might have preferred slavery, as in the West Indies, but the various work processes in the northern economy gave the worker too much autonomy and power. Slavery was therefore impossible. Employers had to raise wages and promise unhindered access to land at no cost to the employee. A freer world was born along with a peasant class of small farmers in New England and most of New Netherland. Although the peasantry was subject to feudal constraints in Rensselaerwyck and New France, it was far less exploited in these regions than in contemporary Europe.

As we saw, the centre of the Atlantic world-system, and even of the world economy, began to move to London during the seventeenth century. From this standpoint, northeastern North America was a distant periphery that supplied fish, furs, and wood. By 1660, however, given the economic and social history of the Atlantic seaboard and its integration into the Atlantic market, it was already evident that this region was destined to become something more than a mere periphery. Here, a free peasant class developed while merchants and their ships took part in the Atlantic trade. This was a crucial factor because a free peasantry enabled the productive forces to develop and created an internal market, while the merchant class began to accumulate capital. We can understand the importance of this in light of André Gunder Frank's remarks in relation to development and underdevelopment. He points out that 'the greater the wealth available for exploitation [in the seventeenth and eighteenth centuries], the poorer and more underdeveloped the region today; and [conversely] the poorer the region was [as] a colony, the richer and more developed it is today.'[3] Bolivia, Santo Domingo, and Surinam were coveted prizes compared to New France or New Holland. Investments in the first three were enormous, and their maritime traffic was far greater than in the north. These colonies exported minerals, sugar, tobacco, and cotton – products much sought after on the world market. These exports covered the cost of importing European products. This was not the case in New Holland, nor particularly in New England, which did not even have furs to offer. These 'poor' colonies had to get hold of specie somehow in order to balance their constant deficit situation. This is what stimulated the New Amsterdam merchants to get involved in trade with Virginia and the West Indies and prompted, more especially, the New England merchants to enter into the Atlantic trade triangle. Once integrated into trading networks where they would be able to control the terms of exchange, merchants could accumulate capital at the expense of the producing regions.

The 'rich' regions, which produced sugar, gold, cotton, and tobacco, all adopted slavery. The planters made fortunes. In the long term, however, there was a price to pay for slave-based prosperity. Because slavery engenders a high degree of resistance in the slave, productive forces are slow to develop, and it is impossible to generate an internal mass-consumer market. Furthermore, it leads to an ecological cul-de-sac. Slave labour as a mode of production condemns a society to a single-staple economy and makes it more or less impossible to engage in advanced husbandry or make use of complex implements. In the long term, this exhausts the soil, which in turn leads to deforestation and finally to erosion. The poverty of the slaves means that an internal market cannot develop. All wealth is concentrated in the hands of a planter minority that buys imported luxury products. Compare this with a free peasantry of the type found in Holland, that is to say, a land-owning peasantry not burdened by feudal relationships. Because it can dovetail its production with market requirements, producing for both internal and external buyers, there is an incentive to reduce self-sufficiency and develop commercial crops or livestock. Instead of being inhibited by social relationships that destroy all initiative, the process whereby producers can specialize and modernize tools and work methods moves steadily forward, and yields increase accordingly.

By 1660, a free peasantry existed on the Atlantic seaboard, providing a basic element of the socio-economic structure of the region. It was already predictable that, in the long term, northeastern North America would move from the periphery to the semi-periphery and become a form of sub-empire in the Atlantic economy.

In terms of development, New France was doubly handicapped from the outset. For one thing, geography worked against it. The periodic freeze-up of the Saint Lawrence River prevented the colony from entering the Atlantic trade triangle and the circulation that led to the accumulation of capital. Social factors also worked against it. The seigneurial regime had a constricting effect on the peasantry. In the early period, the yoke was reasonably light since every possible inducement had to be used to attract workers. Once settlement began to take root, the regime became more and more confining. By the nineteenth century, when there began to be too many people for the available land, the seigneurial system had become a veritable strait-jacket, discouraging any attempt to develop productive forces. This confining structure had already been put in place by 1663, just at the end of the period we have been considering.

The time will come when we will once more set off in our canoe and cover a further segment of this historical journey. But for the moment, let us be content with replenishing our provisions of sagamité.

Notes

ABBREVIATIONS

Annales ESC	*Annales Économie, Société, Civilisation*
CERM	Centre d'Études et de Recherches Marxistes
CIEE	Centre Inter-universitaire d'Études Européennes
DRCHNY	*Documents Relative to the Colonial History of the State of New York*
JEH	*Journal of Economic History*
JR	*The Jesuit Relations and Allied Documents*
NNN	*Narratives of New Netherland, 1609-1664*
PP	*Past and Present*
RAPQ	*Rapport de l'archiviste de la province de Québec*
RAQ	*Recherches amérindiennes au Québec*
RHAF	*Revue d'Histoire de l'Amérique Française*
CA	*The Children of Aataentsic: A History of the Huron People to 1660*

MANUSCRIPT SOURCES

Archives Nationales, Paris, Archives des colonies, series C[11] and F[3]

PREFACE

1 Braudel, *Civilisation matérielle, économie et capitalisme,* 3:12, 14, 28-9.

CHAPTER 1:
EUROPE IN TRANSITION

1 Léon, *Histoire économique et sociale du monde,* 2:100. Slicher Van Bath, *The Agrarian History of Western Europe,* 198.
2 Léon, *Histoire économique et sociale du monde,* 1:544.
3 Ibid., 563-4.
4 Braudel, *Civilisation matérielle et capitalisme,* 1:33.
5 Jennings, *The Invasion of America,* 21. Braudel, *Civilisation matérielle, économie et capitalisme,* 3:338.
6 Chaunu and Gascon, *Histoire économique et sociale de la France,* 1:7.
7 K.H.D. Haley, *The Dutch in the Seventeenth Century,* 22.
8 J.U. Nef in Crouzet, 'Angleterre et France au 18e siècle,' 256.
9 Cipolla, 'L'échec italien,' 8.
10 Marie-Victorin, *Flore laurentienne,* 345.
11 J. De Vries, *The Dutch Rural Economy,* 87.
12 Wallerstein, *The Modern World System,* 1:98.
13 J. De Vries, *The Economy of Europe,* 48-51. Wallerstein, *The Modern World System,* 1:166.

14 J. De Vries, *The Economy of Europe*, 48-51.

15 Frank, *L'accumulation mondiale 1500-1800*, 114.

16 Idem.

17 Hilton, 'Qu'entend-on par capitalisme?' 193.

18 Chaunu and Gascon, *Histoire économique et sociale de la France*, 1:336-7.

19 Dobb, *Études sur le développement du capitalisme*, 208-9. Hobsbawn, 'The General Crisis of European Economy,' 48.

20 J. De Vries, 'On the Modernity of the Dutch Republic,' 191-202. J. De Vries, *The Dutch Rural Economy*, 140, 185.

21 J. De Vries, *The Dutch Rural Economy*, 213.

22 Ibid., 270.

23 Ibid., 203.

24 K.H.D. Haley, *The Dutch in the Seventeenth Century*, 16.

25 J. De Vries, *The Economy of Europe*, 95.

26 Barbour, *Capitalism in Amsterdam*, 88-9.

27 K.H.D. Haley, *The Dutch in the Seventeenth Century*, 29.

28 Vilar, *Or et monnaie dans l'histoire*, 248.

29 J. De Vries, *The Economy of Europe*, 95, 131.

30 Barbour, *Capitalism in Amsterdam*, 67.

31 J. De Vries, *The Economy of Europe*, 100.

32 Barbour, *Capitalism in Amsterdam*, 83.

33 Bois, *Crise du féodalisme*, 363.

34 R. Brenner, 'Agrarian Class Structure,' 62.

35 Chaunu, 'Malthusianisme démographique,' 11.

36 Hill and Postan, *Histoire économique et sociale de la Grande-Bretagne*, 1:286.

37 Idem.

38 Vilar, *Or et monnaie dans l'histoire*, 259.

39 Hill and Postan, *Histoire économique et sociale de la Grande-Bretagne*, 1:311.

40 Idem.

41 Hill and Postan, *Histoire économique et sociale de la Grande-Bretagne*, 1:344-435.

42 Ibid., 370.

43 R. Brenner, 'Agrarian Class-Structure,' 63.

44 R. Brenner, 'The Origins of Capitalist Development,' 77.

45 Hill and Postan, *Histoire économique et sociale de la Grande-Bretagne*, 1:235.

46 Braudel, *Civilisation matérielle et capitalisme*, 1:37.

47 Bois, 'Against the Neo-Malthusian Orthodoxy,' 63-7.

48 Bois, *Crise du féodalisme*, 364.

49 P. Goubert in Labrousse, *Histoire économique et sociale de la France*, 2:98-9.

50 Braudel, *Civilisation matérielle et capitalisme*, 1:89.

51 Meuvret, *Études d'histoire économique*, 19-20.

52 Braudel, *Civilisation matérielle et capitalisme*, 1:55.

53 G. Lefebvre cited by P. Goubert in Labrousse, *Histoire économique et sociale de la France*, 2:146-7.

54 Parker, 'The Social Foundations of French Absolutism,' 84.

55 Porchnev, *Les soulèvements populaires en France*, 560-1.

56 Braudel, *Civilisation matérielle et capitalisme*, 1:250.

57 P. Goubert in Labrousse, *Histoire économique et sociale de la France*, 2:355-6.

58 P. Léon in ibid., 217.

59 Goubert, *L'ancien régime*, 1:59.

60 Ibid., 60-1.

61 Ibid., 61.

62 Chaunu and Gascon, *Histoire économique et sociale de la France*, 1:1.

63 Goubert, *L'ancien régime*, 1:62.

64 P. Léon in Labrousse, *Histoire économique et sociale de la France*, 2:189.

65 Lublinskaya, *French Absolutism*, 138.

66 Goubert, *L'ancien régime*, 1:64.

67 Chaunu and Gascon, *Histoire économique et sociale de la France*, 1:361.

68 Richelieu, Armand Jean du Plessis, duc de, 'Testament politique,' 1:160, cited in Porchnev, *Les soulèvements populaires en France*, 551.

69 Dobb, *Études sur le développement du capitalisme*, 30-1.

70 Parker, 'The Social Foundations of French Absolutism,' 84-7.

71 Anderson, *Lineages of the Absolutist State*, 98.

72 Ibid., 102.

73 Porchnev, *Les soulèvements populaires en France*, 268-99.

74 Hincker, 'Contribution à la discussion,' 63.

75 K.H.D. Haley, *The Dutch in the Seventeenth Century*, 16.

76 Idem.

77 Kupp, 'Note de recherche,' 13-14.

78 Easterbrook and Aitken, *Canadian Economic History*, 27, 29-30.

79 Ibid., 29-32.

80 Kupp, 'Note de recherche,' 15.

81 Jennings, *The Invasion of America*, 97-8.

82 Kupp, 'Note de recherche,' 565-9.

83 Braudel, *Civilisation matérielle et capitalisme*, 1:42.

84 Ibid., 37.

CHAPTER 2:
NORTH AMERICA BEFORE
EUROPEAN SETTLEMENT

1 Boucher, *Histoire véritable et naturelle*, 40-6.

2 *JR* (1664-5), 49:265.

3 Ibid., 261.

4 Champlain, *Oeuvres*, 1:295, 329; 2:508, 519, 526, 863, 881. Sagard, *Le grand voyage du pays des Hurons*, 79 (114), 230-7 (326-36). Cartier, *Voyages en Nouvelle-France*, 100.

5 Champlain, *Oeuvres*, 1:317, 332; 2:511, 524-6, 538, 558, 591, 660-3, 807-17, 839, 842, 857, 858, 913. Sagard, *Le grand voyage du pays des Hurons*, 215-21 (304-14). Radisson, *Voyages*, 104. Cartier, *Voyages en Nouvelle-France*, 97, 114-15.

6 Jacquin, *Histoire des Indiens d'Amérique du Nord*, 62.

7 Van der Donck, *A Description of the New Netherlands*, 45.

8 Idem. Champlain, *Oeuvres*, 2:912, 923.

9 Boucher, *Histoire véritable et naturelle*, 38, 56-7.

10 Rousseau, 'Pierre Boucher, naturaliste et géographe,' 307.

11 Boucher, *Histoire véritable et naturelle*, 38, 56-7.

12 *JR* (1645-6), 29:221-3; (1653-4), 41:127-9;
(1655-6), 42:37, 63-5, 69, 79.

13 Boucher, *Histoire véritable et naturelle*, 54. See also *JR* (1652-3), 40:113-17; (1663-4), 49:39.

14 Boucher, *Histoire véritable et naturelle*, 70.

15 Van der Donck, *A Description of the New Netherlands*, 50.

16 Ibid., 51.

17 D.P. De Vries, 'Voyages from Holland,' 110.

18 Boucher, *Histoire véritable et naturelle*, 71-2. See also *JR*, (1656-7), 43:153; (1662-3), 48:177.

19 Eckert, *The Silent Sky*, 3-4.

20 Boucher, *Histoire véritable et naturelle*, 69.

21 *JR* (1655-6), 42:207; (1659-60), 45:231-3; (1662-3), 48:157.

22 Sagard, *Le grand voyage du pays des Hurons*, 35 (51). See also *JR* (1662-3), 49:155.

23 D.P. De Vries, 'Voyages from Holland,' 38.

24 *JR* (1662-3), 48:155-78. See also Sagard, *Le grand voyage du pays des Hurons*, 222-30 (314-26).

25 Megapolensis, 'A Short Account of the Mohawk Indians,' 171.

26 Bogaert, 'Narrative of a Journey,' 149.

27 Van der Donck, *A Description of the New Netherlands*, 54.

28 Boucher, *Histoire véritable et naturelle*, 75. See also *JR* (1652-3), 40:215; (1656-7), 43:261.

29 *JR* (1635), 8:19.

30 *JR* (1636), 9:167.

31 Boucher, *Histoire véritable et naturelle*, 15-16. See also *JR* (1633), 5:89.

32 Driver, *Indians of North America*, 88.

33 Van der Donck, *A Description of the New Netherlands*, 55.

34 *JR* (1662-3), 48:161-9; (1645-6), 29:219-23; (1656-7), 43:101-3; (1659-60), 45:189-97; (1659-61), 46:277-9; (1662-4), 48:125-7; (1666-7), 50:241-3.

35 Crête, 'La plaine laurentienne,' 20. J.V. Wright, *La préhistoire du Québec*, 23, 101.

36 Meyer, 'Une magistrale mise en cause du 18ᵉ siècle,' 892-3.

37 Driver, *Indians of North America*, 63.
    Jacquin, *Histoire des Indiens d'Amérique
    du Nord*, 37-8. Marienstras, *La résistance
    indienne aux Étas-Unis*, 25, 215.
38 Jennings, *The Invasion of America*, 29.
39 Trelease, *Indian Affairs in Colonial New
    York*, 5. Wood, 'A Sketch of the First
    Settlement,' 64.
40 Jennings, *The Invasion of America*, 26.
41 Ibid., 28.
42 Cartier, *Voyages en Nouvelle-France*, 99-
    104.
43 Heidenreich, *Huronia*, 15. CA, 31-2, 437,
    n. 8.
44 Rousseau, 'Le Canada aborigène,' 50. JR
    (1640), 20:43; (1641-2), 21:187-95.
45 JR (1643-4), 27:47; (1647-8), 33:61-6.
46 JR (1644-5), 28:67.
47 JR (1657-8), 44:245-51.
48 Ibid., 245.
49 In addition to the four previous refer-
    ences, see also (1640), 18:227-35; (1642),
    23:225; (1647-8), 33:69-73, 149-53; (1652-
    3), 40:153-5; (1655-6), 42:219-21; (1659-
    60), 46:67-9; (1660-1), 46:281-3; (1663-4),
    48:275; (1664-5), 49:226; (1666-7), 51:27,
    43.
50 Jacquin, *Histoire des Indiens d'Amérique
    du Nord*, 17.
51 Rousseau, 'Le Canada aborigène,' 44-53.
    Trelease, *Indian Affairs in Colonial New
    York*, 5. Barré and Girouard, 'La plaine
    laurentienne,' 43-51. Jacquin, *Histoire
    des Indiens d'Amérique du Nord*, 43.
    Clermont, 'Le castor et les Indiens
    préhistoriques,' 102.
52 Barré and Girouard, 'La plaine laurenti-
    enne,' 43-5.
53 J.V. Wright, *La préhistoire du Québec*, 18,
    35, 36.
54 Barré and Girouard, 'La plaine laurenti-
    enne,' 43-5.
55 *The American Indians*, (Washington, DC:
    National Geographic Society 1974), cited
    in Jacquin, *Histoire des Indiens
    d'Amérique du Nord*, 38.
56 Sagard, *Le grand voyage du pays des
    Hurons*, 93 (135). See also Sagard,
    Histoire du Canada, 266 (283). JR (1638-
    9), 15:156. Jacquin, *Histoire des Indiens

d'Amérique du Nord*, 37. Heidenreich,
    Huronia, 191-3.
57 Rousseau, 'Pierre Boucher, naturaliste
    et géographe,' 395.
58 Champlain, *Oeuvres*, 2:509. Cartier,
    Voyages en Nouvelle-France, 109, 145.
59 Sagard, *Le grand voyage du pays des
    Hurons*, 98 (141).
60 Driver, *Indians of North America*, 103.
61 Marie-Victorin, *Flore laurentienne*, 855.
62 Idem.
63 Allaire, *Cuisinons nos plantes sauvages*,
    126-30.
64 Heidenreich, *Huronia*; Tooker, *An
    Ethnography of the Huron Indians*.
65 Sagard, *Le grand voyage du pays des
    Hurons*, 104 (150). JR (1646-7), 30:211;
    (1639), 17:113-15.
66 My thanks to Fernando Belo for his
    comments on this subject.
67 JR (1639), 16:225-33; (1634-6), 8:115;
    (1652-3), 38:249.
68 JR (1634-6), 8:115.
69 Champlain, *Oeuvres*, 2:562, 944. Sagard,
    Le grand voyage du pays des Hurons, 80
    (116). JR (1640), 19:125-7; (1652-3),
    40:223; (1655-6), 42:221-3. CA, 32, 437, n.
    8. Clermont, 'L'augmentation de la
    population,' 160. Dickinson, 'The Pre-
    Contact Huron Population,' 173-9.
70 Sagard, *Le grand voyage du pays des
    Hurons*, 80 (115), 81 (117); Sagard,
    Histoire du Canada, 237 (250).
    Champlain, *Oeuvres*, 2:562, 945.
    Heidenreich, *Huronia*, 116.
71 JR (1639), 16:227-9, 17:25-7; (1640),
    19:125. CA, 30, 58, 163. Heidenreich,
    'Huron,' in Trigger, *Northeast*, 368.
72 Heidenreich, *Huronia*, 56.
73 Sagard, *Histoire du Canada*, 227 (238),
    252 (267).
74 Sagard, *Le grand voyage du pays des
    Hurons*, 84 (122).
75 Ibid., 84-99 (122-43). Champlain,
    Oeuvres, 2:569-70, 589.
76 Rousseau, 'Pierre Boucher, naturaliste
    et géographe,' 369-70. On horticulture,
    see Champlain, *Oeuvres*, 2:518, 545, 581-2,
    907.
77 Heidenreich, *Huronia*, 163. See also

Champlain, *Oeuvres*, 2:563-4.

78 Sagard, *Histoire du Canada*, 265 (282-3). Champlain, *Oeuvres*, 2:520.

79 Boucher, *Histoire véritable et naturelle*, 34-7.

80 Sagard, *Le grand voyage du pays des Hurons*, 80-1 (117). Champlain, *Oeuvres*, 2:563.

81 Sagard, *Histoire du Canada*, 251-2 (266); Sagard, *Le grand voyage du pays des Hurons*, 89 (129).

82 Kalm, *Travels in North America*, 363-5. Radisson, *Voyages*, 41.

83 JR (1649-50), 35:175. Champlain, *Oeuvres*, 2:523, 589, 910.

84 Sagard, *Histoire du Canada*, 238 (251). JR (1639), 16:79-81. Van der Donck, *A Description of the New Netherlands*, 97. Driver, *Indians of North America*, 92-3.

85 Champlain, *Oeuvres*, 2:524-5, 538-40, 912.

86 Bogaert, 'Narrative of a Journey,' 142-3. JR (1633-4), 6:295-303.

87 JR (1637), 13:97.

88 Champlain, *Oeuvres*, 2:566, 948. Bogaert, 'Narrative of a Journey,' 143.

89 Sagard, *Le grand voyage du pays des Hurons*, 84 (122-3), 86 (125), 112 (161), 116-24 (167-78), 129 (185), 133-4 (191-2). Champlain, *Oeuvres*, 2:868. Radisson, *Voyages*, 108. JR (1616-29), 4:203-5, (1636), 10:43-7; (1664-5), 49:231.

90 JR (1616-29), 4:203-5; (1657-8), 44:279-89 Sagard, *Le grand voyage du pays des Hurons*, 125 (179). Van der Donck, *A Description of the New Netherlands*, 39.

91 JR (1634-6), 8:261-5.

92 Sahlins, *Âge de pierre*.

93 JR (1636), 10:185-9. Heidenreich, *Huronia*, 134, 223-4.

94 JR (1635), 8:127. See also (1634), 6:235-9.

95 Mauss, *Sociologie et anthropologie*, 148.

96 Idem. Sahlins, *Âge de pierre*, 204.

97 Heidenreich, *Huronia*, 155. CA, 32. Champlain, *Oeuvres*, 2:906, 930. JR (1640), 20:45; (1640-1), 21:189-91.

98 Morgan, *League of the Iroquois*, 47. See also JR (1652-3), 40:145-55.

99 Morgan, *League of the Iroquois*, 439.

100 Champlain, *Oeuvres*, 2:852. See also 2:898-906.

101 Heidenreich, *Huronia*, 227-41; Heidenreich, 'Huron,' 384-5; CA, 62-3.

102 Sagard, *Le grand voyage du pays des Hurons*, 46-7 (67-8). Van der Donck, *A Description of the New Netherlands*, 76. Champlain, *Oeuvres*, 2:946-7.

103 JR (1636), 10:223-5; (1640), 20:19-21.

104 Sagard, *Le grand voyage du pays des Hurons*, 74 (108-9); Sagard, *Histoire du Canada*, 226 (238). See also JR (1640-1), 21:245-9; (1642-5), 27:37-9, 43-5; (1647-8), 33:153-5.

105 Thines and Lempereur, *Dictionnaire général des sciences humaines*, 304.

106 JR (1637), 12:249.

107 Sagard, *Le grand voyage du pays des Hurons*, 129-30 (186).

108 Sahlins, *Âge de pierre*, 318, 324.

109 CA, 135-6.

110 Champlain, *Oeuvres*, 2:572. Sagard, *Histoire du Canada*, 318 (342). JR (1657-8), 44:305-7.

111 Tooker, *An Ethnography of the Huron Indians*, 52-3, 122.

112 Champlain, *Oeuvres*, 2:952-3. Sagard, *Le grand voyage du pays des Hurons*, 123 (176-7).

113 JR (1657-8), 44:305.

114 Sagard, *Le grand voyage du pays des Hurons*, 112 (160). Champlain, *Oeuvres*, 1:312; 2:570, 953.

115 Champlain, *Oeuvres*, 2:571-2, 796. Sagard, *Le grand voyage du pays des Hurons*, 115-16 (165-6). Tooker, *An Ethnography of the Huron Indians*, 122-7.

116 Champlain, *Oeuvres*, 2:573. Sagard, *Histoire du Canada*, 318-19 (341-3). JR (1637), 14:31-5. Driver, *Indians of North America*, 445.

117 JR (1633), 5:221; (1649-50), 35:251; (1660-1), 46:267; (1662-3), 48:65. Sagard, *Le grand voyage du pays des Hurons*, 120 (173); *Histoire du Canada*, 318-20 (341-4).

118 JR (1637), 12:71; (1657-8), 44:281-3.

119 JR (1645-6), 30:79; (1649-50), 35:117-19.

120 Morgan, *League of the Iroquois*, 324. JR (1644-5), 27:259-61; (1649-50), 35:229-33. Radisson, *Voyages*, 62.

121 Sagard, *Le grand voyage du pays des Hurons*, 90 (130).

122 Ibid., 121 (174).
123 Morgan, *League of the Iroquois*, 325.
124 Sagard, *Le grand voyage du pays des Hurons*, 134 (192-3).
125 Morgan, *League of the Iroquois*, 323.
126 Driver, *Indians of North America*, 446.
127 *JR* (1636), 10:233-5; (1645-6), 28:45-55.
128 *JR* (1638-9), 156. See also, concerning the Montagnais, *JR* (1634), 6:243-5.
129 Champlain, *Oeuvres*, 2:582, 919.
130 *JR* (1633), 5:247-9.
131 *JR* (1936), 10:213.
132 Van der Donck, *A Description of the New Netherlands*, 100-1. See also Champlain, *Oeuvres*, 2:574, 583. Megapolensis, 'A Short Account of the Mohawk Indians,' 179-80. *JR* (1645-6), 28:51-5.
133 *JR* (1636), 10:233. See also D.P. De Vries, 'Voyages from Holland,' 96-7.
134 *JR* (1636), 10:251-3.
135 Sahlins, *Âge de pierre*, 236-8.
136 Bogaert, 'Narrative of a Journey,' 146. Champlain, *Oeuvres*, 2:583-4.
137 *CA*, 51. *JR* (1655-6), 42:159-61. Sagard, *Le grand voyage du pays des Hurons*, 153 (219-20).
138 This discussion is based on Foucault, *Surveiller et punir*, 36-72. For a detailed description of ritual Huron torture see *JR* (1637), 13:37-43.
139 Foucault, *Surveiller et punir*, 9.
140 Ibid., 57.
141 Sagard, *Histoire du Canada*, 320 (344).
142 Foucault, *Surveiller et punir*, 65. Hill and Postan, *Histoire économique et sociale de la Grande-Bretagne*, 1:276.
143 *JR* (1652-53), 38:272-3, 277; see also (1645-6), 28:45-55. Champlain, *Oeuvres*, 2:574, 583.
144 Foucault, *Surveiller et punir*, 55.
145 Ibid., 56.
146 D.P. De Vries, 'Voyages from Holland,' 94.
147 *JR* (1616), 3:85.
148 Van der Donck, *A Description of the New Netherlands*, 94.
149 Ibid., 72.
150 Ibid., 76. *JR* (1635), 8:127-9.
151 *JR* (1635), 8:129; (1637), 12:67; (1633), 5:105.
152 Gessain, *Ammassalik ou la civilisation obligatoire*, 35.
153 *JR* (1637), 13:51. See also Champlain, *Oeuvres*, 2:568.
154 *JR* (1638-9), 15:154; see also (1633), 6:25; (1636), 9:279-83; (1657-8), 44:285-7; (1666-7), 50:257. See also Van der Donck, *A Description of the New Netherlands*, 72. Sagard, *Le grand voyage du pays des Hurons*, 125 (179-80). Wooley, 'A Two Years Journal in New York,' 28. Boucher, *Histoire véritable et naturelle*, 92. Champlain, *Oeuvres*, 1:311; 2:569, 795.
155 Barré and Girouard, 'La plaine laurentienne,' 54.
156 Heidenreich, *Huronia*, 164-8.
157 *JR* (1633), 6:25; see also (1634), 6:229.
158 Larocque, 'L'introduction de maladies européennes,' 15.
159 *JR* (1616), 3:109. Tooker, *An Ethnography of the Huron Indians*, 123.
160 Megapolensis, 'A Short Account of the Mohawk Indians,' 174. See also Sagard, *Histoire du Canada*, 318 (342); Sagard, *Le grand voyage du pays des Hurons*, 116-20 (167-73). *JR* (1647-8), 32:275-9; (1657-8), 44:305. D.P. De Vries, 'Voyages,' 55, 93. C. Wooley, 'A Two Years Journal in New York,' 27.
161 Engels, *The Origins of the Family*, 80-93.
162 Godelier, 'Le sexe comme fondement ultime de l'ordre social,' 268-306.
163 *JR* (1633), 5:181.
164 *CA*, 39.
165 *JR* (1635), 8:117-19; (1636), 10:127-31.
166 *JR* (1634), 6:231-9; (1656-70), 44:37-41. See also Marie de l'Incarnation, *Lettres historiques*, 134.
167 *JR* (1637), 13:241.
168 Driver, *Indians of North America*, 341. *CA*, 55. Marie de l'Incarnation, *Lettres historiques*, 134.
169 Driver, *Indians of North America*, 354-7. Champlain, *Oeuvres*, 2:578. *CA*, 79-80.
170 *CA*, 135.
171 Jacquin, *Histoire des Indiens d'Amérique du Nord*, 89-90. Driver, *Indians of North America*, 399.

172 Van der Donck, *A Description of the New Netherlands*, 95. JR (1616), 3:115.

173 JR (1647-8), 33:199.

174 JR (1616), 3:203-5. Champlain, *Oeuvres*, 2:574-7.

175 Champlain, *Oeuvres*, 578. Driver, *Indians of North America*, 354, 357.

176 Sagard, *Le grand voyage du pays des Hurons*, 110 (158-9). See also JR (1637), 13:169-73; (1639), 17:147-9, 179-83, 189-93; (1642-3), 23:157-61; (1645-6), 29:271-5; (1648-9), 34:107-11, 215-19; (1663-4), 48:265-7.

177 JR (1639), 17:195-7.

178 Champlain, *Oeuvres*, 2:519, 574.

179 JR (1636), 10:159.

180 Ibid., 161-5.

181 Ibid., 167-9.

182 Ibid., 171-3.

183 Ibid., 169-71.

184 JR (1635), 8:121-3; (1636), 10:265-9.

185 JR (1635), 8:121; (1636), 10:141-57, 265-9.

186 Champlain, *Oeuvres*, 2:585-7. Sagard, *Le grand voyage du pays des Hurons*, 203-6 (290-5).

187 JR (1636), 8:121. Champlain, *Oeuvres*, 2:585.

188 JR (1636), 10:271.

189 Ibid., 123.

190 JR (1636), 10:169-71.

191 JR (1655-6), 42:165-7.

192 JR (1647-8), 33:189.

193 Ibid., 191-3.

194 JR (1637), 12:61.

195 JR (1636), 10:267.

196 Marcuse, *Eros and Civilisation*, 11, 16, 37.

197 Ibid., 35.

198 Ibid., 37.

199 JR (1639), 16:241-3.

200 JR (1637), 12:51-3.

201 JR (1634), 6:243-5.

202 Marcuse, *Eros and Civilisation*, 39.

203 JR (1657-8), 44:283.

204 JR (1634), 6:283-5. See also JR (1636), 10:177-85; (1637), 12:147-9; (1639), 17:209-10. Sagard, *Le grand voyage du pays des Hurons*, 130 (187).

205 Marcuse, *Eros and Civilisation*, 39-40.

206 Champlain, *Oeuvres*, 1:311. JR (1657-8), 44:283-93. Marie de l'Incarnation, *Lettres historiques*, 32.

207 JR (1636), 10:201-5; (1637), 13:175-7.

208 JR (1657-8), 44:303.

209 JR (1651-2), 37:151-7; (1655-6), 42:141; (1656-7), 43:287-9.

210 JR (1642), 23:171.

211 JR (1637), 13:263.

212 JR (1642), 23:171-6. For other references to dreams, see (1634), 6:181-5; (1637), 12:55-7; (1639), 17:161-3; (1640-1), 21:261-5; (1642), 23:171, 209-21; (1645-6), 30:43-5; (1655-6), 42:65-7, 195-7; (1656-7), 43:267-9; (1661-2), 47:179-81.

213 JR (1657-8), 44:307.

214 JR (1642), 22:291; (1656-7), 43:287-91. Sagard, *Le grand voyage du pays des Hurons*, 129 (186).

CHAPTER 3:
THE QUESTION OF UNEQUAL EXCHANGE

1 Thomas Bottomore, *A Dictionary of Marxist Thought*, 60-1.

2 Amin, *L'accumulation à l'échelle mondiale*, 1:161.

3 Ibid., 104.

4 Bottomore, *A Dictionary of Marxist Thought*, 60-1.

5 Amin, *L'accumulation à l'échelle mondiale*, 2:38-41.

6 Ibid., 13-14.

7 CA, 242.

8 JR (1655-6), 42:61-3.

9 Champlain, *Oeuvres*, 1:341.

10 Barré and Girouard, 'La plaine laurentienne,' 45.

11 CA, 220-1. JR (1660-1), 46:253, 275, 283.

12 JR (1657-8), 44:243-5.

13 Ibid., 245.

14 Jacquin, *Histoire des Indiens d'Amérique du Nord*, 102.

15 Cartier, *Voyages en Nouvelle-France*, 60-1.

16 Ibid., 110.

17 Morgan, *League of the Iroquois*, 472. Cartier, *Voyages en Nouvelle-France*, 83. Trudel, *Histoire de la Nouvelle-France*, 1:90.

18 Champlain, *Oeuvres*, 2:513. Trudel, *Histoire de la Nouvelle-France*, 2:216-17.

19 Morgan, *League of the Iroquois*, 474.
20 JR (1657-8), 44:239-41; (1664-5), 50:37.
21 Cartier, *Voyages en Nouvelle-France*, 110, 124. Trudel, *Histoire de la Nouvelle-France*, 1:152-75.
22 Witthoft, *Indian Prehistory of Pennsylvania*, 43. See also A.W. Crosby, Jr., *The Columbian Exchange*, 122-64.
23 Martin, *Keepers of the Game*, 48.
24 Ibid., 48-9. Larocque, 'L'introduction de maladies européennes,' 19-20.
25 Cartier, *Voyages en Nouvelle-France*, 117-19.
26 Champlain, *Oeuvres*, 2:816. CA, 214-15. Perrot, *Mémoires sur les moeurs*, 9-12.
27 Salwen, 'Indians of Southern New England and Long Island,' 170-1.
28 Martin, *Keepers of the Game*, 40.
29 JR (1616), 3:105.
30 Sagard, *Le grand voyage du pays des Hurons*, 257-8 (366).
31 Bogaert, 'Narrative of a Journey,' 141.
32 JR (1635), 8:87-91.
33 JR (1637), 14:7-9; (1638), 15:19-23; (1640), 19:87-9.
34 JR (1637), 13:85-169.
35 JR (1640), 19:77-9.
36 JR (1639), 16:217-19, 101-3.
37 JR (1640), 19:123.
38 JR (1644-5), 28:41-3.
39 JR (1647), 30:229.
40 Idem.
41 JR (1656-7), 43:291.
42 JR (1657-8), 44:155.
43 JR (1659-60), 45:235; (1660-1), 47:63-5; (1662-3), 48:79-83; (1663-4), 49:139.
44 JR (1669-70), 53:79-83.
45 JR (1660-1), 46:255.
46 JR (1638-9), 5:156; (1643-4), 25:105-7; (1662-3), 48:133-5.
47 JR (1643-4), 25:109.
48 Martin, *Keepers of the Game*, 46.
49 Van der Donck, *A Description of the New Netherlands*, 64, 71-2.
50 JR (1640), 19:233-7.
51 Martin, *Keepers of the Game*, 50. CA, 601.
52 Martin, *Keepers of the Game*, 50.
53 Rousseau, 'Le Canada aborigène,' 41.
54 JR (1639), 16:93.
55 JR (1637), 14:99.

56 JR (1638), 15:33.
57 JR (1637), 12:237; (1655-6), 42:135-7.
58 JR (1636), 9:207.
59 JR (1637), 13:127, 199.
60 JR (1637), 14:51.
61 JR (1639), 16:39.
62 JR (1638), 15:19.
63 JR (1638), 15:37-51.
64 Ibid., 53.
65 JR (1640), 19:91-3. See also ibid., 207-11; (1644-5), 28:41-3.
66 JR (1636), 10:93.
67 JR (1637), 13:131; (1638), 15:23; (1640), 19:213, 233-5; (1640), 20:33.
68 JR (1647), 31:121-3.
69 CA, 499-500.
70 Martin, *Keepers of the Game*, 130-49.
71 JR (1647), 30:281-3.
72 Martin, *Keepers of the Game*, 31.
73 Ibid., 131-4.
74 Ibid., 135-4.
75 Ibid., 141-3. Lescarbot, *Histoire de la Nouvelle-France*, 3:425.
76 Bogaert, 'Narrative of a Journey,' 141.
77 JR (1640-1), 21:211-13.
78 CA, 602.
79 Megapolensis, 'A Short Account of the Mohawk Indians,' 174.
80 JR (1649-50), 35:213. See also Radisson, *Voyages*, 82.
81 Van der Donck, *A Description of the New Netherlands*, 73. See also D.P. De Vries, 'Voyages from Holland,' 118.
82 JR (1633), 5:113-17.
83 Champlain, *Oeuvres*, 1:296-302. See also Trudel, *Histoire de la Nouvelle-France*, 2:157-8.
84 Champlain, *Oeuvres*, 1:388.
85 Ibid., 398, 401, 439. Trudel, *Histoire de la Nouvelle-France*, 2:176, 194.
86 Champlain, *Oeuvres*, 1:332-44, 358-74; 2:502, 816, 822, 829.
87 Ibid., 2:521. CA, 260. Hunt, *Wars of the Iroquois*, 22-6.
88 JR (1640-1), 21:239-41; (1645-6), 29:145-7. Champlain, *Oeuvres*, 1:454, 467; 3:1,046.
89 Champlain, *Oeuvres*, 2:502, 529-37.
90 CA, 365-76.
91 Champlain, *Oeuvres*, 1:366, 397-412, 438; 3:1,006-8.

92 Ibid., 3:398-9.

93 Ibid., 1:397-412; 2:844-53; 3:1,045-50, 1,064.

94 Ibid., 1:404; 3:1,050.

95 Ibid., 1:411-12.

96 *JR* (1633), 6:7.

97 Champlain, *Oeuvres*, 1:404; 3:1,050.

98 Lanctot, *Histoire du Canada*, 1:162.

99 *JR* (1616-29), 4:207.

100 Lanctot, *Histoire du Canada*, 1:173.

101 'Articles accordés par le Roy à la Compagnie de la Nouvelle-France' [Articles of the Compagnie de la Nouvelle-France aproved by the King], C11A-1, Fo. 80, 82V-83R. Trudel, *Histoire de la Nouvelle-France*, 2:298.

102 Lanctot, *Histoire du Canada*, 1:177, 179, 180.

103 Lublinskaya, *French Absolutism*, 216-19.

104 Leblant, 'Le commerce compliqué des fourrures canadiennes,' 60-1.

105 La Chesnaye, 'Mémoire, 1677,' F³2, Fo. 03R.

106 'Articles accordés entre les Directeurs et associés en la Compagnie de la Nouvelle-France: et les députés des habitants du pays agrées et confirmés par le Roi' [Clauses agreed between the directors and associates of the Compagnie de la Nouvelle-France: and the representatives of inhabitants of countries certified and confirmed by the King] C11A-1, Fo. 212R-228R.

107 Trudel, *La seigneurie des Cent-Associés*, 176-7. Lanctot, *Histoire du Canada*, 1:239.

108 'Ordonnance du 6 septembre 1645,' cited in Trudel, *La seigneurie des Cent-Associés*, 176-7; also cited in Lanctot, *Histoire du Canada*, 1:241.

109 Aubert de la Chesnaye, 'Mémoire,' F³2, Fo. 03v.

110 *JR* (1645-6), 28:155-7.

111 'Arrêt du 27 Mars 1647, portant Réglement concernant les habitants du pays de Canada' [Decree of 27 March 1647 on the regulation regarding inhabitants of the country of Canada], C11A-1, Fos. 237R-240R. See also Lanctot, *Histoire du Canada*, 1:241. Innis, *The Fur Trade in Canada*, 39. Trudel, *La*

112 La Chesnaye, 'Mémoire, 1677,' F³2, Fo. 04R-05R.

113 Hamelin, *Économie et société en Nouvelle-France*, 53.

114 *JR* (1637), 12:243; (1644-5), 27:253-7, 279-81.

115 Idem.

116 *JR* (1644-5), 27:279-81.

117 *JR* (1637), 12:253.

118 *JR* (1633), 5:267.

119 Idem.

120 *JR* (1637), 12:249.

121 *JR* (1633), 5:249-57; (1637), 12:249-55.

122 *JR* (1637), 12:257.

123 *JR* (1633), 5:265.

124 Sahlins, *Âge de pierre*, 337.

125 Mauss, *Sociologie et anthropologie*, 199.

126 Dechêne, *Habitants et marchands*, 172-3.

127 Kupp, 'Quelques aspects de la dissolution,' 367-71. Condon, *New York Beginnings*, 13-17.

128 *CA*, 344-9, 465.

129 Trelease, *Indian Affairs in Colonial New York*, 46.

130 *CA*, 344-9.

131 Condon, *New York Beginnings*, 27.

132 DeRassières cited in Condon, *New York Beginnings*, 103.

133 Leach, *The New Northern Colonial Frontier*, 21. Nissenson, *The Patroon's Domain*, 22.

134 D.P. De Vries, 'Voyages from Holland,' 99.

135 Trelease, *Indian Affairs in Colonial New York*, 50.

136 Nissenson, *The Patroon's Domain*, 81-2. See also Kupp, 'Fur Trade Relations,' 109, 143.

137 D.P. De Vries, 'Voyages from Holland,' 89.

138 *JR* (1645-6), 28:105. *NNN*, 261. Kupp, 'Fur Trade Relations,' 118, 142, 196.

139 Van Laer, *Van Rensselaer Bowier Manuscripts*, 320.

140 'Report on the Condition of the Colony of New Netherland in 1638,' *DRCHNY*, 1:106-7.

141 Trelease, *Indian Affairs in Colonial New York*, 61, 112-13, 118.

142 Anonymous, 'Journal of New

Netherland,' 273. See also DRCHNY, 1:182.

143 Van Laer, *Van Rensselaer Bowier Manuscripts*, 685.

144 Van Laer, *Van Rensselaer Bowier Manuscripts*, 512, 683, 689, 698, 723. Trelease, *Indian Affairs in Colonial New York*, 132.

145 Trelease, *Indian Affairs in Colonial New York*, 134.

146 'Secret case: West India Company Report of the Amsterdam Chamber of the West India Company ... Respecting the Swedes,' DRCHNY, 1:592.

147 Trelease, *Indian Affairs in Colonial New York*, 118.

148 JR (1645-6), 28:112; see also 104-15, 136-40. NNN, 235-50, 251-4, 255-64.

149 JR (1644-5), 27:247-57.

150 Frederickson and Gibb, *La chaîne d'alliance*, 10. 'The Honble William Johnson's second speech to the Sachems and Warriors of the confederate nations, 24th June 1755,' DRCHNY, 6:969-70; 'Propositions of the Mohawks. Minutes of the Court of Fort Orange, Sept. 6, 1659,' DRCHNY, 13:110; 'Final Answer given to the Mohawks at their first Castle Kaghnuwage ... Sept. 24, 1659,' DRCHNY, 13:112; 'Conference held at Fort Orange (Albany) between the Director-General and the Senecas, 25th July, 1660,' DRCHNY, 13:184; 'Council Minutes, Indian Conference at Fort Orange, Jan. 22, 1661,' DRCHNY, 13:191.

151 Trelease, *Indian Affairs in Colonial New York*, 118. Van Laer, *Van Rensselaer Bowier Manuscripts*, 351.

152 'Propositions of the Mohawks,' DRCHNY, 13:109.

153 'Final Answer given to the Mohawks at their first Castle Kaghnuwage ... Sept. 24, 1659,' DRCHNY, 13:112-14.

154 NNN, 273; see also DRCHNY, 1:182.

155 'Order That no offence shall be given to the Indians under severe penalty ... Sept. 27, 1659,' DRCHNY, 13:114. 'Conference held ... 25th July, 1660,' DRCHNY, 13:184-5.

156 Ibid., 184-6.

157 'Mr. Peter Schagen to the States General, the Island of Manhattan pur-chased, Amsterdam, November 5, 1626,' DRCHNY, 1:37. Jennings, *The Invasion of America*, 132. Savard, *Le sol américain*, 26-7. See also 'Patent to Messrs Godyn and Blommaert for a Tract of Land on Delaware Bay, 15th of July, 1630,' DRCHNY, 1:43; 'Appendix to the despatch of Messrs Joachimi and Brasser, received 11th June 1633,' DRCHNY, 1:56; 'Answer to the Remonstrance of the Dutch Ambassadors ... April 1632,' DRCHNY, 1:58; 'The Assembly of the XIX to the States General, 25th October 1634,' DRCHNY, 1:94; 'New Project of Freedoms and Exemptions, without date, file, entitled West Indie, 1630-1635,' DRCHNY, 1:100, n. 33; 'Appendix received from My Lord Saye, Read 9th August 1642,' DRCHNY, 1:128; 'Indian deed for an island in Hudson's river, opposite Bethlehem, called Long or Mahicander's Island, 8th Feb., 1661,' DRCHNY, 13:193; Van Laer, *Van Rensselaer Bowier Manuscripts*, 159.

158 JR (1655-6), 42:109-11; see also (1647), 31:99-101; (1652-3), 40:143-7.

159 JR (1642-3), 24:271-81.

160 'Articles accordés par le Roy à la Compagnie de la Nouvelle-France' [Articles of the Compagnie de la Nouvelle-France approved by the King], Article 17, C11A-1, Fo. 83R.

161 JR (1634), 6:103-5; (1635), 8:49-51.

162 Ibid., 8:15.

163 CA, 568-70, 613, 628.

164 JR (1642), 22:311; see also (1637), 12:255; (1639), 16:35.

165 JR (1642-3), 25:27.

166 Lanctot, *Histoire du Canada*, 1:234.

167 Kalm, *Travels in North America*, 1:268. D.P. De Vries, 'Voyages from Holland,' 113.

168 CA, 208.

169 Rousseau, 'Le Canada aborigène,' 55-6.

170 JR (1643-4), 27:37.

171 Sagard, *Le grand voyage du pays des Hurons*, 92-3 (134).

172 JR (1640-1), 21:239-41.

173 CA, 353.

174 Ibid., 357.

175 Ibid., 358.

176 Ibid., 354. *JR* (1647-8), 33:67.

177 *CA*, 803.

178 Ibid., 213.

179 Ibid., 354. Hunt, *The Wars of the Iroquois*, 117-20.

180 D.P. De Vries, 'Voyages from Holland,' 113. Brasser, 'Mahican,' 202-3.

181 *JR* (1645-6), 28:275-7.

182 Wood, 'Sketch of the First Settlement,' 64-6. Megapolensis, 'A Short Account of the Mohawk Indians,' 172.

183 *JR* (1647), 31:89. Wood, 'Sketch of the First Settlement,' 66. *CA*, 337.

184 *JR* (1642), 22:307; (1644-5), 28:47.

185 Sagard, *Le grand voyage du pays des Hurons*, 88 (127), 250-2 (354-9). *JR* (1645-6), 29:145-7.

186 *JR* (1640), 20:19-21.

187 *CA*, 288-90.

188 *JR* (1636), 10:301-5.

189 *CA*, 423.

190 Ibid., 325.

191 Sagard, *Histoire du Canada*, 166 (170).

192 Sagard, *Le grand voyage du pays des Hurons*, 116 (166-7).

193 *CA*, 374.

194 Ibid., 844.

195 Sagard, *Histoire du Canada*, 166-7 (170).

196 Trudel, *Histoire de la Nouvelle-France*, 2:213.

197 *CA*, 404-5.

198 Sagard, *Le grand voyage du pays des Hurons*, 126-8 (180-5). *JR* (1656-7), 43:147-9; (1638-9), 15:154; (1656-7), 43:147-9. Kalm, *Travels in North America*, 1:298.

199 Sagard, *Le grand voyage du pays des Hurons*, 186 (266-7). *CA*, 374.

200 Sagard, *Histoire du Canada*, 320 (344), 332 (357).

201 Dechêne, *Habitants et marchands*, 168. Kupp, 'Fur Trade Relations,' iv.

202 *JR* (1644-5), 27:293; (1633), 5:113-17; (1651-2), 38:141. See also Marie de l'Incarnation, *Lettres historiques*, 17 March 1650, 58.

203 Michaelius, 'Letter of Reverend Jonas Michaelius,' 122-33.

204 Megapolensis, 'A Short Account of the Mohawk Indians,' 172. See also 'Letter from the Same Affairs at Esopus, 1662,' *DRCHNY*, 13:228.

205 Michaelius, 'Letter of Reverend Jonas Michaelius,' 128.

206 Bogaert, 'Narrative of a Journey,' 153-4; see also ibid., 129-62 and especially 141, 148, 149.

207 Michaelius, 'Letter of Reverend Jonas Michaelius,' 130.

208 Bogaert, 'Narrative of a Journey,' 145-54.

209 D.P. De Vries, 'Voyages from Holland,' 95.

210 Megapolensis, 'A Short Account of the Mohawk Indians,' 176.

211 Ibid., 173. See also Radisson, *Voyages*, 65. *JR* (1655-6), 42:155-7.

212 Megapolensis, 'A Short Account of the Mohawk Indians,' 173. *CA*, 617-18.

213 Sagard, *Le grand voyage du pays des Hurons*, 67 (97-8).

214 Trelease, *Indian Affairs in Colonial New York*, 127. 'Conference held at Fort Orange,' *DRCHNY*, 13:184-6.

215 *CA*, 618.

216 *JR* (1647-8), 33:203-7.

217 *JR* (1634-6), 8:57-9.

218 Bogaert, 'Narrative of a Journey,' 142, 146, 153.

219 Van Laer, *Van Rensselaer Bowier Manuscripts*, 483-4. Trelease, *Indian Affairs in Colonial New York*, 43. *CA*, 618.

220 *CA*, 618.

221 Bogaert, 'Narrative of a Journey,' 149, 151.

222 Delftschaven Archives, no. 97, Rotterdam Archives. Information forwarded by Th. J. Kupp to Marcel Trudel and reported in Trudel, *La seigneurie des Cent-Associés*, 185.

223 Trudel, *La seigneurie des Cent-Associés*, 185. *JR* (1647), 27:99.

224 *JR* (1647-8), 32:187.

225 Dechêne, *Habitant et marchands*, 142-3.

226 *JR* (1656-7), 44:59.

227 'Narrative of Governor de Courcelles' Voyage to Lake Ontario, 1671,' *DRCHNY*, 9:84. See also La Chesnaye, 'Mémoire sur le prix du castor, 1670' [Report on

the price of beaver], CIIA-3, Fo. 150R-
151R.

228 JR (1616-29), 29:207. See also CA, 360.
'Règlement pour la traite des Sauvages
par M. de Tracy, à Québec, 25 juillet
1665' [Regulation for trade with the
Indians, Monsieur de Tracy, at Quebec,
25 July 1665], F³3, Fo. 325R.

229 Sagard, Histoire du Canada, 251 (266).

230 CA, 358-62.

231 Sagard, Le grand voyage du pays des
Hurons, 98 (142).

232 JR (1662-3), 48:129. Radisson, Voyages,
41. Marie de l'Incarnation, Lettres historiques, 26 August 1644, 33.

233 CA, 409. See also D.P. De Vries,
'Voyages from Holland,' 117.

234 Champlain, Oeuvres, 3:986. Van Laer,
Van Rensselaer Bowier Manuscripts, 247,
426, 474, 511, 565.

235 Anonymous, 'Journal of New
Netherland,' 1:182.

236 Trelease, Indian Affairs in Colonial New
York, 98.

237 JR (1640-1), 21:37.

238 D.P. De Vries, 'Voyages from Holland,'
113.

239 JR (1642-3), 24:295; (1643-4), 26:237-41.

240 Trelease, Indian Affairs in Colonial New
York, 135.

241 'Report of the Committee of the States
General on the Affairs of New
Netherland, 1650,' DRCHNY, 1:388, 389,
392.

242 'Remonstrance of New Netherland ...
addressed by the people of New
Netherland, July 20, 1649,' DRCHNY,
1:311; see also DRCHNY, 1:427.

243 'Letter from Directors to Stuyvesant ...
June 6th, 1653,' DRCHNY, 14:206.

244 'Reply of the West India Company to
the answer of the H.P. Stuyvesant, 1666,'
DRCHNY, 2:496.

245 JR (1648-9), 34:123; see also (1647-8),
32:179-83; (1649-50), 35:219-22.

246 JR (1651-2), 38:67.

247 'Resolution to provide the Mohawks
with a moderate amount of powder and
lead, lest they apply therefore to the
English,' DRCHNY, 13:35. JR (1662-3),

48:77.

248 Trelease, Indian Affairs in Colonial New
York, 118, 131.

249 JR (1647), 32:21.

250 Kupp, 'Fur Trade Relations,' 118-21.
Braudel, Civilisation materiélle,
économie et capitalisme, 3:211.

251 JR (1640-1), 20:221. See also Marie de
l'Incarnation, Lettres historiques, 24
August 1641, 28.

252 JR (1642-3), 24:291.

253 JR (1642), 22:269; see also (1648-9),
34:137.

254 JR (1642), 22:307.

255 JR (1643-4), 27:71; see also (1659-60),
45:302-15.

256 JR (1633), 5:231; (1661-2), 47:185, 199;
(1662-3), 48:61-3. Marie de
l'Incarnation, Lettres historiques, 26
August 1644, 34; 10 August 1662, 142.
'Letter from the same to the same.
Affairs at the Esopus; evils arising from
the unlimited sale of liquor to the
Indians, 5 Sept. 1662,' DRCHNY, 13:228.

257 Trelease, Indian Affairs in Colonial New
York, 51.

258 Van der Donck, A Description of the
New Netherlands, 75. 'Letter from the
same to the same,' DRCHNY, 13:228.

259 Ordinance forbidding the sale of alcohol to Amerindians, 1641, 1643, 1645,
1647, 1648, 1654, 1656, 1657, see Flick,
History of the State of New York, 298,
338. Scott, 'New Amsterdam's Taverns
and Tavern-Keepers,' 9. Wood, 'Sketch
of the First Settlement,' 74.

260 JR (1633), 5:231; see also (1645-6), 29:79-
81.

261 JR (1645-6), 29:77-9; (1636), 9:207.

262 Trudel, La seigneurie des Cent-Associés,
320-8.

263 Marcuse, Eros and Civilization, 71.

264 Dechêne, Habitant et marchands, 158.

265 Ibid., 158-9.

266 JR (1633), 5:231, (1662-3), 48:63.

267 Marie de l'Incarnation, Lettres historiques, 26 August 1644, 34. See also JR
(1657-8), 44:277-81.

268 Dailey, 'The Role of Alcohol,' 53.

269 JR (1634), 6:283, 259, 279, 283.

270 Denton, *A Brief Description of New York*, 7.
271 JR (1645-6), 29:153-5.
272 JR (1633), 5:231.
273 Trelease, *Indian Affairs in Colonial New York*, 70.
274 'Propositions of the Mohawks,' DRCHNY 13:108-9.
275 JR (1661-2), 47:141.
276 Ibid., 185.
277 JR (1662-3), 48:63.
278 JR (1645-6), 29:77-8.
279 D.P. De Vries, 'Voyages from Holland,' 95.
280 Sagard, *Histoire du Canada*, 252-3 (267).
281 Martens, 'Une hypothèse sur les wampums,' 54-5. Van der Donck, *A Description of the New Netherlands*, 56, 78, 93. D.P. De Vries, 'Voyages from Holland,' 95. Wooley, 'A Two Years Journal in New York,' 32.
282 Van der Donck, *A Description of the New Netherlands*, 78.
283 Martens, 'Une hypothèse sur les wampums,' 54.
284 JR (1636), 9:173-5.
285 Idem. See also (1637), 13:151; (1638), 15:37; (1638-9), 15:158; (1645-6), 29:53-5. Noël, *Art décoratif et vestimentaire des Amérindiens*, 161.
286 Bogart, 'Currency Crisis in New Amsterdam,' 6. Van der Donck, *A Description of the New Netherlands*, 93.
287 Idem.
288 De Voe, *The Market Book*, 29.
289 Bogart, 'Currency Crisis in New Amsterdam,' 6.
290 Van der Donck, *A Description of the New Netherlands*, 93.
291 JR (1641-2), 21:268-72.
292 JR (1642-3), 24:273.
293 Wood, 'Sketch of the First Settlement,' 76.
294 JR (1653-4), 41:43.
295 JR (1643-4), 27:29-33.
296 JR (1643-4), 27:25-7. Hunt, *The Wars of the Iroquois*, 108-9.
297 JR (1643-4), 27:25-7.
298 JR (1642), 23:225.
299 JR (1640), 20:51-3; (1640-1), 21:203-19;

(1642), 11:307-11, 23:179-81.
300 JR (1647-8), 32:179-83.
301 JR (1643-4), 27:63.
302 JR (1643-4), 27:63-9; (1644-5), 28:39-45.
303 JR (1645-6), 28:279.
304 JR (1643-4), 27:25-7.
305 JR (1644-5), 28:57.
306 JR (1645-6), 28:148-50, 315, n. 16; (1644-5), 27:247-55.
307 JR (1645-6), 29:247.
308 JR (1647-8), 33:73.
309 JR (1647-8), 33:119-21.
310 CA, 731.
311 Ibid., 737-9. JR (1647-8), 33:69-71; (1649), 34:225-7.
312 JR (1647-8), 33:81-3.
313 JR (1648-9), 34:99.
314 JR (1648-9), 34:123-5.
315 JR (1636), 34:123-37. D.P. De Vries, 'Voyages from Holland,' 94.
316 JR (1648-9), 34:137.
317 JR (1648-9), 34:125-31, 145, 227-9.
318 JR (1648-9), 34:197.
319 JR (1648-9), 34:197-9.
320 JR (1650-1), 36:177.
321 JR (1648-9), 34:223; (1649-50), 35:109-11.
322 JR (1657-8), 44:251.
323 JR (1653-4), 41:77-9. CA, 822-3. See also, Barbeau, *Huron and Wyandot Mythology*, 361-5, 368-9, 375-9.
324 JR (1649-50), 35:209-11.
325 JR (1650-1), 36:116.
326 JR (1651-2), 37:181; (1652-3), 40:223.
327 JR (1650-1), 36:193-5.
328 JR (1651-2), 37:109-11.
329 JR (1657-8), 44:149-53.
330 Idem; see also JR (1652-3), 40:157.
331 Trelease, *Indian Affairs in Colonial New York*, 118.
332 JR (1653-4), 41:51-65.
333 JR (1656-7), 43:115-25.
334 JR (1655-6), 42:33; (1656-7), 43:117-21; (1657-8), 44:187-9.
335 JR (1651-2), 37:259.
336 'Secret case: West India Company Report ... respecting the Swedes,' DRCHNY 1:592. Trelease, *Indian Affairs in Colonial New York*, 109. Van Laer, *Van Rensselaer Bowier Manuscripts*, 483-4.
337 JR (1655-6), 42:113; see also ibid., 177,

179-83; (1647-8), 33:63-5; (1653-4), 41:81-3.

338 JR (1655-6), 42:181.

339 JR (1655-6), 42:111-13.

340 JR (1656-7), 44:49-51.

341 JR (1661-2), 47:147.

342 JR (1661-2), 47:145-7.

343 Hunt, *The Wars of the Iroquois*, 145.

344 JR (1663-4), 49:141; see also (1660-1), 47:107.

345 JR (1662-3), 48:77. Radisson, *Voyages*, 92.

346 JR (1662-3), 48:77.

347 JR (1663-4), 49:141.

348 'Secret case: West India Company Report ... respecting the Swedes,' DRCHNY 1:592. Hunt, *The Wars of the Iroquois*, 131-44. Jennings, 'The Indian Trade of the Susquehanna Valley,' 407.

349 JR (1662-3), 48:77; (1663-4), 49:141-9.

350 JR (1649-50), 35:199-205; see also Donnelly, *Thwaites' Jesuit Relations*, 133.

351 JR (1651-2), 38:45-7. Bourque, *Classes sociales et question nationale*, 85-7.

352 JR (1651-2), 38:47-9.

353 JR (1648-9), 34:87-91, 127-9.

354 Hunt, *The Wars of the Iroquois*, 109.

355 Ibid., 115, 125.

356 JR (1652-3), 40:213-17.

357 JR (1659-60), 45:235.

358 JR (1662-3), 48:127; see also (1657-8), 44:245-9; (1659-60), 45:43-5, 219-21, 243-5; (1666-7), 50:21-5, 301, 303-5.

359 CA, 350-1.

360 JR (1635), 8:57.

361 D.P. De Vries, 'Voyages from Holland,' 90.

362 Van der Donck, *A Description of the New Netherlands*, 50.

363 Kalm, *Travels in North America*, 1:277-8. See also Marie-Victorin, *Flore laurentienne*, 517-18.

364 R. Parent in Hamelin et al. *Histoire du Québec*, 56-7.

365 La Chesnaye, 'Mémoire, 1677,' F²2, Fo. 02R.

366 Cartier, *Voyages en Nouvelle-France*, 107, 110, 149.

367 Leblant, 'Le commerce compliqué des fourrures canadiennes au début du 17ᵉ siècle,' 59.

368 Trudel, *Histoire de la Nouvelle-France*, 2:264, 265, 272, 297, 335, 431, 433.

369 JR (1616-29), 4:207-9. Trudel, *Histoire de la Nouvelle-France*, 2:287.

370 JR (1616-29), 4:207-9. Trudel, *Histoire de la Nouvelle-France*, 2:431.

371 JR (1616-29), 4:207. CA, 336. Trudel, *Histoire de la Nouvelle-France*, 2:431.

372 Trudel, *Histoire de la Nouvelle-France*, 2:431. See also Trudel, *La seigneurie des Cent-Associés*, 24.

373 Campeau, *Les finances publiques de la Nouvelle-France*, 8-15. Salone, *La colonisation de la Nouvelle-France*, 51. Lanctot, *Histoire du Canada*, 1:225. Innis, *The Fur Trade in Canada*, 39.

374 La Chesnaye, 'Mémoire, 1677,' F³2, Fo. 03R.

375 Trudel, *La seigneurie des Cent-Associés*, 1:184.

376 Christensen, *Colonial New York*, 1-160.

377 Marie de l'Incarnation, *Lettres historiques*, 17 September 1660, 119; 23 September 1660, 123-4.

378 Martin, *Keepers of the Game*, 16.

379 Clermont, 'Le castor et les Indiens préhistoriques,' 5.

380 JR (1634), 6:299.

381 Clermont, 'Le castor et les Indiens préhistoriques,' 6.

382 JR (1634), 6:301.

383 Van der Donck, *A Description of the New Netherlands*, 97, 100. Washburn, *The Indian and the White Man*, document 11:31.

384 Malone, 'Changing Military Technology,' 56-8.

385 Washburn, *The Indian and the White Man*, document 11:28-34; document 12:35-9.

386 Van der Donck, *A Description of the New Netherlands*, 96.

387 'Propositions of the three Mohawk castles ... June 16, 1657,' DRCHNY, 13:72-3; 'Propositions of the Mohawks ... Sept. 6, 1659,' 13:109.

388 JR (1656-7), 43:185.

389 JR (1635), 8:115.

390 CA, 412. Heidenreich, *Huronia*, 151-2. Bibeau, 'Les palissades des sites iroquoiens,' 192.

391 Marie de l'Incarnation, *Lettres historiques*, 10 September 1646, 49.
392 CA, 413.
393 Ibid., 410.
394 Ibid., 425.
395 Sagard, *Le grand voyage du pays des Hurons*, 92-3 (134).
396 JR (1638-9), 15:157; (1643-4), 27:63-7; (1644-5), 28:39-45; (1648-9), 34:197-9.

CHAPTER 4:
HURONIA AND IROQUOIA

1 JR (1635), 8:47-51; (1639), 17:21-7; (1639), 17:21-7, 45-9; (1640-1), 21: 143-5.
2 JR (1633), 5:259-61; (1636), 10:241-7.
3 JR (1633), 5:261.
4 Trudel, *Histoire de la Nouvelle-France*, 2:339, 391.
5 JR (1639), 17:9-15; (1644-5), 28:63-5.
6 JR (1640-41), 21:141; (1642), 23:19-21; (1647-8), 33:75-7; (1648-9), 33:252-3, 256-7.
7 My analysis of missionary and Huron interrelationships is based on two articles by Pierre Bourdieu: 'Genèse et structure du champ religieux,' 295-334, and 'Une interprétation de la théorie de la religion,' 3-21.
8 JR (1635), 8:123-5.
9 JR (1636), 10:197-201; (1637), 13:103-5.
10 JR (1648-9), 34:207-8. See also (1638-9), 15:158.
11 Bourdieu, 'Genèse et structure du champ religieux,' 318.
12 JR (1647), 31:125. See also (1640), 19:213-15; (1645), 29:31-3; (1651-2), 38:39-41; (1653), 39:261, 40:23.
13 JR (1636), 10:117-21.
14 JR (1637), 13:199-201.
15 JR (1638-9), 15:158; (1639), 16:241-53, 17:9-53.
16 Radisson, *Voyages*, 93. Trudel, *Histoire de la Nouvelle-France*, 2:384-92.
17 JR (1634), 6:145.
18 Ibid., 145-7.
19 JR (1635), 8:11-15.
20 JR (1642-3), 23:271; (1643-4), 26:35-7; (1644-5), 27:139-41; (1660-1), 46:197.
21 JR (1635), 8:75.
22 JR (1636), 9:283-91; (1637), 12:241-55;

(1639), 16:33-5; (1642), 22:309-11. CA, 547.
23 JR (1649-50), 35:233-5.
24 JR (1635), 8:113; for fireworks, see also (1637), 11:67-9.
25 JR (1638), 15:139; (1639), 17:39.
26 JR (1642), 23:23; (1640-1), 20:221-31; (1645-6), 29:179-81.
27 JR (1638), 15:137-9; (1640), 19:127-35; (1640-1), 21:141-5; (1642), 23:19-27; (1643-4), 26:201-15; (1645-6), 29:179-81; (1647-8), 33:75-7; (1648-9), 33:254-5, 34:223-5. CA, 666, 669, 681.
28 JR (1635), 8:113; (1638), 15:121-3; (1653-4), 41:109-11.
29 JR (1637), 12:107-8; (1638), 15:17-19, 121; (1650-1), 37:39; (1666-7), 50:299. Gagnon, *La conversion par l'image*, 15-46.
30 JR (1634), 6:181.
31 JR (1634), 7:189.
32 JR (1637), 12:141-3; (1638), 15:139; (1639), 17:119; (1646), 30:67-9.
33 JR (1647-8), 33:217-23.
34 JR (1634), 7:101.
35 JR (1634), 7:131.
36 JR (1634), 7:131-7.
37 JR (1634), 7:131; (1636), 10:13; (1639), 17:11.
38 JR (1637), 13:103-5, 14:27-9; (1647-8), 33:203-5, 217-19.
39 Sagard, *Le grand voyage du pays des Hurons*, 110-11 (158-9). JR (1637), 13:169-71; (1639), 17:147, 179-89; (1642), 23:159; (1648-9), 34:107-9, 217.
40 JR (1637), 13:181.
41 JR (1636), 10:185-9, 197-209; (1637), 13:179-83, 213-17; (1640), 19:81-3; (1661-2), 47:177-81.
42 JR (1635), 8:89; (1637), 13:165, 219; (1638), 15:115; (1640), 19:91-5, 20:81-5.
43 JR (1637), 13:101-5; (1639), 17:47-9.
44 JR (1637), 12:71-5, 13:105; (1642), 22:293-5; (1647-8), 33:203-7.
45 JR (1636), 8:251-3; (1638), 15:13-17, 23-5, 33-5; (1642-3), 24:25-7.
46 JR (1638), 15:29.
47 JR (1638), 15:29-31. See also (1637), 14:37.
48 JR (1637), 12:85-91, 13:213-15, 14:7-11, 17.
49 JR (1638), 15:17-19.
50 JR (1637), 14:9.

51 *JR* (1638), 15:49.
52 Idem.
53 *JR* (1637), 13:215-17.
54 *JR* (1638), 15:21; (1655-6), 42:73.
55 *JR* (1640), 19:153, 175-7, 193-5, 213-17, 20:27-9, 61-3, 73-5; (1640-1), 21:177; (1642), 23:141-3; (1644), 25:109-13.
56 *JR* (1640), 20:67-9.
57 Ibid., 47-8.
58 Ibid., 51-3.
59 Ibid., 73-5.
60 *JR* (1640-1), 21:179.
61 Ibid., 205.
62 Ibid., 205-17.
63 *JR* (1640), 19:209-11; (1642), 23:179-81.
64 *JR* (1643-4), 27:25.
65 *JR* (1640), 19:135; (1645-6), 29:179-81.
66 *JR* (1644-5), 28:57.
67 *CA*, 473-4.
68 Ibid., 478.
69 Ibid., 476. *JR* (1633), 5:255.
70 Ibid., 241.
71 Idem.
72 *JR* (1637), 14:17.
73 Ibid., 53.
74 *JR* (1637), 12:247.
75 Larocque, 'L'introduction de maladies européennes,' 22.
76 *JR* (1637), 12:243-5.
77 Ibid., 251.
78 *JR* (1639), 16:219.
79 *JR* (1648-9), 34:227.
80 *JR* (1639), 16:59-61, 17:61-3.
81 *JR* (1637), 13:167-9.
82 *JR* (1638-9), 15:187-9.
83 *JR* (1640), 19:123.
84 *JR* (1642), 23:23-5, 101-3.
85 *JR* (1645-6), 30:23.
86 *JR* (1647-8), 32:179, 33:69.
87 Ibid., 33:69.
88 *JR* (1648-9), 34:227.
89 Idem. See also (1648-9), 33:227, 34:83.
90 *JR* (1637), 12:89-91, 14:7-9, 41-3; (1639), 17:189-91; (1640), 19:219-27; (1662-3), 48:123.
91 *JR* (1636), 9:283-5; (1637), 12:47.
92 *JR* (1636), 9:283; (1637), 12:41.
93 Ibid., 75.
94 *JR* (1638), 14:231-3.
95 *JR* (1636), 9:233.

96 Marie de l'Incarnation, *Lettres historiques*, 3 September 1640, 23-4. Groulx, 'Missionnaires de l'Est en Nouvelle-France,' 62-5. See also *JR* (1647-8), 32:213-15.
97 *JR* (1639), 16:251.
98 *JR* (1645-6), 29:257-9; (1647-8), 33:141-3.
99 *JR* (1637), 13:209.
100 *JR* (1639), 17:11.
101 *JR* (1638), 15:77.
102 Idem.
103 *JR* (1640), 19:247-51.
104 *JR* (1640-1), 21:157-9.
105 *JR* (1638), 15:95-9.
106 *JR* (1640), 19:151.
107 *JR* (1640), 20: 63-5; (1640-1), 21:155-7.
108 *JR* (1640), 19:137-45.
109 *JR* (1638), 15:115-17.
110 *JR* (1639), 17:47-9.
111 *JR* (1638), 15:121.
112 *JR* (1640), 19:211-27.
113 Ibid., 211-15.
114 Ibid., 245-7.
115 *JR* (1640), 20:63.
116 *JR* (1640), 19:249-51.
117 *JR* (1639), 17:51-5.
118 *JR* (1640-1), 21:155.
119 *JR* (1641-2), 21:161-3; (1642), 23:43-67.
120 *JR* (1639), 17:33, 95; (1642-3), 24:237-9.
121 *JR* (1640-1), 20:231, 21:147-9; (1642-3), 24:239-41, 25:25-7.
122 *JR* (1645-6), 29:277-9.
123 *JR* (1642), 23:27.
124 Ibid., 199-201.
125 *JR* (1642-3), 25:27. See also 24:233-9, (1644-5), 28:89-91.
126 *JR* (1642), 23:81-3.
127 Ibid., 89-91.
128 *JR* (1643-4), 25:111.
129 *JR* (1643-4), 26:265-7; (1645-6), 29:273-9, 30:75.
130 *JR* (1637), 13:127, 14:15.
131 *JR* (1637), 13:141.
132 *JR* (1645-6), 29:277-9.
133 *JR* (1644-5), 28:87-9.
134 *JR* (1647-8), 33:141; (1645-6), 29:257-9.
135 *JR* (1648-9), 34:217.
136 *JR* (1648-9), 34:105-7.
137 *JR* (1645-6), 28:87.
138 *JR* (1639), 17:53.

139 JR (1640), 19:127-9.
140 JR (1639), 17:37-9.
141 Ibid., 25-7; (1640), 20:51-3.
142 Ibid., 57-61.
143 JR (1640-1), 21:235.
144 JR (1642), 23:105-7.
145 JR (1643-4), 27:69; see also 105-9.
146 Ibid., 111.
147 JR (1655-6), 42:73.
148 Bourdieu, 'Une interprétation de la théorie de la religion,' 9.
149 JR (1637), 14:9.
150 M. Weber, Wirtschaft und Gesellschaft, 1:385, cited by Bourdieu, 'Une interprétation de la théorie de la religion,' 9.
151 Bourdieu, 'Genèse et structure du champ religieux,' 313.
152 Bourdieu, 'Une interprétation de la théorie de la religion,' 9.
153 Bourdieu, 'Genèse et structure du champ religieux,' 315.
154 Bourdieu, 'Une interprétation de la théorie de la religion,' 10.
155 JR (1636), 10:231-3.
156 Ibid., 303.
157 JR (1643-4), 26:307.
158 JR (1647-8), 33:205.
159 JR (1642), 23:125.
160 Ibid., 187.
161 Ibid., 129.
162 JR (1635), 8:95.
163 CA, 424.
164 JR (1634), 6:181.
165 Bourdieu, 'Genèse et structure du champ religieux,' 298.
166 JR (1642), 23:193.
167 JR (1647-8), 32:195-219; (1650-1), 37:51-61.
168 Marie de l'Incarnation, Lettres historiques, 35, 52, 55.
169 JR (1647), 31:155, 32:49-53.
170 JR (1639), 17:51. See also Marie de l'Incarnation, Lettres historiques, 1 September 1639, 22.
171 JR (1645-6), 30:19-21; see also (1643-4), 26:217-57.
172 JR (1642), 23:109.
173 JR (1642), 23:73; see also (1638), 15:107; (1642), 23:63, 73, 193; (1643-4), 26:229; (1647-8), 32:215-19.
174 JR (1650-1), 37:59.
175 JR (1647-8), 32:217.
176 JR (1645-6), 29:75.
177 JR (1645-6), 30:39.
178 Idem.
179 Sagard, Histoire du Canada, 318; Sagard, Le grand voyage du pays des Hurons, 119 (171).
180 JR (1657-8), 44:281.
181 JR (1662-3), 48:169; (1645-6), 39:30.
182 JR (1637), 12:69-71.
183 Marcuse, Eros and Civilization, 16.
184 Ibid., 12, 38.
185 Ibid., 31-5.
186 Olivier, Les enfants de Jocaste, 67; see also 32, 65-72, 162-5, 176, 181.
187 Godelier, 'La pensée de Marx et d'Engels,' 112-13.
188 JR (1635), 7:295-7; (1642), 23:141-3; (1645-6), 29:273-5.
189 JR (1639), 17:115-17; (1640), 20:61; (1642), 23:67; (1645-6), 30:23-5; (1647-8), 32:195-9.
190 JR (1642-3), 23:267.
191 JR (1643-4), 26:287.
192 JR (1645-6), 30:47.
193 JR (1645-6), 29:273-9.
194 JR (1644), 26:219-21; (1656-7), 43:215-17.
195 JR (1640-1), 21:77; (1651-2), 38:63-7.
196 JR (1633), 5:259; (1640), 19:125; see also the index under 'saint,' 73:309.
197 JR (1642), 23:151; (1644-5), 28:47-55.
198 JR (1642), 23:187.
199 Idem.
200 JR (1640), 13:217-21.
201 JR (1645-6), 30:61-3.
202 JR (1642), 23:135-7.
203 JR (1645-6), 30:103-7.
204 JR (1645-6), 29:193; (1647-8), 32:199.
205 JR (1648-9), 34:217.
206 Ibid., 105.
207 Ibid., 217.
208 JR (1657-8), 44:297.
209 JR (1637), 12:61.
210 JR (1639), 17:131-3.
211 JR (1640), 19:211.
212 JR (1648-9), 34:111.
213 JR (1656-7), 43:283-5.
214 Marcuse, Eros and Civilization, 35-8, 65-6.
215 JR (1642), 23:53.

216 Ibid., 93.
217 JR (1639), 17:209.
218 Ibid., 201; (1636), 10:167.
219 JR (1645-6), 29:75-7.
220 Marcuse, *Eros and Civilization*, 38-9.
221 Champlain, *Oeuvres*, 512. Sagard, *Le grand voyage du pays des Hurons*, 51 (75).
222 JR (1637), 13:51.
223 Castilla Del Pino, 'Sexualité et pouvoir,' 13.
224 JR (1638), 14:235.
225 JR (1645-6), 29:187-9.
226 JR (1642), 23:187-91.
227 JR (1639), 16:251; (1640-1), 21:135-7; (1643-4), 27:65.
228 JR (1639), 16:41; (1642-3), 24:47; (1655-6), 42:147. See also (for the Iroquois) (1656-7), 44:37.
229 JR (1637), 13:141.
230 JR (1637), 14:17-19.
231 JR (1645-6), 30:33.
232 JR (1642), 23:173-5.
233 Ibid., 193.
234 Ibid., 163-5.
235 JR (1643-4), 27:23.
236 JR (1647-8), 33:183-5.
237 JR (1643-4), 25:119-23; (1638), 15:107-9; (1642), 23:63; (1642-3), 24:47-9; (1642), 23:71-3; (1643-4), 26:229; (1647-8), 32:215.
238 Sagard, *Histoire du Canada*, 319.
239 Sagard, *Le grand voyage du pays des Hurons*, 120 (173).
240 Sagard, *Histoire du Canada*, 319; Sagard, *Le grand voyage du pays des Hurons*, 120-1 (173).
241 JR (1645-6), 29:79.
242 Sagard, *Le grand voyage du pays des Hurons*, 117 (169). JR (1642), 22:287-9.
243 JR (1642), 22:289.
244 JR (1655-6), 42:135, 147.
245 JR (1634), 6:181-5.
246 JR (1639), 17:153-5.
247 Ibid., 169-201.
248 Ibid., 167.
249 Ibid., 171.
250 Ibid., 175.
251 Ibid., 179.
252 Ibid., 185.
253 Ibid., 189-91.
254 JR (1640-1), 21:163; (1647), 31:157.

255 JR (1634), 6:187-9, 7:127-35; (1635), 7:279-81, 8:123-5, 145-7. My thanks to Alain Beaulieu for having suggested this line of research.
256 JR (1640-1), 21:161.
257 JR (1642), 23:47.
258 Ibid., 49.
259 Ibid., 51.
260 Ibid., 87.
261 JR (1647), 31:133; (1647-8), 33:211-13.
262 JR (1643-4), 27:71.
263 JR (1642), 23:55-7.
264 JR (1637), 13:197-9, 227; (1640), 19:219-23.
265 JR (1642), 23:189-91.
266 JR (1639), 17:191.
267 JR (1637), 13:127; see also (1634), 7:133-5; (1639), 17:9-11.
268 Driver, *Indians of North America*, 396-402.
269 JR (1637), 13:73, 37-83; (1638-9), 15:187. See also Champlain, *Oeuvres*, 527-8, 823.
270 JR (1637), 13:75.
271 Ibid., 55. See also Radisson, *Voyages*, 37.
272 JR (1637), 13:55-7.
273 Ibid., 79.
274 Weinmann, 'Le cannibalisme pour demain?' 27.
275 JR (1644-5), 27:137.
276 JR (1645-6), 29:235.
277 Ibid., 235-7.
278 JR (1639), 17:131; (1644-5), 28:49-51.
279 JR (1640), 19: 213-15; (1645-6), 29:33-5; (1651-2), 38:37-9.
280 JR (1642), 23:185.
281 JR (1639), 17:137-9.
282 JR (1644-5), 28:85-9.
283 JR (1649), 34:105-9.
284 JR (1634), 6:181; (1644-5), 28:47-9.
285 JR (1642), 23:187; (1644-5), 28:55-7.
286 Ibid., 47-55.
287 JR (1637), 13:169.
288 Ibid., 169-71.
289 JR (1637), 13:171.
290 JR (1644-5), 28:53.
291 Champlain, *Oeuvres*, 2:585.
292 JR (1633), 5:231.
293 JR (1636), 9:207.
294 JR (1640), 19:135-7.
295 JR (1642), 23:127.
296 Ibid., 67.

297 *JR* (1639), 17:117; see also 41-3.

298 *JR* (1642), 23:141-3.

299 Ibid., 135.

300 *JR* (1645-6), 30:23-7; (1647-8), 32:199.

301 *JR* (1640), 20:61-5; (1642), 23:53-7; (1637), 14:99-105.

302 *JR* (1637), 13:217-21.

303 *JR* (1640-1), 21:77-9; (1647-8), 32:215-19, 33:231-3.

304 *JR* (1642), 23:191-7.

305 Ibid., 137-9, 163-5.

306 *JR* (1643-4), 26:171-81; (1637), 12:253-7.

307 *JR* (1642-3), 25:35-7.

308 *JR* (1643-4), 26:303-5.

309 *JR* (1645-6), 29:273-5.

310 Idem.

311 *JR* (1642), 23:155.

312 *JR* (1648-9), 34:107.

313 *JR* (1640-1), 21:75-9; (1649-50), 35:165-7.

314 *JR* (1645-6), 30:25.

315 *JR* (1645-6), 30:27.

316 Ibid., 29-31.

317 *JR* (1647-8), 33:231.

318 Idem.

319 Idem.

320 *JR* (1636), 9:95-7.

321 *JR* (1655-6), 42:135; (1648-9), 34:225-7.

322 *JR* (1663-4), 49:151-3; (1651-2), 38:61-3; (1652-3), 40:161-2; (1655-6), 42:41, 57-9; (1656-7), 43:263-5, 313; (1664-5), 49:257.

323 *JR* (1654-6), 41:213-15; (1663-4), 49:151-3.

324 *JR* (1653-4), 41:87-9.

325 *JR* (1656-7), 43:103.

326 Idem.

327 *JR* (1657-8), 44:151.

328 *JR* (1652-3), 38:247-9.

329 *JR* (1656-7), 43:297-9. Radisson, *Voyages*, 122.

330 *JR* (1659-60), 45:207.

331 *JR* (1669-70), 54:81.

332 *JR* (1656-7), 44:21.

333 *JR* (1656-7), 43:293-5.

334 *JR* (1662-3), 48:169-71.

335 *JR* (1656-7), 43:293-5.

336 Radisson, *Voyages*, 38-9, 40-3, 52, 59-61, 63, 77, 85. See also *JR* (1647), 30:255-7; (1647-8), 34:115; (1649-50), 35:247-51; (1652-3), 40:131-41; (1655-6), 42:107-11, 187-91. *CA*, 827.

337 *JR* (1647-8), 32:173-5; (1659-60), 46:85-7.

338 *JR* (1656-7), 43:295. See also Radisson, *Voyages*, 58, 72, 73, 76, 77.

339 *JR* (1655-6), 42:187-9. Radisson, *Voyages*, 121.

340 *JR* (1655-6), 42:137. See also (1648-9), 34:117-19; (1649-50), 35:247-9; (1656-7), 43:299-301.

341 *JR* (1660-1), 47:53. Radisson, *Voyages*, 43.

342 *JR* (1662-3), 48:169-73.

343 *JR* (1655-6), 42:57.

344 *JR* (1659-60), 45:102.

345 *CA*, 837-40.

346 Ibid., 286. *JR* (1640-1), 21:201; (1656-7), 44:37-9.

347 *CA*, 83.

348 Morgan, *League of the Iroguois*, 70-5.

349 Megapolensis, 'A Short Account of the Mohawk Indians,' 176. D.P. De Vries, 'Voyages from Holland,' 94.

350 *JR* (1655-6), 42:109-11; (1669-70), 53:183-5.

351 Megapolensis, 'A Short Account of the Mohawk Indians,' 177-8. D.P. De Vries, 'Voyages from Holland,' 96.

352 Van der Donck, *A Description of the New Netherlands*, 103.

353 *JR* (1656-7), 43:289-91, 307-9.

354 Radisson, *Voyages*, 93.

355 *JR* (1655-6), 42:31-3; (1656-7), 43:99, 101, 103.

356 *JR* (1647), 30:221-3; (1649-50), 35:167-9; (1652-3), 40:129-33; (1655-6), 42:151; (1656-7), 43:287-9, 307-9.

357 Trelease, *Indian Affairs in Colonial New York*, 118.

358 *JR* (1656-7), 43:107-9.

359 *JR* (1657-8), 44:149-53; (1652-3), 40:219.

360 *JR* (1657-8), 44:165-7.

361 *JR* (1660-1), 47:111.

362 *JR* (1650-1), 37:35-9; (1652-3), 40:179-81; (1655-6), 42:229; (1660-1), 46:275-7; (1662-3), 48:75-9, 101-3, 131-3; (1664-5), 49:231-3; (1666-7), 51:43-5, 53-5.

363 *JR* (1655-6), 42:57, 179-81.

364 *JR* (1653-4), 41:91-129.

365 *JR* (1655-6), 42:61-83.

366 Ibid., 95-7.

367 Ibid., 87.

368 *JR* (1656-7), 43:297.
369 *JR* (1655-6), 42:91.
370 Ibid., 127-9.
371 Ibid., 39-41, 43-5, 119-21.
372 Ibid., 229-33; (1656-7), 43:99-103, 179-85.
373 *JR* (1656-7), 127-55; (1657-8), 44:185-7.
374 *JR* (1656-7), 43:147-51.
375 Ibid., 147-67.
376 Ibid., 171.
377 *JR* (1655-6), 42:95-7; (1656-7), 43:147-61, 179-81; (1657-8), 44:185-7, 225.
378 *JR* (1656-7), 43:297-305, 44:21-41.
379 *JR* (1656-7), 43:297.
380 *JR* (1655-6), 42:153-7.
381 *JR* (1656-7), 44:37.
382 *JR* (1655-6), 42:139-41.
383 Ibid., 153-67.
384 *JR* (1656-7), 43:297.
385 *JR* (1655-6), 42:187; (1656-7), 44:25. Marie de l'Incarnation, *Lettres historiques*, 9 September 1655, 92; October 1661, 134.
386 *JR* (1653-4), 41:119.
387 *JR* (1663-4), 49:107.
388 *JR* (1656-7), 43:297-9.
389 *JR* (1655-6), 42:187.
390 *JR* (1656-7), 43:215-17.
391 M. Weber, *Wirtschaft und Gesellschaft*, 2:893, cited in Bourdieu, 'Genèse et structure du champ religieux,' 302.
392 *JR* (1659-60), 46:109-11.
393 *JR* (1655-6), 42:201-3.
394 *JR* (1656-7), 43:283-5.
395 Ibid., 309.
396 Ibid., 299.
397 *JR* (1655-6), 42:201-3.
398 *JR* (1656-7), 43:299.
399 Ibid., 313-15.
400 Ibid., 289-91. Radisson, *Voyages*, 115.
401 *JR* (1657-8), 44:153.
402 Ibid., 157-9.
403 *JR* (1659-60), 45:191.
404 *JR* (1661-2), 47:141-5.
405 Ibid., 195.
406 Trelease, *Indian Affairs in Colonial New York*, 127-8, 134.
407 *JR* (1660-1), 47:93.
408 *JR* (1663-4), 49:103.
409 *JR* (1662-3), 48:99.
410 *JR* (1660-1), 46:199.
411 *JR* (1665-6), 50:145-7.

CHAPTER 5:
CONQUER AMERICA AND CONQUER THE ATLANTIC

1 Innis, *The Cod Fisheries*, 69. Kupp, 'Fur Trade Relations,' 7-8.
2 'To the High and Mighty Lords States General of the United Netherlands,' DRCHNY, 2:511.
3 J. De Vries, *The Economy of Europe*, 101-2. Deyon, 'La concurrence internationale des manufactures lainières,' 21.
4 J. De Vries, *The Economy of Europe*, 113-15. Wallerstein, *The Modern World System*, 1:277.
5 Frank, *L'accumulation mondiale 1500-1800*, 120.
6 Idem. See also J. De Vries, *The Economy of Europe*, 100.
7 Deyon, 'La concurrence internationale des manufactures lainières,' 21. Wilson, 'Cloth Production and International Competition,' 104.
8 Hill and Postan, *Histoire économique et sociale de la Grande-Bretagne*, 1:288. Bailyn, *The New England Merchants*, 16. Eggleston, *The Transition of Civilization*, 2. Davis, *The Rise of the Atlantic Economies*, 131.
9 Hill and Postan, *Histoire économique et sociale de la Grande-Bretagne*, 1:345.
10 Ibid., 316.
11 Bailyn, *New England Merchants*, 4.
12 See among others the listed works of C. Nish, A. Van der Donck, D.S. Smith, E.B. Greene, and V.B. Harrington.
13 C. Carroll, *The Timber Economy of Puritan New England*, 80-2.
14 Diamond, 'From Organization to Society,' 470.
15 'Resolution of the States General urging the colonization of New Netherland,' DRCHNY, 1:106. See also 'Mr. Joachimi to the States General, October 25, 1642,' DRCHNY, 1:135.
16 'Proposed articles for the colonization and trade of New Netherland,' DRCHNY, 1:110-14.
17 'Secretary Van Tienhoven's answer to the remonstrance from New

Netherland,' DRCHNY, 1:423. See also JR (1646), 28:108.

18 'Proposed articles,' DRCHNY, 1:114. See also Condon, *New York Beginnings*, 153-4.

19 'Appendix received from My Lord Saye, Read 9th August 1642,' DRCHNY, 1:128-9.

20 'New Amstel, on the Delaware River, from 1659 to 1662,' DRCHNY, 2:187-95.

21 'Proposed articles,' DRCHNY, 1:110.

22 NNN, 259. Kilpatrick, *The Dutch Schools of New Netherland*, 132.

23 'Extract from a letter of Director Stuyvesant ... September 1659,' DRCHNY, 13:107-8.

24 Bailyn, *The New England Merchants*, 16-17.

25 JR (1635), 8:9-11; (1651-2), 38:63-5.

26 Government of Quebec, *Annuaire du Québec, 1968-69*, (Quebec City: Queen's Printer, 1914-80), 174.

27 La Chesnaye, 'Mémoire, 1677,' F³2, Fo. 03R.

28 Debien, 'Engagés pour le Canada,' 190.

29 Marie de l'Incarnation, *Lettres historiques*, 26 August 1644, 30. Also cited in Innis, *Select Documents in Canadian Economic History*, 285-6. Debien, 'Engagés pour le Canada,' 191.

30 Diamond, 'From Organization to Society,' 458.

31 J.B. Wright, *The Cultural Life of the American Colonies*, 56. Radisson, *Voyages*, 79.

32 JR (1659-60), 45:191-201. Marie de l'Incarnation, *Lettres historiques*, 60, 72, 99, 137.

33 Harvey, 'Stagnation économique en Nouvelle-France,' 8.

34 Van der Donck, *A Description of the New Netherlands*, 123.

35 Braudel, *Civilisation matérielle, économie et capitalisme*, 2:213.

36 D. Smith, 'The Demographic History of Colonial New England,' 171.

37 Ibid., 165.

38 JR (1636), 9:139; (1642-3), 23:27; (1652-3), 40:217; (1659-60), 45:193; (1662-3), 48:177. Marie de l'Incarnation, *Lettres historiques*, 10 August 1662, 147.

39 Hill and Postan, *Histoire économique et sociale de la Grande-Bretagne*, 1:265.

40 Charbonneau, *Vie et mort de nos ancêtres*, 133.

41 J. De Vries, *The Dutch Rural Economy*, 109-10.

42 Goubert, *Cent mille provinciaux*, 62.

43 Thomas and Anderson, 'White Population, Labor Force and Extensive Growth,' 650-1.

44 Marie de l'Incarnation, *Lettres historiques*, 30 August 1650, 64. JR (1642-3), 24:159-61.

45 C. Carroll, *The Timber Economy of Puritan New England*, 61.

46 Marie de l'Incarnation, *Lettres historiques*, 26 August 1644, 29. Also cited in Innis, *Select Documents in Canadian Economic History*, 285. See also Kalm, *Travels in North America*, 1:272.

47 Boucher, *Histoire véritable et naturelle*, 141.

48 JR (1662-3), 48:177.

49 Van der Donck, *A Description of the New Netherlands*, 66.

50 Lockbridge, 'Land Population and the Evolution of New England Society,' 66.

51 Dechêne, *Habitants et marchands*, 271-3. JR (1636), 9:155.

52 JR (1633), 6:29; (1650-1), 36:165; (1652-3), 40:215; (1659-60), 45:191-3. Marie de l'Incarnation, *Lettres historiques*, 4 October 1656, 95.

53 D.P. De Vries, 'Voyages from Holland,' 91.

54 Ibid., 99.

55 Champlain, *Oeuvres*, 2:839.

56 NNN, 261.

57 C. Carroll, *The Timber Economy of Puritan New England*, 48. Salwen, 'Indians of Southern New England and Long Island', 170-1.

58 JR (1652-3), 40:215.

59 JR (1642-3), 23:307-9; (1652-3), 40:215; (1662-3), 48:173. Marie de l'Incarnation, *Lettres historiques*, 10 August 1662, 147.

60 JR (1662-3), 48:177. The passenger pigeon has since become extinct.

61 JR (1652-3), 40:217.

62 D.P. De Vries, 'Voyages from Holland,'

30, 100. Van der Donck, *A Description of the New Netherlands*, 28-50.

63 Van der Donck, *A Description of the New Netherlands*, 96. 'Information respecting the Land in New Netherlands, 1650,' DRCHNY, 1:369. See also D.P. De Vries, 'Voyages from Holland,' 98-9 and Kalm, *Travels in North America*, 1:267.

64 D. Brown, *Bury My Heart at Wounded Knee*, 12.

65 D.P. De Vries, 'Voyages from Holland,' 118.

66 JR (1659-60), 45:191-5.

67 Kalm, *Travels in North America*, 1:266-8, 270.

68 Ibid., 285-6.

69 Braudel, *Civilisation matérielle et capitalisme*, 1:100. Braudel, *Civilisation matérielle, économie et capitalisme*, 1:107.

70 Meuvret, *études d'histoire économique*, 20.

71 Braudel, *Civilisation matérielle, économie et capitalisme*, 1:106.

72 Dechêne, *Habitants et marchands*, 345. JR (1636), 9:155-7

73 Goubert, *Cent mille provinciaux*, 99.

74 Braudel, *Civilisation matérielle, économie et capitalisme*, 1:67.

75 C. Carroll, *The Timber Economy of Puritan New England*, 58-9.

76 Ibid., 57.

77 Ibid., 75.

78 Bailyn, *The New England Merchants*, 23-7.

79 C. Carroll, *The Timber Economy of Puritan New England*, 35-7.

80 Bailyn, *The New England Merchants*, 76-7.

81 C. Carroll, *The Timber Economy of Puritan New England*, 75. Bailyn, *The New England Merchants*, 47.

82 C. Carroll, *The Timber Economy of Puritan New England*, 8-9.

83 Ibid., 20.

84 Ibid., 86.

85 Braudel, *Civilisation matérielle, économie et capitalisme*, 1:318.

86 C. Carroll, *The Timber Economy of Puritan New England*, 86.

87 Ibid., 77, 94.

88 Bailyn, *The New England Merchants*, 78.

89 Ibid., 62-71.

90 C. Carroll, *The Timber Economy of Puritan New England*, 87, 137.

91 Bailyn, *The New England Merchants*, 83. Easterbrook and Aitken, *Canadian Economic History*, 65.

92 Braudel, *Civilisation matérielle, économie et capitalisme*, 3:174.

93 Frank, *L'accumulation mondiale 1500-1800*, 122.

94 J. De Vries, *The Economy of Europe*, 120.

95 Ibid., 130-1.

96 Braudel, *Civilisation matérielle, économie et capitalisme*, 3:189.

97 Idem.

98 J. De Vries, *The Economy of Europe*, 136.

99 Braudel, *Civilisation matérielle, économie et capitalisme*, 3:189.

100 Idem. J. De Vries, *The Economy of Europe*, 131.

101 Braudel, *Civilisation matérielle, économie et capitalisme*, 3:89.

102 J. De Vries, *The Economy of Europe*, 132.

103 Braudel, *Civilisation matérielle, économie et capitalisme*, 3:103.

104 Condon, *New York Beginnings*, 145.

105 Braudel, *Civilisation matérielle, économie et capitalisme*, 3:198.

106 Bachman, *Peltries or Plantations*, 50-1.

107 Braudel, *Civilisation matérielle, économie et capitalisme*, 3:45, 197, 198.

108 'Subject reference for the assembly of the XIX, 1638,' DRCHNY, 1:110.

109 'Subjects for consideration of the Assembly of the XIX, 1643,' DRCHNY, 1:135-6; 'Report of the Committee of the States General on the affairs of New Netherland,' DRCHNY, 1:389; see also DRCHNY, 1:155.

110 Van der Donck, *A Description of the New Netherlands*, 129. Flick, *History of the State of New York*, 2:38. Michaelius, 'Letter of Reverend Jonas Michaelius,' 131. De Voe, *The Market Book*, 34.

111 'Cap't Mason to (Mr. Secretary Coke), April 2, 1632,' DRCHNY, 3:16-17.

112 Bachman, *Peltries or Plantations*, 66.

113 Emmer, 'History of the Dutch Slave Trade,' 732.

114 J. De Vries, *The Economy of Europe*, 138.

115 Braudel, *Civilisation matérielle*,

économie et capitalisme, 3:198.

116 Emmer, 'History of the Dutch Slave Trade,' 737.

117 Braudel, *Civilisation matérielle, économie et capitalisme*, 3:198. J. De Vries, *The Economy of Europe*, 138-41.

118 Hill and Postan, *Histoire économique et sociale de la Grande-Bretagne*, 1:373, 376-7.

119 D.P. De Vries, 'Voyages from Holland,' 82.

120 Reed, 'Transaction Costs and Differential Growth,' 189.

121 Andrews, *The Colonial Period of American History*, 3:50.

122 Johnson, *The Law Merchant and Negotiable Instruments*, 5.

123 Bachman, *Peltries or Plantations*, 84. Flick, *History of the State of New York*, 2:40. Tustin, 'Development of the Salt Industry,' 40.

124 'Petition of certain Dutch merchants to the States General, 1651,' DRCHNY, 1:436.

125 'Secret resolution of the States General, p. 23,' DRCHNY, 1:437.

126 Emmer, 'History of the Dutch Slave Trade,' 737.

127 'Reply of the West India Company to the answer of the H.P. Stuyvesant, 1666,' DRCHNY, 2:496.

128 Braudel, *Civilisation matérielle, économie et capitalisme*, 3:220.

129 'To the High and Mighty Lords States General of the United Netherlands,' DRCHNY, 2:511-14. The figure of 25,000 sailors employed on the Brazil coast is surely exaggerated. According to Braudel, the world-wide Dutch fleet numbered about 50,000 sailors c. 1670. *Civilisation matérielle, économie et capitalisme*, 3:159.

130 J. de Vries, *The Dutch Rural Economy*, 111-14. Kula, *Théorie économique du système féodal*, 71. Wilson, 'The Decline of the Netherlands,' 26.

131 Ibid., 24.

132 J. De Vries, *The Economy of Europe*, 123.

133 Braudel, *Civilisation matérielle, économie et capitalisme*, 3:221.

134 Ibid., 161.

135 Kupp, 'Could the Dutch Commercial Empire have Influenced the Canadian Economy?' 387; Kupp, 'Quelques aspects de la dissolution,' 366.

136 Braudel, *Civilisation matérielle, économie et capitalisme*, 2:138, 367.

137 Braudel, *Civilisation matérielle, économie et capitalisme*, 3:295.

138 Delafosse, 'La Rochelle et le Canada,' 470. JR (1655-6), 42:31; (1659-60), 45:31.

139 Marie de l'Incarnation, *Lettres historiques*, 10 September 1652, 86. JR (1652-3), 40:79-81.

140 Easterbrook and Aitken, *Canadian Economic History*, 63.

141 Ibid., 62-3.

142 Marie de l'Incarnation, *Lettres historiques*, 17 September 1660, 119; 23 September 1660, 123-4; 30 August 1650, 60; 17 September 1660, 119. Also cited in Innis, *Select Documents in Canadian Economic History*, 287-8.

143 Marie de l'Incarnation, *Correspondences*, 1 September 1652, 479. Also cited in Trudel, *La seigneurie des Cent-Associés*, 270.

144 JR (1642-3), 23:279. See also (1659-60), 45:221.

145 JR (1652-3), 40:215.

146 Trudel, *La seigneurie des Cent-Associés*, 271.

147 JR (1655-6), 42:225-9.

148 Trudel, *La seigneurie des Cent-Associés*, 271.

149 Ibid., 270-1. Radisson, *Voyages*, 134-72.

150 Marie de l'Incarnation, *Lettres historiques*, 25 June 1660, 97-119. JR (1659-60), 45:245-61. Trudel, *Histoire de la Nouvelle-France*, 1:260-1.

151 Boucher, *Histoire véritable et naturelle*, 137. Marie de l'Incarnation, *Lettres historiques*, 1 September 1652, 87; JR (1664-5), 50:81-3.

152 D.P. De Vries, 'Voyages from Holland,' 125.

153 Van der Donck, *A Description of the New Netherlands*, 29.

154 Bogart, 'New Amsterdam's Windmills Made History,' 5.

155 De Voe, *The Market Book*, 17.

156 Ibid., 29.

157 Ibid., 44. Stokes, *The Iconography of Manhattan Island*, 1:123.

158 Bogart, 'New Amsterdam's Windmills Made History,' 7-10.

159 Trudel, *La seigneurie des Cent-Associés*, 231.

160 Ibid., 212.

161 'Ordonnance de M. Raudot,' C11A-28, Fo. 365R.

162 'Explication sur le traité fait avec le sieur Rozée et Compagnie' [Explanation of the treaty concluded with Sieur Rozée and Company], C111A-1, Fo. 315R.

163 Trudel, *La seigneurie des Cent-Associés*, 238.

164 C11A-1, Fo. 288R and V, October 1661.

165 Boucher, *Histoire véritable et naturelle*, 137. Marie de l'Incarnation, *Lettres historiques*, 13 September 1651, 61. Dechêne, *Habitants et marchands*, 142-3.

166 Van der Donck, *A Description of the New Netherlands*, 93.

167 De Voe, *The Market Book*, 29, 36.

168 Bogart, 'Currency Crisis in New Amsterdam,' 6.

169 Finegan, 'Colonial Schools and Colleges in New York,' 169.

170 Wood, 'Sketch of the First Settlement,' 14-16.

171 Braudel, *Civilisation matérielle et capitalisme*, 1:371. Van der Donck, *A Description of the New Netherlands*, 37. *JR* (1645-6), 28:106. Stokes, *The Iconography of Manhattan Island*, 1:119-31.

172 Stokes, *The Iconography of Manhattan Island*, 119-31. Marie de l'Incarnation, *Lettres historiques*, 28 August 1642, 29. *JR* (1650-1), 36:173-5.

173 Van der Donck, *A Description of the New Netherlands*, 22.

174 C. Carroll, *The Timber Economy of Puritan New England*, 8-9.

175 Van der Donck, *A Description of the New Netherlands*, 22.

176 Carroll, *The Timber Economy of Puritan New England*, 27.

177 Van der Donck, *A Description of the New Netherlands*, 21-2, 61. See also Wood, 'Sketch of the First Settlement,' 3.

178 Van der Donck, *A Description of the New Netherlands*, 18.

179 Ibid., 51. D.P. De Vries, 'Voyages from Holland,' 110. *JR* (1662-3), 48:179.

180 Marcuse, *Eros and Civilization*, 216.

181 Braudel, *Civilisation matérielle, économie et capitalisme*, 1:317-18.

182 Van der Donck, *A Description of the New Netherlands*, 60. D.P. De Vries, 'Voyages from Holland,' 28.

183 Boucher, *Histoire véritable et naturelle*, 16.

184 Van der Donck, *A Description of the New Netherlands*, 97-8.

185 Ibid., 96.

186 Séguin, *La civilisation traditionelle de l'habitant*, 560-5. C. Carroll, *The Timber Economy of Puritan New England*, 63. Van der Donck, *A Description of the New Netherlands*, 41. Kalm, *Travels in North America*, 1:269.

187 Idem. Van der Donck, *A Description of the New Netherlands*, 24.

188 Kalm, *Travels in North America*, 1:269.

189 Washburn, *The Indian and the White Man*, document 20:63-6.

190 Salwen, 'Indians of Southern New England and Long Island,' 170.

191 Wood, 'Sketch of the First Settlement,' 66.

192 W. Simons, 'Narragansett,' 170.

193 Ibid., 172. Washburn, 'Seventeenth-Century Indian Wars,' 89-92.

194 Kalm, *Travels in North America*, 1:270. Jennings, *The Invasion of America*, 122.

195 Anonymous, 'Journal of New Netherland,' 273. The same document can be found in *DRCHNY*, 1:182. D.P. De Vries, 'Voyages from Holland,' 97-8.

196 Ibid., 98.

197 Anonymous, 'Journal of New Netherland,' 276.

198 Idem.

199 D. Brown, *Bury My Heart at Wounded Knee*, 2-3.

200 D.P. De Vries, 'Voyages from Holland,' 115-17.

201 Ibid., 118.

202 'The Eight men to the Amsterdam Chamber of the West India Company, October 28, 1644,' *DRCHNY*, 1:209-13.

203 Flick, *History of the State of New York,*
    1:304-19. De Voe, *The Market Book,* 34.
    Trelease, *Indian Affairs in Colonial New
    York,* 126-31. Ellis et al., *A Short History
    of New York State,* 23. 'Proposals by the
    Esopus Indians, September 4, 1659,'
    DRCHNY, 3:106-7.
204 J. Duffy, *Epidemics in Colonial America,*
    cited in Johnson, *The Law Merchant and
    Negotiable Instruments,* 58.
205 Bogart, 'Currency Crisis in New
    Amsterdam,' 6-7.
206 I have based my discussion largely on
    G.F. Stanley's excellent article, 'The First
    Indian "Reserves" in Canada,' 178-85.
    See also Groulx, 'Missionnaires de l'Est
    en Nouvelle-France,' 55-6. JR (1656-7),
    43:221.
207 JR (1645-6), 29:75-81; (1649-50), 35:237-9.
208 JR (1637), 12:221.
209 T.J.C. Brasser, 'The Coastal
    Algonquians,' 78.
210 Tooker, 'History of Research,' 5.
211 Marie de l'Incarnation, *Lettres his-
    toriques,* 26 August 1637, 93. See also JR
    (1650-1), 37:77-9; (1653-4), 41:139-41;
    (1663-4), 49:75-7.
212 JR (1642-3), 24:23.
213 JR (1637), 12:79.
214 JR (1649-50), 35:237.
215 Idem. Marie de l'Incarnation, *Lettres
    historiques,* 10 September 1646, 43.
216 JR (1650-1), 36:193-5.
217 JR (1639), 16:77-9.
218 JR (1642-3), 24:23-5; (1659-60), 45:39-41.
219 JR (1642-3), 24:21; (1647), 31:155-7; (1653-
    4), 41:139.
220 JR (1652-3), 40:241.
221 JR (1639), 16:251; (1645-6), 29:73-5.
222 JR (1647-8), 33:177-9.
223 JR (1663-4), 49:79.
224 JR (1642-3), 24:47-9; see also (1649-50),
    35:241. Marie de l'Incarnation, *Lettres
    historiques,* 44.
225 JR (1653-4), 41:143; see also (1660-1),
    47:53-5.
226 JR (1648-9), 34:111.
227 JR (1656-7), 43:243-9.
228 Marie de l'Incarnation, *Lettres his-
    toriques,* 1647, 55-6.

229 Brenner, 'To Pray or to Be Prey,' 140.
230 JR (1659-60), 45:37.
231 Ibid., 41-3.
232 Sagard, *Le Grand voyage du pays des
    Hurons,* 77 (112). JR (1635), 8:127-9.
233 JR (1656-7), 43:271-3.
234 Boucher, *Histoire véritable et naturelle,* 98.
235 JR (1634), 6:231.
236 Van der Donck, *A Description of the
    New Netherlands,* 98. Sagard, *Le grand
    voyage du pays des Hurons,* 66 (96-7),
    70 (102), 72 (105). Boucher, *Histoire
    véritable et naturelle,* 98, 114-15. Driver,
    Indians of North America, 342. Jacquin,
    *Histoire des Indiens d'Amérique du
    Nord,* 55-6.

CHAPTER 6:
THE REBIRTH OF
EUROPEAN SOCIETIES
IN NORTH AMERICA

1 'Ordonnance du Gouverneur de Lauzon
  qui oblige tous les Français à se rendre à
  leur travail avec leurs armes à feu'
  [Ordinance issued by Governor Lauzon
  forcing all Frenchmen to go to work
  bearing firearms], RAPQ, 1924-5, 390,
  cited in Harris, *The Seigneurial System
  in Early Canada,* 205.
2 Rocher, 'The Relations between Church
  and State in New France,' v-viii.
3 Ibid., viii, 23.
4 Marie de l'Incarnation, *Lettres historiques,* 26 August 1644, 30; 13
  September 1651, 64-5.
5 'Titre pour la fondation des Religieuses
  hospitalières Québec, avril 1639'
  [Founding charter for the Hospitalière
  nuns of Quebec, April 1639], C11A-1, Fo.
  117R.
6 'Titre de l'Établissement des Religieuses
  Ursulines à Québec, mai 1639'
  [Founding charter for the Ursuline
  nuns of Quebec, May 1639], C11A-1, Fo.
  158R.
7 D'Argenson, letter of 14 October 1658,
  cited in Dechêne, *Habitants et
  marchands,* 79, n. 106. See also Leclerc,
  'Le mariage sous le régime français,' 52.

8 'Articles accordés entre les Directeurs et associés en la Compagnie de la Nouvelle France et les députés des habitants du dit pays, 6 mars 1645,' C¹¹A-1 Fo. 213R, 212R-228R; 'Confirmation de la concession accordée aux Religieuses hospitalières de Québec de 24 arpents de terres situés sur la rivière St Charles le 16 avril 1642,' C¹¹A-1 Fo. 128R-129R; 'Concession accordée par la Compagnie de la Nouvelle-France au sr Beauvais pour les Ursulines de Québec de douze arpents de terre ..., 15 janv 1637,' C¹¹A-1 Fo. 160R; 'Concession accordée aux Religieuses ursulines de six Arpents ou environ de terres ..., 28 sept 1639,' C¹¹A-1 Fo. 163R; 'Concession de l'isle de Montréal par la Compagnie de la Nouvelle-France ... à Pierre Chevrier ... et Jerosme Le Royer sieur de la Dauversiere ..., 7 déc 1640,' C¹¹A-1 Fo. 190R-194R.

9 Lanctot, *Histoire du Canada*, 1:210-11.

10 *JR* (1643-4), 27:84.

11 Trudel, 'Les obligations des censitaires,' 37-41.

12 Marie de l'Incarnation, *Lettres historiques*, 13 September 1651, 64.

13 Trudel, 'Les obligations des censitaires,' 41.

14 Ibid., 3-41 for the basic details that follow. See also Rocher, 'Relations between Church and State in New France,' 32-5, 53, 198 and Harris, *The Seigneurial System in Early Canada*, 21-5.

15 Bois, *Crise du le féodalisme*, 352-5. Monière, 'L'utilité du concept de mode de production,' 497; see also 483-502.

16 Nissenson, *The Patroon's Domain*, 171-2.

17 Rife, 'Land Tenure in New Netherland,' 67-8.

18 Ibid., 70-1. Van Laer, *Van Rensselaer Bowier Manuscripts*, 755-7, 771.

19 Nissenson, *The Patroon's Domain*, 819. Bachman, *Peltries or Plantations*, 95-139. Leach, *The Northern Colonial Frontier*, 21. Trelease, *Indian Affairs in Colonial New York*, 43. Condon, *New York Beginnings*, 127. Sutherland, *Population Distribution in Colonial America*, 64.

20 Anonymous, 'Journal of New Netherland,' *DRCHNY*, 1:182 and also in *NNN*, 274.

21 'Proposed Articles for the Colonization and Trade of New Netherland,' *DRCHNY*, 1:110-14. See also Rife, 'Land Tenure in New Netherland,' 63.

22 'Draft of Freedoms and Exemptions for New Netherland,' *DRCHNY*, 1:401-5.

23 Flick, *History of the State of New York*, 1:247-8.

24 Rife, 'Land Tenure in New Netherland,' 53.

25 Ibid., 55-6.

26 Ibid., 60.

27 Trudel, *Initiation à la Nouvelle-France*, 193.

28 Wood, 'Sketch of the First Settlement,' 85-6.

29 De Voe, *The Market Book*, 41.

30 Anonymous, 'Journal of New Netherland' (1638), *NNN*, 273. See also *DRCHNY*, 1:182 and D.P. De Vries, 'Voyages from Holland,' 100.

31 Braudel, *Civilisation matérielle, économie et capitalisme*, 3:335.

32 Ibid., 345.

33 Genovese, *Économie politique de l'esclavage*, 50, 62, n. 4, 104.

34 Jane and Vigneras, *The Journal of Christopher Columbus*, cited in W.E. Washburn, *The Indian and the White Man*, 2-5.

35 Braudel, *Civilisation matérielle, économie et capitalisme*, 3:375.

36 Diamond, 'From Organization to Society,' 462.

37 Van der Donck, *A Description of the New Netherlands*, 98.

38 Trelease, *Indian Affairs in Colonial New York*, 37.

39 Van der Donck, *A Description of the New Netherlands*, 103.

40 McManus, *A History of Negro Slavery in New York*, 1-22. See also McKee, *Labor in Colonial New York*, 114-69.

41 Van Laer, *Correspondence of Jeremias Van Rensselaer*, cited in McManus, *A History of Negro Slavery in New York*, 5. Michaelius, 'Letter of Reverend Jonas Michaelius,' 129.

42 'Short digest of the excesses and highly injurious neglect which New Netherland has experienced ... January 27, 1650,' DRCHNY, 1:335. McManus, *A History of Negro Slavery in New York*, 13-15.

43 Trudel, *L'esclavage au Canada français*, 3-5. See also JR (1633), 5:197-9.

44 Boucher, *Histoire véritable et naturelle*, 161.

45 Debien, 'Engagés pour le Canada,' 191, 197-8.

46 Ibid., 203.

47 Ibid., 191.

48 Dechêne, *Habitants et marchands*, 56.

49 Mondoux, 'Les hommes de Montréal,' 75. Daveluy, 'Le drame de la recrue de 1653,' 166-7.

50 Debien, 'Engagés pour le Canada,' 193.

51 Ibid., 179, 193.

52 Braudel, *Civilisation matérielle, économie et capitalisme*, 3:340.

53 Diamond, 'From Organization to Society,' 463-4.

54 Ibid., 467.

55 D.P. De Vries, 'Voyages from Holland,' 36, 125.

56 Dechêne, 'La croissance de Montréal,' 172.

57 'Arrét pour défense à tous habitants de la Nouvelle-France d'en sortir sans le congé du Gouverneur, 12 mars 1658' [Decree forbidding all inhabitants of New France from leaving without the Governor's permission, 12 March 1658], C11A-1, Fo. 301R-303R.

58 'Secretary Van Tienhoven's answer to the remonstrance from New Netherland, November 29, 1650,' DRCHNY, 1:428.

59 Dechêne, *Habitants et marchands*, 69.

60 Ibid., 272.

61 Séguin, *La civilisation traditionelle de l'habitant*, 152-4.

62 Boucher, *Histoire véritable et naturelle*, 162.

63 'Information respecting the Land in New Netherland, 1650,' DRCHNY, 1:369. Van der Donck, *A Description of the New Netherlands*, 129.

64 D.P. De Vries, 'Voyages from Holland,' 91.

65 Dechêne, *Habitants et marchands*, 393.

66 Moogk, 'In the Darkness of a Basement,' 403.

67 McKee, *Labor in Colonial New York*, 32.

68 'Petition of the Walloons and French to Sir Dudley Carleton, February 5, 1622,' DRCHNY, 3:9-10.

69 Marx, *Capital*, 839-40.

70 Bridenbaugh, *Cities in the Wilderness*, 1:107-12.

71 De Voe, *The Market Book*, 28.

72 Ibid., 49. McAnear, 'The Place of Freemen in Old New York,' 418.

73 Kilpatrick, *The Dutch Schools of New Netherland*, 128-40.

74 Bailyn, *The New England Merchants*, 37-8.

75 Trudel, 'Les débuts d'une société,' 202.

76 La Chesnaye, 'Mémoire, 1677,' F^{3}2, Fo. 04v.

77 Lanctot, 'Position de la Nouvelle-France,' 526.

78 Bridenbaugh, *Cities in the Wilderness*, 98.

79 Van der Donck, *A Description of the New Netherlands*, 135.

80 Bourdieu and Passeron, *La reproduction*, 19.

81 Trudel, 'Les débuts d'une société,' 186-7.

82 Ibid., 193-202.

83 Bailyn, *The New England Merchants*, 38.

84 Van der Donck, *A Description of the New Netherlands*, 54.

85 Fitchen, *New World Dutch Barn*, 1-23, 77, 115.

86 Stokes, *The Iconography of Manhattan Island*, 87.

87 W.V.H., 'Early Dutch Brought Santa to America,' 6.

88 Bourdieu and Passeron, *La distinction*, 546.

89 Ibid., 545-6.

90 D.P. De Vries, 'Voyages from Holland,' 87.

91 Van der Donck, *A Description of the New Netherlands*, 130.

92 Bridenbaugh, *Cities in the Wilderness*, 1:68.

93 Flick, *History of New York State*, 1:237-8.

94 'Report of the Committee of the States General on the Affairs of New Netherland, 1650,' DRCHNY, 1:389.

95 D.P. De Vries, 'Voyages from Holland,' 101.

96 *JR* (1645-6), 28:106.

97 Johannes Megapolensis, 'A Short Account of the Mohawk Indians,' cited in Pratt, *Religion, Politics and Diversity*, 6-7. See also *NNN*, 392-3.

98 Flick, *History of the State of New York*, 2:14-15.

99 Anonymous, 'Journal of New Netherland' (1638), 272.

100 Pratt, *Religion, Politics and Diversity*, 9-10, 23.

101 Flick, *History of the State of New York*, 2:18, 20.

102 Rocher, 'The Relations between Church and State in New France,' 63-4.

103 *JR* (1642-3), 23:287-9.

104 Rocher, 'The Relations between Church and State in New France,' 69.

105 *JR* (1664-5), 50:85-7.

106 Rocher, 'The Relations between Church and State in New France,' 75-7.

107 Leclerc, 'Le mariage sous le régime français,' 34.

108 Kilpatrick, *The Dutch Schools of New Netherland*, 81.

109 Marie de l'Incarnation, *Lettres historiques*, 1653, 90; see also 3 September 1640, 23, 24; 10 September 1646, 49. *JR* (1650-1), 36:173-5.

110 Lockbridge, 'L'alphabétisation en Amérique 1650-1800,' 504-6.

111 Kilpatrick, *The Dutch Schools of New Netherland*, 228-9.

112 Trudel, *La population du Canada en 1663*, 146, 151.

113 LeRoy Ladurie, *Paysans du Languedoc*, 647.

114 Furet and Ozouf, 'L'alphabétisation en France,' 490-1. See also Stone, 'Literacy and Education in England,' 69-139.

115 Furet and Ozouf, 'L'alphabétisation en France,' 491.

116 'Arrêt du 27 mars 1647, portant réglement concernant les habitants du pays de Canada' [Decree of 27 March 1647 on the regulation concerning the inhabitants of Canada], C11A-1, Fo. 237R-240R.

117 Trudel, *La seigneurie des Cent-Associés*, 175, 191-2.

118 Ibid., 244-9.

119 *JR* (1659-60), 45:35-45.

120 Trudel, *Histoire de la Nouvelle-France*, 1:246-8, 336-8, 357-8.

121 Flick, *History of the State of New York*, 1:280.

122 Ibid., 301-7.

CONCLUSION

1 *JR* (1637), 13:179.

2 Paré, 'Chapeaux Bagg.' This Master's thesis (Université du Québec à Montréal) merits publication.

3 Frank, *Lumpen bourgeoisie: Lumpen développement*, 19, cited in R. Brenner, 'Origins of Capitalist Development,' 86-92. See also Frank, *L'accumulation mondiale, 1500-1800*, 306.

Bibliography

ABBREVIATIONS

Annales ESC   *Annales Économie, Société, Civilisation*

CERM   Centre d'Études et de Recherches Marxistes

CIEE   Centre Inter-universitaire d'Études Européennes

DRCHNY   *Documents Relative to the Colonial History of the State of New York*

JEH   *Journal of Economic History*

JR   *The Jesuit Relations and Allied Documents*

NNN   *Narratives of New Netherland, 1609-1664*

PP   *Past and Present*

RAPQ   *Rapport de l'archiviste de la province de Québec*

RAQ   *Recherches amérindiennes au Québec*

RHAF   *Revue d'Histoire de l'Amérique Française*

CA   *The Children of Aataentsic: A History of the Huron People to 1660*

MANUSCRIPT SOURCES

Archives Nationales, Paris, Archives des colonies, series $C^{11}$and F^{3}

PRINTED SOURCES

An asterisk (*) precedes works containing printed sources.

Acta Historiae Neerlandicae: Studies on the History of the Netherlands. La Haye, Boston, London: Martinus Nijhoff 1978

Adair, E.R. 'The French Canadian Seigneury.' *Canadian Historical Review* 35 (1954):187-207

Allaire, Denise. *Cuisinons nos plantes sauvages.* Montreal: Éditions de l'Aurore 1977

Amerman, Richard H. 'Medical Beginnings in New Netherland.' *De Halve Maen* 31, no. 2 (July 1956):10-11

—. 'Medical Practices in New Netherland.' *De Halve Maen* 31, no. 4 (January 1957):7-9

Amin, Samir. *L'accumulation à l'échelle mondiale.* 2 vols. Paris: 10/18 1970

—. *L'échange inégal et la loi de la valeur.* Paris: Anthropos 1973

Anderson, Perry. *Lineages of the Absolutist State.* London: NLB 1974

Andrews, Charles M. *The Settlements* and *England's Commercial Period of American History.* Vol. 3 and Vol. 4 of *The Colonial Period of American History.* New Haven: Yale University Press 1964

Angelo, Henry and Charles L. Shedd. 'A Note on Berdache.' *American Anthropologist* 57 (1955):121-6

* Anonymous. 'Journal of New Netherland.' In *NNN*, J. Franklin Jameson, 265-84. New York: Charles Scribner 1909. Also in *DRCHNY*, edited by E.B. O'Callaghan, 1:180-90. Albany: A. Weed 1856-77

Assiniwi, Bernard. *Histoire des Indiens du Haut et du Bas-Canada.* 3 vols. Montreal: Leméac 1974

Axtell, James. *The European and the Indian: Essays in the Ethnohistory of Colonial North America.* New York: Oxford University Press 1981

Bachman, Van Cleaf. *Peltries or Plantations: The Economic Policies of the Dutch West India Company in New Netherland, 1623-1639.* Baltimore: Johns Hopkins University Press 1969

Bailey, A.G. *The Conflict of European and Eastern Algonkian Cultures, 1504-1700: A Study in Canadian Civilization.* 2nd ed. Toronto: University of Toronto Press 1969

Bailyn, Bernard. *The New England Merchants in the Seventeenth Century.* New York: Harper & Row, Torchbooks 1964

Banfield, A.W.F. *Les mammifères du Canada.* Quebec: National Museums of Canada and Presses de l'Université Laval 1974

Barbeau, C.M. *Huron and Wyandot Mythology with an Appendix Containing Earlier Published Records.* Anthropological series 11, memoir 80, Department of Mines, Geological Survey, Canada. Ottawa: Government Printing Bureau 1915

Barber, Elinor G. *The Bourgeoisie in 18th-Century France.* Princeton: Princeton University Press 1967

Barbour, Violet. *Capitalism in Amsterdam in the 17th Century.* Baltimore: Johns Hopkins University Press 1950

Barré, Georges and Laurent Girouard. 'La plaine laurentienne, les Iroquois: Premiers agriculteurs.' *RAQ* 7, no. 1-2 (1978):43-54

Barriault, Yvette. *Mythes et rites chez les Indiens Montagnais.* La Société historique de la Côte Nord. Quebec: Laflamme 1971

Bartsch, Werner. 'Gnaws – a Canadian Sequel to "Jaws."' *Maclean's,* 23 October 1978, 14-16

Behar, L. 'Lois de population et science démographique.' *La Pensée,* no. 186 (April 1976):3-26

—. 'Surpopulation relative et reproduction de la force de travail.' *La Pensée,* no. 176 (August 1974):9-29

Berkhofer, Robert F. *Salvation and the Savage: An Analysis of Protestant Missions and American Indian Response, 1787-1862.* New York: Atheneum 1972

Berne, Eric. *Games People Play.* New York: Ballantine Books 1977

Bertaux, Daniel. *Destins personnels et structure de classe.* Paris: Presses Universitaires de France 1977

Bibeau, Pierre. 'Les palissades des sites iroquois.' *RAQ* 10, no. 3 (1980):189-97

Bloch, Marc. *Seigneurie française et manoir anglais.* Paris: Association Marc Bloch 1960

* Bogaert, Harmen Meyndertsen van den. 'Narrative of a Journey into the Mohawk and Oneida Country, 1634-35.' In *NNN*, J. Franklin Jameson, 137-62. New York: Charles Scribner 1909

Bogart, John A. 'Currency Crisis in New Amsterdam.' *De Halve Maen* 32, no. 1 (April 1957):6-7

—. 'The Furtrade in New Netherland.' *De Halve Maen* 34, no. 2 (July 1959):9-10

—. 'New Amsterdam's Windmills Made History.' *De Halve Maen* 35, no. 2 (July 1960):5-6, 9-

10; 35, no. 3 (October 1960):7-8, 10

Bois, Guy. 'Against the Neo-Malthusian Orthodoxy.' *PP*, no. 79 (May 1978):60-9

—. *Crise du féodalisme*. Cahiers de la Fondation nationale des sciences politiques, no. 202. Paris: Éditions de l'École des hautes études en sciences sociales 1976

—. 'A Reply to Professor Brenner Symposium, Agrarian Class Structure and Economic Development in Pre-Industrial Europe.' *PP*, no. 79 (May 1978):55-69

Bottomore, Thomas. *A Dictionary of Marxist Thought*. Cambridge: Harvard University Press 1983

Bouchard, Russel. *Les armes de traite*. Quebec: Boréal Express 1976

* Boucher, Pierre. *Histoire véritable et naturelle des moeurs et productions du pays de la Nouvelle-France vulgairement dite le Canada* (1664). Boucherville: Société historique de Boucherville 1964

Bourdieu, Pierre. *La distinction, critique sociale du jugement*. Paris: Éditions de Minuit 1979

—. 'Genèse et structure du champ religieux.' *Revue française de sociologie* 12, no. 3 (1971):295-334

—. 'Une interprétation de la théorie de la religion selon Max Weber.' *Archives européennes de sociologie* 12 (1971):3-21

Bourdieu, Pierre, Jean-Claude Chamboredon, and Jean-Claude Passeron. *Le métier sociologue*. Paris: Mouton-Bordas 1968

Bourdieu, Pierre and Jean-Claude Passeron, *La reproduction: Elements pour une théorie du système d'enseignement*. Paris: Éditions de Minuit 1970

Bourque, Gilles. *Classes sociales et question nationale au Québec, 1740-1840*. Montreal: Éditions Parti-pris 1970

Bourque, Gilles and Anne Légaré. *Le Québec: La question nationale*. Paris: Maspero 1979

Brasser, T.J. 'The Coastal Algonquians: People of the First Frontiers.' In *American Indians in Historical Perspective*, edited by Leacock and Oestreich. New York: Random House 1971

Brasser, T.J.C. 'Mahican.' In *Northeast*, edited by B.G. Trigger. Vol. 15 of *Handbook of North American Indians*. Washington, DC: Smithsonian Institution 1978

Braudel, Fernand. *Les structures du quotidien, Les jeux de l'échange* and *Le temps du monde*. Vol. 1, Vol. 2, and Vol. 3 of *Civilisation matérielle, économie et capitalisme, xvᵉ – xviiiᵉ siècle*. Paris: A. Colin 1979

—. *Civilisation matérielle et capitalisme, xvᵉ – xviiiᵉ siècle*. Vol. 1. Paris: A. Colin 1967

—. 'Histoire et sociologie.' In *Traité de sociologie*, edited by G. Gurvitch, 1:83-98. Paris: Presses Universitaires de France 1958

—. *La Méditerranée et le monde méditerranéen à l'époque de Philippe II*. 2nd ed., rev. and corr. 2 vols. Paris: A. Colin 1966

—. 'Prices in Europe from 1450 to 1750.' In *The Economy of Expanding Europe in the 16th and 17th Centuries*, edited by E.E. Rich and Charles Wilson. Vol. 4 of *The Cambridge Economic History of Europe*. Cambridge: Cambridge University Press 1967

Brebner, John Bartlet. *The Explorers of North America*. New York: Meridian Books 1933

Brenner, Elise M. 'To Pray or to Be Prey: That is the Question. Strategies for Cultural Autonomy of Massachusetts Praying Town Indians.' *Ethnohistory* 27, no. 2 (Spring 1980):135-51

Brenner, Robert. 'Agrarian Class-Structure and Economic Development in Pre-Industrial Europe.' *PP*, no. 70 (February 1976):30-75

—. 'The Origins of Capitalist Development: A Critique of Neo-Smithian Marxism.' *New Left Review*, no. 104 (July-August 1977):25-93

Bridenbaugh, Carl. *Cities in the Wilderness: Urban Life in America, 1625-1742*. New York: Capricorn Books 1964

—. *The Colonial Craftsman*. Chicago: University of Chicago Press, Phoenix Books 1964

—. *Myths & Realities: Societies of the Colonial South*. New York: Atheneum 1965

Brown, Dee. *Bury My Heart at Wounded Knee: An Indian History of the American West*. New York: Holt, Rinehart and Winston 1970

Brown, George W., Marcel Trudel, and André Vachon. *Dictionnaire biographique du Canada*. Vol. 1. Quebec: Presses de l'Université Laval 1967

Bruhat, Jean. 'La révolution française, problèmes de passage du féodalisme au capitalisme.' *La Pensée*, no. 187 (June 1976):3-4

Burt, A.L. 'The Frontier in the History of New France.' In *Canadian Historical Association, Report of the Annual Meeting, 1940*, 93-9. Toronto: University of Toronto Press 1940

Campeau, Lucien. *Les finances publiques de la Nouvelle-France sous les Cent-Associés*. Montreal: Bellarmin 1975

* —, ed. *La premiére mission d'Acadie (1602-1616)*. Quebec: Presses de l'Université Laval 1967

Carroll, Charles F. *The Timber Economy of Puritan New England*. Providence: Brown University Press 1973

Carroll, Peter N. *Puritanism and the Wilderness: The Intellectual Significance of the New England Frontier, 1629-1700*. New York: Columbia University Press 1969

* Cartier, Jacques. *Voyages en Nouvelle-France*. Montreal: Éditions Hurtubise-HMH 1977

Castilla del Pino, C. 'Sexualité et pouvoir.' In *Sexualité et pouvoir*, edited by A. Verdiglione, 13. Paris: Payot 1976

CERM. *Dictionnaire économique et social*. Paris: Éditions Sociales 1975

—. *Sur le féodalisme*. Paris: Éditions Sociales 1971

—. *Sur le mode de production asiatique*. Paris: Éditions Sociales 1969

* Champlain, Samuel de. *Oeuvres de Champlain*. Edited by C.H. Laverdière (1870). Reprinted with introduction by G.E. Giguére. 3 vols. Montreal: Éditions du Jour 1973

Chapdelaine, Claude. 'L'ascendance culturelle des Iroquoiens du Saint-Laurent.' *RAQ* 10, no. 3 (1980):145-52

Charbonneau, Hubert. *Vie et mort de nos ancêtres, étude démographique*. Montreal: Presses de l'Université de Montréal 1975

Chaunu, Pierre. 'Malthusianisme démographique et malthusianisme économique.' *Annales ESC* 27, no. 1 (January-February 1972):1-19

Chaunu, Pierre and Richard Gascon. *1450-1660: L'état et la ville*. Vol. 1 of *Histoire économique et sociale de la France*. Paris: Presses Universitaires de France 1977

Chaussinand-Nogaret, Guy. 'Capital et structure sociale sous l'ancien régime.' *Annales ESC* 25, no. 2 (March-April 1970):463-76

Christensen, Gardell Dano. *Colonial New York*. Camden, NJ: Thomas Nelson & Sons 1969

Cipolla, C.M. 'L'echec italien.' In *Transition du féodalisme à la société industrielle: L'échec de l'Italie de la Renaissance et des Pays-Bas du 17ᵉ siècle*, edited by P.M. Hohenberg and F. Frantz, 7-9. Montreal: Centre inter-universitaire d'études européennes 1975

—, ed. *The Fontana Economic History of Europe: The Sixteenth and Seventeenth Centuries*. London: Collins, Fontana Books 1974

Claiborne, Robert. *Les premiers américains*. Translated from the English by Simon Noireaud. Netherlands: Time-Life International 1973

Clastres, Pierre. *Recherches d'anthropologie politique*. Paris: Éditions du Seuil 1980

—. *La société contre l'état*. Paris: Éditions de Minuit 1974

Clermont, Norman. 'L'augmentation de la population chez les Iroquoiens préhistoriques.' *RAQ* 10, no. 3 (1980):159-64

—. 'Le castor et les Indiens préhistoriques de la Haute-Mauricie, un problème d'identification.' *RAQ* 4, no. 1 (1974):4-8

—. 'Une figure iroquoise, Garakontié.' *RAQ* 7, no. 3-4 (1978):101-7

—. 'L'identité culturelle iroquoienne.' *RAQ* 10, no. 3 (1980):139-44

—. 'La plaine laurentienne: Le sylvicole initial.' *RAQ* 7, no. 1-2 (1978):31-42

—. 'Que étaient les Attikamègues?' *Anthropologica* 16, no. 1 (1974):59-74

Clermont, Norman and Claude Chapdelaine. 'La sédentarisation des groupes non-agriculteurs dans la plaine de Montréal.' *RAQ* 10, no. 3 (1980):153-8

Comeau, Robert, ed. *Économie québécoise*. Montreal: Les Cahiers de l'Université du Québec 1969

Condon, Thomas J. *New York Beginnings: The Commercial Origins of New Netherland*. New York: New York University Press 1968

Cooper, J.P. 'In Search of Agrarian Capitalism.' *PP*, no. 80 (August 1978):20-65

Crête, Serge-André. 'La plaine laurentienne, les premiers habitants.' *RAQ* 7, no. 1-2 (1978):19-30

Crosby, A.W., Jr. *The Columbian Exchange: Biological and Cultural Consequences of 1492*. Westport, CT: Greenwood Press 1972

Crouzet, François. 'Angleterre et France au 18ᵉ siècle, essai d'analyse comparée de deux croissances économiques.' *Annales ESC* 21, no. 2 (March-April 1966):254-91

Dailey, R.C. 'The Role of Alcohol among North American Indian Tribes as Reported in the Jesuit Relations.' *Anthropologica* 10, no. 1 (1968):45-54

Daveluy, Marie-Claire. 'Le drame de la recrue de 1653.' *RHAF* 7, no. 2 (September 1953):157-71

Davis, Ralph. *The Rise of the Atlantic Economies*. London: Weidenfeld and Nicolson 1977

Debien, Gabriel. 'Engagés pour le Canada au XVIIᵉ siécle vus de La Rochelle.' *RHAF* 6, no. 2 (September 1952):177-223; 6, no. 3 (December 1952):374-407

Dechêne, Louise. 'La croissance de Montréal au 18ᵉ siècle.' *RHAF* 27, no. 2 (September 1973): 168-79

—. *Habitants et marchands de Montréal au XVIIᵉ siècle*. Paris and Montreal: Plon 1974

Delafosse, M. 'La Rochelle et le Canada au XVIIᵉ siècle.' *RHAF* 4, no. 4 (March 1951):469-511

Delâge, Denys. 'Canada et New York 1608-1750.' M.A. thesis, Université de Montréal 1968

—. 'Les structures économiques de la Nouvelle-France et de la Nouvelle-York.' *L'actualité économique* (April-June 1970):67-118

De la Morandière, Charles. *Histoire de la pêche française de la morue dans l'Amérique septentrionale*. 3 vols. Paris: G.P. Maisonneuve et Larose 1962

* Denton, Daniel. 'A Brief Description of New York Formerly Called New Netherlands' (London 1670). In *Historic Chronicles of New Amsterdam, Colonial New York and Early Long Island*, edited by Cornell Jaray, 2:1-57. Port Washington, NY: Ira J. Friedman 1968

Desrosiers, Léo Paul. *Iroquoise: 1534-1646*. Vol. 1. Montreal: Institut d'histoire de l'Amérique française 1947

De Voe, Thomas F. *The Market Book Containing a Historical Account of the Public Markets in the Cities of New York, Boston, Philadelphia and Brooklyn with a Brief Description of Every Article of Human Food Sold Thereon. The Introduction of Cattle in America and Notices of Many Remarkable Specimens*. New York: printed for the author, 1862

* De Vries, David Pieterz. 'Voyages from Holland to America, 1632-1644. Short Historical and Journal Notes of Several Voyages' (Hoorn 1655). Translated from the Dutch for the New York Historical Society by Henry C. Murphy (1810-82). In *Historic Chronicles of New Amsterdam, Colonial New York and Early Long Island*, edited by Cornell Jaray 1-136. Port Washington, NY: Ira J. Friedman 1968

De Vries, Jan. *The Dutch Rural Economy in the Golden Age, 1500-1700*. New Haven: Yale University Press 1974

—. *The Economy of Europe in an Age of Crisis, 1600-1750*. Cambridge: Cambridge University Press 1876

—. 'An Inquiry into the Behavior of Wages in the Dutch Republic and Southern Netherlands, 1580-1800.' In *Acta Historiae Neerlandicae: Studies on the History of the Netherlands*. La Haye, Boston, London: Martinus Nijhoff 1978

—. 'On the Modernity of the Dutch Republic.' *JEH* 33, no. 1 (March 1973):191-202

—. 'The Role of the Rural Sector in the Development of the Dutch Economy, 1500-1700.' *JEH* 31, no. 1 (March 1971):266-8

Deyon, Pierre. 'La concurrence internationale des manufactures lainières aux 16ᵉ et 17ᵉ siècles.' *Annales ESC* 27, no. 1 (January 1972):20-32

—. *Le mercantilisme.* Paris: Flammarion 1969

Diamond, Sigmund. 'Le Canada français au XVIIᵉ siècle: Une société préfabriquée.' *Annales ESC* 16, no. 2 (March-April 1961):317-54

—. 'An Experiment in "Freudalism": French Canada in the Seventeenth Century.' *William and Mary Quarterly*, 3rd series, 18 (1961):3-34

—. 'From Organization to Society: Virginia in the Seventeenth Century.' *American Journal of Sociology* 63, no. 5 (March 1958):457-75

—. 'Old Patterns and New Societies: Virginia and French Canada in the Seventeenth Century.' In *Sociology and History*, edited by W.J. Cahnman and S. Boscoff, 170-90. New York: Free Press of Glencoe 1964

—, ed. *The Creation of Society in the New World.* Chicago: Rand McNally 1963

Dickinson, John A. 'The Pre-Contact Huron Population. A Reappraisal.' *Ontario History* 72, no. 3 (September 1980):173-9

Dobb, Maurice. *Études sur le développement du capitalisme.* Paris: Maspero 1969

Dobb, Maurice and Paul M. Sweezy, eds. *Du féodalisme au capitalisme: Problémes de la transition.* 2 vols. Paris: Maspero 1977

Domar, Evsey D. 'The Causes of Slavery or Serfdom: A Hypothesis.' *JEH* 30, no. 1 (March 1970):18-32

Donnelly, Joseph P. *Thwaites' Jesuit Relations, Errata and Addenda.* Chicago: Loyola University Press 1967

Douglas, James. *New England and New France: Contrasts and Parallels in Colonial History.* Toronto and New York: W. Briggs & Putnam's Sons 1913

Douville, Raymond and Jacques Donat Casanova. *La vie quotidienne en Nouvelle-France.* Paris: Hachette 1964

Driver, Harold E. *Indians of North America.* Chicago: University of Chicago Press 1969

Duffy, John. *Epidemics in Colonial America.* Baton Rouge: Louisiana University Press 1959

Duffy, J. 'Smallpox and the Indians in the American Colonies.' *Bulletin of the History of Medicine* 25, no. 4 (July-August 1951):324-41

* Dutch Settlers' Society of Albany. *Deacon's Account Book, 1652-1664.* Albany: n.p., n.d.

—. *Yearbook 1928-1929.* Vol. 4. Albany: n.p., n.d.

—. *Yearbook 1944.* Vol. 20. Albany: n.p., n.d.

Easterbrook, W.T. and Hugh G.J. Aitken. *Canadian Economic History.* Toronto: Macmillan 1967

Easterbrook, W.T. and M.H. Watkins. *Approaches to Canadian Economic History.* Carleton Library, no. 31. Toronto: McClelland & Stewart 1967

Eccles, W.J. *The Canadian Frontier, 1534-1760.* Toronto: Holt, Rinehart & Winston 1969

Eckert, Allan W. *The Silent Sky: The Incredible Extinction of the Passenger Pigeon.* Dayton, OH: Landfall Press 1965

* Éditions du Jour. *Relations des Jésuites contenant ce qui s'est passé de plus remarquable dans les missions des pères de la Compagnie de Jésus dans la Nouvelle-France, 1611-1672.* Reprint of the 1858 edition. 6 vols. Montreal: Éditions du Jour 1972

Eggleston, Edward. *The Transition of Civilization from England to America in the Seventeenth Century.* Boston: Beacon Press 1959

Ellis, D.M., J.A. Frost, H.C. Syrett, and H.J. Carman. *A History of New York State.* New York: Cornell University Press 1967

Emmanuel, A. *L'échange inégal*. Paris: Maspero 1969

Emmer, Pieter C. 'The History of Dutch Slave Trade: A Bibliographical Survey.' *JEH* 32, no. 2 (June 1972):728-47

Engels, Freidrich. *L'origine de la famille, de la propriété et de l'état*. Paris: Éditions Sociales 1954

—. *The Origins of the Family, Private Property, and The State*. Translated by Ernest Untermann. Chicago: Charles H. Kerr 1902

Fine, Ben. 'On the Origins of Capitalist Development.' *New Left Review*, no. 109 (May-June 1978):88-95

Finegan, Thomas E. 'Colonial Schools and Colleges in New York.' *Proceedings of the New York State Historical Association* 16 (1917):168-82

Fitchen, J. *New World Dutch Barn*. Syracuse: Syracuse University Press 1968

Flick, A.C., ed. *History of the State of New York*. 10 vols. New York: Columbia University Press 1933-7

Foucault, Michel. *Surveiller et punir: Naissance de la prison*. Paris: Gallimard 1975

Frank, André Gunder. *L'accumulation mondiale 1500-1800*. Paris: Calmann Levy 1977

Fredrickson, N. Jaye and Sandra Gibb. *La chaîne d'alliance, l'orfèvrerie de traite et de cérémonie chez les Indiens*. Ottawa: Musées nationaux du Canada 1980

Frégault, Guy. 'La Nouvelle-France à l'époque de Marie de l'Incarnation.' *RHAF* 18, no. 2 (September 1964):167-75

Fumoleau, René. *As Long as this Land Shall Last – A History of Treaty 8 and Treaty 11, 1870-1939*. Toronto: McClelland & Stewart 1973

Furet, François. 'Le catéchisme révolutionnaire.' *Annales ESC* 26, no. 2 (March-April 1971):255-89

Furet, François and Jacques Ozouf. 'L'alphabétisation en France, 17ᵉ-19ᵉ siècles.' *Annales ESC* 32, no. 3 (May-June 1977):488-502

Gagné, Gérard. 'La paléontologie humaine en Amérique du Nord: un aperçu.' *RAQ* 12, no. 1 (1982):3-12

Gagnon, François Marc. *La conversion par l'image, un aspect de la mission des Jésuites auprès des Indiens du Canada au XVIIᵉ siècle*. Montreal: Bellarmin 1975

—. '"Ils se peignent le visage ... ," réaction européenne à un usage indien au XVIᵉ et au début du XVIIᵉ siècles.' *RHAF* 30, no. 3 (December 1976):363-81

Gauthier, Florence. 'Théorie de la voie unique de la révolution bourgeoise ou négation de la révolution française.' *La Pensée*, no. 187 (June 1976):38-48

Genovese, Eugene D. *Économie politique de l'esclavage*. Paris: Maspero 1968

* Geronimo. *Mémoires de Geronimo*. Paris: Maspero 1975

Gessain, Robert. *Ammassalik ou la civilisation obligatoire*. Paris: Flammarion 1969

Gindin, Claude. 'Chronique historique, la pensée historique de Jean Meuvret, quelques-uns de ses enseignements.' *La Pensée*, no. 169 (June 1973):92-102

Giraud, Marcel. *Le Métis canadien, son rôle dans l'histoire des provinces de l'Ouest*. Paris: Institut d'ethnologie 1945

Godelier, Maurice. *Horizon, trajets marxistes en anthropologie*. Paris: Maspero 1973

—. 'Modes de production, rapports de parenté et structures démographiques.' *La Pensée*, no. 172 (December 1973):7-31

—. 'La pensée de Marx et d'Engels aujourd'hui et les recherches de demain.' *La Pensée*, no. 143 (February 1969):92-120

—. 'Le sexe comme fondement ultime de l'ordre social et cosmique chez les Baruya de Nouvelle-Guinée, mythe et réalité.' In *Sexualité et pouvoir*, edited by A. Verdiglione, 268-306. Paris: Payot 1976

Goubert, Pierre. *La société*. Vol. 1 of *L'ancien régime*. Paris: A. Colin 1969

—. *Les pouvoirs*. Vol. 2 of *L'ancien régime*. Paris: A. Colin 1973

—. *Cent mille provinciaux au xviie siècle.* Paris: Flammarion 1968

Grabill, Wilson H., Clyde V. Kiser, and Pascal K. Whelpton. *The Fertility of American Women.* New York: J. Wiley & Sons 1958

Greene, Evarts B. and Virginia B. Harrington. *American Population before the Federal Census of 1790.* New York: Columbia University Press 1932

Grenon, Michel and Régine Robin. 'À propos de la polémique sur l'ancien régime et la révolution: Pour une problématique de la transition.' *La Pensée,* no. 187 (June 1976):5-30

Griffiths, Naomi. *The Acadians: Creation of a People.* Toronto: McGraw-Hill Ryerson 1973

Groulx, Lionel. 'Missionaires de l'Est en Nouvelle-France. Réduction et séminaires indiens.' *RHAF* 3, no. 1 (June 1949):45-72

Guibert, Elizabeth. 'Statut idéologique du possible en histoire.' *La Pensée,* no. 187 (June 1976):49-53

Guy, Camil. *Le canot d'écorce à Weymontaching.* Musée national de l'homme, bulletin no. 20. Montreal: Éditions de l'Aurore 1977

Hale, John R. *L'âge des découvertes.* Alexandria, vt: Time-Life 1970

Haley, Alex. *Racines.* 2 vols. Paris: J'ai Lu 1976

Haley, K.H.D. *The Dutch in the Seventeenth Century.* London: Thames and Hudson 1972

Hall, Peter, ed. *The Penguin World Atlas.* Harmondsworth: Penguin Books 1974

Hamelin, Jean. *Économie et société en Nouvelle-France.* Quebec: Presses de l'Université Laval 1960

Hamelin, Jean, ed., with S.A. Crête, R. Parent, J. Mathieu, A. Garon, N. Voisine, and R. Jones. *Histoire du Québec.* Montreal: France-Amérique 1977

Hargous, Sabine. *Les Indiens du Canada.* Paris: Ramsay 1980

Harris, Richard Colebrook. *The Seigneurial System in Early Canada: A Geographical Study.* Quebec: Presses de l'Université Laval 1966

Hartz, Louis. *The Founding of New Societies: Studies in the History of the United States, Latin America, South Africa, Canada and Australia.* New York: Harcourt, Brace and World 1964

Harvey, Pierre. 'Stagnation économique en Nouvelle-France.' *L'actualité économique* (October- December 1961):537-48

Hecht, Robert A. *Continents in Collision: The Impact of Europe on the North American Indian Societies.* Washington, DC: University Press of America 1980

Hecksher, Eli Filip. *Mercantilism.* London: Allen & Unwin 1955

Hedrick, U.P. *A History of Agriculture in the State of New York.* New York: Hill and Wang 1966

Heidenreich, Conrad E. *Huronia. A History and Geography of the Huron Indians, 1600-1650.* Toronto: McClelland & Stewart 1971

—. 'Huron.' In *Northeast,* edited by B.G. Trigger. Vol. 15 of *Handbook of North American Indians.* Washington, DC: Smithsonian Institution 1978

Heidenreich, Conrad E. and Arthur J. Ray. *The Early Fur Trades: A Study of Cultural Interaction.* Toronto: McClelland & Stewart 1976

Henripin, Jacques. *La population canadienne au début du xviiie siècle: Nuptialité, fécondité, mortalité infantile.* Paris: Presses Universitaires de France 1954

Hill, Christopher. *Reformation to Industrial Revolution, 1530-1780.* Vol. 2 of *The Pelican Economic History of Britain.* Harmondsworth: Penguin Books 1969

Hill, C. and M.M. Postan. *Des origines au 18e siècle.* Vol. 1 of *Histoire économique et sociale de la Grande-Bretagne.* Paris: Seuil 1977

Hill, Christopher and James and Edgell Richword. *The English Revolution 1640.* London: Lawrence & Wishort 1949

Hilton, Rodney H. 'A Crisis of Feudalism, Symposium, Agrarian Class Structure and Economic Development in Preindustrial Europe.' *PP,* no. 80 (August 1978):3-19

—. 'Qu'entend-on par capitalisme?' In *Du féodalisme au capitalisme: Problémes de la transi-*

tion, edited by M. Dobb and P.M. Sweezy, 1:177-95. Paris: Maspero 1977

Hincker, François. 'Contribution à la discussion sur la transition du féodalisme au capitalisme: La monarchie absolue française.' In *Sur le féodalisme*, CERM, 61-66. Paris: Éditions Sociales 1971

Hobsbawm, Eric. 'Du féodalisme au capitalisme.' In Vol. 2 of *Du féodalisme au capitalisme: Problèmes de la transition*, edited by M. Dobb and P.M. Sweezy, 7-15. Paris: Maspero 1977

—. 'The General Crisis of European Economy in the 17th Century.' *PP*, no. 5 (May 1954):33-53; no. 6 (November 1954):44-65

—. *Industry and Empire: From 1750 to the Present Day*. Vol. 3 of *The Pelican Economic History of Britain*. Harmondsworth: Penguin Books 1969

Hohenberg, Paul M. and Frederick Krantz, eds. *Transition du féodalisme à la société industrielle: L'échec de l'Italie de la renaissance et des Pays-Bas du XVIIe siècle*. Montreal: Actes du premier colloque international du CIEE 1974

Hunt, George. *The Wars of the Iroquois: A Study in Intertribal Relations*. Madison: University of Wisconsin Press 1960

Innis, Harold A. *The Cod Fisheries: The History of an International Economy* (1940). Toronto: University of Toronto Press 1978

—. *The Fur Trade in Canada* (1930). Toronto: University of Toronto Press 1967

* —. *Select Documents in Canada, Economic History, 1497-1783*. Toronto: University of Toronto Press 1929

Jacquin, Philippe. *Histoire des Indiens d'Amérique du Nord*. Paris: Payot 1976

Jaenen, Cornelius J. 'Amerindian Views of French Culture in the Seventeenth Century.' *Canadian Historical Review* 55, no. 3 (September 1974):261-91

—. *Friend and Foe: Aspects of French-Amerindian Cultural Contact in the Sixteenth and Seventeenth Centuries*. Toronto: McClelland & Stewart 1976

* Jameson, J. Franklin. *Narratives of New Netherland, 1609-1664*. New York: Charles Scribner 1909

Jane, C. and L.A. Vigneras, eds. *The Journal of Christopher Columbus*. New York: Clarkson, N. Potter 1960

* Jaray, Cornell. *Historic Chronicles of New Amsterdam, Colonial New York and Early Long Island*. 2 vols. Port Washington, NY: Ira J. Friedman 1968

Jeannin, Pierre. *L'Europe du nord-ouest et du nord aux 17e et 18e siècles*. Paris: Presses Universitaires de France, Nouvelle Clio 1969

Jeffreys, C.W. *The Picture Gallery of Canadian History*. Toronto: Ryerson Press 1942

Jenness, Diamond. *Indians of Canada*. Toronto: University of Toronto Press 1977

Jennings, Francis. 'The Indian Trade of the Susquehanna Valley.' *Proceedings of the American Philosophical Society* 110, no. 6 (December 1966):406-24

—. *The Invasion of America, Indians, Colonialism and the Cant of Conquest*. Williamsburg: University of North Carolina Press 1975

Jennings, Jesse D. *Prehistory of North America*. 2nd ed. New York: McGraw-Hill 1974

Jetté, René. 'La stratification sociale: Une direction de recherche.' *RHAF* 26, no. 1 (June 1972):35-51

Johnson, Adrian. *America Explored: A Cartographical History of the Exploration of North America*. New York: Viking Press 1974

Johnson, Harry M. *Sociology: A Systematic Introduction*. New York: Harcourt, Brace 1960

Johnson, Herbert Alan. *The Law Merchant and Negotiable Instruments in Colonial New York, 1664 to 1730*. Chicago: Loyola University Press 1963

Jones, E.L. 'Agricultural Origins of Industry.' *PP*, no. 40 (July 1968):58-71

Jury, Wilfrid and Elsie McLeod-Jury. *Sainte-Marie aux Hurons*. Montreal: Bellarmin 1980

* Kalm, Pehr. *Voyage de Pehr Kalm au Canada en 1749*. Translated by J. Rousseau, G. Bethune, and P. Morisset. Montreal: P. Tisseyre 1977

* Kalm, Peter (Pehr). *Travels in North America.* English version of 1770 edition, revised by A.B. Benson. 2 vols. New York: Dover Publications 1966

Kammen, Michael. *Colonial New York: A History.* New York: Charles Scribner 1975

Kapesh, An Antane (Anne André). *Je suis une maudite sauvagesse.* Montreal: Leméac 1976

—. 'Ces terres dont nous avions nommé chaque ruisseau.' *RAQ* 5, no. 2 (1975):3

Kerr, D.G.G. *A Historical Atlas of Canada.* Don Mills, ON: Thomas Nelson (Canada) 1966

Kilpatrick, W.A. *The Dutch Schools of New Netherland and Colonial New York.* Bulletin no. 12. Washington, DC: United States Bureau of Education 1912

Kula, Witold. *Théorie économique du système féodal.* Paris: Mouton 1970

Kupp, Th. Jan. 'Could the Dutch Commercial Empire Have Influenced the Canadian Economy during the First Half of the Eighteenth Century?' *Canadian Historical Review* 52, no. 4 (December 1971):367-88

—. 'The Fur Trade Relations, New Netherlands-New France: A Study of the Influence Exerted by the Fur Trade Interests of Holland and New Netherlands on the Settlement of New France during the Years 1600 to 1664.' Ph.D. thesis, University of Manitoba 1968

—. 'Note de recherche: Le développement de l'intérêt hollandais dans la pêcherie de la morue de Terre-Neuve; L'influence hollandaise sur les pêcheries de Terre-Neuve au 17ᵉ siècle.' *RHAF* 27, no. 4 (March 1974):565-9

—. 'Quelques aspects de la dissolution de la compagnie de M. De Monts, 1607.' *RHAF* 24, no. 3 (December 1970):357-74

Labrousse, E., P. Léon, P. Goubert, J. Bouvier, C. Carrière, and P. Harsen. *Des derniers temps de l'âge seigneurial aux préludes de l'âge industriel, 1660-1784.* Vol. 2 of *Histoire économique et sociale de la France.* Paris: Presses Universitaires de France 1970

Lamontagne, Roland. 'Géohistoire du Canada.' *RHAF* 28, no. 4 (March 1965):534-40

Lanctot, Gustave. *Des origines au régime royal.* Vol. 1 of *Histoire du Canada.* Montreal: Beauchemin 1960

—. 'Position de la Nouvelle-France en 1663.' *RHAF* 11, no. 4 (March 1958):517-32

Larocque, Robert. 'L'introduction de maladies européennes chez les autochtones des XVIIᵉ et XVIIIᵉ siècles.' *RAQ* 12, no. 1 (1982):13-24

Lavallée, Louis. 'Les archives notariales et l'histoire sociale de la Nouvelle-France.' *RHAF* 28, no. 3 (December 1974):385-401

Le Roy Ladurie, Emmanuel. 'Note critique: en Haute-Normandie, Malthus ou Marx?' *Annales ESC* 33, no. 1 (January-February 1978):115-24

—. *Les paysans de Languedoc.* Paris: SEVPEN 1966

—. 'A Reply to Professor Brenner.' Paper presented at symposium, Agrarian Class Structure and Economic Development in Pre-industrial Europe. *PP*, no. 79 (May 1978):55-9

—. *Le territoire de l'historien.* Paris: Gallimard 1973

Leach, Douglas Edward. *The Northern Colonial Frontier, 1607-1763.* New York: Holt, Rinehart and Winston 1966

Leacock, E.B. and L. Oestreich. *American Indians in Historical Perspective.* New York: Random House 1971

Leblant, Robert. 'Le commerce compliqué des fourrures canadiennes au début du 17ᵉ siècle.' *RHAF* 26, no. 1 (June 1972):53-66

Leclerc, P.A. 'Le mariage sous le régime français.' *RHAF* 13, no. 2 (September 1959): 230-46; 13, no. 3 (December 1959):374-401, 525-43; 14, no. 1 (June 1960):34-60; 14, no. 2 (September 1960): 226-45

* Législature du Québec. *Collection de manuscrits contenant lettres, mémoires et autres documents historiques de la Nouvelle-France.* Vol. 1. Quebec: Imprimerie A. Côté 1883

Léon, Pierre. *Les hésitations de la croissance.* Vol. 2 of *Histoire économique et sociale.* Paris: A. Colin 1978

—. *L'ouverture du monde xive-xvie siécle.* Vol. 1 of *Histoire économique et sociale.* Paris: A. Colin 1977

* Lescarbot, Marc. *Histoire de la Nouvelle-France.* Vol. 3. Toronto: Champlain Society 1914

Lévy-Bruhl, Henri. *Histoire juridique des sociétés de commerce en France aux xviie et xviiie siécles.* Paris: Éditions Donat-Mont-Chrestien 1938

Lockbridge, Kenneth. 'L'alphabétisation en Amérique 1650-1800.' *Annales* ESC 7 (May-June 1977):504-6

—. 'Land, Population and the Evolution of New England Society, 1630-1790.' PP 39 (April 1968):62-80

Lublinskaya, A.D. *French Absolutism: The Crucial Phase, 1620-1629.* Cambridge: Cambridge University Press 1968

McAnear, Beverley. 'The Place of the Freeman in Old New York.' *New York History* 21 (October 1940):418-30

McCullum, Hugh and Karmel. *This Land Is Not For Sale.* Toronto: Anglican Book Centre 1975

Macdonald, L.A. 'France and New France: The Internal Contradictions.' *Canadian Historical Review* 52, no. 2 (June 1971):121-43

McEvedy, Colin. *The Penguin Atlas of Modern History (to 1815).* Harmondsworth: Penguin Books 1972

McKee, Samuel, Jr. *Labor in Colonial New York, 1664-1776.* Port Washington, NY: Ira J. Friedman 1935

Mackintosh, W.A. 'Economic Factors in Canadian History.' In *Canadian Economic History,* edited by W.T. Easterbrook and M.H. Watkins, 1-15. Toronto: McClelland & Stewart 1967

* McLuhan, T.C., ed. *Pieds nus sur la terre sacrée.* Paris: Denoël-Gonthier 1974

McManis, Douglas R. *Colonial New England.* Toronto: Oxford University Press 1975

McManus, Edgar J. *A History of Negro Slavery in New York.* Syracuse: Syracuse University Press 1966

McManus, John C. 'An Economic Analysis of Indian Behavior in the North American Fur Trade.' JEH 32, no. 1 (March 1972):36-53

Malone, P.M. 'Changing Military Technology among the Indians of Southern New England, 1600-1677.' *American Quarterly* 25 (1973):56-8

Mandel, Ernest. *Traité d'économie marxiste.* 4 vols. Paris: 10/18 1962

Mandrou, Robert. *La France aux xviie et xviiie siècles.* Paris: Presses Universitaires de France 1967

—. *Louis xiv et son temps, 1661-1715.* Vol. 10 of *Peuples et civilisations.* Paris: Presses Universitaires de France 1973

Marcuse, Herbert. *Eros and Civilization.* Boston: Beacon Press 1966

—. *Eros et civilisation.* Paris: Éditions de Minuit 1963

* Marie de l'Incarnation, Mère. *Lettres historiques de la Vénérable Mère Marie de l'Incarnation sur le Canada.* Edited by B. Sulte. Quebec: L'Action sociale 1927

* —. *Marie de l'Incarnation, ursuline (1599-1672): Correspondance.* Edited by Guy Oury. Solesmes, France: Abbaye Saint-Pierre 1971

Marie-Victorin, Frère. *Flore laurentienne.* 2nd ed. Montreal: Presses de l'Université de Montréal 1964

Marienstras, Élise. *La résistance indienne aux États-Unis du xvie au xxe siècle.* Paris: Gallimard/Julliard 1980

Martens, Francis. 'Une hypothèse sur les wampums.' RAQ 4, no. 3 (June 1974):52-7

Martin, Calvin. *Keepers of the Game: Indian Animal Relationships and the Fur Trade.* Berkeley: University of California Press 1978

Marx, Karl. *Le capital.* Paris: Éditions Sociales 1973

—. *Capital: A Critique of Political Economy.* Edited by Frederick Engels, translated by Samuel Moore and Edward Aveling. New York: Random House, Modern Library 1906

Mauro, Frédéric. *L'expansion européenne, 1600-1870*. Paris: Presses Universitaires de France, Nouvelle Clio 1967

Mauss, Marcel. *Sociologie et anthropologie*. Paris: Presses Universitaires de France 1973

* Megapolensis, Johannes. 'A Short Account of the Mohawk Indians.' In *NNN*, J. Franklin Jameson, 163-80. New York: Charles Scribner 1909

Meuvret, Jean. *Études d'histoire économique: Recueil d'articles*. Cahiers des Annales, no. 32. Paris: A. Colin 1971

Meyer, Jean. 'Une magistrale mise en cause du 18ᵉ siècle: L'Europe des lumières de P. Chaunu.' *Annales ESC* 29, no. 4 (July-August 1974):888-902

*Michaelius, Jonas. 'Letter of Reverend Jonas Michaelius, 1628.' In *NNN*, J. Franklin Jameson, 117-33. New York: Charles Scribner 1909

Mondoux, Soeur. 'Les hommes de Montreal.' *RHAF* 2, no. 1 (June 1948):59-80

Monière, Denis. 'L'utilité du concept de mode de production des petits producteurs pour l'historiographie de la Nouvelle-France.' *RHAF* 29, no. 4 (March 1976):483-502

Moogk, Peter N. 'In the Darkness of a Basement: Craftsmen's Associations in Early French Canada.' *Canadian Historical Review* 57, no. 4 (December 1976):399-438

Morgan, Lewis Henry. *League of the Iroquois*. Secaucus, NJ: Citadel Press 1972

Morris, Richard B. *Government and Labor in Early America*. New York: Harper & Row 1965

Morse, Eric W. *Fur Trade Canoe Routes of Canada, Then and Now*. Toronto: University of Toronto Press 1969

Myers, Gustavus. *A History of Canadian Wealth*. Toronto: J. Lewis & Samuel 1972

Nef, John U. *Industry and Government in France and England, 1540-1640*. New York: Cornell University Press 1964

Nell, E.J. 'Population, the Price Revolution and Primitive Accumulation.' *Peasant Studies* 6, no. 1 (1977):32-40

* New York, State of. *Census 1855: Introduction to the Census of the State of New York for 1855*. Albany: [s.n.] 1857

Nish, Cameron. *Les bourgeois-gentilshommes de la Nouvelle-France, 1729-1748*. Montreal: Fides 1968

Nissenson, S.G. 'The Development of a Land Registration in New York.' *New York History* 20, no. 1 (January 1939):16-42

—. *The Patroon's Domain*. New York: Columbia University Press 1937

Noël, Michel. *Art décoratif et vestimentaire des Amérindiens du Québec, xvrᵉ et xvrrᵉ siècles*. Montreal: Leméac 1979

North, Douglas C. and Robert Paul Thomas. 'The Rise and Fall of the Manorial System: A Theoretical Model.' *JEH* 31, no. 4 (December 1971):777-83

Norton, Thomas Elliot. *The Fur Trade in Colonial New York, 1686-1776*. Madison: University of Wisconsin Press 1974

* O'Callaghan, E.B., ed. *The Documentary History of the State of New York*. 4 vols. Albany: Weed Parsons & Co. 1849-51

* —, ed. *Documents Relative to the Colonial History of the State of New York*. 14 vols. Albany: A. Weed 1856-77

Oleson, T.J. *The Norsemen in America*. Ottawa: Canadian Historical Association 1963

Olivier, Christiane. *Les enfants de Jocaste, l'empreinte de la mère*. Paris: Denoël-Gonthier 1980

Oury, Dom. G.M. *Madame de la Peltrie et ses fondations canadiennes*. Quebec: Presses de l'Université Laval 1974

—. *Marie de l'Incarnation*. 2 vols. Quebec: Presses de l'Université Laval 1973

Parain, Charles and Pierre Vilar. *Mode de production féodal et classes sociales en système précapitaliste*. Les Cahiers du CERM. Paris: Éditions Sociales 1971

Paré, Hélène. 'Chapeaux Bagg' (titre provisoire). M.A. thesis in progress, Université de Québec à Montréal

Parent, Raynald. 'Inventaire des nations amérindiennes au début du 17ᵉ siècle.' *RAQ* 7, no. 3-4 (1978):5-20

Parker, David. 'The Social Foundations of French Absolutism 1610-1630.' *PP*, no. 53 (November 1971):66-89

* Perrot, Nicolas. *Mémoire sur les moeurs, coustumes et relligion* (sic) *des sauvages de l'Amérique septentrionale*. Mémoires pittoresques de la Nouvelle-France, no. 1. Leipzig: Librairie A. Franck 1865. Reprint. Montreal: Éditions Elysée 1973

Pilon-Lé, Lise. 'Le régime seigneurial au Québec: Contribution à une analyse de la transition au capitalisme.' Manuscript, Anthropology Department, Université Laval, Quebec

Polanyi, Karl. *The Great Transformation: The Political and Economic Origins of our Time*. Boston: Beacon Press 1967

Polanyi, Karl, Conrad M. Arensberz, and Harry W. Pearson. *Trade and Market in the Early Empires*. New York: Free Press 1957

Porchnev, Boris. *Les soulèvements populaires en France de 1623 à 1648*. Paris: SEVPEN 1963

Postan, M.M. *Essays on Medieval Agriculture and General Problems of the Medieval Economy*. Cambridge: Cambridge University Press 1973

—. *The Medieval Economy and Society: An Economic History of Britain in the Middle Ages*. London: Weidenfeld and Nicolson 1972

Postan, M.M. and John Hatcher. 'Population and Class Relations in Feudal Society.' Paper presented at symposium, Agrarian Class Structure and Economic Development in Pre-industrial Europe. *PP*, no. 78 (February 1978):24-37

Posthumus, N.W. *Inquiry into the History of Prices in Holland*. Publications of the International Scientific Committee on Price History. 2 vols. Leiden: E.J. Brill 1946

Potter, David M. *People of Plenty: Economic Abundance and the American Character*. Chicago: University of Chicago Press, Phoenix Books 1961

Powell, Summer Chilton. *Puritan Village: the Formation of a New England Town*. New York: Anchor Books 1965

Pratt, John Webb. *Religion, Politics and Diversity: The Church-State Theme in New York History*. Ithaca: Cornell University Press 1967

Québec, Gouvernement du. *Annuaire du Québec, 1968-1969*. Quebec: Éditeur officiel du Québec 1969

* Radisson, Pierre-Esprit. *Journal 1682-1683. Les débuts de la Nouvelle-France*. Montreal: Stanké 1979

* —. *Voyages of Peter Esprit Radisson Being an Account of his Travels and Experiences among the North American Indians, from 1652 to 1684* (Boston 1885). Edited by Gideon D. Scull. Reprint. New York: Burt Franklin 1967

Ray, Arthur J. and Donald Freeman. *Give us Good Measure: An Economic Analysis of Relations between the Indians and the Hudson's Bay Company before 1763*. Toronto: University of Toronto Press 1978

Ray, Arthur J. *Indians in the Fur Trade: Their Role as Hunters, Trappers and Middlemen in the Lands Southwest of Hudson Bay, 1660-1870*. Toronto: University of Toronto Press 1974

Recherches internationales à la lumière du marxisme. *Premières sociétés de classes et mode de production asiatique*. Special no. 57-8 (January-April 1967)

Reed, Clyde. 'Transaction Costs and Differential Growth in Seventeenth-Century Western Europe.' *JEH* 33, no. 1 (March 1973):177-90

Renaud, Paul E. *Les origines économiques du Canada*. Mamers: Gabriel Enault 1928

Rey, Pierre Philippe. *Les alliances de classes*. Paris: Maspero 1976

—. *Colonialisme, néo-colonialisme et transition au capitalisme*. Paris: Maspero 1971

Rich, E.E. 'Fur Trade.' *Economic History Review* 7 (1966):307-28

—. 'Trade Habits and Economic Motivation among the Indians of North America.' *Canadian Journal of Economics and Political Science* 26, no. 1 (February 1960):35-53

Rich, E.E. and Charles Wilson. 'The Economy of Expanding Europe in the 16th and 17th Centuries.' In Vol. 4 of *The Cambridge Economic History of Europe*. Cambridge: Cambridge University Press 1967

Richet, Denis. 'Croissance et blocages en France du xvᵉ au xviiiᵉ siècle.' *Annales ESC* 23, no. 4 (July-August 1968):759-87

Rife, Clarence White. 'Land Tenure in New Netherland.' In *Essays in Colonial History*, presented to C.M. Andrews by his students, 41-73. New Haven: Yale University Press 1931

Robin, Régine and Michel de Certeau. 'Débat: Le discours historique; les institutions de l'histoire; histoire, psychanalyse et sémiotique; l'histoire et le réel.' *Dialectiques*, no. 14, 1976:42-62

Rocher, Guy Arthur. 'The Relations Between Church and State in New France During the Seventeenth Century: A Sociological Interpretation.' PH.D. thesis, Harvard University 1957

* Rochmenteix, Père Camille, ed. *Relations par lettres de l'Amérique septentrionale, années 1709 et 1710*. Paris: Letouzey & Ané 1904

Romig, Edgar Franklin. 'The English and Low-Dutch School-Master.' *New York Historical Society Quarterly* 43, no. 2 (April 1959):149-59

Rostow, W.W. 'The Beginnings of Modern Growth in Europe: An Essay in Synthesis.' *JEH* 33, no. 3 (September 1973):547-79

Rousseau, Jacques. 'Le Canada aborigène dans le context historique.' *RHAF* 18, no. 1 (June 1964):39-63

—. 'Pierre Boucher naturaliste et géographe.' In *Histoire véritable et naturelle ... de la Nouvelle-France* (1664), Pierre Boucher, 262-400. Boucherville: Sociéte Historique de Boucherville 1964

Roy, Raymond and Hubert Charbonneau. 'Le contenu des registres paroissiaux canadiens du xviiᵉ siècle.' *RHAF* 30, no. 1 (June 1976):85-97

Ryerson, Stanley B. *The Founding of Canada: Beginnings to 1815*. Toronto: Progress Books 1963

* Sagard, Gabriel. *Dictionnaire de la langue huronne*. Paris: Denys Moreau 1632. In Vol. 4 of *Histoire du Canada*, Gabriel Sagard. Paris: Librairie Tross 1866

* —. *Le grand voyage du pays des Hurons*. Montréal: Éditions Hurtubise-HMH 1976

* —. *Histoire du Canada et voyages que les Frères mineurs recollets y on faicts pour le conversion des infidèles depuis l'an 1615*. 4 vols. Paris: Edwin Tross 1866

Sahlins, Marshall. *Âge de pierre, âge d'abondance: L'économie des sociétés primitives*. Paris: Gallimard 1976

Salone, Émile. *La colonisation de la Nouvelle-France*. Paris: E. Guilmoto 1906. Reprint. Montreal: Boréal Express 1970

Salwen, B. 'Indians of Southern New England and Long Island: Early Period.' In *Northeast*, edited by B.G. Trigger. Vol. 15 of *Handbook of North American Indians*. Washington, DC: Smithsonian Institution 1978

Savard, Rémi. 'L'autodétermination des peuples autochtones.' *Le Devoir*, 25 March 1980

—. *Le sol américain: Propriété privée ou terre-mère*. Montreal: Hexagone 1981

Scott, Kenneth. 'New Amsterdam's Taverns and Tavernkeepers.' *De Halve Maen* 39, no. 1 (April 1964):9-10, 15; no. 2 (July 1964):9-10, 15; no. 3 (October 1964):13-15; no. 4 (January 1965):11-12, 15; 40, no. 1 (April 1965):11-12, 14

Séguin, Robert Lionel. *La civilisation traditionnelle de l'habitant aux 17ᵉ et 18ᵉ siécles*. Montreal: Fides 1967

Sherwood, Warren George. 'The Patroons of New Netherland.' *New York History* 12, no. 3 (July 1931):271-94

* Shortt, Adam. *Documents Relating to Canadian Currency: Exchange and Finance during the*

French Period. Ottawa: F.A. Acland, King's Printers 1925

Simons, W. 'Narragansett.' In *Northeast*, edited by B.G. Trigger. Vol. 15 of *Handbook of North American Indians.* Washington, DC: Smithsonian Institution 1978

Simonis, Yvan. 'Le cannibalisme des Iroquois: Comportement social, environnements, structures de l'esprit.' *Anthropologie et sociétés* 1, no. 2 (1977):107-22

Sjoberg, Gideon. *The Preindustrial City.* New York: Free Press 1965

Slicher Van Bath, B.H. *The Agrarian History of Western Europe A.D. 500-1850.* London: Edward Arnold 1963

Smith, Daniel Scott. 'The Demographic History of Colonial New England.' *JEH* 32, no. 1 (March 1972):165-83

Smith, Wallis. 'The Fur Trade and the Frontier: A Study of an Inter-Cultural Alliance.' *Anthropologica* 15, no. 1 (1973):21-35

Soboul, Albert. *La révolution française.* 2 vols. Paris: Éditions Sociales 1962

—. 'Sur un article d'Antoine Pelletier ou comment des historiens refont l'histoire.' *La Pensée*, no. 187 (June 1976):36-7

—. 'Sur l'article de Michel Grenon et Régine Robin.' *La Pensée*, no. 187 (June 1976):31-5

Stanley, George F.G. 'The First Indian "Reserves" in Canada.' *RHAF* 4, no. 2 (September 1950):178-210

—. 'The Indians and the Brandy Trade during the Ancien Regime.' *RHAF* 6, no. 4 (March 1953):489-505

—. 'The Policy of "Francisation" as Applied to the Indians during the Ancien Regime.' *RHAF* 3, no. 3 (December 1949):333-48

* Stokes, I.N.P. *The Iconography of Manhattan Island, 1408-1909.* 6 vols. New York: Robert H. Dodd 1915-28

Stone, Lawrence. 'The Educational Revolution in England, 1560-1640.' *PP*, no. 28 (July 1964):4-80

—. 'Literacy and Education in England, 1640-1900.' *PP*, no. 42 (February 1969):69-139

Styron, William. *The Confessions of Nat Turner.* New York: Signet Books 1968

Sutherland, Stella H. *Population Distribution in Colonial America.* New York: Columbia University Press 1936

Tehanetorens. 'Migration of the Iroquois.' In *Tales of the Iroquois.* Rooseveltown, NY; Cornwall, ON: Akwesasne Notes, Mohawk Nation 1976

Terray, Emmanuel. *Le Marxisme devant les sociétés primitives.* Paris: Maspero 1972

Thines, G. and A. Lempereur. *Dictionnaire général des sciences humaines.* Paris: Éditions universitaires 1975

Thomas, R. and T. Anderson. 'White Population, Labor Force and Extensive Growth of the New England Economy in the Seventeenth Century.' *JEH* 33, no. 3 (September 1973):650-67

* Thwaites, Reuben G., ed. and trans. *The Jesuit Relations and Allied Documents.* 73 vols. Cleveland: Burrows Brothers 1896-1901

Tooker, Elisabeth. *An Ethnography of the Huron Indians, 1615-1649.* Bureau of American Ethnology, bulletin 190. Washington, DC: Smithsonian Institution 1962

—. 'History of Research.' In *Northeast*, edited by B.G. Trigger. Vol. 15 of *Handbook of North American Indians.* Washington, DC: Smithsonian Institution 1978

Trelease, Allen W. *Indian Affairs in Colonial New York: The Seventeenth Century.* New York: Cornell University Press 1960

Trigger, Bruce. *The Children of Aataentsic: A History of the Huron People to 1660.* 2 vols. Montreal: McGill-Queen's University Press 1976. Quoted material cited from first paperback edition, McGill-Queen's University Press 1987

Trigger, Bruce G., ed. *Northeast.* Vol. 15 of *Handbook of North American Indians.* Washington, DC: Smithsonian Institution 1978

Trudel, Marcel. *Atlas historique du Canada français.* Quebec: Presses de l'Université Laval 1961
—. *Le comptoir, 1604-1627.* Vol. 2 of *Histoire de la Nouvelle-France.* Montreal: Fides 1966
—. *Les débuts du régime seigneurial au Canada.* Montreal: Fides 1974
—. 'Les débuts d'une société: Montréal, 1642-1663. Étude de certains comportements sociaux.' *RHAF* 23, no. 2 (September 1969):185-208
—. *L'esclavage au Canada français.* Quebec: Presses de l'Université Laval 1960
—. *Initiation à la Nouvelle-France.* Montreal: Holt, Rinehart & Winston 1968
—. 'La Nouvelle-France.' *Cahiers de l'Académie canadienne-française,* no. 2 (1957):25-50
—. 'Les obligations des censitaires à l'époque des Cent-Associés.' *RHAF* 27, no. 1 (June 1973):3-41
—. *La population du Canada en 1663.* Montreal: Fides 1973
—. *La seigneurie des Cent-Associés, 1: Les événements.* Vol. 3 of *Histoire de la Nouvelle-France.* Montreal: Fides 1979
—. *Les vaines tentatives, 1524-1603.* Vol. 1 of *Histoire de la Nouvelle-France.* Montreal: Fides 1963
Tustin, E.B., Jr. 'The Development of the Salt Industry.' *New York Historical Society Quarterly* 33, no. 1 (January 1949):39-50
* Van der Donck, Adriaen. *A Description of the New Netherlands.* Edited by Thomas F. O'Donnell. Amsterdam: Evert Niewenhof 1655. Reprint, translated by Jeremiah Johnson (1841). Syracuse: Syracuse University Press 1968
Van der Wee, H. 'Prices and Wages as Development Variables: A Comparison between England and Southern Netherlands, 1400-1700.' In *Acta Historiae Neerlandicae: Studies on the History of the Netherlands.* La Haye, Boston, and London: Martinus Nijhoff 1978
Van Deventer, David. *The Emergence of Provincial New Hampshire, 1623-1741.* Baltimore: Johns Hopkins University Press 1976
Van Laer, A.J.F., ed. *Van Rensselaer Bowier Manuscripts.* Albany: State University of New York Press 1908
Vaughan, Aldent. *New England Frontier: Puritans and Indians, 1620-1675.* Toronto: Little Brown 1965
Verdiglione, Armando, ed. *Sexualité et pouvoir.* Paris: Payot 1976
Vilar, Pierre. 'Croissance économique et analyse historique.' In *Première conférence internationale d'histoire économique,* 35-82. Stockholm, Paris: École des Hautes Études en Sciences Sociales 1960
—. 'Débats et combats, histoire marxiste, histoire en construction, essai de dialogue avec Althusser.' *Annales ESC* 28, no. 1 (January-February 1973):165-98
—. 'Histoire sociale et philosophie de l'histoire.' *La Pensée,* no. 118 (November-December 1964):64-77
—. *Or et monnaie dans l'histoire, 1450-1920.* Paris: Flammarion 1974
—. 'Problems of the Formation of Capitalism.' *PP,* no. 10 (November 1956):15-38
Vincent, Sylvie and Bernard Arcand. *L'image de l'Amérindien dans les manuels scolaires du Québec.* Montreal: Éditions Hurtubise-HMH 1979
Wabeke, Bertus Harry. *Dutch Emigration to North America, 1624-1860.* New York: Netherlands Information Bureau 1944
Wallerstein, Immanuel. *Capitalist Agriculture and the Origin of the European World Economy, 16th Century.* Vol. 1 of *The Modern World System.* New York: Academic Press 1974
—. *Mercantilism and the Consolidation of the European World Economy, 1600-1750.* Vol. 2 of *The Modern World System.* New York: Academic Press 1980
Washburn, W.E. 'Symbol Utility and Aesthetics in the Indian Furtrade.' In *Aspects of the Fur Trade: Selected Papers of the 1965 North American Fur Trade Conference,* 50-4. St. Paul: Minnesota Historical Society 1967
—. 'Seventeenth-Century Indian Wars.' In *Northeast,* edited by B.G. Trigger. Vol. 15 of

Handbook of North American Indians. Washington, DC: Smithsonian Institution 1978

* —, ed. *The Indian and the White Man.* New York: Anchor Books 1964

Watkins, M.H. 'A Staple Theory of Economic Growth.' In *Approaches to Canadian Economic History,* edited by W.T. Easterbrook and M.H. Watkins, 49-73. Carleton Library no. 31. Toronto: McClelland & Stewart 1967

Watkins, Mel, ed. *Dene Nation: The Colony Within.* Toronto: University of Toronto Press 1977

Weber, Max. *Wirtschaft und Gesellschaft.* Tubingen: J.C.B. Mohr (P. Siebeck) 1922

Weinmann, Heinz. 'Le cannibalisme pour demain?' *Le Devoir,* 3 May 1980

Williams, Eric. *Capitalism and Slavery.* New York: Capricorn Books 1966

Wilson, Charles. *Economic History and the Historian: Collected Essays.* London: Weidenfeld and Nicolson 1969

—. *La république hollandaise des Provinces-Unies.* Paris: Hachette 1968

—. 'Taxation and the Decline of Empires, an Unfashionable Theme,' 'The Decline of the Netherlands,' and 'Cloth Production and International Competition in the Seventeenth Century.' In *Economic History and the Historian: Collected Essays.* London: Weidenfeld and Nicolson 1969

Wissler, Clark. *Histoire des Indiens d'Amérique du Nord.* Paris: R. Laffont 1969

Witthoft, John. *Indian Prehistory of Pennsylvania.* In Martin, *Keepers of the Game.* Berkeley: University of California Press 1978

GameWood, Silas. 'A Sketch of the First Settlement of the Several Towns on Long Island with their Political Condition, to the End of the American Revolution' (Brooklyn 1828). In *Historic Chronicles of New Amsterdam, Colonial New York and Early Long Island,* edited by Cornell Jaray, 2:1-205. Port Washington, NY: Ira J. Friedman 1968

* Wooley, Charles. 'A Two Years' Journal in New York and Part of its Territories in America.' In *Historic Chronicles of New Amsterdam, Colonial New York and Early Long Island,* edited by Cornell Jaray, 1:1-97. Port Washington, NY: Ira J. Friedman 1968

Wright, James B. *The Cultural Life of the American Colonies, 1607-1763.* New York: Harper & Row, Torchbooks 1962

Wright, J.V. *La préhistoire de l'Ontario.* Ottawa: Musées nationaux du Canada; Montreal: Fides 1981

—. *La préhistoire du Québec.* Ottawa: Musées nationaux du Canada; Montreal: Fides 1980

—. *Visages de la préhistoire du Canada.* Ottawa: Musées nationaux du Canada; Montreal: Fides 1981

W.V.H. 'Early Dutch Brought Santa to America.' *De Halve Maen* 30, no. 4 (January 1956):6

Zoltvany, Yves F. *The French Tradition in America.* New York: Harper & Row 1969

Index

Acadia, 33, 99

Agriculture: among Amerindians, 47, 160-1; in England, 8-9, 18, 23; in Europe, 5; in France, 24-6; in Holland, 8-9, 12-14; in Huron society, 50-1, 69; by settlers, 251-2

Alcohol: effect on Amerindian societies, 136-40, 297; and trade practices of Europeans, 136-8

Algonkian group of tribes: as allies of Hurons, 96; as traders, 45-6, 94, 95

Algonkins: economic changes due to fur trade, 121; and epidemics, 86, 87; and fur wars, 143

Amerindians: and agriculture, 47, 160-1; and alcohol, 136-40, 297; children, treatment of, 50, 180-1, 204, 294; decision-making, 61-2; dispossession of, 36-7; as domestic servants, 312; economic system, based on redistribution of goods, 52-3, 55-7, 124; economic system, changes in, 333-6; economic system, effect of unequal exchange on, 81, 120-30, 122-3, 124-5; and epidemics, 85-93; health of, before European influence, 67-8, 85; and hospitality, 53, 253; intertribal relationships, 56-7; and leisure, 52; origins, 43; population, 5, 43-4; and reservations, 290-7; and settlers, 253, 285-6, 325-6; and slavery, 314, 315; subsistence activities, 46-8; trade routes, traditional, 46, 82-3; as traders, 120-32, 155. *See also* Algonkins; Hurons; Iroquois; Mahicans; Micmacs; Mohawks; Montagnais; Neutrals

Amsterdam, 6, 15-16, 17

Andacwander ritual, 70-1, 170, 201, 205

Anglo-Dutch wars, 110, 148-9, 231, 266, 269, 273

Animals. *See* Livestock; Wildlife

Antwerp, 6

Architecture, in northeastern North America, 324-5

Arthabaskan language, 45

Artisans: France, 28, 30; as production force in 16th century, 7-8; status in colonies, 319-20

Asia, and Dutch traders, 16, 264, 267, 273

Baltic region: domination by Dutch traders, 31; and economic world-system in 17th century, 4

Banks: France, 29; Holland, 17

Baptism, of Amerindians, 90, 170, 179. *See also* Conversion, of Amerindians

Barter, as form of exchange in New France, 280

Beaver: as currency, 141-2, 280; depletion of, 130, 155, 284; epidemics among, 92; as principal export of colonies, 259; value per skin, 156

Birds, 38-9

Bison, 37

Black slaves, 312, 314, 315-16

Body, attitude towards, in Huron society, 76-7, 198

Bourgeoisie: England, 19-20, 21-4; France, 27, 29, 30-1; Holland, 17; Italy, 11; in northeastern North America, 322

Brazil, and Dutch traders, 16, 264, 266

Brébeuf, Jean de (Father), 72, 86, 90-1, 146

Britain. *See* England

British traders. *See* English traders

Brûlé, Étienne, 125, 175-6

Cannibalism, in Huron society, 64, 66, 213

Canoes, 51

Capital: accumulation, 4, 7, 79; merchant, 29-30, 80, 81

Capitalism: development of, 4; and economic expansion in 16th-century Europe, 4; in England, 18-24; in France, 24-31; in Holland, 12-18; in Italy, 11; and mode of production, 9. *See also* Capital; Labour

Caribou, 38, 92

Cartier, Jacques, 82, 83-4

Celebrations. *See* Feasts; Rituals

Cereals, production by: Amerindians, 47; France, 25; Holland, 14

Ceremonial exchange, in Huron society. *See* Redistribution of goods

Champlain, Samuel de: and Amerindian guides, 84; and Amerindian trade rituals, 96-8, 103; and fur wars, 94, 142; and Hurons, 96-7; and Iroquois, 95, 96; and murder of Étienne Brûlé, 175-6; and support of Jesuits in New France, 118-19

Charter of Freedoms and Exemptions, 106, 108, 305

Chaumonot, Father, 90-1, 187, 233

Children: in Amerindian society, 50, 58, 59-60, 204; education of, 180-1

Children, treatment of: in Christian tradition, 204-5, 294-5

Clan system, in Huron society, 58, 201

Class system: in England, 18-19, 21-4; in New France, 303-5; in New Netherland, 323-4

Coal, as energy source, 7, 21

Cokayne Plan, 240

Colonists. *See* Settlers

Colonization, of northeastern North America: economics of, 3-4; by England, 31, 32, 33, 34, 35; by France, 32, 33, 34, 35; by Holland, 31, 32, 33, 34, 35; *See also* New England; New France; New Netherland; Settlers

Colonizing wars, in northeastern North America. *See under* Wars

Communauté des Habitants, 101, 131

Compagnie de Caën, 98, 118, 125, 156

Compagnie de la Nouvelle-France, 98

Compagnie des Cent Associés: lack of profitability of, 157; and monopoly of fur trade in New France, 100, 157; origins, 98; and seigneurial system in New France, 304; subsidy of Roman Catholic Church in New France, 329; and trade advantage for Amerindian converts, 167

Compagnie des Habitants, 100, 101, 247, 279

Conjuncture: definition, 6; and European economic cycles, 4-6

Consumer industries: England, 20-1; France, 26; Holland, 14

Conversion, of Amerindians: psychology of, 235-6; and social destabilization, 186-93; and trade price advantage, 119, 167, 184

Conversion, of Hurons by Jesuits: as goal of French missionaries, 125; process of, 178-94; and protection from Iroquois, 146; and purchase of firearms, 120, 136, 144, 167, 184. *See also* Jesuits; Roman Catholic Church

Cooling, global, in 17th century, 5

Copper, as trade item, 54, 107

Corn, 47

Cottage industry mode of production: England, 8, 17, 18, 20; France, 26, 28. *See also* 'Putting out'

Credit, by French merchants to Hurons, 103

Currency: beaver, 141-2, 280; of France, 29; gold, 141, 142; of Holland, 17; silver, 141,

142; wampum, 140-1, 280-1
Cycles, economic. *See* Economic cycles

Deer, 37, 40, 155
Dependency, of Amerindians on
Europeans, 78, 81, 132-3
Diet: of Amerindians, 138; of Dutch, 14, 15;
of Europeans, 257; of settlers, 252-7
Diseases. *See* Epidemics
Division of labour. *See under* Labour
Divorce, 58
Divorce, in Huron society, 202, 295
Dogs, 51
Donnacona (Iroquois chief), 83-4
Dorchester Company, 243, 246
Draperies, new. *See* 'New draperies'
Dreams, in Huron society, 71-5, 205-7
Dutch East India Company, 16th century,
263-4; trading network, 16, 263-4
Dutch traders: and alcohol, sale of, 139;
and Amerindians, 108-16, 126-31; com-
pared with French traders, 127, 128-31;
dominance of fur trade, 336-7; and
firearms, sale of, 118, 128, 135, 136; and
fur wars, 104, 154; and Hudson River
route, 33, 96, 103; and Iroquois, 110-16;
and slave trade, 266; trade network,
262-74. *See also* Dutch East India
Company; Dutch West India
Company; Holland; New Netherland;
New Netherland Company
Dutch West India Company: bankruptcy
of, 267; and copper, sale of, 107; internal struggles, 105-6; and monopoly of
fur trade, 105, 108; and New
Netherland, 108, 244-5, 264, 266, 302,
309; origins, 16, 105; and patroonships,
305-8; and profits from fur trade, 157;
and purchase of land from
Amerindians, 116-17; and slave trade,
315-16

Economic expansion: and capitalism, x; of
European world-system, 6-7; in 16th
century, 4
Economics, world-system theory, x, 3-4
Economy: Amerindian, 81, 122-3, 124-5,
129-30, 333-7; European, 4-6
Ecosystem, of northeastern North
America: before European
settlement, 37-41; exploitation by set-
tlers, 282-6, 338. *See also* Forests;
Wildlife
Education: of Amerindians, attempts by
missionaries, 180-1; in Holland, 14; in
Huron society, 58, 59-60; in New
France, 330; in New Netherland, 329-30
Elk, 40
Emigration: from England, 34, 240, 243-4,
245-6; from Holland, 17, 34
'Enclosure' of land: in England, 19, 20, 22,
34; in France, 26
Energy sources: coal, 7, 21; wind-driven, 7;
wood, 27
England: agricultural methods, 8-9, 18, 23;
bourgeois revolution (1640-50), 19, 21-
4; capitalism, 10, 18-24; colonization
activities, 31, 32, 33, 34, 35, 258-9, 260;
economy in 17th century, x, 5, 241; and
emigration to northeastern North
America, 19, 34, 240, 243-4, 245-6, 258-
9; energy sources, 7; and fur trade, 99;
mode of production, 18-19; and protectionist measures against Dutch, 22-3,
240, 262, 267, 268-9, 273; shipbuilding,
7. *See also* English traders; New
England
Epidemics. *See also* Diseases; Smallpox
Epidemics, among Amerindians: blamed
on Jesuits' witchcraft, 171-3,
177-8; during fur wars, 145; effect on
Amerindian society, 85-93; influenza,
86-7; smallpox, 86, 87; as viewed by
Jesuits, 152
Epidemics, in Europe, 258
Epidemics, and wildlife, 91-2
Europe, Eastern, and feudalism, 11-12
Europe, Northwestern: economic condi-
tions, 4, 6-7; population, 5
Europeans. *See* Dutch traders; English
traders; French traders; Settlers
Exchange: commercial, between
Europeans and Amerindians, 82; ritual,
between French traders and Hurons,

97, 102-3; terms of, between Europeans and Amerindians, 80; types of, 79; unequal, among Amerindian tribes, 122, 130; unequal, between Europeans and Amerindians, 78, 79, 81-2, 123, 334, 336. *See also* Trading

Expansion, economic. *See* Economic expansion

Fallow system (of agriculture), 14

Famine: among Hurons, 87, 144-5, 146, 147, 162; in France, 25-6; unknown among Amerindians before European contact, 46, 47

Farm animals. *See* Livestock

Farming, and conflict with Amerindian land use, 285-6

Feast of the Dead, 73-4, 124, 162, 218

Feasts, in Huron society, 52, 76

Feudal mode of production: in Eastern Europe, 11-12; in Holland, 12; in Italy, 11; replacement by capitalistic mode, 9; Spain, 10-11. *See also* Feudalism

Feudalism: in England, abolition of, 22; in France, 24-5. *See also* Feudal mode of production

Finance, and economic world-system theory, 4

Finance industry: in France, 29; in Holland, 17

Firearms: illegal sale of, to Amerindians, 132, 133; and Iroquois superiority in war, 133-5, 144, 147, 151; sale by Dutch, 118, 128, 134-5, 135; sale by French, to converts only, 91, 120, 144, 167, 335-6; sale to Amerindians, 159-60

Fish: abundance in northeastern North America, 39-40, 41; as staple food in Holland, 15

Fishing: and fur trade, 82; in Huron society, 51

Fishing industry: of England, 32; of France, 29, 32; of Holland, 15, 31-2

Force, military. *See* Military force

Forests: depletion by colonists, 282-3; in early 17th century North America, 37; and growth of lumber industry in New England, 259-62

Fort Nassau, 105

Fort Orange: as Dutch trading post, 93, 108, 113, 127; origins, 105; and patroonships, 307-8; and sale of firearms to Iroquois, 134-5; settlement of, 248; transformation into municipality, 311

Forts, and fur trade, 94

France: agriculture, 24-6; and capitalism, 10, 24-31; class system, 24-6, 30-1; colonization activities, 32, 33, 34, 35, 84; economy in 17th century, x, 5, 7; emigration to European countries, 34-5, 242; emigration to New France, 246-9; energy sources, 27; government, 30-1; peasants, 241-2; population in 16th century, 24; population in 17th century, 5-6; religious wars, 242; shipping industry, 274-5. *See also* French traders; New France

Free trade, in furs: in New France, 94-5, 101; in New Netherland, 105

French traders: assimilation of Amerindian culture, 96-8, 125; compared with Dutch traders, 116-17, 127, 128-31; effect on Amerindian societies, 116; and fur trade in New France, 93-103. *See also* France; New France

Fronde, La, 30-1, 101

Fur production. *See* Production, of furs

Fur trade: and changes in Amerindian society, 56-7, 69, 78, 189; company profits, 155-8; and economy of New France, 275, 276; France, 33, 95; Holland, 33; production volume, 129; and seigneurial system in northeastern North America, 308-9; use of existing Amerindian trade networks, 55; wars, 142-54. *See also* Dutch traders; English traders; French traders

Fur wars. *See under* Fur trade

Generosity, and Amerindian trade alliances. *See* Redistribution of goods

Giving, code of, in Amerindian society. *See* Redistribution of goods

Gold: as currency, in New Netherland, 141, 142; and 16th-century economy, 5

Goods. *See* Trade goods

Government: of England, 22; of France, 30-1; of Holland, 17; in Huron society, 60-3; of New France, 331-2; of New Netherland, 332

Great Britain. *See* England

Guilds: England, 8, 21, 22; Holland, 16; Italy, 11; responsibilities of, 7-8

Health, of Amerindians, before contact with Europeans, 67-8, 85

Holland: agriculture, 8-9; capitalism, 10, 12-18; colonization activities, 31, 32, 33, 34, 35; and development of North America, x; economy, x, 5, 6, 7-9, 241, 272, 273-4; emigration from, 34; energy sources, 7; and fur trade, 157; immigration to, 17; imports, 15-16; land ownership in, 12-13, 14; as major power in 17th century, 239, 263; mode of production, 7-9, 12, 17; and Navigation Acts, 22-3, 262, 267, 268-9, 273; and New Sweden, conquest of, 150; religious tolerance, 17; shipbuilding, 7; standard of living, 17-18, 34; trade network, 239; war with England, 23, 148-9, 231, 266, 269, 273. *See also* Dutch traders; Dutch West India Company; New Netherland

Homesteading. *See* Settlers

Horses, 160

Horticulture: Amerindian, 47; Dutch, 14

Hudson, Henry: and Dutch fur trade, 33, 103; and sale of alcohol to Amerindians, 137

Hudson River, as trade route to interior, 96

Huguenots: autonomy in La Rochelle (France), 30; emigration to North America, 35, 247-8; in Holland, 17; and religious wars in France, 99

Hunting, by Hurons, 51, 159

Huron group of tribes, 49-50

Huron society, before European influence: agricultural methods, 50-1, 69; body, attitude towards, 76, 198; and cannibalism, 64, 66, 213; character, 66-7; chiefs,

role of, 60-3; children, treatment of, 59-60, 294-5; and clan system, 58, 201; curing societies, 69, 70; and dancing, 76-7; description, 49-77; and diseases, attitude towards, 207-8; division of labour, 50, 59-60; and dreams, 71-5; economy, pre-fur trade, 53-7; and education, attempts by missionaries, 201-2; family relations, 58-9; and feasts, 52, 76-7; geographic distribution, 49-50; giving, code of, 52-3, 63; health of, before settlement of Europeans, 67-8, 85; hospitality, 53; houses, 49; hunting, 51; and inheritance, 58; justice system, 62; language, 56; leisure activities, 52; and matrilinear kinship systems, 57-9; medical knowledge, 70; men, role of, 50, 69; and nature, 73; paternity, 58-9; personal property, 51-2; political system, 60-3; population in early 17th century, 44, 49; and redistribution of goods, 52-3, 56-7, 63; sexual freedom, 59, 69, 70-1, 77, 125, 201, 203-4; social relations, 56-66, 76-7; subsistence activities, 50-2; and tobacco, 51; torture, role of, 63-6, 211-13; trade routes, traditional, 82; as traders, 53-7; and war, 56, 60, 62, 63; and wealth, 51-2, 55, 58; witchcraft, belief in, 73; work, 50-2

Hurons, under French influence: abandonment by, 147-8, 149; alliance with traders, 96-7; ambivalent attitude towards, 126; dependence on, 145-6, 172; destruction of, 146-7; economy, changes due to fur trade, 121-5, 158; and epidemics, 85-93, 86, 87, 171-8, 177-8; and famine, 87, 144-5, 146, 147, 162; first contact, 54, 94; and fur trade, 94, 95, 102, 123, 129, 130, 142, 158-62; and fur wars, 142-54; and Iroquois, 118, 144-54; and Jesuits, attitude towards, 89-90, 169, 171-5, 217, 231; and Jesuits, disruptive effect of, 89, 194-224; and ritualism, growth of, 162; and rituals, exclusion of converts from, 190, 191; sale of firearms to converts only, 91, 120, 144, 167, 335-6; and unequal

exchange, 78, 79, 81-2, 123, 125, 130
Ice age, in 17th century, 5
Illegal trading. *See* Smuggling
Illness, attitude towards: Huron, 207-10; Jesuit, 210-11
Incas, 86
Indentured servants: in New France, 317-18, 329; prevalence in northeastern North America, 312
India, economic position in 17th century, x
Indians, North American. *See* Amerindians
Industrial Revolution, and textile industry, 272
Infant mortality: among North American settlers, 250, 253-4; in Huron society, 67-8
Inflation, in 16th century Europe, 5, 6, 7
Inheritance, in Huron society, 58
Interest rates, Dutch, 17
Intermarriage, between French men and Huron women, 202-3
Interpreters, 124, 125
Inuit, 43, 45
Iron. *See* Metal
Iroquois: and captives, assimilation of, 225-8; and Christianity, attitude towards, 229-30; cruelty of, 146; and Dutch traders, 110-16; and epidemics, 87, 88, 92-3, 93; and firearms, 134-5, 144, 147, 151; and French, after destruction of Huronia, 148-54; and fur trade, 129, 148, 158; and fur wars, 144-54; and Hurons, 118, 144-54; and intertribal warfare, 95, 122-3, 224-5; and Jesuits, relations with, 232-8; resistance to European settlement, 84; war chiefs, power of, 228-9
Iroquois group of tribes, 46
Iroquois society, before European influence: geographic distribution, 46; languages, 45; population, 44; sub-groups, 46; subsistence activities, 46; trade routes, 82
Italy: bourgeoisie, 11; capitalism, 11; economy, x, 5, 6; feudal mode of production, 11; and guilds, 11; and production

of luxury products, 8
Jesuits: abandonment of Hurons, 148, 149; and accusations of witchcraft by Amerindians, 89-90, 169, 171-5, 217, 231; arrival in New France, 118; and competition with traditional religion, 164-71; conversion, methods, 167-9, 178-94; and destabilization of Huron society, 164-211, 214, 218-24, 334-5; as disease carriers, 90, 92; and education of Amerindians, attempts at, 180-1; and firearms, as incentive to conversion, 167, 184; and Hudson Bay, exploration of, 83; and Iroquois, after destruction of Huronia, 148-54; and *Jesuit Relations*, 48-9, 166; and reservations, 291-7; and sexual repression among Amerindians, 201-4; and support of fur wars, 142-3, 145; symbiotic relationship with French traders, 119, 163, 166; and torture, attitude towards, 211-13; and trade, assuring advantages for converts, 166, 167, 172, 173, 184, 195; as traders, 101
Jogues, Isaac (Father), 87, 91, 110, 123, 173, 186, 245, 252

Kidnapping, of Amerindians, 83, 109

La Rochelle: and financing of Compagnie des Habitants, 101; and religious wars in France, 99; and rivalry between French port cities, 98
Labour: of Amerindians, 158, 160-1; and capital, 7-9; and Dutch *fabrieken*, 16-17; in Holland, 15-17; need for, in northeastern North America, 311-20, 339-40; slavery, 4, 312-14, 315-16, 319; unequal exchange of, between Europeans and Amerindians, 79-80. *See also* Wage-earners; Workers
Labour, division of: among Amerindian tribes, 120-3; change in Amerindian society, 81; and decline of guild system, 16, 17, 21; in Dutch agriculture, 13; in English textile industry, 20; in France, 27; in Huron society, 59-60; interna-

tional, and economic world-system theory, 4; in pre-European North America, ix

Lalement, Gabriel (Father), 40, 110, 135, 146

Lalemant, Jérôme (Father), 143, 187, 191, 214-17

Land, Amerindian, cultivated by settlers, 251-2

Land ownership: comparison of European and Amerindian concepts, 117; in England, 18, 22, 23, 34; in France, 24-6; in Holland, 12-13, 14; in Huron society, 51-2; in New France, 303-5; in New Netherland, 305-11; in North America, 251

Land quality, in North America, 251

Languages, Amerindian: knowledge of, by French, 127; variety of, 45

Laval, Monseigneur de, 137, 297

Le Jeune, Father, 39, 55, 119, 135, 155, 166-7, 171

Le Mercier, Father, 131-2, 143

Le Moyne, Simon (Father), 224, 233, 237

Literacy: in Holland, 14; in northeastern North America, 330-1

'Little ice age' (17th century), 5

Livestock farming: in France, 26; in Holland, 12, 13; by settlers, 252

Lumber industry, as economic resource for New England, 259-62

Mahicans: and conflict with Iroquois, 104, 122-3, 151; and Dutch traders, 104

Manhattan (Dutch fort), 105

Manhattans, and sale of land to Dutch, 116-17

Manufacturing: and economic world-system theory, 4; in England, 23; in France, 27-8; in Holland, 16-17

Maps, of northeastern North America, creation of, 84

Market economy, in northeastern North America, 322

Markets, and development of capitalism, 4

Marriage: among Hurons, under Jesuit rule, 295-6; in traditional Huron society, 58, 59

Mass production, in England, 20

Matrilinear kinship systems, among Hurons, 53

Mayas, 47

Medicine, Amerindian, 88, 170, 207-9

Mediterranean region, and economic world-system in 17th century, 4

Megapolensis, Johannes (Pastor), 39, 93, 229-30

Men, role of, in Huron society, 50, 69

Merchant capital, 29-30, 80, 81

Merchants: in New Amsterdam, 278-9; in New France, 279; and profits, 80; relationship with Jesuits in New France, 119

Metal, as replacement for Amerindian materials, 132-3, 161

Metals, precious. *See* Gold; Silver

Métayage: France, 25, 27; New Netherland, 306, 307

Métis, 300

Mexico, population decline in 17th century, 5

Michaelius, Jonas (Pastor), 117, 127, 128

Micmac group of tribes, 45

Micmacs: and epidemics, 86; and fur trade, 82, 95, 121; intertribal relations, 122

Middle Ages, and feudal mode of production, 12-13

Military force, use by Europeans against Amerindians, 78, 83, 104, 122, 124-5

Missionaries: Dutch, 117; financial support of, 165, 166; French, 118-19; influence on French traders, 125. *See also* Jesuits

Mohawks: and Dutch traders, 104, 113; and firearms, 134-5; and intertribal wars, 95, 104, 287; and objection to sale of alcohol, 139; prostitution by women, 93; as traders, 96, 224

Monarchy: England, 22, 30; France, 29, 30-1; Holland, 30

Monopoly, of fur trade: with Amerindians, 80; and Dutch West India Company, 105; in New France, 94, 100-2, 157; and New Netherland Company, 105; and Société des Marchands, 95

Montagnais: and belief in witchcraft by Jesuits, 89; economic changes due to fur trade, 121; epidemics, 86, 88; as traders, 94, 95, 132

Montagnais group of tribes, 45

Montmagny, Governor, 101, 120

Montreal, as trading post, xi, 95

Moors, in Spain, 10

Moose, 38, 40-1

Names: changing of, in traditional Huron society, 205; places, in northeastern North America, 324

Native rights, and land purchases by Dutch traders from Amerindians, 117

Natives. *See* Amerindians

Nature, and man, balance of, and unequal exchange of goods between Amerindians and Europeans, 78, 81, 154

Navigation Acts, 22-3, 262, 267, 268-9, 273

Navy, French, 28, 99

Netherlands. *See* Holland; New Netherland

Neutral group of tribes, 46

Neutrals: defeat by Iroquois, 147; and epidemics, 88; and fur wars, 143; and trade with Hurons, 53, 54

New Amsterdam: capture by British, 269; development of independent merchants, 278-9; origins, 105; urbanization of, 281. *See also* New Netherland

'New draperies': England, 17; Holland, 17; and Industrial Revolution, 272

New England: Amerindian population, 44; economic depression of 1640, 260; immigration to, 258-9; and slavery, 316; trade with Europe, 260-1; trade with West Indies, 261-2

New England Company, 246

New France: currency, 280; economic development by mid-17th century, 274-7, 278; government, 331-2; immigrants, 317-18; and indentured servants, 317-18, 319; population, 276; and relations with Amerindians, 117-20; and religious institutions, 281, 328-9; and seigneurial system, 341; and slavery,

316; transition from trading post to colony, 302-5

New Netherland: colonization, 302; currency, 280; economic role of, in Dutch trading network, 266; epidemics among Amerindians, 88; exports, 266, 268; and fur trade, 103-16, 142; government, 310-11, 332; loss to Great Britain, 269-72; as part of Dutch trading network, 262-74; and relations with Amerindians, 117; and religious institutions, 327-8; as secular society, 117; as secular state, 229; and seigneurial system, 305-10; settlement of, 108, 244, 245, 248; and slavery, 315-16; trade with Virginia, 268; wars between settlers and Amerindians, 287-90. *See also* New Amsterdam

New Netherland Company: and Fort Nassau, 104; origins, 103-4. *See also* Dutch traders

New Sweden, conquest by Dutch, 150

New Sweden Company, 107

Newfoundland, and French fishing industry, 29, 32

Noordse Company (Northern Company), 104

North America: colonization, economics of, 3; conquest of, and 16th century economic expansion, 4; economy in 17th century, x, 4; and English immmigrants, 34; population, 5, 43-4

Northern Company, 104

Origin of the family, private property and the state, The, 68

Ossossané (Huron village), 181, 183, 184, 185, 186

Pandemics. *See* Epidemics

Paris, population of, 27

Passenger pigeon (*Ectopistes migratorius*), 38

Patroons: and Dutch fur trade, 106; in New Netherland, 305-8. *See also* Seigneurial system

Peace, and trade, among Amerindians, 110-13

Peasants: Eastern Europe, 11-12; England, 18, 19; France, 24-6, 30; Holland, 9, 12-13, 14; in New France, 303-5; in New Netherland, 306, 309-10; in North America, 250
Peat industry, in Holland, 15
Piece work. *See* Cottage industry mode of production
Plymouth Company, 243
Population: Amerindian, 43, 88; and economic world-system theory, 4; English, in North America, 246; in Europe, 5, 249-50; French, in St. Lawrence Valley in mid-17th century, 247; Holland, 17; New England in 1663, 247; New France in 1663, 247; New Netherland in 1663, 247; North America, 5, 243, 249-50, 253; Spain, 35
Portugal, x, 6, 32
Precious metals. *See* Gold; Silver
Prices: and Amerindian trade practices, 103; and economic world-system theory, 4; and effect on 16th-century European economies, 6; of furs, 109, 131; and inflation, in 16th century, 4
Prisons, 295
Private property, and conflict with Amerindian land use, 285-6
Production, of furs, 129, 142
Production systems: development of, 7-9; and development of capitalism, 4; and labour in 16th century, 8
Profits: of fur-trading companies, 156; and inflation in 16th century, 4; and merchant capital, 80
Proletariat. *See* Workers
Prostitution, by Mohawk women, 93
Protectionist measures. *See* Monopoly; Navigation Acts
Puritans, 86, 242
'Putting out' (England). *See* Cottage industry mode of production

Quebec: capture by Jarvis Kirke, 99; as trading post, 33, 93, 94, 127

Ragueneau, Father, 74, 93, 152-3

Rates of exchange, among Amerindian tribes, 57
Rats, and introduction of ticks to North America, 92
Raw materials, and economic world-system theory, 4
Recollets (French missionaries), 118, 119, 125
Redistribution of goods, in Huron society, 52-3, 56, 58-9, 63, 73-4, 124, 190-1
Reformation: in England, 20; in Holland, 14
Religion: in England, 22, 34; in France, 30, 35; in Holland, 17; in Huron society (*see under* Hurons); in New France, 328-9; in New Netherland, 326-8
Reservations, for Amerindians, 290-7, 337
Revolution, England (c. 1640-58), 19, 21-4
Richelieu, Cardinal, 98, 99
Rituals, in Huron society, 190, 197-8, 200-1
Roman Catholic Church: and England, 20; and French fur trade, 98-9; and Holland, 14; and New France, 247, 302-3, 328-9. *See also* Jesuits; Religion
Rule of giving. *See* Giving, code of
Russia, trade with Holland, 239

Sachem (peace chief), 60-3, 69, 189, 228
Sagamité, 54, 102
Sainte-Marie-among-the-Hurons, 146, 164, 174
Salt, and fishing industry, 32
Schools. *See* Education
Scientific discoveries, use by Jesuits as proof of European superiority, 169
Sealife, in early 17th century North America, 40
Seigneurial system: in New France, 303-5; in New Netherland, 106-7. *See also* Patroons
Serfdom, in Eastern Europe, 11-12
Settlers: Dutch, and patroons, 106-7; economic activities, 259-60; and fur trade, 100-2, 242-3; in New England, 258-9; in New France, 99, 100-1, 118; in north-eastern North America, 242-50; standard of living, 253; in Virginia, 258-9
Sexual freedom, in Huron society, 59, 69, 70-1, 77, 125

Sexual repression, of Hurons under Jesuits, 201-2, 295
Sexual roles, in Huron society, 59-60, 69
Shaman: role of, in Huron society, 72, 73, 75, 164-5; undermining of authority by Jesuits, 169-71
Sharing, in Huron society. *See* Redistribution of goods
Sheep-raising: in England, 19, 20; in Spain, 10
Shipbuilding: in Holland, 7, 16; in North America, 260, 261
Shipping industry: in England, 22-3; in France, 28-9; in Holland, 15-16, 22-3, 33-4; in Spain, 11
Ships, commercial: Dutch, 7; English, 7
Silver: as currency, 141, 142; production drop in second half of 16th century, 5; and 16th-century economic expansion, 4
Slave trade: and Dutch West India Company, 16, 266, 315-16; and France, 29
Slavery: in northeastern North America, 312-14, 315-16, 340-1; and 16th-century economic expansion, 4
Smallpox, 86, 87, 93. *See also* Epidemics
Smuggling, of furs, 131
Social customs, European, in northeastern North America, 325
Social services, in Holland, 17-18
Société des Marchands, 95, 98, 118
Société Notre-Dame de Montréal, 302
Sorcery. *See* Witchcraft
South America: conquest of, 4; demographic changes, 43; and economic world-system in 16th century, 4; population, 5
Spain: economy in 16th century, 6; economy in 17th century, x, 5, 10; feudal mode of production, 10-11; shipping, decline in, 11
St. Lawrence River, as shipping lane, 275-6
Standard of living: England, 23; France, 26, 28; Holland, 17-18, 34; of settlers, 253
Stuyvesant, Pieter: and end of Dutch monopolistic trade practices, 109; and sale of firearms to Iroquois, 135; and settlement of New Netherland,

245; and slavery in New Netherland, 316; and trade with Iroquois, 113
Sweden: economic position in 17th century, x; settlements in North America, 254-7; as significant presence in development of North America, x
Swedish traders, and sale of firearms to Iroquois, 135, 136

Taxes: Britain, 18; England, 19, 22; France, 25, 26, 27; Holland 13; New France, 304-5
Technological transfer: between Europeans and Amerindians, 133; and trade, 81
Technology, use by Jesuits as proof of European superiority, 168
Textile industry: England, 23, 240, 241; France, 26, 28; Holland, 17, 272; Spain, 10-11; in 16th century, 8; in 17th century, 8
Thirty Years' War, 240
Tobacco, in Huron society, 51
Torture: in European society, 64-6; in Huron society, 63-6; view of Jesuits, 211-14
Tourte. *See* Passenger pigeon
Tourterelle. *See* Passenger pigeon
Trade. *See* Smuggling
Trade, in Amerindian society: and code of giving, 57; intertribal, 53-7; and peace, 110-13; as political activity, 56-7; routes, ownership of, 55
Trade, with Europeans: and epidemics among Amerindians, 86, 87; and technological transfer, 81
Trade goods, and unequal exchange, 132-3, 156
Trade routes, Amerindian, used by Europeans, 82-3
Trading activities, international: by England, 23; by France, 28-9; by Holland, 15-16
Trapping, as labour-intensive activity, 158-60
Tribes, Amerindian, 45-6
Trigger, Bruce G., xi, 48, 228
Turkeys, 38, 155

Unequal exchange, between Europeans and Amerindians. *See under* Exchange
United East India Company, 104, 105
Urbanization: England, 19, 23; France, 19; Holland, 14-15, 17
Van der Donck, Adriaen, 88, 93, 230-1, 249, 251
Van Rensselaer, Killiaen: and fur trade in New Netherland, 106, 107, 108, 109; and patroonships in New Netherland, 106, 306, 307, 308
Van Tweenhuyzen, Lambert, 33; and company, 103
Verenigde Oostindische Company (United East India Company), 104
Vimont, Father, 88, 111, 118, 136, 187
Virginia: economy of, 278; emigration to, 244, 258-9; as English colony, 31, 106; trade with New Netherland, 268
Vryheden ende Exemptien. *See* Charter of Freedoms and Exemptions

Wage-earners: and Dutch East India Company, 16; in England, 18, 19; in France, 26, 30; in Holland, 14-15, 16; in New Netherland, 312; in North America, 250. *See also* Labour; Workers
Wages: and economic world-system theory, 4; in 16th century, 4, 8
Wampum: and Amerindian trade routes, 82, 104; as currency, 54, 140-1, 280-1
Wapiti (*Cervus canadensis*), 37-8, 41
War chiefs, 60, 62, 228-9
Wars: colonizing, 281-2, 286-90; and depletion of natural resources, 334; fur, 142-54; and New France, and interference with settlement, 248
Wars, in Huron society: increase of, due to fur trade, 62; participation of Europeans as condition of trade, 97; revenge as motive for, 63; and social prestige, 56; war chiefs, role of, 60, 62
Water routes, and trade networks, 54
Wealth: and exploitation of natural resources, 81; in Huron society, 51-2, 55, 58; unequal distribution of, due to fur

trade, 189
Weapons. *See* Firearms
Whales, 40
Whaling industry, and Holland, 15, 32
Wild cow. *See* Wapiti
Wildlife: destruction by colonists, 283-4; in early 17th-century North America, 37-42; and epidemics, 92; as food of settlers, 252-3. *See also names of specific animals*
Wind-driven energy sources, in Holland, 14
Witchcraft, Jesuits accused of, by Hurons, 87, 89, 171-3, 236
Women, Amerindian: change in status due to fur trade, 69; as converts, 235; increase in workload of, due to fur trade, 161; and marriage to French traders, 125
Women, European, status of, 68
Women, in Huron society: childbirth, 68; and children, 68; sexual freedom, 59, 69, 125; as shaman, 69; status of, 59, 68, 69; subsistence activities, 50
Women, in Iroquois society, 68, 228
Wood: as energy source, 27; as New England export product, 260-1
Wool production, in England, 20, 239-40
Work: in Huron society, 50-2; in 16th-century Europe, 8
Workers: in England, 18, 23-4; in France, 27; in Holland, 15. *See also* Labour; Wage-earners
World-system theory, in economics, x, 3-4
Writing, use by Jesuits as proof of European superiority, 168